ESSAY WRITING

METHODS AND MODELS

Rebecca C. Mann
Pete M. Mann

Wilkes Community College

WADSWORTH PUBLISHING COMPANY
Belmont, California

A Division of Wadsworth, Inc.

To Jennifer and Alison, with love

English Editor: Angela Gantner
Editorial Assistant: Julie Johnson
Production: Cece Munson, The Cooper Company
Print Buyer: Randy Hurst
Interior and Cover Designer: Janet Bollow
Copy Editor: Steven Gray
Compositor: Omegatype Typography
Cover: © 1989 Jim Salvati, The Image Bank

Printed in the United States of America

1 2 3 4 5 6 7 8 9 10—94 93 92 91 90

LIBRARY OF CONGRESS CATALOGING-IN-PUBLICATION DATA

Mann, Rebecca C.
  Essay writing, methods and models / Rebecca C. Mann, Pete M. Mann.

       p.   cm.
  ISBN 0-534-12168-3
   1. English language—Rhetoric.   2. Essays—Authorship.   3. College readers.   I. Mann, Pete M.   II. Title.
PE1471.M26   1989
808′.042—dc20

89-36503
CIP

CONTENTS

List of Readings   xi
Preface   xiii

PART ONE: METHODS   1

CHAPTER 1   **GETTING STARTED**   3

Prewriting   4
  Journal   4
  Freewriting and Focused Freewriting   5
  Looping   8
  Cubing   10
  Inventory   13
Focusing   14
  Audience   16
  Purpose   19
  Organization   20
Journal Suggestions   21

CHAPTER 2 **DEVELOPING A THESIS** 23

Characteristics of a Thesis Statement 24
Components of a Thesis Statement 24
   General Thesis Statement 25
   Focused Thesis Statement 32
Prewriting Activities 42
Journal Suggestions 42

CHAPTER 3 **DEVELOPING THE ESSAY** 43

Organization 44
   Climactic Order 45
   Spatial Order 46
   Chronological Order 49
   Strategies of Exposition 49
Paragraphs 51
   Making a Point 52
   Supporting the Point 53
Providing Support 56
   Characteristics of Support 56
   How Support Works 57
   Levels of Support 57
   Developing Support 59
Making Writing Specific 60
   Action Verbs 60
   Sensory Words 61
Developing Coherence 65
   Transitions 65
   Repetition of Key Words and Ideas 69
   Pronouns 71
Achieving Unity 72
Journal Suggestions 74

CHAPTER 4 **INTRODUCTIONS AND CONCLUSIONS** 77

Introductions 77
   Funnel Introduction 78
   Contrast Introduction 79
   Anecdotal Introduction 83
Conclusions 85
   Summary Conclusion 85
   Inverted Funnel Conclusion 86
Journal Suggestions 88

CHAPTER 5   **REVISING THE ESSAY**   89

Revision Techniques   90
    Global Revision   90
    Peer Revision   91
    Local Revision   92
Revising the Introduction and the Thesis   93
Revising Organization   93
Revising Support   94
    Revising Thesis Support   95
    Revising Paragraph Support   97
Checking for Coherence   102
Checking for Unity   103
Revision Checklist   104
Journal Suggestions   106

CHAPTER 6   **EDITING THE ESSAY**   107

Editing Sentence Structure and Grammar   110
    Sentences   110
    Fragments   111
    Run-ons (R-O) and Comma Splices (CS)   112
    Parallelism (//)   114
    Modifiers   116
    Subject–Verb Agreement (S–V)   118
    Verb Tense   122
    Review of Pronouns   125
Editing Diction   130
    Connotation   131
    Slang   132
    Clichés   132
    Pretentious Words   133
    Vague Words   135
    Sexist Language   136
    Point of View   139
    Wordiness   142
Editing Punctuation and Mechanics   147
    End Punctuation (., ?, !)   148
    Colon (:)   149
    Semicolon (;)   150
    Comma (,)   151
    Dash (—)   153
    Hyphen (-)   153
    Ellipsis Points (. . .)   154

Parentheses ( )   155
Apostrophe (')   156
Quotation Marks (" ")   158
Capitalization   161
Abbreviations   164
Numbers   165
Journal Suggestions   167

PART TWO: MODELS 169

CHAPTER 7   **DESCRIPTION**   171

Journal Suggestions   171
Guidelines   173
Topic   173
Observation   175
Focus   176
Support   178
Readings   180
    Student Essay   180
    Professional Essays   181
Writing Assignments   195
    Prewriting   196
    Revising   197

CHAPTER 8   **EXAMPLE**   199

Journal Suggestions   200
Guidelines   202
Topic   203
Organization and Development   204
    Extended Example   205
    Multiple Examples   205
Support   205
Thesis   206
Readings   210
    Student Essay   210
    Professional Essays   212
Writing Assignments   224
    Prewriting   225
    Revising   226

CHAPTER 9   **PROCESS ANALYSIS**   227

Journal Suggestions   229
Guidelines   230
Topic   231
Support   233
Organization   234
Thesis   239
Readings   241
  Student Essay   241
  Professional Essays   242
Writing Assignment   254
  Prewriting   255
  Revising   256

CHAPTER 10   **CLASSIFICATION**   259

Journal Suggestions   260
Guidelines   261
Topic   261
Principle of Classification   263
Special Features of Classification Essays   266
  Classes   267
  Characteristics   267
  Balance   267
Thesis   267
Readings   274
  Student Essay   274
  Professional Essays   275
Writing Assignment   289
  Prewriting   290
  Revising   291

CHAPTER 11   **COMPARISON AND CONTRAST**   293

Journal Suggestions   293
Guidelines   295
Topic   295
Bases of Comparison or Contrast   296
Organization   299
  Whole Method   299
  Point-by-Point Method   300
  Student Essays   301

Balance 303
Thesis 303
Readings 306
    Student Essay 306
    Professional Essays 308
Writing Assignment 316
    Prewriting 317
    Revising 318

CHAPTER 12   **DEFINITION** 319

Journal Suggestions 320
Ways of Defining 322
    Dictionary Definitions 322
    Extended Definitions 322
Guidelines 323
Topic 324
Standard Meaning 324
Purpose 325
Strategies of Development 325
    Development by Examples 325
    Development by Contrast 326
    Development by Function 327
Thesis 327
Readings 330
    Student Essay 330
    Professional Essays 331
Writing Assignment 350
    Prewriting 351
    Revising 352

PART THREE: APPLICATIONS 353

CHAPTER 13   **APPLYING WRITING SKILLS** 355

Using Writing Skills in Other College Courses 355
Getting Started 356
    Focusing 357
    Prewriting 357
Writing to Learn 358
    Taking Notes 358
    Textbook Outlining 363

Responding to Essay Questions   365
  Subject Knowledge   365
  Effective Writing   365
  Anticipating Essay Questions   366
  Taking an Essay Exam   367
Summaries, Reports, and Reviews   373
  Summaries   374
  Reports   377
  Reviews   381
The Research Paper   383
  Choosing a Topic   385
  Limiting the Topic   387
  Preparing a Working Bibliography   388
  Developing a Working Thesis   390
  Taking Notes   391
  Developing an Outline   397
  Writing a Draft of Your Paper   399
  Incorporating Sources   400
  Format for Writing Research Papers   402
Sample Research Paper   406
Journal Suggestions   412

Index   413

LIST OF READINGS

DESCRIPTION

A Busy Room	Anne Conner 180
China Still Lifes	William Gass 181
My Father, the Prince	Phyllis Theroux 188
Twenty-seven-twenty-two	Bob Greene 192

EXAMPLE

Freedom of Speech: Another Look	Gordon Chatterton 210
The Peter Principle	Laurence J. Peter and Raymond Hull 212
Elvira's Story	Flora Mancuso Edwards 217
Courtship Through the Ages	James Thurber 219

PROCESS ANALYSIS

How to Start an Intravenous Infusion	Judith Heck 241
How to Cook Dried Pasta So You Can Taste It	Corby Kummer 242
Ode to Makeup	Irene Egan 247
The Maker's Eye: Revising Your Own Manuscripts	Donald Murray 250

CLASSIFICATION

My Three Roles   Martha Howard   274
Friends, Good Friends—and Such   Judith Viorst   275
   Good Friends
Buying a Pickup Truck   Noel Perrin   279
Cinematypes   Susan Allen Toth   286

COMPARISON AND CONTRAST

Hands   Lynn Fredericks   306
The Transaction: Two Writing   William Zinsser   308
   Processes
That Lean and Hungry Look   Suzanne Britt   310
Venezuela for Visitors   John Updike   312

DEFINITION

Freedom   Sandy Faw   330
About Men   Gretel Ehrlich   331
The Mail of the Species   William Swanson   335
On Boxing   Joyce Carol Oates   339

PREFACE

One of the key observations we have made, both in learning to write ourselves and in teaching composition, is that writing is both a recursive and a linear activity. Writing is recursive or process-oriented in that writers and teachers cannot say precisely where and how to begin a piece of writing and likewise cannot say that a piece of writing is ever finished. There always seems to be something else we can do to a piece of writing to make it better.

On the other hand, practically all writing is linear or product-oriented. We write in order to finish a piece of writing. The report has to be written—that is, finished—as does the essay, the letter to Mom, the program for the PTA meeting, the autobiography on the job application, and so forth. Consequently, as writers, regardless of our status, we are forever caught in the tension of needing to produce and of needing to explore and express.

For these reasons, we believe that this text is a viable rhetoric and reader for students in freshman composition. In fact, the title of the text, *Essay Writing: Methods and Models*, reflects a basic choice English instructors confront when selecting a text: the dilemma of process versus product. This text is our attempt to resolve that dilemma. In it, we attempt to lead students through the exploratory, expressive stage of the writing process, as well as through the linear, product-oriented phase that accompanies most writing activity. *Essay Writing: Methods and Models* will enable students to understand and use the writing process to accomplish a wide variety of writing tasks.

The text is divided into three distinct parts that deal in detail with the essential components of writing and with their application to writing tasks in the academic community.

Part One describes the methods writers use to create completed compositions. Chapter 1, "Getting Started," takes a detailed look at the writing process. Students are shown that writing is a recursive process that depends on the interaction of numerous factors and activities. They are encouraged to experiment with a variety of prewriting strategies, and they are also made aware of the importance of audience, purpose, and organization in the development and completion of a writing task.

Chapter 2, "Developing a Thesis," moves students beyond the prewriting stage of the writing process and helps them understand the necessity of developing a working thesis for an essay. The material in this chapter analyzes the content and structure of effective thesis statements and presents numerous opportunities for students to critique thesis statements and to develop thesis statements of their own for essays on specific topics.

Chapter 3, "Developing the Essay," takes a close look at methods for organizing material within the body of an essay. It also presents valuable information on paragraph construction, the need for high-quality support of the thesis statement, and the importance of developing coherence and achieving unity in writing. These concepts are supported with numerous examples and exercises that will help students learn to incorporate these strategies in their own writing. Guidelines, models, and strategies for writing introductions and conclusions are contained in Chapter 4.

Chapter 5, "Revising the Essay," focuses on the necessity to "resee" one's writing and to evaluate it in relation to audience, purpose, thesis, support, organization, coherence, and unity. Students are shown that revision is an integral component—if, indeed, not the most important part—of the writing process.

Chapter 6, "Editing the Essay," is the final chapter in Part One. The material in this chapter focuses on the conventions of Standard Written English (SWE) and helps students understand that use of these conventions will enable them to communicate with their readers. This chapter provides information about various topics including sentence structure, pronoun usage, subject–verb agreement, parallelism, punctuation, and mechanics.

Part Two of the text focuses on standard expository strategies that writers use to present information in support of a thesis. These include description, example, process analysis, classification, comparison and contrast, and definition. Unlike many texts, which provide a minimum of information about using expository strategies, each chapter in Part Two of *Essay Writing: Methods and Models* provides detailed guidelines for using a particular strategy and supports these with numerous and varied examples and exercises.

In each chapter, students are led step-by-step through the process of developing an essay based primarily on the expository strategy under investigation. The process includes selecting, narrowing, and focusing a topic; developing a thesis statement; and supporting the thesis with adequate specifics in an appropriate organizational scheme. Each chapter in Part Two also includes general and contextual writing assignments and accompanying prewriting activities. The variety of assignments allows students to work independently, developing purpose, audience, and organizational format, or to work in a guided writing environment, with audience and purpose either stated or implied.

Finally, each chapter in Part Two includes one student essay and three professional essays, all of which clearly and directly illustrate the use of a particular expository strategy. The professional essays were selected according to two criteria: (1) clear, effective use of a particular rhetorical strategy; and (2) high interest level for students. Students will enjoy and be challenged by the content of these outstanding essays, *and* they will be able to discern quickly and easily the authors' uses of particular expository strategies in support of their essays' theses.

Part Three of *Essay Writing: Methods and Models*, entitled "Applications," represents the ideal result of any writing course. As composition instructors, our primary objective is to make a difference in how our students write once they leave our classes.

The long chapter constituting Part Three is entitled "Applying Writing Skills." It focuses on standard academic, job-related, and personal writing tasks. The material in this chapter leads students to apply the components of the writing process to specific writing tasks. Students can make any writing activity easier and its result more effective by identifying the audience, clarifying the purpose, and completing one or more prewriting activities. Revising drafts and editing for clarity of expression will further enhance the readability and effectiveness of a piece of writing.

The application of these strategies varies for each writing task. Chapter 13 shows students how to apply these elements of the writing process to various writing tasks, including note taking, essay exams, summaries, reports, reviews, and research papers. The chapter lets students see how the methods for writing in Part One and the models for writing in Part Two work together in relation to specific writing tasks to enable writers to complete their writing tasks effectively and with a significant degree of confidence and ease.

Essay Writing: Methods and Models is a clear, direct, exercise-oriented guide to prewriting techniques and to basic rhetorical principles and patterns. The abundance of clear, simple examples and focused, task-specific exercises works well with typical college freshmen and with nontraditional students. The "methods" and "models" arrangement of material in the text provides for maximum flexibility in the classroom. Instructors may select and present the prewriting techniques and rhetorical principles contained in Part One in any order they choose. Likewise, instructors may vary the order of the rhetorical patterns contained in Part Two of the book.

ACKNOWLEDGMENTS

We are grateful to the following reviewers, who made helpful comments and suggestions:

Peter D. Adams, Essex Community College

Rebecca S. Argall, Memphis State University

Barbara Baxter, Memphis State Technical Institute

Linda Doran, Volunteer State Community College

Linda R. Eastburn, Linn-Benton Community College

Jean M. English, Tallahassee Community College

Adam Fischer, Coastal Carolina Community College

John Hagaman, Western Kentucky University

Jim Hanlon, Shippensburg University of Pennsylvania

Paul D. Hauser, Kirkwood Community College

Kathleen E. Kiefer, Colorado State University, Ft. Collins

John B. Little, Pima Community College

James A. Moore, East Central University

Randall L. Popken, Tarleton State University

Nancy Posselt, Midlands Technical College

Duane H. Roen, University of Arizona

B. Alice Rogers, Nashville State Technical Institute

Joyce Swofford, Clayton State College

Dene Kay Thomas, University of Idaho

Patricia W. Wright, Wayne Community College

In addition, we want to thank our colleagues for their ideas and encouragement: Blair Hancock, Lola Knox, Ann Moffett, Brenda Moore, the late Edith Murphy, and Dianne Wagner.

P A R T O N E

METHODS

✎ CHAPTER ONE

GETTING STARTED

Taking a trip to the beach this weekend would require some special planning on your part. You might begin by choosing a place to stay and making reservations. You might also clean your car, check the oil, and get a full tank of gas. You might even find a road map and get some extra cash. Imagine making these plans, getting into your car on Friday afternoon, and realizing an hour down the road that you had forgotten to pack. There you are: perfect destination, a place to stay, but no toothbrush, bathing suit, suntan lotion, or radio. You aren't likely to think to yourself, "Oh well, somehow I will get by. Maybe I'll run into someone I know who will lend me a bathing suit!"

Now think about writing assignments. How many times have you had a particular topic in mind, sat down to write, and found you had nothing to say? You probably sat there staring at the paper and finally started writing, just hoping that the right ideas would pop up.

Writing projects, like a beach trip, require careful preparation in order to be successful. There are several ways you can prepare to achieve the successful completion of a writing assignment. Collectively, these activities are called *prewriting and focusing*. Following are several guidelines and methods for prewriting and focusing. Be sure to try them all, and complete the exercises for each. Afterward, the trip will be less stressful, more productive, and maybe even fun.

✎ PREWRITING

Prewriting includes many of the thinking and writing activities necessary before you can begin to prepare a first draft of a writing assignment. Most writers go through a series of mental discovery activities prior to beginning to write. These activities help them to develop a focus and to generate ideas for writing. It is also possible (and advisable) to supplement these mental discovery activities with written activities that encourage the flow of ideas and provide a written record of the results of the discovery process. Prewriting, then, consists of written activities you perform in order to get to the point of writing a draft.

Remember, however, that writing is a recursive activity. During the process of producing a finished piece of writing, you may adjust, fine-tune, delete, rewrite, and augment one or more of the paragraphs or one or more of the ideas. Consequently, prewriting doesn't apply exclusively to the beginning of the writing process. You may find that you also need to use prewriting techniques at various stages along the way to a finished piece of writing.

Does all of this sound hard? It is! Good writing is hard work and requires patience, diligence, and thought. Following are some ways to make the task easier by becoming comfortable with the prewriting part of the writing process. As you gain familiarity with some of these prewriting methods and learn to use them regularly, you will find not only that they help you get started with a writing task but that they also make writing a little easier. For many writers, the hardest part of writing is the first part—getting started.

JOURNAL

Journal keeping, a prewriting activity, is a well-established method of generating ideas for writing and of producing material useful in specific writing tasks. Keeping a journal is a very private activity, and doing it successfully requires some self-discipline. However, it is also very rewarding. It offers you an opportunity to express and record your thoughts and feelings in a safe, noncritical, and unrestricted manner. It can also serve as a source of ideas—even inspiration—for completing required writing tasks. And just as important, journal writing, if practiced regularly, helps to demystify the act of writing and to make writing an accessible, reliable, and comfortable method of self-expression.

Keeping a journal, like other prewriting activities, is a relatively simple, straightforward process. The following guidelines will enable you to begin to practice the art of journal keeping:

- Use a spiral notebook or loose-leaf binder.
- Write regularly (daily is best) in your journal.
- Write for a predetermined minimum amount of time, and longer if you can; write for at least ten minutes during each journal-writing session.
- Write on a variety of subjects, and include your feelings, opinions, and ideas.
- Be alert to topics for journal-writing sessions; ideas may come from conversations, class discussions and lectures, daily news reports, books and magazines, movies—even from memories and dreams.
- Be only moderately concerned with the correctness of your journal writing; grammar, punctuation, and spelling can be corrected later, if necessary.
- Review your journal entries periodically; such review can produce new ideas for future journal entries, remind you of a previous entry you may want to develop further, or simply impress you with the amount of writing you've produced.

These journal-keeping guidelines will enable you to record your thoughts, ideas, and feelings in a safe and rewarding manner. The writing that you accumulate in your journal can also become a source of ideas and information for other writing activities. Figure 1.1, a sample page from a student journal, shows what a journal entry might look like.

FREEWRITING AND FOCUSED FREEWRITING

Freewriting and focused freewriting are two of the easiest ways to begin the prewriting process. Both of these prewriting techniques require that you write regularly, according to a few simple guidelines.

Freewriting   A key purpose of freewriting is to produce a certain quantity of writing or to write for a specified amount of time on particular subjects. Your instructor may ask you to freewrite for ten minutes at the beginning of each class period and to collect this writing in a notebook. Or you may do this on your own outside class whenever you have a writing assignment to complete. In either case, the guidelines for freewriting are simple:

- Write without stopping for a specified amount of time.
- Or write without stopping until you have produced a specified amount of copy.
- Write about anything you want or need to write about.
- Do not plan, organize, revise, or proofread as you write.

FIGURE 1.1 Sample journal entry

8/27/88

My history prof. asked an interesting question: "Is nuclear disarmament desirable?" That led to other questions. Will ND lead to an increase in ~~conventional~~ conventional warfare? If so, ~~than~~ then we know people are going to be killed. As long as the Super Powers are at a nuclear standoff we know they won't fight a conventional war. Thus no one dies — at least not in war. I didn't say anything but I don't agree. Sooner or later someone will push the button and most of us will die. Why? Just because the button is there. How can I prove this?

Mom called — 2:00 pm — I was napping. She wants me home this weekend to see Uncle Marvin from N.Y. I have to call back on Fri. Who's Uncle Marvin?

Still working on the Eng. essay — I know I'm going to write on the meaning of Freedom! But what will I say ??? Freedom means FREE, but is that possible? Should we be allowed to drive our cars anywhere we want to? Can we dump any garbage anywhere we please? Free?

Freewriting is particularly helpful when you're faced with the feeling that you have nothing to say or when you find it hard to get started on a particular writing assignment. It is always an effective technique for beginning the writing process.

PRACTICE   Set aside time each day for the next three days for an uninterrupted ten-minute stint of freewriting. As you do the freewriting, remember to write continuously for the full ten minutes. Write whatever comes to your mind, even if it is just your name. Many people find that, if they experience writer's block at this point, it helps to write about the block. Or write, "I can't think of anything to say." Try it. Skip the fourth day, and then freewrite again for the next two days. If possible, avoid rereading your writing as you do this exercise. On the seventh day, reread your writing. As you do, you will probably discover some of the following:

1. You wrote a lot of garbage! One day you did write your name over and over.

2. In the midst of all the garbage are one or two sentences or parts of sentences that catch your eye. Mark them in some way; an asterisk or highlighting pen works well. You may be able to use some of these highlighted ideas in later assignments. In addition, these words or phrases may be worthy of more writing. If this is the case, you may want to try focused freewriting on these ideas.

3. Most important, you do have things to say. Knowing this should lessen your anxiety about future writing assignments.

4. Add your own discoveries about your freewriting in the spaces provided here:

   _____

   _____

   _____

   _____

Focused Freewriting   The second type of freewriting is called *focused* or *guided freewriting*. Perhaps you have been given a list of topics and you must choose one of these for your next writing assignment. A freewriting exercise in which you focus on your chosen subject will help you discover things to say about that subject as well as to identify a central or main idea to develop in an essay about the topic. The guidelines for focused freewriting are the same as those for freewriting. Figure 1.2 shows an example of focused freewriting.

PRACTICE   Your instructor may give you a particular subject for this focused freewriting exercise. If not, come up with your own topic or try one of the ones listed here. Again as you do this, remember to write for at least ten minutes, and don't worry about spelling or grammatical errors. Just write!

Topics

How to bathe a dog

Your favorite time of the year

How you plan to relax when you get home today

House plants you have liked or killed or grown

The last time you listened to the radio

The focused freewriting idea you liked best from your freewriting exercise

LOOPING

Looping, another prewriting activity, at first resembles focused freewriting. The first step in looping is to write freely and rapidly on a specific subject for six minutes. As with freewriting, you concentrate during this phase on getting thoughts down on paper, without worrying about grammar or organization.

After writing for six minutes, read what you have written and underline what you believe to be the central or best idea contained in this piece of writing. This central idea, whether it is a sentence or part of a sentence, is called the *dominant statement*.

On another sheet of paper, write a sentence that summarizes the dominant statement from your first loop. Then do another six minutes of focused freewriting based on this statement. This is the second loop.

Repeat this process a third time. Select the dominant statement from the second bout of focused freewriting, write a sentence that summarizes it, and then freewrite for another six minutes about this dominant statement. This is the third loop.

After the third loop, reread all of your writing. By the time you finish rereading it, you will see some central or focused idea that can be used

FIGURE 1.2   Sample focused freewriting

FREEDOM

I've decided to write my essay about freedom — what it really means. The big question I'm facing is can we really be free — can we have total freedom and still have some form of society or community or order — maybe not — maybe freedom is relative some how or other — can there be degrees of freedom — levels of freedom — and what would this depend on and who would decide how much freedom is OK and how much is not and then what's the worse that can happen if we have total freedom? Has there ever been a society that tried this and what happened and where and how long did it last? I don't know how I would find out; maybe look in the library, but I'm not sure I have the time. I think I want to say that freedom is perfect, but human beings are not so maybe we can't have total freedom. What will we have?

as the subject of an essay. Thus you have found something to write about—something to say.

PRACTICE   Select one of the following topics, and do a practice looping exercise based on it:

> Your fear of writing
>
> What you remember about your high-school English class
>
> Your worst vacation
>
> The problems of being a parent
>
> Your most memorable Christmas Eve
>
> A topic of your own choosing

As you complete this activity, remember the following points:

- This exercise works best if you try at least three loops. If, after you have completed three loops, you still have trouble finding something to write about, try looping one or two more times. The extra time and effort will be worthwhile if they help you find a focus for your essay.
- Don't concern yourself with mistakes and corrections as you write the loops. Prewriting is for your benefit. It doesn't matter how many words are misspelled, how many sentences are left fragmented, or how many commas are omitted. Concentrate only on committing your thoughts to paper.
- Several sheets of paper are helpful for this exercise—at least one for each loop.

CUBING

Cubing, a prewriting activity developed by Peter Elbow, assumes that you have reached the point where you have in mind a subject that you want or need to write about. You then explore this subject from six points of view: description, comparison, association, analysis, application, and persuasion.

Perhaps it will help to imagine the six sides of a cube. On each side of the cube is a different mini-writing assignment or way to explore the subject. Each mini-writing assignment actually requires you to respond to your subject from a particular perspective.

When you finish all of the responses, you will have examined your topic from six different perspectives. Then reread what you have written. It is likely that one of the six perspectives will offer an insight into the subject that you feel you can develop in more detail. The writing you did on that perspective thus provides material for you to develop as the focus of the first draft of the writing assignment. Figure 1.3 is an example of a cubing exercise.

PRACTICE

Pick your own topic or select one of the following subjects for this cubing exercise:

| school | marriage | your favorite short story |
| work | swimming | best friends |

Then write about each of the following "sides of the cube," using the subject you just chose. NOTE: These writings work best as timed activities. Allow three to five minutes for writing about each of the six perspectives. You will spend approximately twenty minutes generating ideas as you complete a cubing exercise.

A. **Describe it.** Look closely at your subject, and record what you see. If it is an abstract term (for example, *marriage*), your description will have a different tone than it will have if your subject is a more tangible one (such as *swimming*). Don't worry about that. Just concentrate on writing swiftly about the perspective on this side of the cube.

B. **Compare it.** What does it resemble? Remember, comparison can include likenesses *and* differences.

C. **Associate it.** What or whom do you think of when you think about this subject? Does it make you think of certain times, people, places, or events?

D. **Analyze it.** Tell how it is made, constructed, or formed; and if possible, identify what it is made of.

E. **Apply it.** How can this subject be used? What can you do with it?

F. **Argue for it or against it.** Be sure to choose only one position. Give reasons why you are for or against it.

When you finish looking at your subject from these six perspectives, you will have some idea of which perspective has the greatest potential for being developed into a paragraph or essay. As with all prewriting activities, keep two things in mind:

1. This is a prewriting activity. The goal is to develop a focus for writing and to generate ideas—not to produce a finished piece of writing.

FIGURE 1.3 Sample cubing exercise

<u>Describe it</u> freedom seems to be a state of being. It's like a way of living and relating to the world and everybody in it. It's liberated and unrestricted, or at least I think it ought to be.

<u>Compare it</u> freedom is like any other political system in that it is a political system. It differs from all others in that its primary objective is to let people do and be what they want to do and be.

<u>Associate it</u> freedom makes ~~it~~ me think of a vacation with no obligations and no responsibilities and the opportunity to go and do as I please. Why? Should it? Too Silly?

<u>Analyze it</u> freedom is made up of a set of beliefs that says people have the right to control their own lives. and this right comes just from the fact that we are human beings. Freedom exists when people choose to exercise these rights. Is this right?

<u>Apply it</u> the primary use of freedom is to let people be and become what they want to be and become. This also will help society since everyone will be the most and best possible.

<u>Argue for or against it</u> I'll argue for freedom since in my opinion it's the best way to live to take the fullest advantage of life. Also, other people feel the same way and try to get it, as can be seen in the news.

2. Keep all your cubing responses. You may want to use your response to another side of the cube at a later stage of completing the writing assignment. Or perhaps, in the process of examining the subject from these six perspectives, you may have written something that suggests a new idea or approach to the subject. Finally, there just may be some gem in this prewriting activity that is worth keeping for future reference.

INVENTORY

The prewriting technique called *inventory* requires you to take an inventory of your knowledge, beliefs, and feelings about a particular subject. As you take the inventory, you record the information you generate. The inventory then becomes a means to develop a focus for writing about the topic, as well as a source of information and ideas for completing the writing assignment.

Two methods of conducting the inventory are possible: brainstorming and clustering. Like cubing, both brainstorming and clustering assume that you have already settled on a general subject with which to begin.

Brainstorming   Brainstorming is primarily a listing activity. When you brainstorm a subject, you jot down all the ideas, words, and phrases that come to mind as you think about the subject. This exercise works best if you concentrate on quantity. Try to list as many different words or phrases as you can about the subject. When you have finished, look over the list and identify the dominant words or ideas contained in it.

PRACTICE   This exercise can be fun to do as a group. Form a group of three or four fellow writers. Appoint one person to serve as the recorder. After you agree on a topic, begin brainstorming. As your group thinks of words and phrases that relate to the topic, the recorder (who can also brainstorm while recording) writes these down. After ten minutes, stop and pass the paper around; or if possible, photocopy the page for each person in the group. It will be interesting to see how many different ideas the group produces about the topic. After you see the results of the group's brainstorming activity, you may want to write about the topic from a perspective that is entirely different from the one you originally had.

To complete this exercise, choose one of the topics from the following list. Try to make the choice a group decision.

holidays	stress	exercise
violence on the nightly news	the college library	cafeteria food
campus slang	date rape	

Clustering Clustering, another form of inventory taking, differs only slightly from brainstorming. In this prewriting activity, you again concentrate on the general subject and record any ideas you have that relate to the subject. But with clustering, you develop the relationships among your ideas as you record them. Begin by writing your topic in the center of a blank sheet of paper. Then draw a box around the topic. Next, write the main ideas you have about the topic at random around the topic, and draw a box or circle around each main idea. Then connect each main idea to the topic with a straight line. Finally, jot down your ideas about each main idea. Draw lines around these ideas, and connect them to the appropriate main ideas. When you finish this prewriting activity, you will have clustered several main ideas around the general topic. You will also have clustered various subordinate ideas around each main idea. One of these clusters can be used to provide a direction or focus for your writing. Figure 1.4 is an example of a clustering activity.

PRACTICE Either develop your own topic or select one of the following for this exercise. Write the topic you select in the center of a blank sheet of paper, draw a box around the topic, and then cluster your ideas around the topic. Remember to connect ideas to main ideas and main ideas to the topic.

a pastime	movies	your favorite relative
a class you dislike	best friends	your job

FOCUSING

Developing a focus for a piece of writing simplifies the writing process and enables you to write more creatively and effectively. The focusing process actually consists of three separate components: audience, purpose, and organization. Identifying your audience, establishing your purpose, and developing a form of organization for a particular writing task will help you move effectively toward a completed piece of writing.

FIGURE 1.4   Sample clustering activity

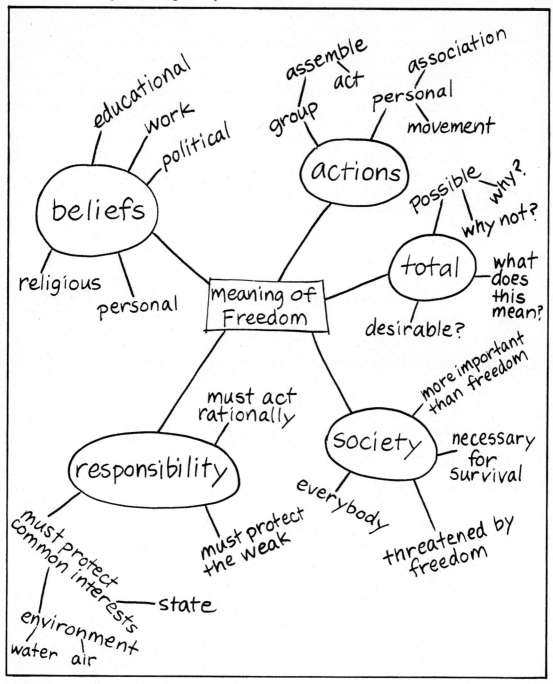

AUDIENCE

Identifying and analyzing your audience constitute an important part of the focusing process. The same information presented to different audiences might require different forms of presentation. Suppose that you have been asked to explain the K-mart Blue Light Special to an eight-year-old American child and to an adult Mexican tourist. Your task in both cases is the same, but your explanation to the young American will differ considerably from your explanation to the Mexican adult.

Clearly, analyzing your audience can have a significant effect on a particular writing task. Audience analysis can help you make the following decisions about a writing assignment:

- Length of the writing
- Depth of the writing
- Tone
- Point of view
- Use of examples
- Level of technicality

Finally, audience analysis has the added benefit of making writing less difficult. It's easier to write *to someone* about something than it is just to write about something.

Personal Audience Personal settings for writing are those in which you are writing for yourself. These can be in the form of journals, diaries, notes to yourself, and even grocery lists. This kind of writing, according to author and writing theorist Linda Flower, is often referred to as *writer-based prose*. In this type of writing, you are not under any obligation to make your writing clear and logical, or to communicate to anyone other than yourself. Consequently, you are free to say whatever you want to say in whatever order you want to use and at whatever level of detail you wish. The only standard for judging the quality of your own writer-based prose is whether or not it makes sense to you and whether or not it allows you to express your thoughts and feelings adequately.

Invoked Audience Often when you write, particularly in academic settings, your audience is not clearly defined. Generally, of course, your audience is your teacher, who will read and evaluate your writing. Still, it is helpful to know who your audience is before you start writing. Knowing that you have an audience to write for enables you to focus your writing in order to make it suitable for that audience.

If, for example, you are assigned to write an essay about the personal growth experienced by King Lear in Shakespeare's *King Lear,* you have an invoked audience. Your teacher does not say "write this paper to me." But as you begin to write the paper, you realize that you are addressing it to your instructor. You may also realize that you are writing it to or for the larger academic community, which includes your classmates and may also include other teachers and perhaps people outside your class and/or your school.

Regardless of which concept of audience comes to mind as you write the essay, you are identifying a potential reader or readers of your essay. Invoking an audience for your writing may strike you as artificial. But even though that may be true, it highlights the need all writers have to write to an audience (reader). Knowing who your audience is before you start writing is helpful and perhaps essential, since this knowledge enables you to focus your writing.

Invoking an audience helps you answer these very important questions:

■ How long does your audience expect this writing assignment to be?
■ Does the reader(s) expect it to be typed or handwritten?
■ Does the reader(s) expect it to contain just your personal views? materials from authorities in the field? both?
■ What does the reader(s) expect in terms of tone, point of view, and level of technicality?

Let's suppose that the previously mentioned topic on *King Lear* is your subject for a writing assignment. You might first want to identify your audience. The audience in this case is your teacher. Next, you would want to analyze this audience in terms of the particular writing assignment. You might ask these questions:

1. How long does my instructor expect this essay to be?

2. Does he/she expect it to be typed or handwritten?

3. Does he/she expect it to contain documentation or just my personal views and opinions?

4. What tone should I use? Should the essay have a formal, detached tone or a more personal tone?

5. What about point of view? Should the essay be written from the formal third-person point of view or from the more subjective first-person point of view?

You may be writing this essay for a teacher who is considered to be a Shakespearian scholar. If so, your essay will probably not add any information to this teacher's knowledge about *King Lear*. Perhaps, though, this teacher is making the assignment in order to evaluate your comprehension of the play. Therefore, the level of technicality of your essay may need to be scholarly—not so as to present new information to your teacher about the play, but to demonstrate your level of understanding of the play. Remember that audience questions such as these should be considered regardless of whether or not your teacher mentions them when making an assignment.

Here's one additional point to remember when working on a writing assignment that requires an invoked audience. Keep your writing interesting. No one likes to be bored—not even teachers who make writing assignments! Therefore, your writing should be interesting and lively.

Public Audience A third type of audience analysis is very much like market research. The first step in this type of analysis is to understand the product—that is, to know what you are going to write about. The next step is to identify your audience or, in business terms, to define and analyze your market. Once you know who will be reading your writing, attempt to describe that audience. Here are some basic variables involving readers that are relevant to this type of audience analysis:

- Age
- Sex
- Educational level
- Interests
- Knowledge of the subject
- Prejudices in favor of or against the subject

Your description of your audience in terms of these basic characteristics will help you direct your writing to your reader. As you develop your description, try to create a mental image of your reader. Then imagine that you are talking directly to this person or group. Gradually, you'll discover that your writing begins to accommodate itself to particular audiences. As your audiences vary, you'll notice corresponding shifts in tone and in point of view, as well as changes in complexity of sentence structure and in the technical content of your writing.

PRACTICE   The following activities provide opportunities for you to write on the same topics for different audiences. As you begin each exercise, remember to ask some or all of the audience analysis questions about each audience. Keep your written responses short—no more than one paragraph each.

1. Explain to a prospective employer and then to your grandmother why you chose your vocation.

2. First tell your girlfriend or boyfriend and then your seven-year-old brother what you think is important in a good marriage.

3. Tell your diary and then your father why you failed chemistry (or some other course) last semester.

PURPOSE

Once you have identified your audience, you can begin to determine the purpose of the writing. *Purpose* generally refers to the goal of a piece of writing, and as such it makes clear just what you want a specific piece of writing to accomplish.

Usually, when people write essays, they want to accomplish one of two things: to inform readers or to persuade readers. Informing readers means conveying information to them. Most of the writing on the front page of a newspaper is of this type. By reading the articles that appear on this page, we can get a lot of information about numerous people, places, and events. Generally, these articles do not contain opinions of the writers, nor do they attempt to persuade us to agree with the content of the writing. Their primary purpose is to present information.

Instructors sometimes ask you to write essays of this type. For example, in a history class you might be assigned to write a term paper in which your primary purpose is to identify and describe the major changes in public sanitation in the United States during the nineteenth century. Your purpose in this writing assignment does not require you to express an opinion about these changes, to determine the relative merit of the changes, or even to evaluate the impact of the changes on the quality of life of nineteenth-century Americans. Rather, you are simply to inform: to identify and describe the changes.

Persuasive writing, unlike informative writing, attempts to persuade or convince the reader that the writer's position concerning a particular subject is valid or true. The inside of the front page of most newspapers contains this kind of writing. The editorial page contains articles (essays) that clearly express the writers' views about particular matters. Although these essays do, to some extent, present information about particular topics, their primary purpose is to provide interpretations of or draw conclusions about these topics. In doing so, these writers develop specific positions in relation to the topics and then attempt to demonstrate that their interpretations or conclusions are correct.

The earlier topic for a student essay, maintaining that King Lear experienced personal growth in the course of the play, requires persuasive writing. It is undeniable, of course, that Lear experienced numerous events during the play. It is not a foregone conclusion, however, that these experiences led to personal growth on the part of King Lear. Therefore, the writer of this essay must use the facts given in the play, along with an appropriate interpretation of them, to support this assertion.

PRACTICE   Complete each of the following exercises:

1.   Write a paragraph in which your purpose is to *inform* your reader of what constitutes proper conduct in a job interview.

2.   Write a paragraph in which your purpose is to *persuade* your reader that proper conduct is important in a job interview.

3.   Write either an informative paragraph or a persuasive paragraph on a topic of your choosing.

ORGANIZATION

Once you have identified the audience and established the purpose of a particular writing task, you must determine how to organize the presentation of information so that your writing addresses the audience appropriately and accomplishes its purpose.

In essay writing, *organization* refers to the order or arrangement in which information about the topic is presented. Generally, essays follow a rather simple but highly effective organizational pattern consisting of three parts: introduction, body, and conclusion. Each of these components serves a particular function in essay writing.

Introduction   Most essays begin with one or more introductory paragraphs. Short essays of 800 words or less usually begin with a one-paragraph introduction. Longer essays may contain two or more introductory paragraphs.

The introductory paragraph serves several functions. It gets the reader's attention, identifies the subject of the writing, presents background information about the subject, and (in some cases) presents the thesis statement of the essay. You will learn more about writing introductions in Chapter 4. Once the subject is introduced, the essay proceeds to the second part—the body.

Body   The body of the essay clarifies and supports the position taken toward the topic in the thesis statement. Generally, the body of an essay consists of two or more paragraphs. Each of these paragraphs makes a point about the thesis of the essay and then supports the point in the remainder of the paragraph.

Conclusion   Typically, an essay ends with a summary or concluding paragraph. As with introductions, conclusions may consist of one or more paragraphs, depending on the length of the essay. The conclusion reminds the reader of the thesis or main point of the writing and provides a summary of the supporting information that has been presented in the body of the essay. In addition, the conclusion may call for action on the part of the reader. Good conclusions assure the reader that the writer is aware of what must be said and has said it. Chapter 4 provides additional information on how to write effective conclusions.

PRACTICE   Journal keeping is a helpful practice and a valuable resource for all writers. You may want to consider keeping a journal as a part of your learning activity in this course. Begin by following the journal-keeping guidelines explained in this chapter.

Each chapter of this book includes a section entitled "Journal Suggestions." These sections provide an opportunity for you to focus your journal-writing activity on a specific component of the writing process. As you work your way through each chapter, review the journal suggestions; then consider using one or more of the suggested issues as topics for entries in your journal.

 ## JOURNAL SUGGESTIONS

Temporarily focus the writing in your journal on the subject of how you write. Particular issues you might write about in your journal include the following:

- What kinds of writing do you routinely do? Is all of your writing done for academic assignments? Do you write letters—to teachers, to friends, to business correspondents, to editors of newspapers?
- How do you begin writing? Do you have a special place where you feel comfortable writing? If you have a writing assignment, do you spend much time thinking about it before you actually begin?
- Is there a certain time of the day when you seem to do your best writing? Do you write better under pressure—for example, the night before the writing is due? Or do you allow yourself time to write, rewrite, and revise over a period of several days before an assignment is due?
- How do you feel about your writing? Are you comfortable with writing assignments? Is writing an activity you enjoy, tolerate, or dread? In your journal, analyze and explain your feelings about your writing.

C H A P T E R   T W O

DEVELOPING A THESIS

"Get to the point." Sometimes you actually make this statement; other times you want to, but don't. But in most situations we want people to get to the point, whether they're writing to us or speaking to us. And there is a good reason for this. It is important (and often essential) to know the point of any communication transaction, in order to make sense of what we read and hear.

In rhetorical terms, the point of a communication transaction is referred to as the *thesis* or the *thesis statement*. The thesis statement summarizes the purpose of a communication transaction.

We have trained ourselves to listen for the point in oral communication and to look for the point in a piece of expository writing. For example, you always look for the point when you read articles in your favorite magazines. If you see an article in *Working Woman* entitled, "How to Have More Free Time," you quickly scan the first couple of paragraphs until you locate the point (thesis) of the article. Then you decide whether or not to invest the time and effort required to read the article.

If the thesis attracts or interests you, you may choose to read the article. If the thesis does not appeal to you, you will probably skip the article and look for one that has a more interesting thesis (point).

And that brings us to another dimension—the contractual one—of what we mean by a thesis statement. Let's say that you are interested in the article entitled "How to Have More Free Time." The thesis, located near the end of the second paragraph, says, "Yes, you can add extra time to your day if you organize well, avoid interruptions, and keep control of your schedule."

The author has offered you a contract. She has presented you with goods that you may either purchase or pass up. If you buy—that is, if you decide to read the article—you are in effect purchasing the article the author has offered for sale. The price you pay is the time and energy you invest in reading what she has written. Neither of these, of course, can be refunded, if you should decide later that the article was not worth your investment after all.

But what if, after looking at the goods (the thesis statement), you buy and then the goods are simply not delivered? You read the thesis statement, which promises to show you three ways to get more free time, but the author instead writes about saving money on groceries, finding good restaurants, and having a hectic daily schedule. You may find some or all of this interesting, but you may also be annoyed because you invested your time and effort to learn about something (how to have more free time) that the author never really talked about.

Simply put, the author failed to honor the terms of the contract: she did not deliver the goods you agreed to purchase. Writers have a serious responsibility to honor such agreements, which is one reason why you as a writer must develop your thesis statements carefully. You must be certain that your thesis statements clearly and accurately present the points you want to make.

CHARACTERISTICS OF A THESIS STATEMENT

In order for you to develop effective thesis statements, it is important to know their three primary characteristics:

- A thesis statement is a statement; it is not a question.
- Generally, a thesis statement appears in a single sentence; however, a thesis may be presented in two or more consecutive sentences.
- A thesis statement comes at or near the end of the introduction of the essay. In short essays of 500 words or less, the thesis statement is usually the last sentence of the introductory paragraph.

COMPONENTS OF A THESIS STATEMENT

Every thesis statement contains a topic and a controlling idea. Thesis statements consisting exclusively of these two components are called *general thesis statements.*

In addition, a thesis statement may contain a third component: a plan of development. A thesis statement that contains a topic, a controlling idea, and a plan of development is called a *focused thesis statement*. A plan of development may also be contained in a separate sentence following the general thesis statement, in the introductory paragraph or paragraphs of the essay.

Thus, the components of general and focused thesis statements are as follows:

General Thesis

Topic
Controlling idea

Focused Thesis

Topic
Controlling idea
Plan of development

GENERAL THESIS STATEMENT

As we have just seen, the general thesis statement contains two components: a topic and a controlling idea.

Topic   The topic of a general thesis statement identifies the subject of the essay; it tells what the writing is about. As an example, the topic in the following general thesis statement is underlined:

Example

<u>French lamps</u> can be the solution to a variety of decorating problems.

Obviously, this essay is about French lamps. In fact, if the author writes about any other topic, we will be annoyed by the digression.

Here are some additional general thesis statements, in each of which the topic is underlined:

Examples

When I went back to school, my <u>family</u> had to make several difficult adjustments.

My teenage <u>daughters</u>, Jennifer and Alison, have caused me to reexamine many of my convictions.

My <u>grandmother</u>, who lived to be 95, taught me many important lessons about life.

PRACTICE   Find and underline the topic in each of the following general thesis statements:

1.   Success is a misunderstood word.

2.   My parents are very supportive people.

3. The most difficult thing I have had to do in college is to balance studying with the demands of my part-time job.

4. My friend Heather is a lazy person.

5. Flying is always a terrifying experience for me.

6. Much to my surprise, sociology is now my favorite subject.

7. The movie we saw last night, *Murder on Elm Street*, was terrible.

8. Beagles are difficult dogs to train.

9. I like cold weather for several reasons.

10. The book *Gone with the Wind* was much better than the movie.

PRACTICE   Thesis statements are not easy to write. In fact, the first draft of a thesis statement is rarely suitable "as is" for inclusion in the final draft of an essay.

Most writers spend considerable time and effort developing workable thesis statements. One of the methods they use to accomplish this consists of working their way through one or more prewriting activities until they have developed a suitable thesis statement for whatever they're attempting to write.

Perhaps you can benefit from this process, too. Select one of the following general topics or a topic of your own devising, and freewrite about it for four minutes. Once you have completed the freewriting, read what you have written and underline one or more topics mentioned in the freewriting that might serve as the topic of a thesis statement for an essay on that subject.

Topics

My favorite class is _____

The most important current event is _____

One thing I would never do is _____

At this point in life, I should _____

A kind of television program we could do without is _____

A social issue our government should spend more money, effort, or time

on is _____

Controlling Idea   The second essential component of a general thesis statement is the controlling idea. The controlling idea, like the topic, may consist of one or more words. It, too, can be easily identified in a general thesis statement. As an example, the controlling idea in the following general thesis statement is underlined:

Example   Goldfish, for a variety of reasons, are <u>ideal pets</u>.

"Ideal pets," the controlling idea in this general thesis statement, assures us that the content of this essay will be dedicated to showing why goldfish are great pets. In fact, we would not expect to find anything here about the negative features of goldfish as pets.

   From this example, it appears that the controlling idea in a general thesis statement actually controls or determines the content of the body of the essay. The controlling idea invites certain material to be included in the essay and keeps irrelevant material out of the essay.

PRACTICE   Locate and underline the controlling idea in each of the following general thesis statements:

1.   By following these simple steps, you can replace the fletching on your arrows and continue to shoot the same shafts.

2.   Much to my surprise, I realized that my life is controlled by these powerful passions.

3.   Of the many jobs I've had, painting, assembling furniture cases, and working as a brake-press operator have been the most satisfying.

4.   Justice, important to all of us but difficult to define, means different things to different people.

5.   Being a den mother for my young daughter's Brownie troop was very different from what I had expected.

6.   These three steps to good putting will improve your golf game and reduce your score.

7.   I liked "General Principles of Physical Chemistry," my second chemistry course at North Carolina State University, for several reasons.

8.   Many small differences between my husband's hands and my hands give subtle clues to our differing personalities.

9. Naples' citizens, poverty, and rich history made my hometown back in the States seem part of another planet rather than another country.

10. Although there are many types of life insurance policies, there are only two types of life insurance.

PRACTICE   You just practiced identifying the controlling idea in a series of thesis statements. Now you will practice developing controlling ideas, by using the prewriting activity known as *clustering*. If you're unsure about how to do this, review the discussion of clustering in Chapter 1.

Select a topic from the following list or come up with your own topic. Once you have chosen it, write the name of the topic in the center of a blank sheet of paper, and draw a box around it. Then give yourself three to five minutes to list ideas about the topic that you think should be included in an essay on the subject. Once you have clustered these ideas around the topic, review each one to see if one or more of them could serve as the controlling idea of a thesis statement for an essay on the topic.

Topics

College absence policy

The cure for the federal budget deficit

Boxing—an honorable sport?

My hometown

Adolescence

Selecting a suitable career

For example, the cluster shown in Figure 2.1 was developed in the course of a search for a controlling idea about the topic "College honor code." Notice that each circled item would work as the controlling idea of a thesis statement for an essay on the topic "College honor code." Thus, we could produce at least three different thesis statements from this cluster:

1. The college honor code is outdated.

2. The college honor code leads to the development of honest adults.

3. The college honor code builds character.

The following essay contains a general thesis statement. The supporting paragraphs in the body of the essay properly apply and develop the controlling idea contained in the general thesis statement. The controlling idea is underlined.

FIGURE 2.1   Sample cluster

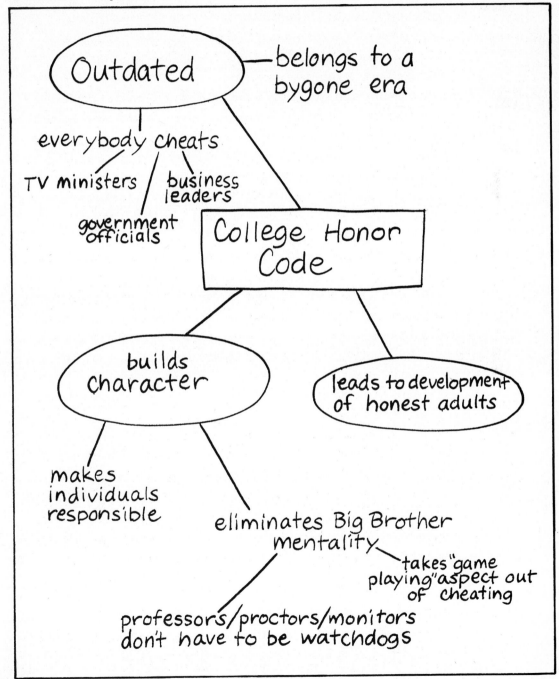

Student
Essay

Introductory
paragraph

Thesis
statement

Supporting
paragraphs

STAR WARS VERSUS *EXCALIBUR*, Mary Jones

Scanning the entertainment section of the newspaper, John searched desperately for a movie to occupy a rainy Saturday afternoon. Looking for anything without the words *star, galaxy,* or *outer space* in the title, his eyes soon fell upon an advertisement for *Excalibur,* a movie dealing with the legend of King Arthur and the Knights of the Round Table. Tired of space-war movies saturated with special effects, John figured that *Excalibur* would be an enjoyable change of pace. He was not disappointed and found the movie to be excellent, but he was startled by the number of similarities between *Excalibur* and the classic space-war movie, *Star Wars.* Despite the obvious differences of location and time, *Star Wars* and *Excalibur* contain some basic similarities.

The movie *Excalibur* tells the story of one of the most classic of all love triangles. This is the one between King Arthur, his wife Guinevere, and his best friend Lancelot. Arthur dearly loves both of them, and Guinevere deeply loves her idealistic husband, but she is drawn to the chivalrous, brave knight, Lancelot. Lancelot is torn by his feelings for the wife of his best friend but eventually admits his love to Guinevere. She returns it, and they are discovered by Arthur. Arthur is shattered by the affair but continues to love and fight for both of them.

The love triangle in *Star Wars* involves the naive farm boy turned fighter pilot Luke Skywalker, a powerful princess and senator named Leia, and a swashbuckling mercenary, Han Solo. Luke falls in love with Leia the first time he sees her and proves his love by saving her life several times. Leia sees Luke as more of a younger brother than a sweetheart, and she eventually falls in love with Han Solo, Luke's best friend. Luke is jealous of the relationship between Han Solo and Leia, but he endures it since he cares for them both.

One of the central characters in *Excalibur* is Merlin, the magician who advises Arthur. Merlin is a wizard who lives backward in time and, therefore, knows what will happen in Arthur's future. Midway through the story, Merlin is captured by Morgana, an evil sorceress.

However, Merlin continues to appear to Arthur when he is in serious trouble to offer his advice. It is Merlin who first helps Arthur wield the magic sword Excalibur that gives him the power to rule Camelot.

Excalibur's Merlin is comparable to *Star Wars'* Obi Wan Kenobi. Obi Wan is one of the last surviving members of a brotherhood of warriors known as the Jedi. He instructs Luke in the ways of the Jedi so he will be able to fight against the evil empire. Obi Wan gives Luke a light saber that had belonged to his father and teaches him how to use it. Midway through *Star Wars,* Obi Wan is killed by Darth Vader, the wicked representative of the empire, but continues to appear to Luke and advise him in desperate situations.

The evil element in *Excalibur* is represented equally by a mother and son, Morgana and Mordred. Morgana, who is Arthur's sister and the mother of their son Mordred, is intent on destroying Arthur. She teaches Mordred to hate Arthur and eventually spurs him to claim his father's throne. Arthur refuses and fights Mordred. Their battle ends as a duel between Arthur and Mordred, in which they kill each other.

In *Star Wars,* the ultimate evil in the universe is personified by Darth Vader. Darth Vader, who is Luke Skywalker's father, is obsessed with destroying the rebel faction that is rising against the empire. He uses every means available to him to see that his wishes are carried out. Once a Jedi, Darth Vader allowed the lure of power to entice him into his evil position. He is hated and feared by all who know him or know about him, and he is capable of using his powers as a Jedi to get his way.

Conclusion   *Star Wars* and *Excalibur* are both excellent movies and should be seen once for sheer enjoyment. If seen again, though, it is interesting to analyze the similarities existing between the two and to note that what Malory thought was an exciting plot several centuries ago still works today.

COMMENT: Notice that the controlling idea in the general thesis statement of this essay suggests that there are basic similarities in the movies *Star Wars* and *Excalibur.*

FOCUSED THESIS STATEMENT

Often, writers choose to use thesis statements that are more developed. A general thesis statement can be elaborated by the addition of a *plan of development*. When a thesis statement contains a plan of development, as well as a topic and a controlling idea, it is called a *focused* thesis statement. As an example, the plan of development in the following focused thesis is underlined:

Example   Goldfish make ideal pets because they <u>eat very little, are never noisy, and require no house training.</u>

The plan of development in a focused thesis statement suggests how the body of the essay will be developed. In fact, the plan of development is a brief or miniature outline of the body of the essay. In the goldfish example, we can assume that the writer will write about the small amount of food goldfish eat, how well behaved they are, and how easy they are to take care of.

PRACTICE   Each of the following sentences contains a plan of development and is, therefore, a focused thesis statement. Underline the plan of development in each of these focused thesis statements.

1. The United States space program consists of three primary areas of activity: manned flight, unmanned deep-space probes, and scientific and applications satellites.

2. Genene Hayes is a great hair stylist because she's relaxed, friendly, and very good at what she does.

3. To see the differences clearly, contrast what the Oldsmobile Delta 88 and the Toyota Corolla two-door sedan offer in comfort, convenience, and cost.

4. The basic steps involved in making a lamp consist of assembling the necessary parts, putting the frame together, and wiring the socket.

5. You will become a faster, more effective reader if you learn how to scan what you read, find the main idea, and identify transition words.

6. Simple guidelines for courteous and efficient telephone usage include learning basic greetings, correct responses, and appropriate closings to conversations.

7. The nature of black holes is revealed by a study of their physical properties and their formative process.

8. Over the years, there has been general agreement that some classic forms and colors and certain combinations of these represent beauty.

9. Planning a wedding can be an easy and enjoyable task if you give yourself plenty of time, establish a budget, and prepare a guest list.

10. Just as an athlete prepares for the grueling challenge of competition, a pregnant woman needs to prepare her body for childbirth by eating properly, resting adequately, and exercising appropriately.

PRACTICE   Creating a plan of development for inclusion in a thesis statement requires careful thought about the possible structure and development of the essay. Once you have worked out a topic and a controlling idea, you can focus on designing a plan of development to include in the thesis statement. Selected prewriting activities can be very helpful in determining what information you should include in the body of the essay and what order you should use to organize the material in support of your thesis.

Cubing is a particularly effective technique for creating a plan of development. It enables you to look at a topic and its accompanying controlling idea from six perspectives and, thereby, to see at least six different ways of developing the topic. If you're unsure about what's involved in cubing, review the discussion of cubing in Chapter 1.

Begin by composing a thesis statement that contains just a topic and a controlling idea. Once you have a thesis statement containing a topic and a controlling idea, respond to the questions on the six sides of the cube. Then analyze your responses and determine whether two or more of them might work as components of a plan of development for this thesis statement. The following sample exercise reviews how to carry out the steps of cubing for a particular thesis statement.

Sample: Cubing Exercise   Here is how one person used cubing to create a plan of development for a thesis statement that supports (controlling idea) a woman's right to obtain an abortion (topic).

A.   Describe it.
Example   Abortion is the act of terminating a pregnancy by killing the fetus by surgically removing the fetus from the womb. (I may have to check on the accuracy of this.)

B. Compare it.

Example
It's a lot like a DNC. (Is this the right abbreviation? Check it.) The procedure is about the same. My sister had a DNC and a good friend of mine confided in me that she had an abortion two years ago. From listening to them talk, it sounds like these are very similar procedures. But they felt differently about them. My sister didn't mind letting people know about her DNC, but my friend told me that I was only the fifth person who knew about her abortion.

C. Associate it.

Example
I associate abortions with child abuse, poverty, and orphans. It seems to me that one way to avoid these tragedies is to let women abort so that fewer unwanted children are born.

D. Analyze it.

Example
Abortions are performed by physicians in proper medical settings. This means that patients receive good care and run few medical risks. Also, patients receive counseling and psychological and emotional support.

E. Apply it.

Example
Abortions have several uses. They give women more control over their lives. They also help to control the population and to decrease the number of unwanted children.

F. Argue for or against it.

Example
I'm for a woman's right to a safe abortion, regardless of circumstances. Women need to be in charge of their own bodies; after all, their bodies are *their* bodies. As for women electing to use this as a form of birth control, I don't agree. No woman in her right mind would prefer to have an abortion as opposed to some less painful, less complicated, and less expensive method of birth control.

COMMENT: This cubing activity enabled the writer to develop the following thesis statement, in which the plan of development is underlined:

Example
A woman's right to obtain an abortion should be protected, since it ensures that women who have abortions will receive proper medical care and that fewer unwanted children will be born.

The following essay contains a focused thesis statement. The supporting paragraphs in the body of the essay show a proper application of the plan of development contained in the focused thesis statement. The plan of development is underlined.

**Student
Essay**

Introductory
paragraph

INTERSTATE EATING, Donald Scott

The interstate highway system has made automobile travel easy and fast. However, these new highways have created a crisis for the discerning traveling diner. No longer can one whip into "Mom's Diner" while passing through a town, because no longer does one travel through towns. Such friendly, cozy, distinctive restaurants have been replaced by standardized, boring interstate eating establishments. These interstate eating establishments are a growth industry and have proliferated at an astounding rate. On the more-traveled interstates, it is rare to find an interchange without at least one such restaurant. With this great number of eating establishments, one would expect diversity. This, however, is not the case. In fact, the sameness of interstate restaurants is such that all of them can be classified as fast-food, coffee shop, or truck-stop eateries.

Focused
thesis
statement

Supporting
paragraphs

Fast-food restaurants have become very common along the interstate highway system. These include such chains as Wendy's, McDonald's, and Hardee's. They specialize in burgers and other sandwiches. The customer generally has to place and pick up his order; he is also expected to clear his table when finished. The advantage of fast-food restaurants is their ability to provide a meal quickly and economically. The disadvantages include the limited choice of food fare and the lack of dining comfort.

The next category of restaurants along interstates is the coffee shop. This group includes Denny's, Howard Johnson's, and some independent restaurants. Coffee shops have table service, and some have non-smoking areas. Their menus are varied and include numerous short-order meals. Also, these restaurants usually have lunch and dinner specials. The food is of good quality, and a meal usually costs from five to seven dollars. The advantages of coffee shops are good service and comfortable dining. One disadvantage is that many of them close at night.

The last category of interstate restaurants is the truck stop. The modern truck stop is the creation of the major oil companies. Originally, truck stops were built for truckers, but now tourists make up quite a bit of these restaurants' trade. Truck stops have both table service and buffet meals. The food quality is low—about the equivalent of frozen TV dinners. The prices are quite high in relation to value. Typically, a meal costs from six to eight dollars in a truck-stop restaurant. The only advantage of truck-stop restaurants is their twenty-four-hour availability.

Conclusion   Almost everyone has eaten in the types of restaurants described here as interstate eating establishments. One may or may not like this type of dining, but cloverleaf cuisinaries do not depend on repeat business. So, should one journey on the interstate highways, he has the choice of eating at the fast-food restaurants with time-saving service and economical prices, the coffee shop with table service and a varied menu, or the truck stop with greasy food, exorbitant prices, and all-night availability.

COMMENT: The thesis statement of this essay suggests that there are basically three types of eating establishments along interstates, which it then names. The body of the essay provides discussion of these three types of interstate eating establishments. Thus, the plan of development in this focused thesis statement is actually a miniature outline of the body of the essay.

PRACTICE   Underline the plan of development in each of the following essays' focused thesis statements, and answer the question following each essay.

Student Essay

Introductory paragraph

Focused thesis statement

BEAUTY: A DEFINITION, Virginia Stover

Semantics really come into play when one attempts to define the word beauty. *Webster's Dictionary* says that beauty is the quality attributed to whatever pleases or satisfies the senses or mind, thus making it an individual matter. For example, to some people, roses are beautiful. Others, however, may associate a red rose and its cloying scent with sickness or death; to their mind, then, the rose is unpleasant. In spite of such conflicts, there is, nevertheless, general agreement that some classic forms, colors, and certain types of behavior represent beauty.

Supporting paragraphs

Beauty is found in form. Whether it is the very studied looks of a high-fashion model or the unconsciously formed grace of a classically shaped shell, there is beauty in line. Pleasing shapes and lines are found in architecture, from the pristine spire of a country church steeple to an exotic Turkish minaret. A horse of good conformation has graceful lines and to me is beautiful. There are bountiful other examples of beauty in the animal kingdom that have good form, such as birds, butterflies, streamlined fish, and deer. One only has to look about in nature to see beauty in form.

Color is a marvelous medium for portraying beauty. The movie *Fantasia* is a prime example of this. Disney's use of color in this movie is superb. Mother Nature also gives gorgeous displays of beauty through color. I can lose myself by looking up into green trees. The varied shades of the green leaves, when gently touched by the wind, change from a soft green to silvery green. When there is blue sky for a background, the effect can only be described as beautiful. Last winter, I was awed by the colors of an ice storm. A light rain had fallen and then quickly frozen. Occasionally the sun would pop out from behind the cloudy, gray sky, causing the whole landscape to sparkle in pink, gray, and silver. The colors created a magnificent scene that over-whelmed me. The beauty of color can be a moving experience.

"Pretty is as pretty does" and "beauty is only skin deep" are over-used ways of saying that a pleasant and cheerful attitude toward life gives beauty to the person who radiates these qualities. I remember meeting and getting to know a homely woman, whom, because of her kindness, gentleness, and unassuming ways, I came to consider beau-tiful. On the other hand, I have known physically attractive people who were so unpleasant that I thought of them as being just that— unpleasant. For me, their insensitive attitudes overshadowed their good looks. Much personal beauty comes from within, from the soul, and is evidenced in a person's attitude. If this condition occurs, then we see beauty.

Conclusion

That old homily, "Beauty is in the eye of the beholder," says it all. Anything that I have referred to as beauty can be negated by a bad experience. Although a well-formed horse has beauty, the person who has just been thrown by one probably has a different opinion. I can only conclude by agreeing with *Webster's Dictionary* that beauty is indeed an individual choice.

RESPONSE: In a brief paragraph, explain how the supporting paragraphs of this essay follow the plan of development contained in the focused thesis statement of the essay.

_____

_____

_____

_____

_____

_____

Student Essay

Introductory paragraph

Focused thesis statement

Supporting paragraphs

BLACK HOLES, Frank White

Almost everyone has heard of "black holes" in space, but most people do not know what these actually are. Contrary to popular assumption, a black hole is not a void; rather, it is a solid object. This fact, as well as other information about the nature of black holes, is revealed by a study of their physical properties and their formative process.

A black hole is a celestial body with gravity so strong that light waves cannot escape from it—hence, the designation "black." The speed required to escape from a black hole's gravitational field is greater than the speed of light. A black hole creates a three-dimensional gravity hole into which anything nearby will fall. Black holes attract nearby stars, dust, and gas, and are surrounded by accretion disks of captured material. As the material in an accretion disk spirals into a black hole, it becomes heated by compression and emits X rays. X rays, which are more energetic than visible light, can escape from black holes and are the only means of observing black holes.

A black hole is the corpse of a dead star that has exhausted its thermonuclear fuel and collapsed. If a star is large enough (at least three times as massive as the sun), it will, when it burns out, collapse under the influence of its own gravity until the nuclei of its atoms actually touch each other. The resulting compact sphere, estimated to be about ten miles in diameter, is so dense that a thimble full of it would weigh billions of tons on the earth. Since the gravitational attraction between objects varies directly with their masses and inversely with the distance between them, the presence of so much material within such a small volume creates extreme gravitational forces within and near a black hole. Black holes increase in gravitational power as they increase in mass by capturing nearby material.

Conclusion   Most large stars will eventually become black holes. These bizarre objects will, therefore, become quite common in future millennia.

RESPONSE: Does having a focused thesis statement for this essay make it easier for the reader to anticipate and understand the content of the essay? Explain your response.

_____

_____

_____

_____

_____

_____

PRACTICE   Following are ten general thesis statements. Rewrite each of these in the space provided so that each is transformed into a focused thesis statement. To accomplish this, you will need to add a plan of development to each general thesis statement. For example, the general thesis statement, "My first year of college was a very chaotic one for me," can be rewritten as the focused thesis statement, "My first year of college was very chaotic for me because of a hectic class schedule, new living arrangements, and uncertain work hours."

1. My first party in America was nothing like what I had dreamed it
    would be.

    _____

    _____

    _____

2. If you want to save time when bathing your dog, just follow these
    simple steps.

    _____

    _____

    _____

3. My garden this past summer was more productive than I ever
    imagined it would be.

    _____

    _____

    _____

4. I had several close calls during my year in driver's education
    class.

    _____

    _____

    _____

5. Although I've seen many movies, three in particular are my
    favorites.

    _____

    _____

    _____

6. My friend Harry seems unaware of his unique limitations.

_____

_____

_____

7. My wife's grandmother has several unusual habits.

_____

_____

_____

8. I have some very unpleasant memories about my days as a finish sander at Southern Furniture Company.

_____

_____

_____

9. Three experiences this past year have reshaped the course of my life.

_____

_____

_____

10. You, too, can bake a delicious German chocolate cake if you follow these simple steps.

_____

_____

_____

PREWRITING ACTIVITIES

1. Assume that you have decided to write a history term paper on the rise of labor unions in the United States. You know that unions began in an effort to obtain fair wages, benefits, and improved working conditions for laborers. Develop drafts of both a general thesis statement and a focused thesis statement for this research paper.

2. As you develop these thesis statements, decide whether your audience is a personal audience, an invoked audience, or a public audience. How will the particular audience for this piece of writing influence the content of the writing?

3. Finally, consider the purpose of this research paper. Will you attempt to convince (persuade) your reader of something, or will you be primarily concerned with informing your reader of the reasons for the rise of labor unions in the United States?

 ## JOURNAL SUGGESTIONS

Issues that you might write about in your journal include the following:

- Look back through your journal at some of the issues you have written about in the past few weeks. Are any of these issues you would like to explore more fully? If so, focus your journal writing on that issue(s).
- Prewriting, or getting started, was the subject of Chapter 1 of this text. Now that you've had some experience with some of the prewriting strategies, what do you think? Does one of the prewriting strategies especially appeal to you as a way to get started on a writing assignment? Explain why you think this prewriting technique works best for you.
- Some beginning or reluctant writers are timid about writing thesis statements; they are hesitant to assert their opinions on paper. Is this a problem for you? Can you think of writing situations you've encountered where you found it either difficult or uncomfortable to take a stand about an idea? Recount that experience in your journal.

DEVELOPING THE ESSAY

We tend to judge writing based on the degree to which it informs us. In fact, we sometimes say that a piece of writing says nothing. Other times, we say that a piece of writing says very little. And sometimes we say that a particular piece of writing is good—that it communicates.

Two things in particular determine whether or not a piece of writing communicates: the quality of material it contains, and the manner in which the material is presented. The quality of material and the manner of its presentation are directly related to the rhetorical concepts of organization, support, unity, and coherence.

The following paragraph is underdeveloped. To begin with, it lacks adequate support for its topic sentence. In addition, it lacks unity and coherence. Finally, it is poorly organized.

Example   GOODBYE, NUMOO

Saying goodbye to my favorite cat was one of the most difficult things I've ever done. I knew, however, that the veterinarian was right. We had had her for thirteen years. She was a superb cat. He said that her kidneys had failed and there was no hope for her. My daughters used to dress her in doll clothes and stroll her in their baby carriage. If she had been a person, she would have gone on dialysis. I dug her grave. It rained that afternoon.

This paragraph has been revised so that it is well-organized, coherent, and unified. Additional support for the topic sentence has also been included.

Example   <u>GOODBYE, NUMOO</u>

Saying goodbye to NuMoo, my favorite cat, was one of the most difficult things I've ever done. To begin with, she had been in our family since she was a kitten, which was thirteen years ago. During that time, she had been a superb cat. She was calm and self-assured. It didn't bother her when my daughters dressed her in doll clothes and strolled her in their baby carriage. Likewise, she insisted on having us nearby each time she had kittens. The veterinarian said that her kidneys had failed and that there was no hope for her. If she had been a person, and we think she was awfully close, she would have gone on dialysis. The veterinarian put her to sleep on a rainy Saturday after-noon. I dug her grave by the fence in the backyard, and we told her goodbye and Godspeed.

ORGANIZATION

The rhetorical concept referred to as *organization* is primarily concerned with the presentation and arrangement of the content of essays. All of us who have had some writing experience know that there is no set way to present information in an essay. Each time we write, we are forced to determine how we will organize the information we intend to present.

Fortunately, there are several ways to organize and present information, and all of these can be learned and then used to accomplish specific writing tasks. These methods of organization include the following:

- Climactic order
- Spatial order
- Chronological order
- Strategies of exposition

As you become familiar with each of these methods of organization, you will recognize how each might be used to organize an essay or a paragraph within an essay, based on the purpose, audience, and content of the writing.

CLIMACTIC ORDER

Often—particularly in conversation—we organize our comments on a particular topic in their order of importance. All of us have had conversations where somebody made assertions such as the following:

Example   There are several things you need to do today. You really ought to make an appointment with the dentist to have that tooth looked at. Also, you need to take that shirt back to Sears and order a larger size. But whatever you do, don't forget to call your mom and tell her that we will be there for dinner on Sunday.

Now, having read this conversational excerpt, answer the following questions about it:

1. Of the chores the person is being reminded to do, which one is most important?

_____

2. Where in the list of chores is this most important chore?

Check one: _____ first _____ second _____ last

3. Why does this chore appear in this position in the list?

_____

4. What word or words does the speaker use to emphasize the importance of this chore?

_____

The information in this communication transaction is arranged in climactic order. That is, the most important information is presented last, since whatever is presented last receives the most emphasis. For this reason, this method of organization is often referred to as *emphatic order.*

Climactic organization is generally signaled by the use of certain emphatic words and terms, such as the following:

- Most important . . .
- The last and most important . . .
- The chief . . .
- The primary . . .

Inclusion of key emphatic terms such as these will signal to your reader that you have arranged the material in climactic order—from least important to most important.

PRACTICE   The following paragraph is organized climactically. However, emphatic words and terms that signal climactic order have been omitted. Rewrite the paragraph to include appropriate emphatic terms.

Example   LIBRARY BLUES

Spending an unproductive morning trying to study in the college library left me feeling very depressed. To begin with, I forgot to bring my biology notes, so I was unable to study for the midterm, which is scheduled for next Friday. I also had some trouble using the card catalog. I'm accustomed to the Dewey decimal system, but this library uses the Library of Congress classification system. Consequently, I never found the Poe biography that I needed for the term paper I'm writing in American Literature. I accidentally dropped a contact lens in the lavatory in the library restroom. Now, I'll have to call my parents and ask them to have my optometrist send me a new one. That will be a hassle for them.

SPATIAL ORDER

Generally, we use spatial order as a means of organization when we are describing an object or a place. Spatial organization follows a particular spatial sequence that allows the writer to present details about an object or a place in a specific order. The details of the description can be organized from top to bottom, from left to right, from inside to outside, or in some other way. For example, you might describe the den in your house from left to right as you enter from the dining room. The following paragraph, which the writer later developed into an essay that appears in Chapter 7 of this text, illustrates spatial order.

Example   A BUSY ROOM

It is not difficult for a stranger to my house to locate my teenage daughters' bedroom. To begin with, there are two posters taped to the

outside of the door. The top poster is a picture of Chicago Bears'
football star Jim McMahon, and the bottom poster is a picture of
Spuds McKenzie. Inside the room to the left is a cosmetics table. There
are two small, white stools in front of the table, and a long, lighted
wall mirror spans the entire width of the tabletop. The mirror, however, has very little space where reflection is possible because it has
been covered with pictures, phone numbers, and banners. Somehow, in
spite of all this, the girls manage to see themselves, because the
clutter on the table makes it obvious that they spend many hours here
drying hair, painting nails, and applying makeup. The tabletop is a
mad assortment of hair curlers, hair dryers, combs, brushes, and
curiously shaped bottles holding fingernail polish, blush, eye shadow,
lipstick, mousse, hair spray, and suntan lotion. Interspersed among
these items are assorted earrings, bracelets, Coke cans, and chewing
gum wrappers. To the right of this table are two unmade beds, with
nightgowns and teddy bears peeping out from the tumble of blankets
and bedspreads. One pillow lies on the floor next to an empty take-
home pizza box. The second bed is covered in papers from a draft of
some assignment. Sticking out from under the papers are two books,
several note cards, a calculator, and a pen. This array leads the eye to
the desk, which is on the right side of the room, opposite the cosmetics table. The desktop is curiously clean and orderly, with only an
empty Coke can beside a neat stack of magazines and an address book.
Next to the desk is a large, yellow bean bag, which is covered with two
jean jackets, several shirts, jeans, a pink-and-white-striped towel, a
pair of gray sweatpants, and two unmatched socks. To describe this
room as interesting is certainly an understatement, but my daughters
love it and don't want me to bother a thing in it.

PRACTICE   After completing one of the following writing practices, ask a classmate
to read what you have written and then to draw a simple diagram or
sketch of the area you have described, including its most significant
features. When the sketch is completed, compare it to your written
description of the area. Is it a reasonably accurate diagram of the area

you described? Are there problems with the diagram? If so, are the problems a result of inadequate detail in your written description?

1. Write a spatially organized paragraph that describes a place you are familiar with. Determine the audience and purpose of the writing before you begin to write.

2. Write a spatially organized paragraph that describes either the reading room or the reference room in your college library. Imagine that your audience for this piece of writing is beginning college freshmen, and that the paragraph will be part of the description of the college library contained in the student government association's freshman orientation handbook.

_____

_____

_____

_____

_____

_____

_____

_____

_____

_____

_____

_____

_____

_____

_____

CHRONOLOGICAL ORDER

Sometimes, the details of a particular piece of writing lend themselves to ordering by time—that is, to chronological arrangement. If, for example, you were reporting your activities for this past weekend, you might begin by relating what you did Friday night, then Saturday morning, then Saturday afternoon, and so on, through Sunday evening. This would result in a chronological arrangement of your activities over the weekend.

You can also use chronological order to write about more varied, less personal topics. A review of world events from 1930 until the start of World War II could certainly be arranged in a time-order sequence, as could the steps of the process used in making glass.

Regardless of the subject matter, chronological order is an effective method of organization for writing about or presenting information about a wide range of topics. The chronological arrangement of any material will be more effective if it includes certain key words and phrases that signal time order. The most frequently used of these are the ordinal numbers: first, second, third, and so on. Here are some other frequently used time-order words: *initially, in the beginning, to begin with, after that, subsequently, later, then, finally.*

STRATEGIES OF EXPOSITION

Often as we interact with the surrounding world, we do so in accordance with certain patterns of thought and discourse that enable us to take in information about the world we live in, process this information, and then present it in ways that others can understand and respond to.

You know what a strategy is: football teams devise and practice complicated strategies with the goal of scoring (or preventing) touchdowns. Similarly, writers plan strategies of exposition with the goal of arranging and presenting (that is, *exposing*) their thoughts about a subject.

The most common and useful strategies of exposition, sometimes called *rhetorical patterns*, are the following:

- Description
- Example
- Process analysis
- Classification
- Comparison and contrast
- Definition

Chapters 7 through 12 of this book are devoted to a close examination of each of these strategies in turn. We use these strategies daily and in a variety of situations to aid us in thinking, speaking, and writing. Consider, for example, the task of selecting a head of lettuce at the produce counter in the grocery store. Few people actually buy the first head of lettuce they see in the lettuce bin; rather, they compare and contrast the heads of lettuce there in order to select the greenest, largest, firmest head available. In doing so, they have adopted the strategy known as *comparison and contrast*. In other situations, the same strategy may be used for very different purposes. For example, responding to an essay question on a history exam might require you to use the same rhetorical pattern, as does this question:

Example   Discuss the differences in the industrial resources available to the North and to the South at the beginning of the American Civil War.

Again, you would rely on using the comparison and contrast rhetorical strategy to answer the question satisfactorily.

Most people use these strategies of exposition regularly and well in thinking and speaking. However, using them in writing is somewhat more difficult, since there, unlike in conversation, the writer cannot receive immediate feedback from the reader that would enable the writer to alter or clarify misunderstood comments quickly. In writing, you must present your ideas fully and clearly, making sure that the reader can understand you without the benefit of further explanation.

Therefore, it is essential that you become proficient in using these strategies of exposition in your writing. Part Two of this book presents explanations and examples of the six major expository strategies. As you work your way through the activities in Part Two, you will learn how to use exposition strategies effectively to accomplish your own writing goals.

The following guide to sample student essays in Part Two will help you to better understand how the strategies of exposition enable writers to present information clearly and effectively. You can use the following guide to refer quickly to these essays.

Strategy	Model Student Essay	Chapter
Description	"A Busy Room"	7
Example	"Freedom of Speech: Another Look"	8
Process Analysis	"How to Start an Intravenous Infusion"	9
Classification	"My Three Roles"	10
Comparison and Contrast	"Hands"	11
Definition	"Freedom"	12

PARAGRAPHS

The basic unit of essay writing is the paragraph. This means that the information contained in an essay is organized and presented in graphically distinct rhetorical entities, which are referred to as *paragraphs*. We even speak of the essay as being a collection of specific types of paragraphs. Generally, we refer to these as follows:

■ Introductory paragraphs
■ Body paragraphs
■ Concluding paragraphs

Most short essays, as you know, contain an introductory paragraph, two or more body paragraphs, and a concluding paragraph. Longer essays may begin with two or more introductory paragraphs and end with two or more concluding paragraphs. In college writing, most of the essays you'll be asked to write will be relatively short. For an example of an effective introductory paragraph, see the first paragraph of "A Busy Room," in Chapter 7, page 180.

Like essays, paragraphs consist of different types of component material. The typical paragraph contains a topic sentence and details that support the topic sentence. While the topic sentence is just that—a single sentence—the details that support it are contained in several sentences, generally two or more, that collectively make up the body of the paragraph. The third paragraph of "Hands" in Chapter 11, page 307, is a strong paragraph. Notice its clear topic sentence and effective supporting detail.

Examine the paragraph about paragraphs that you have just read, and answer the following questions about it:

1. Does this paragraph about paragraphs have a topic sentence?

   _____

2. If so, identify the topic sentence and write it in the space that follows.

   _____

   _____

3. List the details in the paragraph that support its topic sentence.

   _____

   _____

   _____

   _____

   _____

   _____

   _____

   Not all paragraphs in essays conform to the pattern of a topic sentence supported by details. Introductory and concluding paragraphs generally do not contain topic sentences. Instead, they are constructed according to different sets of principles. The introductory paragraph of "Paint," in Chapter 11, page 302, is a short but effective beginning for this essay. Chapter 4 explains how to write introductory and concluding paragraphs.

MAKING A POINT

Since most paragraphs begin with (or at least contain) a topic sentence, it is important to know how to write topic sentences. Topic sentences consist of a topic and the writer's idea about that topic. Consequently, the topic sentence makes a point about the topic of the paragraph, as can be seen in the following examples of topic sentences. In each of these, the topic is underlined with a single line and the point about the topic is underlined with double lines.

Examples   Our president has some rather strong views about negotiating with terrorists.

John, my roommate, left the kitchen in a mess.

Mr. Jefferson gave several reasons for favoring a strong federal government.

For examples of effective topic sentences, see paragraphs 2, 3, and 4 of "How to Start an Intravenous Infusion," in Chapter 9, pages 241–242.

SUPPORTING THE POINT

Support for the topic sentence is the second major component of paragraphs. Generally, the body of a paragraph—that is, everything that comes after the topic sentence—supports the topic sentence. Such support proves, clarifies, and explains the point the writer is making about the topic.

Effective support has several unique characteristics, including the following:

- It consists of particulars that are clearly related to the point of the writing.
- These particulars are details, reasons, and facts.
- The particulars are contained in sentences that make up the body of the paragraph.

The following paragraph contains a topic sentence and supporting details. It illustrates the interrelatedness of these two components in generating clear, effective paragraphs.

Example   KEYBOARDING SKILLS NECESSARY

Keyboarding skills have become essential for most people, both in school and in the workplace. Today, schoolchildren begin using computers as early as in kindergarten. Computers help them learn to read, do math, and even acquire basic writing skills. By the middle grades, some students are writing computer programs and many are doing word processing. Throughout high school and in college, students do much of their work on computers, including spreadsheets in accounting courses, document creation in word-processing courses, programming in computer science courses, and experiments in science courses. Many of these same applications continue in the workplace, while others begin there. Airline reservationists, hotel clerks, telephone operators, and many salespeople must use computers to keep track of information, produce reports, and interact with clients and customers. All of these activities, of course, require keyboarding. Thus the need for keyboarding skills is widespread.

PRACTICE   The following paragraphs lack adequate and concrete details. Rewrite each paragraph in the space provided so that each contains sufficient specifics to support the topic sentence of each paragraph adequately.

GOOD FRIENDS

Good friends are special in some unique, unexpected ways. To begin with, good friends are honest. Secondly, good friends are reliable. You can count on them in almost any instance to be there when you need them. Good friends are also helpful in real and tangible ways. Finally, good friends have staying power. You can expect them to be close to you for years to come.

_____

_____

_____

_____

_____

_____

_____

_____

BUYING A CAR

Buying a new car is a rather serious business and requires careful attention to details. First, determine what size and type of car you need. Then compile a list of the options you would like to have on the car. Once you have made these decisions, find out what is available from various dealers. Next, begin making price comparisons. Finally, make your choice, finalize the deal, and make financing arrangements. Drive carefully!

PROVIDING SUPPORT

Support constitutes the bulk of the material in the body of an essay. Perhaps the simplest definition of *support* is material in the body of an essay that clarifies and backs up the thesis statement of the essay. This limited definition provides some understanding of the concept of support, as the following example illustrates:

Example   Today was an unusually good day for me. To begin with, my boss gave me a raise from $175.00 per week to $190.00 per week. After lunch, I received an unexpected phone call from my father's lawyer in Omaha telling me that I was heir to my great-uncle's estate. Then, on the way to my car after work, I found a ten-dollar bill on the sidewalk. Finally, when I got home, my wife told me that she was taking me to dinner at Glenn's, my favorite restaurant.

An analysis of this paragraph will provide you with some understanding of the rhetorical concept of support. The paragraph begins by making a point—namely, "Today was an unusually good day for me." This statement may or may not be true. At most, it is just this writer's opinion, and someone else might disagree with it. However, in order to pass an informed judgment on the accuracy of this statement, the reader must have the facts. In rhetorical terms, we say that the statement must be supported, and that is what the rest of the paragraph is about. The remainder of the paragraph consists of one fact right after another, each of which serves to support the opening statement. In addition, each fact is rather specific. The raise is from $175.00 per week to $190.00 per week. That's specific. And the writer found a ten-dollar bill. That's specific, too.

CHARACTERISTICS OF SUPPORT

We can identify four general characteristics of support:

- Support is facts; it is never generalizations.
- Support is often sense-oriented so that the reader can see, hear, feel, smell, and taste the supporting details contained in a piece of writing.
- Support produces concrete images in the mind of the reader.
- Support most often follows a topic sentence or a thesis statement.

HOW SUPPORT WORKS

Support consists of details and facts that are generally referred to as *specifics*. We'll use the term *specifics* when referring to elements of support. Specifics, regardless of how general and abstract or how detailed and concrete they are, always do one thing: they create images in the mind of the reader.

Obviously, the more detailed and concrete the specific is, the more detailed and concrete will be the image it creates in the mind of the reader. If, for example, you hear or read the word *cat*, you automatically, without any conscious effort on your part, form an image of a cat in your mind. And that's how specifics work in writing. Each time we encounter a detail—that is, a fact—in a piece of writing, we automatically form a mental image of that detail. If the fact is very general, we conjure a concrete specific, which means that we have to supply the missing details. In the case of the specific *cat*, we supply such things as the color and size of the cat. If the writer had written "black cat," however, we would already know the color of the cat and therefore would not have to supply it ourselves. Rather, we would immediately form the mental image of a black cat, based on the writer's words. If the writer had said "big black cat," we would know the approximate size of the cat, and accordingly we would form a mental image of a big, black cat.

And this is one of the key reasons you write—to re-create reality for your reader. The more specifically and concretely you write, the more uniform will be the resulting reality (the images your writing creates in the minds of your readers). If you write "cat," some of your readers will see a black cat, while others will envision a white cat, and still others will imagine a calico cat. If, however, you write "black cat," all of your readers will envision a black cat. Thus, the images created in the minds of your readers will be very similar rather than widely divergent.

Since your aim as a writer is to present an accurate picture of your subject, it is important that you be specific enough in your writing to ensure that the images your writing creates in the minds of your readers are virtually the same for all of your readers.

LEVELS OF SUPPORT

Essay writing requires two levels of support: thesis support and paragraph support. While it is true that every sentence in your essay must support the thesis statement, it is impractical and even confusing to write with this goal in mind. A better approach is to divide support into separate levels or types and to write from these perspectives.

Thesis Support   The first level of support in essay writing is thesis support. Thesis support is provided by making sure that the topic sentence of each paragraph in the body of the essay supports the thesis statement. The following example, which includes the thesis statement and the topic sentences of the body paragraphs of an essay entitled "My Grandmother," illustrates this point:

Example

General thesis

My grandmother taught me many things, all of which have helped to make me a better person.

Topic sentence of body paragraph 1

My grandmother was obsessed with attending to details.

Topic sentence of body paragraph 2

My grandmother firmly believed that honesty is the greatest of virtues.

Topic sentence of body paragraph 3

Finally, I learned from my grandmother that thrift is just as important as the amount of money one earns.

Notice that the topic sentence of each of these body paragraphs directly supports the thesis statement of the essay. Thus, we can conclude that this essay has thesis-level support.

Paragraph Support   Paragraph support is a matter of ensuring that the topic sentence of each paragraph in the body of the essay is adequately supported by the rest of the information contained in each paragraph. As you write each body paragraph, you must focus on providing support for the topic sentence of that paragraph. The following example provides support for body paragraph 2 from the previous example entitled "My Grandmother":

Example

Topic sentence

Support

My grandmother firmly believed that honesty is the greatest of virtues. She often said to me that "an honest person will never go hungry." On one occasion, she questioned me about some toy soldiers she saw on the dresser in my bedroom. She wanted to know why there were more there than usual. I told her that I had traded for them at school, and she immediately asked if I had played fairly. Another time, she asked me what I had for lunch at school that day. I hesitated and didn't answer. She questioned me, and I soon admitted that I had gone without lunch and bought two Hershey's candy bars at Ralph's Grocery on my way home from school. Her face looked sad, and I could see that she was disappointed with me. She told me that I must never do that again, since the seventy-five cents she gave me each day was for my lunch and spending it for candy was the same thing as telling a lie.

For additional examples of effective support, see paragraphs 2 and 4 of "My Three Roles," in Chapter 10, pages 274–275, and paragraphs 2, 3, and 4 of "A Busy Room," in Chapter 7, pages 180–181.

DEVELOPING SUPPORT

Support in an essay includes various types of information, such as the following:

■ Statistics
■ Names
■ Dates
■ Examples
■ Quotations
■ Ideas

The addition of these types of details makes writing specific and thereby provides support for the point of the writing.

The following sentences contain vague generalizations that fail to communicate effectively:

Examples

1. Mr. Goforth has some weird ideas about the nature of human beings.

2. I really like fast food.

3. My teenage daughters give me lots of things to worry about.

4. I usually spend my Saturdays doing rather mundane things.

5. I like some of my courses better than others.

Here are revisions of these vague, general sentences, each one enhanced by the inclusion of clear, detailed specifics:

Examples

1. Mr. Goforth, who has some weird ideas about the nature of human beings, believes that everybody is greedy, self-centered, and egotistical.

2. Although I like almost all fast food, my favorites are McDonald's Chicken McNuggets and Wendy's Quarter-Pounder.

3. I worry that my teenage daughters Jennifer and Alison don't always eat right and don't always do their homework.

4. I spend my Saturdays doing my laundry at the Soap Opera, buying groceries at Culler's Market, and cleaning my apartment.

5. Although I enjoy all of my courses, I particularly like calculus and physics.

MAKING WRITING SPECIFIC

Two ways to make your writing more specific are to use action verbs and to use sensory words.

ACTION VERBS

Most verbs indicate action. However, some verbs also signify the quality of the action, as well as the action itself. These verbs are generally referred to as *action verbs*. Here are two sentences that show the effect of replacing a more general verb with an action verb:

Example   The old man <u>walked</u> across the street.

The old man <u>hobbled</u> across the street.

PRACTICE   Replace the vague verbs in the following sentences with more specific action verbs. Use the spaces provided to rewrite the sentences.

1. Martha brought the car to a sudden stop.

_____

_____

_____

2.   The radio was playing loudly.

_____

_____

_____

3.   She ate her lunch hurriedly.

_____

_____

_____

4.   The pitcher threw the ball across the plate.

_____

_____

_____

5.   The cowboy walked slowly down the dusty street and then quickly took his gun from its holster when the tumbleweed came around the corner of the saloon.

_____

_____

_____

SENSORY WORDS

Much of what we know about the world we learn through our senses. Writing that appeals to our senses is generally informative and easy to comprehend. You can add sensory vividness to your writing by using words that appeal to some or all of the senses. By doing so, you enable your reader to hear, taste, smell, touch, and see your subject. Here are two sentences that show the effect of incorporating sensory words in the description:

Example   The <u>corn on the cob</u> looked delicious.

The <u>steaming, yellow ears of sweet corn</u> looked delicious.

And here are two more that illustrate a similar intensification of meaning:

Example   Mary seemed to have a bad cold.

Mary's red, swollen eyes, flushed cheeks, and barking cough testified to a bad cold.

PRACTICE   Add sensory words to the following dull sentences to make the writing more specific. Use the spaces provided to rewrite the sentences.

1. Our neighbor's lawn needed mowing.

_____

_____

2. My mom's special cheesecake is very tasty.

_____

_____

3. The skating rink was hot and crowded.

_____

_____

4. The drive through the mountains was relaxing.

_____

_____

5. My dad painted our game room a very pretty color.

_____

_____

6. The truck made noise as it rolled across the street.

_____

_____

7. The smell of oranges always reminds me of Christmas.

_____

_____

8. The talking of the students drowned out the teacher's voice.

_____

_____

9. Her dress looked flattering.

_____

_____

10. Honey has a sweet taste.

_____

_____

PRACTICE   Rewrite the following vague, general sentences, using action verbs and sensory words to make the writing more detailed and specific. Use the space provided after each sentence for the rewrite.

1. My apartment is a mess.

_____

_____

2. The boy rode his tricycle down the sidewalk.

_____

_____

3. The dinner my boyfriend cooked for us was not very appealing.

_____

_____

4. My hometown has numerous historic sites.

_____

_____

5. It was easy to tell when my father was angry.

_____

_____

6. Our senior prom was rather blah.

_____

_____

7. My senior English teacher was a very unusual person.

_____

_____

8. There are several vocations that interest me.

_____

_____

9. My dog can do a number of tricks.

_____

_____

10. The old man walked across the busy street.

_____

_____

DEVELOPING COHERENCE

In addition to including concrete and detailed specifics, good writing presents these specifics in a smooth, integrated, and logical fashion. Rhetorically speaking, writing must have coherence. *Coherence* means that each sentence and each paragraph are related in a clear, integrated, and logical way to the sentences and paragraphs that precede and follow them. The coherence of the information presented leads the reader evenly and with minimum effort from sentence to sentence and from paragraph to paragraph. In summary, the writing flows; it is rarely choppy, jerky, or jolting.

Coherence is usually achieved by using a combination of the following three coherence devices:

- Transitional words and phrases
- Repetition of key words and ideas
- Pronouns

TRANSITIONS

Smooth, logical movement from idea to idea, sentence to sentence, and paragraph to paragraph can be aided by the use of transitional devices. Transitional devices are particular words and phrases that show relationships between sentences within paragraphs and between paragraphs in an essay. Although we routinely use transitional devices in conversation, we tend to omit or overlook them when we write. Therefore, to achieve coherence in our writing, we must make a special effort to include transitional words and phrases.

The following paragraph contains no transitional words or phrases. Despite having a strong topic sentence and adequate supporting details, it lacks something. The ideas and sentences in the body of the paragraph are not related or connected by means of transitional words and phrases.

Example   THE FUTURE OF SOCIAL SECURITY

Social security benefits, so important to many Americans, may be threatened by the aging population of the United States. Social security recipients are supported by the largest work force in the history of this nation. The work force is peopled by baby boomers, most of whom are now in their late thirties and early forties. As these folks move into retirement, the U.S. labor force will shrink, and the number of people qualifying for social security benefits will increase. There will be fewer wage earners contributing to the social security fund and more retirees drawing from the fund. Social security funds may be inadequate to meet the demand for benefits.

Here's the paragraph again, but this time it contains appropriate transitional words and phrases. Notice that including these transitional devices serves to connect the writing by establishing relationships among the specifics contained in the paragraph.

Example   THE FUTURE OF SOCIAL SECURITY

Social security benefits, so important to many Americans, may be threatened by the aging population of the United States. Currently, social security recipients are supported by the largest work force in the history of this nation. The work force is peopled by baby boomers, most of whom are now in their late thirties and early forties. As these folks move into retirement, the U.S. labor force will shrink, and the number of people qualifying for social security benefits will increase. Simultaneously, there will be fewer wage earners contributing to the social security fund and more retirees drawing from the fund. As a result, social security funds may be inadequate to meet the demand for benefits.

There are five basic types of transitional words and phrases:

- Addition words
- Time words
- Contrast words
- Illustration words
- Conclusion words

Words of all five types establish relationships between the ideas and facts that they connect.

Addition Words   Addition words connect details by adding one detail to another. Common addition words include *first, second, third, also, furthermore, in addition, next, another,* and *last.* The addition words in the following example paragraph appear in bold print.

Example   There are several reasons why I finally made up my mind to go to college. **First of all,** I had always wanted to go to college. It's just something that I had put off doing. **Second,** my job was getting the best of me. I had worked in the same position and for the same company for twelve years. It was clear to me that I would never get an advancement. The **third** reason I decided to go to college was to take advantage of the free tuition program offered by my company. I figured that if they were willing to pay the bill, I'd be foolish to turn down the chance to get an education. **Last of all,** I just wanted to be able to say that I had a college education.

Time Words   Time words signal a time-order relationship among the details in a piece of writing. Some time words are *first, then, next, later, after that, while, during, meanwhile, now, before,* and *finally.* The time words in the following example paragraph appear in bold print.

Example   Yesterday I did some things that I had been putting off for a while. **First,** I got my hair cut. **Next,** I stopped by the library and turned in some overdue books. **Then** I spoke with the librarian about a summer job for my daughter, who needs to earn some money for college. **After** leaving the library, I went to my service station and ordered a set of tires for my car. Summer vacation is just two weeks away.

Contrast Words   Contrast words indicate a change of direction in the relationships between details. Key contrast words include *however, but, on the other hand, in contrast, instead, rather, although,* and *nevertheless.* The contrast words in the following example paragraph appear in bold print.

Example   Small-town life is quite different from life in a big city. In a small town, everyone either knows neighbors or is related to them. When I go to the grocery store in the small town where I live, I see people I work with, people I go to church with, and people I party with. Every face looks familiar to some extent. **To the contrary,** in the city where I used to live, almost everyone was a total stranger. There, I shopped at a small neighborhood grocery, but I rarely saw a familiar face. Another difference is in shopping hours. In my small town, stores close at 9:00 P.M. every week night. On Sundays, the hours are 1–5 P.M. If I need something at other hours, I have to do without it until the store opens the next day. **In contrast,** I never had to plan to shop at certain hours in the city, because there was always some store open not far away from my apartment, no matter when I needed to shop. I have only lived in this town for three months, **but** already I find I like the quiet, friendly atmosphere here, **even though** there are some inconveniences.

Illustration Words　Illustration words signal the reader that an example is being presented. Some illustration words are *for example, to illustrate, for instance, thus, once,* and *such as.* The illustration words in the following example paragraph appear in bold print.

Example　　In several ways, the American poet Emily Dickinson lived a very unusual life. **For example,** she rarely left her parents' home in Amherst, Massachusetts. Later in life, she became a recluse, known to Amherst residents by her tendency to dress in white. At least **once** she fell in love, but she never married. Instead, she remained at her parents' home. Few of her poems were published in her lifetime, and after her death, many poems were found in strange places, **such as** on the envelopes of letters she had received. Other poems were found written on scraps of paper. Her unusual life and her unusual but beautiful poetry have made her one of America's favorite poets.

Conclusion Words　Conclusion words let the reader know that the information presented has led to a conclusion or resolution. Common conclusion signals include *therefore, in conclusion, hence, consequently, as a result, because, finally, thus,* and *in summary.* The conclusion words in the following example paragraph appear in bold print.

Example　　For me, watching most television is a lot like eating junk food. There are times when I crave a good sitcom, just as there are times when I have to have a bag of potato chips and a Coke. **Indeed,** watching a sitcom is just as relaxing and enjoyable for me as munching on potato chips. And, when I crave junk food, I hate to stop with just a few potato chips and one Coke. **As a result,** I tend to eat the entire bag of chips, and then I find a candy bar or two, or maybe a box of Cracker Jack to eat as well. Although ice cream is not my favorite, if I'm in the junk-food mood, I check the freezer to see if there's any left. I don't usually stop with just one TV sitcom when I'm in the "junk TV mood" either. Instead, I sit down to watch one show, and, before I know it, two or three hours have passed by, and I've watched four or five half-hour shows. **Consequently,** I find that I have to watch my craving for both junk food and junk TV. I have to make sure that, if I give in to the cravings, I don't let either get the best of me.

PRACTICE   The following paragraph lacks transitional words and phrases. Read the paragraph, and supply appropriate transitions in the spaces provided. You may leave a space blank if you do not think that a transitional word or phrase is needed.

ANYTHING GOES

The college drama department's production of *Anything Goes* was very entertaining. _____ the cast was made up of amateurs, there were some outstanding performances. _____ , Bob Smith's portrayal of Billy Crocker was excellent. Mr. Smith's singing ability was well-matched to the role. _____ good performance was given by Melissa Howard as Reno Sweeney. She seemed to capture the spirit of the nightclub performer and delivered her lines with zest and boldness. _____ to these strong performances, the production had other good points. _____ of these were the sets, all of which uniquely captured the essence of the cruise ship, the *S.S. America*. Its realistic-looking smokestack was painted coal black and trimmed in brilliant red. _____ , the production was excellent and the audience loved it.

REPETITION OF KEY WORDS AND IDEAS

In addition to using transitions to achieve coherence in your writing, you can repeat key words and ideas in the writing to help connect the facts and ideas it contains. Be aware, however, that repeating just any word in the writing will not have the same results. Take care to identify and repeat key words, or if you prefer, use synonyms in place of the key words.

In the following paragraph, the key word *essential* is repeated several times. This repetition keeps the reader aware of the main point of the writing throughout the paragraph.

Example   STUDY HABITS

Few students are aware that good study habits are essential for achieving success in college work and not just for getting good grades. To begin with, good study habits are essential for taking notes properly. If you review your notes after each class session, you will discover how you need to improve your note-taking skills. Regular study habits are also essential for maintaining class attendance. Many students do poorly in college because they cut class. One reason students cut class is because they don't do their homework and are anxious about going to class unprepared. Finally, studying well and regularly is essential for getting good grades on tests. Putting off studying until the night before a test may mean that you don't have enough time for an adequate review of all the material covered on the test. Reviewing material regularly would virtually eliminate this problem. These are just some examples that show why proper study habits are essential for achieving success in an academic setting.

PRACTICE   The following paragraph about buying a computer repeats the key word *uses* or a synonym for it several times. Read the paragraph and circle the key word *uses* and each synonym for it that you find.

BUYING A COMPUTER

The key to buying a computer is to know how you plan to use it. Begin by making a list of the three most important ways you think you will use the machine. Then make another list of secondary tasks. Finally, let your imagination run free, and speculate about how you might use the computer to do things you had never thought of before. Record these possible uses in a third list. Now select a computer that you can use for every task on list one and for as many uses on lists two and three as possible. Once you are convinced that you have selected a machine that covers as many of your needs as possible, given the restrictions of your budget, you are ready to make your purchase.

PRONOUNS

Pronouns are yet another way to achieve coherence in writing. Pronouns are words that stand for or take the place of nouns. As such, pronouns connect writing by directing the reader's attention back to the words they replace. The following words are examples of pronouns: *he, she, it, we, you, they, this, that, these, those, other, another,* and *some.* In the following example paragraph, pronouns appear in bold print.

Example   RESTRICTED DRIVING

Drivers under the age of eighteen should be restricted to driving only in certain areas and on certain kinds of roads. Most sixteen-year-olds are too immature to make the types of quick accurate decisions that are often necessary in heavy city traffic. **They** simply do not have enough experience in doing this. **Some,** in fact, have no driving experience beyond a course in driver's education. **Others** have never driven on expressways. Yet when **they** get their driver's license, **they** are free to drive wherever they please—except in New York City, of course. Keeping young drivers out of heavy city traffic and off expressways would certainly improve traffic safety in **these** areas.

PRACTICE   Underline the pronouns that act as transitions in the following paragraph.

COOKING FOR KIDS

Contrary to what most adults think, kids enjoy cooking, and with the right kind of help, many of them can learn to do it quite well. To begin with, children need easy recipes. They have difficulty completing processes that contain subprocesses, such as preparing Mornay sauce for eggs Benedict. However, they can follow single simple processes with relative ease. Some find this challenging, much like working a puzzle. Others are intimidated by it but do well when an adult gives them one task to perform at a time. A few go on to modify simple recipes and create new ones. Overall, however, it is clear that, given the right circumstances, kids love to cook.

ACHIEVING UNITY

Unity means that all material contained in a piece of writing is clearly related to and directly supports the point of the writing. In the case of essay writing, this means that all material contained in the body of the essay is relevant to and supports the thesis statement of the essay. Unrelated, irrelevant sentences disrupt the logic and order of the writing and destroy its unity. Such irrelevant sentences should be revised or deleted.

The following explanations and activities will help you achieve unity in the essays you write. We begin with an example of a paragraph that exhibits unity problems.

Example   SUMMER JOB BLUES

My summer job at Comer's Concrete Supply was less than I hoped it would be. To begin with, I had to go through an extensive training program, which included washing the trucks, running a front-end loader, assisting the receiving clerk, and acting as a receptionist. Of course, there were no raises during the training program. This did help me, however, to understand how a company is run, which is something I will be able to use someday, since I plan to start my own business after I finish college. First though, I have to pass accounting, and that is giving me a lot of trouble. Then I was assigned to the receiving department, but I wasn't allowed to work with invoices and shipping orders. Rather, I spent my time unloading heavy cartons from the backs of hot, dusty trucks. This was not all bad, however, since I worked without a shirt and got a smooth tan. I also built up my muscles, and I was able to impress a few people when I went back to school at the end of the summer. Once I unloaded the trucks, I had to stack the merchandise in the dark, spider-infested warehouse, which was another little feature of the job that I hadn't counted on. All in all, however, I learned a lot on my summer job and I'm glad now that I had the experience and lived through it.

The writer of this paragraph has failed to maintain paragraph-level unity. Several sentences in the paragraph are not directly related to the topic sentence and, therefore, do not support the topic sentence. In order for the writing to be unified, these sentences should be omitted.

Here's the same paragraph but with the irrelevant sentences omitted. Notice that every sentence in the revised paragraph is directly related to and supports the topic sentence. The paragraph now has unity.

Example   SUMMER JOB BLUES

My summer job at Comer's Concrete Supply was less than I hoped it would be. To begin with, I had to go through an extensive training program, which included washing the trucks, running a front-end loader, assisting the receiving clerk, and acting as a receptionist. Then I was assigned to the receiving department, but I wasn't allowed to work with invoices and shipping orders. Rather, I spent my time unloading heavy cartons from the backs of hot, dusty trucks. Once I unloaded the trucks, I had to stack the merchandise in the dark, spider-infested warehouse, which was another little feature of the job that I hadn't counted on.

PRACTICE   Read the following paragraphs, and mark through the irrelevant material in each. When you have deleted all of the irrelevant material, each paragraph should have unity.

A NIGHT IN MAY

I had the shock of my life when a recent trip to my neighborhood convenience store led to a scary adventure. The store is only two blocks from my house, and I often go there when I need a couple of items to complete a recipe. And that's what I did on Tuesday, May 14. I needed cheddar cheese to top the asparagus casserole I was making for dinner. My mother passed the recipe on to me, since it was one of my favorites. I often make it when I'm having guests over, though I had not invited anyone to dinner that evening. As I stood in line at the counter waiting to pay, I saw my car drive away from the store. I ran out into the parking lot just in time to see the unknown driver turn left onto Bridge Street. I ran back into the store, asked to use the phone, and called the police. Within minutes, two policemen arrived and began asking me questions. I was very impressed with their promptness, and now I feel that my taxes may do some good after all, even though I still resent paying them and I'm still convinced that much of our tax money is wasted. The officers then took me home. On the way, they told me that all officers on duty, as well as the county sheriff's department and the highway patrol, had been notified about the theft of my car. And, believe it or not, I had my car back by 10 P.M. that same evening. Once again, I must say that I was impressed with the good work these policemen did in finding and returning my car.

CAMPING FUN

I'm now convinced that planning a camping trip is as important as taking a tent. My girlfriend and I recently went camping on the spur of the moment. We borrowed a tent and a stove and took a couple of blankets. On our way to the campsite, we bought some groceries and a flashlight at a convenience store. Needless to say, we paid exorbitant prices for these things because we bought them at a convenience store. We probably could have saved a lot of money if we had gone to K-mart for the flashlight and to A & P for the groceries. Once at our campsite, our failure to plan ahead really began to show up. I had to use rocks to drive the tent pegs, since I hadn't thought to bring a hammer. Sure, we had a stove, but it was of little use since we didn't have any pots and pans for cooking. Consequently, we packed the stove back in the trunk and ate cold pork and beans, crackers, and hot soft drinks. I couldn't help but remember the Boy Scout motto, "Be prepared," but I had not been a very good scout, so perhaps I remembered the motto just too late. Anyway, my scout leader was not very prepared himself. It often seemed that he made up the rules as he went along.

✎ JOURNAL SUGGESTIONS

Temporarily focus your journal writing on the act of writing. Issues that you might write about in your journal include the following:

■ Several of the practice exercises in this chapter involved rewriting paragraphs. How do you feel about rewriting things you write? Do you generally rewrite writing assignments, or do you tend to turn in your first writing? Do you rewrite other kinds of writing that you do, such as letters to friends? Do you ever look back at writing you have completed and find problems with the writing, such as grammatical mistakes or problems with unity, coherence, or organization?

- Many of the practice exercises in this chapter also involved adding details to writing. How much do you think these exercises will help you improve your writing? Which exercises did you find most helpful?
- Recall some of the academic writing assignments you have had in the past. What is the hardest part of a writing assignment for you—getting started? writing the beginning sentences? ending the essay? organizing what you are writing? Recall a specific assignment, and try to list the difficulties you encountered in completing that assignment.
- In your journal, write a two- to three-sentence description of a personal possession, such as your car, a present you have received, or a room in your house. Then rewrite that description, adding more detail to it. Remember to use sensory details to describe your possession.

INTRODUCTIONS AND CONCLUSIONS

Beginning a writing project, after you've completed selected focusing and prewriting activities, can still be difficult. Finding the right opening sentence and completing the introduction are often perplexing and sometimes immobilizing tasks. Likewise, ending a piece of writing can be troublesome. You know you have to write a summary or concluding paragraph, but the question of how to do it can, once again, result in writer's block.

Fortunately, there are workable, time-saving strategies for dealing with these writing tasks. Following are explanations of several types of introductions and conclusions that incorporate these strategies. Become familiar with and practice using each type. You will then be able to use whichever ones you want for beginning and ending a particular essay.

INTRODUCTIONS

Essays generally begin with one or more introductory paragraphs. Short essays of less than 800 words usually contain just one introductory paragraph. Longer essays may require two or more introductory paragraphs in order to introduce the topic and give the reader adequate background information about it.

A good introduction generally accomplishes three things:

- It gets the reader's attention.
- It provides the reader with background information about the topic.
- It presents the thesis statement of the essay.

An introduction that accomplishes these three tasks has prepared the reader to understand the content of the essay.

Although there are many types of introductions, we will focus on the three that are best suited to the short essay:

- The funnel introduction
- The contrast introduction
- The anecdotal introduction

Any one of these will work well with virtually every type of essay, regardless of the subject matter. Consequently, you can select a particular type of introduction for a particular essay without wondering if you have chosen the wrong type.

FUNNEL INTRODUCTION

The funnel introduction is the most frequently used type of introduction for the short essay. As its name implies, a funnel introduction begins with a broad, general statement about the topic of the essay, and follows this with narrower, more specific statements about the topic. The final sentence in the funnel introduction is usually the thesis statement of the essay. By this point, the topic has been introduced and focused, and the writer has declared a specific position toward the subject.

Here is an example. The following funnel introduction is the first paragraph of an essay entitled "Three Friends."

Example   All of us have friends, some of whom we're closer to than others. These people give our lives meaning and joy. I have many friends, but most of these might be more accurately described as acquaintances. A small number of them are my good friends, and a few of them are very close to me. Of these, three in particular share most of the thoughts and feelings that are truly central to my life. In fact, in many ways, Mary, Emily, and Ashley, my three best friends, really make my life worth living.

PRACTICE   Select one of the following essay topics, or a topic of your own devising, and write a four- to six-sentence single-paragraph funnel introduction for an essay on that topic. Write your introductory paragraph in the space provided.

> Your favorite relative
>
> The savings value of cents-off coupons
>
> The effect of hobbies on your mental health
>
> The excessive health-consciousness of Americans
>
> Selecting a college major
>
> Dreams you have had
>
> The worst experience of your life
>
> [A topic of your own choosing]

_____

_____

_____

_____

_____

_____

_____

CONTRAST INTRODUCTION

Contrast introductions are particularly useful when you want to surprise or startle your reader—that is, when you want to grab your reader's attention. You should not, however, sacrifice honesty in order to do this. Rather, you should develop a contrast that is both true and surprising. This type of introduction is designed to pique a reader's interest at the same time that it presents background information about the topic and states a position toward the subject of the essay.

A contrast introduction begins by presenting a commonly held belief or opinion about a subject. Generally, this position is one that a reader will recognize as being generally true. Following this rather predictable beginning, the writer introduces a contrasting position that will catch the reader's attention and also will serve as the focus for the essay. Usually, the contrasting position is prefaced by a contrast word or phrase—such as *however, on the contrary, contrary to popular opinion (belief), in contrast*—which informs the reader that a new and different position toward the subject is about to be presented. This new position is put forth in the thesis statement, which may or may not include the contrast word or phrase.

Now let's look at an example of a contrast introduction. The following introductory paragraph makes use of this type of introduction to begin an essay entitled "Learning to Drive."

Example   Most young teenagers are convinced that driving is little more than sitting in the driver's seat, turning the ignition, and going easily and simply wherever one chooses. After all, they think, if Mom and Dad can do it, it can't be that complicated. However, most teenagers are surprised and overwhelmed by the complexity of guiding a big box at fast speeds along narrow strips cluttered by other big boxes moving unpredictably at fast speeds along the same narrow strips. Most teenagers, in fact, find that driving is a rather complex, tiring, and anxiety-producing activity that requires training and skill in order to do it smoothly and safely.

As you can see, this contrast introductory paragraph begins by stating a belief common among nondriving teenagers. It then states a contrasting position, which is developed into a thesis statement in the last sentence of the introductory paragraph.

PRACTICE   The statements that follow represent commonly held beliefs and assumptions. Working with another classmate, or as your teacher directs, write a contrasting statement for each of these. For example, given the common idea, "Honesty is the best policy," you might write the following contrast: "In spite of the common assumption that honesty is the best policy, there are numerous situations when telling the truth is wrong."

1.   Marriages are made in heaven.

   _____

   _____

2.   True love is blind.

   _____

   _____

3.   An apple a day keeps the doctor away.

   _____

   _____

4.   You can't judge a book by its cover.

   _____

   _____

5.   Women can have it all—job, school, and home with children.

   _____

   _____

6.   Writing is just like talking.

   _____

   _____

7.   All children are simply adorable.

   _____

   _____

8.   Money is all a person needs to get elected to public office in the United States.

   _____

   _____

9. City life is more exciting than country life.

_____

_____

10. It takes a lot of money to go to college.

_____

_____

PRACTICE   Select one of the following essay topics, or make up a topic of your own, and write a four- to six-sentence single-paragraph contrast introduction for an essay on that topic. Write your introductory paragraph in the space provided.

Learning to swim

Making good grades

Writing an essay

The role of Congress in the United States government

An analysis of Hamlet's soliloquy

Buying a personal computer

Getting through college

Living with a two-year-old

Understanding teenagers

Caring for an elderly relative

[A topic of your own choosing]

_____

_____

_____

_____

_____

_____

_____

_____

_____

_____

_____

_____

_____

ANECDOTAL INTRODUCTION

The third type of introduction common in short essays, known as the anecdotal introduction, begins by relating a short, simple anecdote, or "little story." The anecdote introduces the subject of the essay, provides limited background information about the topic, and concludes with a thesis statement.

The guidelines for preparing anecdotal introductions are simple. The anecdote should be true, brief, and clearly related to the topic. It should end with a statement of the thesis of the essay.

Here is an example of an anecdotal introduction. It constitutes the first paragraph of an essay entitled "Christmas Shopping."

Example   Joe looked down the aisle at the nearly empty cosmetics shelves. His heart sank as he realized that the Windsong cologne that he had planned to buy Jenny for Christmas was no longer there. He had passed by the aisle just last Monday, but he didn't want to take the time to stop and buy it then. Now it's Christmas Eve, the store has sold out of Windsong, and Jenny won't have the gift of his choice for her. As many of us do, Joe had simply put off doing his Christmas shopping until the last minute. As he walked out of the store with a bottle of bubble bath, he promised himself that he would do better next year. This predicament, of course, is avoidable. In fact, anyone can take much of the tension out of Christmas shopping by simply planning ahead, making a gift list, and shopping early.

PRACTICE   Select one of the following essay topics, or formulate a topic of your own, and write a brief, single-paragraph anecdotal introduction for any essay on that topic. If possible, use an incident from your experience as the subject of your anecdote. Write your introductory paragraph in the space provided.

> How not to prepare for a test
> How to paint a room
> The security of social security
> Family relationships
> Highway safety
> Educational reform in public schools
> Good part-time jobs
> Disciplining young children
> Computers and personal privacy
> Why everybody needs a will
> [A topic of your own choosing]

_____

_____

_____

_____

_____

_____

_____

_____

_____

_____

_____

CONCLUSIONS

Just as there are special strategies for writing introductions to essays, there are also useful techniques for preparing conclusions for essays.

Conclusions serve several purposes in essay writing. To begin with, they inform your reader that you have completed your presentation of information in support of your thesis. Second, conclusions provide you with an opportunity to restate your thesis and to summarize your argument by restating the main points in support of your thesis. Finally, conclusions allow you, when appropriate, to ask your reader to take some specific action based on the material you presented in the body of the essay.

Two types of conclusions are particularly suited to the short essay: the summary conclusion and the inverted funnel conclusion. Either type works well as the summary paragraph for most essays, so you should make a point of working with both of them as you continue to write essays. The following explanations of these two types of conclusions as well as the accompanying practice exercises will enable you to prepare an appropriate conclusion for each essay you write.

SUMMARY CONCLUSION

The summary conclusion is best suited for long, complex essays. It usually begins with a restatement of the thesis in other or different words and follows this with a similar restatement of the main points from the body of the essay that were used to support the thesis. As you restate these main points, be careful not to introduce additional points or new material. You made your case in the body of the essay; new material in the summary will only weaken your presentation.

The following example of a summary conclusion is for an essay entitled "Test Taking." This conclusion paragraph restates the thesis from the introductory paragraph of the essay and then reviews the main points presented in the body of the essay.

Example   Remember, then, that your performance on tests is directly related to your knowledge and use of proven test-taking techniques. If you take accurate class notes, anticipate questions, and review thoroughly, you can lower your anxiety about taking tests and improve your test scores.

PRACTICE The following sentences are thesis statements for essays. Select one of these and write a two- to four-sentence summary conclusion for an essay based on the thesis statement. Write your conclusion paragraph in the space provided.

- Although church and school do teach values to children, I am convinced that parental example is the most important teacher of values.
- One of the primary problems created by working and going to school is the added pressure of maintaining good grades.
- As you select a vocation, remember that your work should provide an adequate salary, allow you to use your natural talents, and satisfy your need to make a contribution to society.
- Since some spouses refuse to take their parental responsibilities seriously, the state must force them to do that when there is a separation or divorce.
- Each individual must recognize and accept her responsibility for cleaning up our environment.
- Children, as well as adults, worry about the threat of nuclear war.

_____

_____

_____

_____

_____

_____

_____

_____

INVERTED FUNNEL CONCLUSION

Conclusions may also be written in an inverted funnel format. This type of conclusion begins with a restatement (usually in different words) of the thesis. The restatement of the thesis is followed by more general statements that show the relationship of the thesis to the subject of the essay. Once again, avoid introducing new ideas or information in the conclusion, since these would confuse your reader and weaken the argument presented in the body of the essay.

Now let's turn to an example of this type of conclusion. The following inverted funnel conclusion is for an essay entitled "Achieving Peace of Mind."

Example   Regardless of how we go about it, each of us has the final responsibility for our own peace of mind. Ideally, we will accept this responsibility and discover ways to maintain and perhaps improve our mental well-being. If we do so, we have the assurance that we will live happier, more contented lives.

PRACTICE   The following sentences are thesis statements for essays. Select one of these, and write an inverted funnel conclusion for an essay based on it. Write your conclusion paragraph in the space provided.

- In many ways, planning for retirement is as important as planning one's career.
- Being a good parent requires patience, understanding, and the ability and willingness to discipline.
- As you select a college to attend, remember that program offerings, cost of tuition, and location all have a serious effect on whether or not you will like the school.
- Dreams can tell us a lot about ourselves, if we take the time to learn some simple ways to interpret them.
- Personal preferences in types of music sometimes change as a person gets older.

_____

_____

 ## JOURNAL SUGGESTIONS

Temporarily focus your journal writing on the act of writing. Issues that you might write about in your journal include the following:

■ What problems have you encountered in your writing for this course in the past few weeks? You might want to focus on the aspects of writing covered so far in this text—getting started, formulating a thesis, developing the essay, and writing introductions and conclusions.
■ Do you have writing assignments in other courses? If so, how might you employ the writing techniques you have learned in this course to help you with writing assignments in other courses?
■ Do introductions and conclusions really matter? How important is it to have effective introductions and conclusions? Do you ever read the introduction to an article in a newspaper or magazine to help you decide whether or not to read the article?
■ Look over some of the journal writing you have done recently. Are there any entries you might consider developing into essays? Journal entries characteristically have no beginning or ending sentences. If there is an entry in your journal that you would consider developing into an essay, how would you begin that essay?

REVISING THE ESSAY

The opportunity to revise is the most exciting aspect of essay writing. The chance to make revisions offers you the freedom to experiment, to make mistakes, to change your mind, to correct errors, and to produce your very best work.

Revising your writing is the single most important thing you can do to improve its quality. And this writing-improvement strategy is available to all writers. Generally, writers spend the majority of their writing time revising what they have previously written. You may want to do the same.

Revision does not mean rewriting. Rather, it means working with an existing piece of writing to reshape and refine it so that it is appropriate for its audience and tailored to its purpose. Rarely, if ever, will you find it necessary to discard a piece of writing and start over. Virtually every piece of writing is usable, given the proper revisions. And without question, it is easier (and often more satisfying) to revise than to write or to rewrite.

It is important to recognize that revision is an integral part of the writing process rather than just a random, haphazard "doctoring" of a piece of writing. As you gain experience with the techniques of revision, you will find that revising is an easy and effective way to improve the quality of your writing. Revising your writing leads you to examine and make judgments about what you have written. You must review and evaluate your writing to make sure that it addresses its intended audience, makes a point, and achieves its purpose through effective organization and adequate support.

This chapter presents a brief discussion of the revision process, as well as a revision checklist to guide you as you revise the essays you write. Remember, adequate revision will ensure that you have achieved the following goals:

- You have identified your audience, clarified your purpose, and developed a thesis statement that summarizes the point of the essay.
- The writing is clear and logically organized.
- There is adequate support for the point of the essay.
- The writing is coherent and unified.
- The writing is correct in its usage, mechanics, punctuation, and spelling (see Chapter 6 for additional explanation).

REVISION TECHNIQUES

Three techniques are particularly helpful in the revision process: global revision, local revision, and peer revision. These approaches to revision represent three different "visions" or perspectives toward the writing.

GLOBAL REVISION

When we are involved directly in the act of writing—putting words on paper—our vision is restricted. We see the sentence that's flowing from our pen and, on occasion, the sentence that came just before; but that's about the scope of our perspective while we're in the act of writing.

That scope, of course, is inadequate. From time to time, we need to step back and see the whole. When artists step back from their canvases (as they often do while painting), they are checking for balance, scale, proportion, and color effect. They want to know if, as a whole, the picture works. As writers, we're no different. We need to step back from our writing periodically and take a global look at what we have written in order to see the whole. Is it balanced? Is it properly proportioned? Are essential elements missing? Does the writing as a whole work?

Read the following paragraph. As you do, notice that it has been thoroughly edited and that it is correct in terms of usage, mechanics, spelling, and punctuation.

Example   <u>MY FUTURE</u>

My father is a truck driver. That's fine for him. Of course, he does not want me to be a truck driver. He wants me to go to college. My mother doesn't want me driving a truck, either. She's convinced after having lived with my father that driving a truck is dangerous and difficult work. But all of this makes me wonder how much parents should have to say about the vocations their children choose to pursue. I'm not sure; however, I do plan to give college a try, at least. If it doesn't work out, I think I can fall back on truck driving, since my father knows a lot of people who could help me get started in the business.

Looking at the separate parts of this writing reveals that they are technically correct: there are no punctuation errors, each word group is a sentence, and each sentence is punctuated properly. However, if we see this paragraph globally—as a whole—we quickly realize that it doesn't work. Too many things are unclear, and some are even missing. For example:

- Whom is the writing addressed to? That is, who is its intended audience?
- What is the purpose of the writing? What does the writer want the reader to know?
- Is this purpose summarized as the point of the writing and stated in either a topic sentence or a thesis statement?
- How well organized is the writing? Where does the writing really begin? Where should it end? How can it get from Point A to Point B most effectively?

These are global revision questions, and it is helpful to ask such questions about any piece of writing.

Global revision can be accomplished in a variety of ways. Perhaps the most helpful way is through whole reading.

Whole reading means reading or rereading the writing as an integrated whole. Try to ignore sentence-structure errors, misspellings, and punctuation problems, and instead focus on issues of audience, purpose, and organization. Can you identify the intended audience of the writing? Can you ascertain the writing's purpose? Can you tell what the objective of the writing is? Finally, is the writing organized in such a way that (1) the reader can follow it with little or no effort, and (2) the writing accomplishes its purpose?

PEER REVISION

A second helpful technique for revising is called *peer revision*. Peer revision simply means that you have someone assist you in the revision process. In its simplest form, peer revision consists of having another person read what you have written and then comment on it.

Although peer revision can be this unstructured, it will be more effective if the peer reviewer follows some simple guidelines in reviewing the author's writing:

- Look at, consider, and respond to the whole essay.
- Is the intended audience clear and consistent throughout the essay?
- Do the subject and purpose of the essay become clear within the first few sentences?
- Does the material in the body of the essay make and support points that together achieve the purpose of the writing?
- Do sentences, passages, or even whole paragraphs seem unrelated or contradictory to the purpose of the writing?
- Can improvements be made in the writing's organization?

Peer reviewers often find it easier to focus on restricted, specific questions of usage and style than on the larger and more general issues of the writing process. Perhaps it's easier to point out an error in subject–verb agreement than to make a judgment about whether or not a piece of writing addresses its intended audience. Nonetheless, if it is to be effective, peer review must deal with the essential questions of audience, purpose, and organization, while for the most part ignoring issues of usage, style, mechanics, and punctuation.

LOCAL REVISION

Local revision, another helpful revision technique, requires a shift in focus from the whole to the specific. The objectives of local revision are as follows:

- To check that each paragraph is functional—that is, that each paragraph accomplishes its purpose
- To ensure that introductory paragraphs announce the subject of the writing and present the author's perspective (as expressed, usually, in the thesis statement) toward it
- To confirm that each body paragraph makes a point that is clearly and adequately supported by details contained within the paragraph
- To check sentence by sentence for unity and coherence, taking care to alter or delete irrelevant material
- To perform final editing to correct mistakes in mechanics, usage, punctuation, and spelling (see Chapter 6 for additional explanation)

These techniques and guidelines for revising your writing will help you through the revision process. The remainder of the material in this chapter focuses on specific areas and components of essays that should receive particular attention in the revision process.

REVISING THE INTRODUCTION AND THE THESIS

Review and evaluate your introduction, making sure that it conforms to one of the types of introductions presented in Chapter 4. If, for example, your introduction is a funnel introduction, it should begin with a broad, general statement about your topic, and it should contain a thesis statement. If, on the other hand, you have written a contrast introduction, the first paragraph of your essay must establish a contrast.

Next, review your essay's thesis statement, which you have most likely included in your introductory paragraph. If you have a workable thesis statement, you will be able to answer *yes* to one or more of the following questions:

■ Does your thesis statement take a position toward your subject?
■ Does your thesis statement express an opinion about your subject?
■ Does your thesis statement assert something related to your subject?

In addition, review the introduction and thesis statement of your essay to make sure that you have identified, considered, and addressed your audience appropriately. Finally, review your purpose for writing the essay to ensure that your thesis statement summarizes and expresses the purpose of the writing.

REVISING ORGANIZATION

Organization has to do with the order of presentation of information within an essay. As we discussed in Chapter 3, information may be presented in accordance with any of the following arrangements:

Spatial order

Climactic order

Chronological order

Expository strategies

Review your writing to make sure that you have used one or more of these organizational patterns correctly and effectively to present the information contained in the body of your essay. If, for example, you used climactic order, did you indeed save the most important information until the end of the paragraph or essay? If you used the expository strategy of comparison and contrast to arrange and present information, did you establish clear bases for comparing or contrasting the subjects of your writing?

PRACTICE   The support in the following paragraph is supposed to be arranged chronologically. Review the paragraph, and determine whether the information is indeed presented in chronological order. If you conclude that the material needs to be rearranged, indicate your suggested changes by numbering the sentences in the order in which you think they should appear in the paragraph. You may decide to revise or delete some sentences.

VACATION

Planning ahead helped make our family's summer vacation a splendid success. We began planning our trip right after Christmas. In late April, we bought our airline tickets. First, we decided where we wanted to go, and, after some discussion, we settled on Colorado and the Rocky Mountains. In early February, my dad wrote to the Department of Tourism in Colorado requesting maps of the area and brochures describing interesting things to see and do. But back in January, we talked to some friends who had lived in Denver, and they gave us some tips for getting around the city. Then, as I said earlier, we bought our tickets in late April. My sister and I began saving money for the trip back in March. By June 15, I had seventy-five dollars tucked away. Finally, our departure date arrived, and we got to the airport early. As we sat on the plane waiting to taxi down the runway, I realized how glad I was that for once we had really done our homework.

REVISING SUPPORT

Adequate and appropriate support is essential if you are to make your point in a piece of writing. As we discussed in Chapter 3, support occurs at two levels in essay writing: at the thesis level and at the paragraph level. Revising your writing includes making a careful check to ensure that each body paragraph supports your thesis and that the topic sentence or central idea of each body paragraph is supported by the content of the paragraph.

The adequacy of the evidence or support you use has a serious and profound effect on the quality of the finished piece of writing. Reread each body paragraph in your essay to make sure that the topic sentence of each paragraph is supported by the evidence in the paragraph. Then read each sentence again, focusing on the accuracy of the evidence and details in each sentence. As you read, ask yourself on a sentence-by-sentence basis whether each detail or piece of evidence is as specific as it should be to give your reader a firm and full understanding of your subject and meaning.

REVISING THESIS SUPPORT

You have achieved thesis support when the topic sentence of each paragraph in the body of the essay directly and clearly supports the thesis statement of the essay. The following essay illustrates thesis-level support. The thesis statement in the introductory paragraph is underlined, as is the topic sentence in each body paragraph. As you read the thesis statement and topic sentences of this essay, notice that the thesis is directly and clearly supported by the topic sentences of the body paragraphs.

STUDENT ESSAY

INFLATION   Howard Stover

Economic inflation is the devaluation of the money supply as a standard of purchasing power. It is the result of increasing the amount of currency in circulation without regard to the existing supply of goods and services. Whenever our bureaucrats in Washington fire up the printing presses and arbitrarily place more money into circulation in order to cover national defense, entitlement programs, welfare programs, defaulted guaranteed loans, and other underbudgeted programs, inflation always follows, almost in direct proportion. This economic principle manifests itself somewhat differently in the cases of the typical working family, the retiree on a fixed income, and the investor.

To the typical American family, inflation means that more money is required to purchase the same amount of goods and services that less money purchased formerly. When the family grocery shopper pays $65

INFLATION, continued

for what $55 would have bought the year before, that's inflation! It's the same thing when Junior's teeth-cleaning bill goes up from $25 to $35. How about the family about to consider buying a new car? The one they bought in 1972 cost about $3,000. A comparable one today costs about $8,000. Increased wages and cost of materials in Detroit, you say? Quite true, but what caused those dramatic increases, which were passed on in the cost of the new car? Devaluation of money. How did it happen? More money in circulation. A family sells its home for twice its cost six years before. Have they "beat the system"? Probably not. If they buy another house, it will undoubtedly cost about twice as much as it cost six years before. Even if the wage earner in the family gets a cost-of-living pay increase, it is usually overcompensated by inflated prices and bracket creep. This, then, is inflation for the typical American family.

Inflation to the retiree on a fixed income means fewer goods and services for the same amount of money. Inflation is a nightmare of gross proportions to such a person. He goes into the grocery store with the same $55 he did the year before, but gets less groceries in quantity and/or quality, because he simply does not have the extra $10 to cover inflation that the typical grocery shopper does. Watching the buying power erode each month can indeed be depressing. Inflation means a gradual reduction in his standard of living. First, that dinner theater or concert series has to be canceled in order to pay the utility bills. Next to go are that special weekly lunch out with a friend and that bottle of Spatlese. Later, as purchasing power erodes further, a gradual reduction in

quality and quantity of clothes and other essentials that make for a good, meaningful life takes place. Finally, inflation means dipping into capital from which his income is generated, thereby reducing his already meager income. This is a severe blow indeed and threatens the nucleus of his economic structure, reducing the quality of life even further.

To the investor, inflation is just one of the economic principles with which he must always deal. If he is successful, his portfolio consists of the proper proportion of bonds, money market funds, futures, precious metals, gems, etc. With a thorough knowledge of what inflation actually is and how it affects his investments, he can carefully manipulate acquisitions and liquidations accordingly. Shrewd managerial control of his portfolio can actually make fortunes because of the effects of inflation. Careful application of the principles of leverage can produce greater profits in times of hyperinflation than during times of low inflation. It takes expertise, capital, guts, and a fair amount of luck. It is not always a piece of cake, however. To some investors, inflation has meant huge losses, either because they ignored its existence or because they were unable to predict its effect in a particular market situation. Suppose Investor A buys a $100,000 piece of real estate at 10% down. In five years, he sells it for $200,000 and clears $100,000 because of the inflated value of the property. This represents 1,000% profit based upon his actual down payment, which at an average of 200% per year certainly beats inflation. So, to Investor A, inflation has been a godsend. Investor B buys 100 ounces of gold at $500 per ounce, or $50,000, as an inflation hedge. Two years later, he liquidates at

INFLATION, continued

$350 an ounce at a capital loss of $15,000. Not only has he lost the $15,000, but the $35,000 that he has recovered from the original $50,000 investment is now only worth about $22,000 because of its loss of intrinsic value due to inflation. Not too long ago, gold at $500 an ounce looked good. Investor B sees inflation as most of us do—a devil!

Economic inflation has been with us continuously since the Great Depression of the 1930s. Some so-called experts say that inflation is a condition derived from too much spending, overextended credit, or buying on margin. If any of these could be traced back to its origin, the real culprit, when exposed, would be the condition whereby too many dollars are chasing too few goods and services; and those excess dollars could, in turn, be traced back to the arbitrary printing of new unsecured money by our Treasury Department. To a few people, inflation is just another economic principle that needs to be considered and dealt with when making and policing prudent investments. For the vast majority of people, however, inflation is a terrible thing they don't really understand, even though they are constantly aware that their standard of living is not what it once was because of inflation and its constant diminishing effect upon purchasing power.

You should always review and, if necessary, revise your writing to achieve thesis support. Using the preceding example essay as a guide, read the thesis statement of your essay. Then identify the topic sentence of each body paragraph. As you do so, determine whether each topic sentence supports the thesis statement of the essay. If it does not, consider revising the topic sentence (or sentences) so that each clearly and directly supports the thesis of the essay. If revising one or more topic sentences seems inappropriate, you might consider revising the thesis statement so that it more accurately reflects the main idea supported by the topic sentences contained in the body of the essay.

REVISING PARAGRAPH SUPPORT

Providing paragraph support involves satisfying two criteria:

- Each paragraph in the body of the essay contains a central idea, which is usually expressed in a topic sentence.
- The topic sentence or central idea of each body paragraph is supported by clear, relevant, detailed specifics.

As you review and revise your writing for paragraph support, make sure that these principles guide your writing. Review each body paragraph to ascertain that it contains a topic sentence. Then review the body of each paragraph to make sure that the details it contains support the topic sentence of the paragraph.

As you review the paragraphs in the body of the essay, respond to these questions:

■ Does each paragraph contain a topic sentence?
■ Does the topic sentence of each paragraph include a clearly identified topic and a clear, concise controlling idea?
■ Does each paragraph contain adequate support for the topic sentence of the paragraph?
■ Are the specifics in each paragraph sufficiently detailed?

PRACTICE   Read the following paragraphs. Which one of them does not begin with a topic sentence? In the space provided, write a topic sentence for that paragraph.

CAR TROUBLE

The battery was weak and barely turned the engine. Then, when I finally got it going, I had to pump the brakes several times to bring the car to a stop. The speedometer didn't work either, and the radio speaker buzzed continuously. Finally, the power door locks failed, and a mechanic had to help me get out of the car.

GUITAR BLUES

Learning to play the guitar was a trying experience for me. To begin with, I had to use my father's guitar, which has a very broad fret board. Since I have small hands, it was very difficult for me to reach around the neck. Secondly, my teacher, Mr. Moffett, was rather unreliable. He rarely showed up on time for lessons, and once he didn't show up at all. I waited for him for forty minutes outside the door of his second-floor studio and then called my dad to come pick me up. But the most difficult part of all was memorizing the fingerings for chords. I repeatedly confused finger positions for E flat and B flat, and I still don't know the difference between G minor and G major. All in all, learning to play the guitar proved rather hopeless for me.

_____

_____

PRACTICE   The following paragraphs lack clear, detailed specifics. You will be asked to revise each paragraph so that it contains adequate specifics. We begin with an example paragraph before and after revision.

Example   HOW TO SET OUT A TOMATO PLANT

Setting out a tomato plant is a rather simple task. To begin with, dig a hole. Then place the plant in the hole. You may want to add some fertilizer. Next, cover the plant up with dirt and pack it down. Finally, add some water and then sit back and wait for your first tomato.

HOW TO SET OUT A TOMATO PLANT

Setting out a tomato plant is a rather simple task. To begin with, dig a hole approximately four to six inches deep and twice the diameter of the plant's root ball. Next, add about one teaspoon of either 10-10-10 or 8-8-8 fertilizer to the hole. Be sure to mix the fertilizer in with the loose soil at the bottom of the hole. After adding and mixing the fertilizer, fill the hole at least half full with water. Allow the water to soak into the soil, and then position the tomato plant in the center of the hole. Be sure that the roots of the plant are no more than three to five inches below the soil line. Finally, fill the hole with dirt, packing it gently around the roots and stem of the plant. With regular watering and feeding, you'll be enjoying tomatoes from the plant in about six weeks.

Now provide similar detailed specifics in revising the following two paragraphs. Write your revisions in the space following each paragraph.

CLEANUP

Cleaning my apartment means a lot of work for me. To begin with, I take my clothes and other things to the laundry. Then I mop the floors, empty the trash cans in a couple of rooms, clean the kitchen, and do some dusting. Finally, I clean the bathroom. After that's finished, I tidy the bookshelves, fluff the cushions, and collapse.

_____

_____

_____

_____

_____

_____

_____

_____

_____

_____

_____

_____

_____

_____

COLLEGE EXPECTATIONS

    I must admit that college was nothing like I expected it to be. To
begin with, registration was a hassle. Then I had to buy books, which
no one had told me about. One of the books cost me a day's pay. When I
got to my first class, I was told that it had been canceled. So there I
was back at registration, and it took me a long time to find another
class that was offered at the same hour. Then after I had attended this

new class for some time, somebody told me that it wasn't required in my program. Nevertheless, I decided to stay in the class, since I liked the professor and he was talking about some things I'm interested in. Still, I can't get over how different college is from what I had believed it would be.

_____

_____

_____

_____

_____

_____

_____

_____

_____

_____

_____

_____

_____

_____

_____

_____

CHECKING FOR COHERENCE

In order for your writing to read well, it must be coherent. Writing is coherent when the ideas, sentences, and paragraphs it contains are adequately and appropriately related to each other. As you learned in Chapter 3 there are several ways to achieve coherence in writing, including the following:

- Repetition of key words and ideas
- Use of pronouns
- Use of transitional words and phrases

PRACTICE   Select a paragraph or an essay that you have written in this course. Then read through the piece, and underline any coherence devices you find, including transitional words and phrases, pronouns, and repeated words and ideas. (If necessary, review the section on providing coherence in Chapter 3.)

PRACTICE   The following paragraph lacks coherence. As you read through it, write in coherence devices so that the ideas and sentences it contains are adequately and appropriately related.

A GOOD JOB

A good job for many people means more than just a good salary. A job might also offer flexible working hours and an on-site day-care center. Some insurance companies in New York City are trying flexible hours for their staff. The insurance companies have set a peak time of ten to twelve o'clock. All personnel must be at work during these hours. Six hours a day can be worked at the employee's convenience. Some automotive plants in Detroit have opened day-care centers at the work site. The day-care centers provide care for children and peace of mind for workers. The children can be visited by their parents during work breaks and lunch hour.

CHECKING FOR UNITY

Revising for unity is your opportunity to make an additional check of your writing to ensure that it supports the point (thesis) of the essay. Writing is unified when all information contained in the essay supports and is directly related to the point of the writing. Any information that contradicts or is irrelevant to the point of the writing needs to be revised to support the point or deleted from the essay.

Review your writing for coherence by reading each paragraph separately and carefully. Focus first on the topic sentence of each paragraph. Then read each sentence in each paragraph, and determine if it is related to and supports the topic sentence of that paragraph. Any sentence or sentences that do not support the topic sentence should be revised or omitted.

The following example paragraph lacks unity. Some of the information contained in the paragraph neither directly relates to nor supports the topic sentence of the paragraph. This irrelevant material is underlined.

Example   DON'T BITE

Your next diet will be more successful if you adhere to some simple principles. You may not need to go on a diet. Check with your doctor before you do. First, always think before you eat. Ask yourself if you really are hungry or if you're eating for some other reason. Second, be sure to drink more water as you diet. Dieters often eliminate soft drinks as part of their diet programs but fail to replace these lost fluids with other, more appropriate beverages. Lemonade really doesn't count since it's a natural drink. Coffee is also acceptable. Finally, be prepared to deal with your friends. They may want you to continue to eat normally, particularly if activities you enjoy together include eating such nondiet foods as potato chips, pizza, and ice cream. It should be noted that pizza is really not junk food. Just go light on the cheese and other special, nonvegetable toppings. The next time you diet, keep these principles in mind. They may just help you make your weight-loss goal.

PRACTICE   The following paragraphs lack unity. Read each paragraph carefully, and underline any material that is not directly related to and does not support the thesis statement.

MARIGOLDS

The marigold is a hardy plant that is a joy to most gardeners because it is easy to grow. Of course, not all gardeners would agree with this. Some of my friends claim that daisies are easier to grow than are marigolds. With marigolds, even a novice at gardening can have healthy plants and an abundance of blooms with little effort. There are exceptions to this, as one might expect, but they're rare. Marigolds thrive in summer heat and in the cool of fall. They grow well in poor soil with little water, preferring a hot, sunny area with southern exposure.

CORPORATIONS [an excerpt]

Other distinct characteristics of a corporation are the ownership by stockholders and the limited liability of stockholders. Unlike other forms of business, a corporation is owned by many separate people. Ownership of a corporation is transferable to other people by the sale of stock, without disrupting the normal flow of business operations. Ownership of stock is an investment strategy more people should take advantage of. It provides an effective hedge against inflation and is relatively safe. On the other hand, stockholders are not personally responsible for the debts incurred by the corporation. The only loss a shareholder may incur is the amount of money he or she paid for the stock of the company. Most people are unaware of this. The corporation is responsible for its own acts and obligations.

REVISION CHECKLIST

The following revision checklist is a guide to the revision process. Use the checklist as a guide when you revise the essays you write. As you revise your essays, be sure to respond to each item on the revision checklist.

   I. Look at the whole essay.
      _____ Who is your audience?
      _____ What is the purpose of the writing?
      _____ Is the writing well organized?
  II. Consider having a friend or colleague read and comment on your writing (peer revision). He or she may respond to the same questions as those in item I.
 III. Revise introduction and thesis.
      _____ Does the essay begin with an introductory paragraph?
      _____ Does the essay contain a clearly stated thesis?
      _____ Is the thesis statement near the end of the introductory paragraph?
      _____ Does the thesis statement make a point about or take a position toward the subject of the essay?
  IV. Revise support.
      _____ Does the essay contain two or more body paragraphs?
      _____ Does each body paragraph contain a topic sentence or a central idea?
      _____ Is the topic sentence of each body paragraph adequately supported by clear and vivid specifics?
      _____ Does every sentence in every paragraph relate directly to and support the topic sentence of that paragraph?
      _____ Does the topic sentence of each body paragraph support the thesis statement of the essay?
   V. Check for coherence.
      _____ Are the information and ideas contained in the essay closely related?
      _____ Are most of the sentences within each paragraph related by transitional words and phrases, pronouns, and synonyms?
  VI. Check for unity.
      _____ Does every sentence in each body paragraph relate directly to the topic sentence of the paragraph?
      _____ Does every sentence in each body paragraph support the topic sentence of the paragraph?
 VII. Edit carefully (see Chapter 6 for guidelines).
      _____ Is the punctuation correct?
      _____ Is the usage correct?
      _____ Are the mechanics correct?
      _____ Is the spelling correct?

JOURNAL SUGGESTIONS

Temporarily focus the writing you're doing in your journal on revision. Revision issues that you might write about in your journal include the following:

- What did this chapter make you think about? In your journal, reflect on some of the issues covered in this chapter.
- The first sentence of this chapter may be one you do not agree with. Go back and reread the sentence, and then focus your writing on the act of revision. Is it exciting? Can it be viewed as an exciting aspect of writing? Why or why not?
- Many people hesitate to revise their writing, because they feel that doing so is just a lot of extra work. Based on what you now know about the writing process, explain why revising is not just "extra work" and is, in fact, an essential part of the act of writing.

EDITING THE ESSAY

Editing is the process of correcting problems in sentence structure, grammar, and punctuation in your writing. As a component of the writing process, editing may occur at various points prior to the completion of a writing task. Different writers do their editing in different ways:

- Some writers edit sentence-by-sentence. As one sentence—or even part of one sentence—is written, the writer goes back through the sentence and edits it.
- Some writers edit paragraph-by-paragraph.
- Some writers edit before, during, and after revising sentences or paragraphs.
- Some writers pay no attention to editing decisions until the final draft of the writing. At that time, they edit the paper.

Any or all of these methods are acceptable. The important point to remember is that writing, revision, and editing are very different components of the writing process.

You may have had the experience of submitting a paper after checking and rechecking it for errors in grammar, punctuation, and sentence structure. Then, when it was returned to you, it had a lower grade than you had anticipated, because of poor content or organization. In your zeal to eliminate misspelled words and bad punctuation, you had forgotten to pay sufficient attention to content and organization. When you write, therefore, you have two major areas of concern: what you write, and how you write it. This chapter is about how you write rather than about what you write.

In many ways, it is much easier to talk than it is to write. For one thing, when you are talking to someone, you have a much more relaxed attitude about what you say and how you say it. In informal conversations with friends, you may use jargon, clichés, and euphemisms freely, and you may speak in incomplete sentences. Consider, for example, the following conversation between two people at work:

Example

BILL: Wanna go to lunch?

ALAN: Can't—gotta finish this report.

BILL: Get James to help you this afternoon—we're going to the new Chinese restaurant. You said you wanted to try it.

ALAN: Not me! Musta been somebody else—I hate Chinese food! Tried it once and hated it. I'll never try it again.

While this style is perfectly acceptable in conversation, it is unacceptable in formal writing. Formal writing must conform to a set of standards called *Standard Written English* (SWE). Standard Written English is a set of rules and regulations about sentence structure, grammar, and punctuation that writers must follow.

Think of these rules and regulations as a set of policies. Almost any place you might work has a set of policies or guidelines you must follow. These policies are usually collected in a policy manual, and—depending on your position with the company—you are responsible for reading and interpreting policy, supervising policy, or implementing policy as you go about your duties. Similarly, grammatical rules are a set of policies that you must follow as you write in order to make your writing accessible and intelligible for the typical reader.

The remainder of this chapter provides explanations of some of these guidelines. The chapter also provides excerpts from student writing and exercises that will help you strengthen your skills in applying the guidelines of SWE.

There are several possible ways in which you can use this chapter. You may want to read through the chapter and concentrate on what you know are trouble spots for you. For example, in the past, you may have had papers returned with the abbreviation "R-O" somewhere in the margin. A section in this chapter explains run-on sentences and provides methods of correcting run-on sentences.

You may also use this chapter as a reference when writing your papers. For example, when you finish a draft of a piece of writing, you might want to review appropriate sections of the editing chapter—much as you might use a dictionary to look up the spelling of words. This chapter can be a handy source of information about editing problems.

For some reason, it is much easier to find mistakes in textbook exercises or in someone else's writing than it is in your own writing. Consequently, when you get ready to edit your own writing, you may find that peer reading is a good way to edit your paper. Have a friend, a classmate, or a relative read your writing to check for editing problems. That person may be able to find problems you have overlooked.

PRACTICE   Find a piece of writing that you have done. It can be an essay you wrote for this course or something you wrote for another class. Then exchange papers with a classmate. As you read your classmate's paper, make notes about problems you see in the writing, such as misspelled words, mistakes in grammar, and errors in punctuation.

Another helpful editing strategy is to try to read your writing from another person's point of view. After you finish a piece of writing, put it away for a day or two. If that is impossible, try to get away from it for at least several hours. When you come back to the writing, try to assume another point of view and read your writing as if you had never read it before. This fresh look at your writing may enable you to see problems you had not noticed before.

PRACTICE   Find a piece of writing that is at least one month old. It may be an old essay test, a research paper you did for another course, or a book review. Read the paper very critically, looking for any problem areas. These may include misspelled words, confusing sentences, errors in grammar, or inconsistent punctuation. As you reread the paper, assume the point of view of the teacher who originally graded the writing. Likewise, you might reread the paper from the point of view of a classmate who took the course with you. Ask yourself these questions as you read:

■ Do any sentences leave me wondering what the writer meant?
■ Did the writer leave out information that is important to understanding the point of the writing?
■ Are some places in the paper too wordy and full of information that is not needed to support the point of the paper?

EDITING SENTENCE STRUCTURE AND GRAMMAR

In this section you will review the following elements of sentence structure and grammar:

- Sentences
- Fragments
- Run-ons and comma splices
- Parallelism
- Modifiers
- Subject–verb agreement
- Verb tense
- Pronoun agreement, reference, and point of view

SENTENCES

Standard Written English requires writers to write in sentences. In order for a group of words to be called a *sentence*, it must contain a subject (who or what the sentence is about) and a verb (what the sentence says about the subject), and it must express a complete thought. Sentences begin with a capital letter and end with one of three types of punctuation: a period, a question mark, or an exclamation point.

PRACTICE

Write three sentences on the following lines. Then underline the subject once and the verb twice in each sentence. Make sure that each sentence begins with a capital letter and ends with one of the three types of end punctuation. Then exchange books with a classmate and read and analyze your classmate's sentences. If you disagree about his or her subject and verb choices, have another classmate read and analyze the sentences.

1. _____

_____

_____

2. _____

_____

3. _____

_____

_____

_____

FRAGMENTS

A word group is a sentence if it contains a subject and a verb and if it expresses a complete thought. A word group is called a fragment (frag) if it is missing one or more of these three sentence components but has been punctuated to look like a complete sentence.

PRACTICE Read the following excerpt from a student essay on the three levels of the study of history. Which word group in the excerpt is a fragment?

WAYS TO STUDY HISTORY

   The first level of the study of history is the study of individual events. This helps historians understand what actually happened and how it happened. For example, the causes and effects of the event.

Methods of Finding Fragments Here is a two-stage approach to identifying fragments:

- Read the writing, one sentence at a time, starting at the end of the writing. If you read a group of words that makes no sense, it may be a fragment.
- Next, check to make sure that each word group contains a subject and a verb and expresses a complete thought.

Methods of Correcting Fragments The third "sentence" in the previous student writing is a fragment. Here are two possible ways of correcting this fragment:

- Add a subject and a verb:

Example   For example, historians analyze the causes and effects of the event.

■ Connect the fragment to the sentence that comes either before or after it:

Example   This helps historians understand what actually happened and how it happened, which are the causes and effects of the event.

RUN-ONS (R-O) AND COMMA SPLICES (CS)

A run-on sentence is actually two complete sentences that have been combined without adequate punctuation and/or connecting words. One kind of run-on is called a *comma splice*. Comma splices occur when two complete sentences or two independent clauses are spliced or joined by a comma. Because a comma indicates only a slight pause, it is inadequate for the purpose of combining two sentences or two independent clauses. The following excerpt from a student essay on putting contains both a run-on sentence and a comma splice.

Example   IMPROVE YOUR PUTTING

In order to putt well, you must be able to read the green. First, you must determine the length of your putt this is the distance between your golf ball and the hole. Next, stand two to three feet behind your ball to see which way the green reads. There is an important reason for doing this, the reason is that your golf ball will break either right or left or in one direction and then the other.

Methods of Finding Run-on Sentences   The following two-step method can be used to find run-on sentences:

■ Read your writing aloud, and listen for pauses in your voice.
■ When you hear a pause, check the punctuation to see if it is adequate.

Methods of Correcting Run-ons   The second word group in the student writing is a run-on. The last word group is a comma splice. Here are three possible ways to correct these errors:

■ Make the two complete thoughts two separate sentences:

Example   There is an important reason for doing this. The golf ball will break either right ot left or in one direction and then the other.

■ Combine the two thoughts with either a semicolon or a comma and a joining word (for additional information about these terms, see "Editing Punctuation and Mechanics," page 147):

Example   First, you must determine the length of your putt; this is the
distance between your golf ball and the hole.

■ Make one idea subordinate to the other:

Example   First, you must determine the length of your putt, which is the
distance between your golf ball and the hole.

PRACTICE   Rewrite the following sentence fragments, run-on sentences, and comma
splices so that each is a complete sentence. You may find it necessary to
divide some of these word groups into two or more sentences or to add
or delete words. For example, you might rewrite the fragment, "After
finishing my homework," as "After finishing my homework, I watched
the late movie on television."

1. I traveled extensively in the West during Christmas vacation, I
    plan to spend the summer in New England.

    _____

    _____

2. While watching the ducks land on the lake.

    _____

    _____

3. Drinking coffee never bothers me I find it refreshing.

    _____

    _____

4. To get to the store, go two blocks and turn left. At the stop sign.

    _____

    _____

5. I always pay my bills on time, I can't afford the late charges.

    _____

    _____

6. Mary broke her finger when her tennis racket slipped out of her hand the coach had warned her to tighten her grip; she just didn't take him seriously.

_____

_____

7. If truck drivers were only more courteous.

_____

_____

8. You can't buy that in this state. Regardless of your age.

_____

_____

9. My watch is never right, however, my teacher won't accept that as an excuse for being tardy.

_____

_____

10. Fire is frightening, that's why I'm careful to double check the iron before I leave the house.

_____

_____

PARALLELISM (//)

If items are parallel, they are arranged in similar or balanced form. Items of equal value in sentences must be balanced so that the reader can easily recognize their equivalent status. Faulty parallelism occurs when items or thoughts of equal value in a sentence are not presented in a balanced way, causing the reader to have difficulty seeing the elements these items have in common.

For example, consider the following sentence:

Example   I spent my spring vacation eating, sleeping, and I went to the beach.

In this sentence, the three things that the person did are items that should be balanced. Two of the items are presented in matching –*ing* form. But the last item is presented differently, and this forces the reader to stop and think through the items in order to understand the relationships among them.

Methods of Finding Faulty Parallelism   Most errors in parallelism occur when two or more items are presented in the same sentence. Therefore, if you write a sentence with two or more verbs, descriptive words, or –*ing* words, check to see that the items are presented in parallel constructions.

Methods of Correcting Faulty Parallelism   Here are several ways in which the preceding example sentence can be rewritten so that the items are balanced (that is, parallel):

Examples   ■ I spent my spring vacation eating, sleeping, and having fun at the beach.
■ I spent my spring vacation eating, sleeping, and sunbathing at the beach.
■ On my spring vacation, I ate, slept, and went to the beach.

In the first two revised sentences, all three items are presented in –*ing* form. In the last revision, the three items have been changed to past tense. Either way is correct, because in each instance all three items within the sentence are parallel.

PRACTICE   Correct the faulty parallelism in each of the following excerpts from student writings. Some sentences may have to be divided into two sentences.

1.   I also enjoy many outside activities such as softball, tennis, and just being with family and friends.

_____

_____

_____

2. During my senior year, I received many honors including a scholar-ship to Western University, honor roll for two semesters, and an outstanding student.

_____

_____

3. At present, I am employed by Star Grocery Store. My duties include bagging groceries, stock, and sometimes I fill in as cashier.

_____

_____

4. I couldn't believe my mother actually wanted me to wear the dress, even if it was an heirloom. It was old, faded, and it had a rip.

_____

_____

5. The qualities he liked best about the new president were her person-ality, her rapport with the public, and she had beliefs similar to his own.

_____

_____

MODIFIERS

Modifiers are words or phrases that modify or describe some other word or phrase. In the following sentence, the word _ten_ is a modifier:

Example   I found ten dollars.

Problems known as either dangling modifiers (DM) or misplaced modifiers (MM) are more likely to occur when an entire phrase modifies another word or phrase, as in this sentence:

Example   I found ten dollars walking home.

This sentence is confusing: were the ten dollars walking home or was the speaker walking home? The modifying phrase "walking home" is misplaced, which creates both confusion and unintended humor.

A modifier is called *dangling* when there is no clear word or phrase in the sentence for it to modify, as in the following sentence:

Example   While grilling the hamburgers, a bee stung him.

The sentence is confusing and funny because, as it is written, the reader could assume that the bee was grilling the hamburgers.

Methods of Finding Errors in Modifiers   It is difficult to find errors in modifiers. The person who wrote the sentence about the ten dollars knew exactly what she intended to say. Quite possibly, she could not see the problem with the sentence until someone else pointed it out to her. But there are several methods you can use to find errors in modifiers:

■ Have someone else read your writing, or to try to assume another point of view yourself. Either one of these methods will give you a different perspective on your writing and thus can help you find problems you may have overlooked.
■ If at all possible, let your writing "cool." Allow several hours or a day to intervene between writing and reading what you have written. Time distance from your writing permits a fresh perspective that will enable you to pinpoint sentences or phrases that might be confusing for your reader.
■ Make sure that descriptive words and phrases in each sentence have a logical and clear relationship to some other word or phrase in the sentence.

Methods of Correcting Errors in Modification   Here are three practical ways to correct misplaced or dangling modifiers:

■ Move the modifying phrase closer to the word it modifies:

Example   While walking home, I found ten dollars.

■ Add a subject and verb to the modifying phrase:

Example   While he was grilling the hamburgers, a bee stung him.

■ Place the subject immediately after the modifying phrase:

Example   While grilling hamburgers, he was stung by a bee.

PRACTICE   Rewrite the following sentences to correct problems with misplaced or dangling modifiers. Make sure that the modifying phrase is next to the word it modifies or that it is clearly and logically connected to the word or words in the sentence that it is intended to modify.

1. There were several cars in the parking lot with out-of-state license tags.

   _____

   _____

2. Carrying two suitcases and a camera bag, the airline ticket was hard to dig out of her pocket.

   _____

   _____

3. The public heard last week he had survived a severe heart attack.

   _____

   _____

4. He returned the lawn mower to the repair shop that was still not working properly.

   _____

   _____

5. Walking on the beach, dark angry clouds surrounded us and seemed to touch the water.

   _____

   _____

SUBJECT–VERB AGREEMENT (S–V)

Before you work through the activities on subject–verb agreement, you may find the following brief review of the characteristics of verbs helpful. This review will help you avoid making mistakes in subject–verb agreement. In addition, you will find it helpful for the subsequent section in this chapter on verb tense.

- There are regular and irregular verbs.
- A verb has four principal forms, expressing distinctions in time: the present, the past, the past participle, and the present participle (more will be said about verb tense in the next section of this chapter).
- A verb is called *regular* if the past and past participle forms of the verb are made by adding *–d* or *–ed* to the present form.
- A verb is called *irregular* if the past tense and past participle are not formed in this way (see the following table).

EXAMPLES OF REGULAR AND IRREGULAR VERB FORMS

Present	Past	Past Participle	Present Participle
shout	shouted	shouted	shouting
tickle	tickled	tickled	tickling
laugh	laughed	laughed	laughing
go	went	gone	going
begin	began	begun	beginning
speak	spoke	spoken	speaking

The first three verbs in this table are regular; therefore, the past and past participle are formed by adding *–d* or *–ed*. The last three verbs have past and past participle forms that are quite different; consequently, these are irregular verbs. If you are unsure about whether a verb is regular or irregular, check a dictionary. Many dictionaries give the principal parts of irregular verbs.

The rule for subject–verb agreement is simple: the verb must agree with the subject in number. Therefore, if the subject is singular, the verb must be singular; and if the subject is plural, the verb must be plural.

While the rule itself is simple, applying it is not always easy. Most subject–verb agreement (S–V) mistakes occur in one of the following situations:

- Words come between the subject and the verb:

Example   Methods used to torture criminals in that country [is/are] horrifying.

- There are two or more subjects:

Example   Money and luck [is/are] all John needs to buy the best seat in the house.

- The verb comes before the subject:

Example   Here [is/are] the leftovers.

Indefinite pronouns are used:

Example   Neither of the two kinds of tickets [cost/costs] too much.

Pronouns and Verbs   The words *I, we, you, she, he, it,* and *they* are called *pronouns.* Every noun—person, place, or thing—can be replaced or referred to by a pronoun. In the first of the preceding example sentences, the word *methods* can be referred to as *they.* In the following list, identify the pronoun that could be used for each noun from the example sentences:

Noun	**Pronoun Replacement**
criminals	_____
country	_____
John	_____
house	_____
leftovers	_____

Study the following chart:

Type of Pronoun	**Singular**	**Plural**
first-person	I need	we need
second-person	you need	you need
third-person	he, she, it needs	they need

In the second example sentence, *John* is a noun that can be replaced with the pronoun *he.* From the chart you see that, for third-person singular, the present-tense verb form is *needs.* Choosing pronouns to replace subject words is often helpful in choosing the correct form of the verb.

Methods of Finding and Correcting Errors in Subject—Verb Agreement   Here are four strategies for dealing with problems in subject–verb agreement:

■ Find the subject and the verb in the sentence, and remove any words that come between the subject and the verb. For example, in the sentence, "Methods used to torture criminals in that country [is/are] horrifying," the words that come between the subject and the verb are "used to torture criminals in that country." When you remove these words, the words "Methods [is/are] horrifying" remain. The subject is *methods.* Since *methods* is a noun that can be replaced with the pronoun *they,* the correct form of the irregular verb is *are.*

■ Use plural verbs in sentences that have two or more subjects. For example, in the sentence, "Money and luck [is/are] all John needs to buy the best seat in the house," both *money* and *luck* are subjects of the sentence. Subjects joined by *and* generally take a plural verb. The best way to spot this mistake is to double-check any sentence that has more than one subject to make sure you have chosen the correct form of the verb. In this case, the correct form of the verb is *are*.

But now consider the sentence, "Neither the children nor the father [was/were] found after the tornado swept through the town." When compound subjects are joined by "either . . . or," "neither . . . nor," or "not only . . . but also," the verb should agree with the subject closer to the verb. In this case, the subject *father* is closer to the verb. Since *father* is a singular subject, the verb should also be singular. Therefore, the correct form of the verb is *was*.

■ Determine the subject of the sentence in order to help you decide what verb form to use. This may involve looking past the verb to find the subject. For example, in the sentence, "Here [is/are] the leftovers," the subject is *leftovers*. Since *leftovers* is a plural subject, you must use a plural verb. Therefore, the correct form of the verb is *are*.

■ Use singular verbs with indefinite pronouns. Consider the sentence, "Neither of the two kinds of tickets [cost/costs] too much." The best method of finding and correcting these subject–verb mistakes is to become very familiar with the following list of pronouns. When one of these pronouns is used as a subject, it is considered singular and will always take a singular verb:

one	nobody	nothing	none
anyone	anybody	anything	each
everyone	everybody	everything	either
someone	somebody	something	neither

Therefore, in the preceding example sentence, the correct form of the verb is *costs*.

PRACTICE Revise the following sentences so that the subject and verb in each agree. Write the correct form of the verb in the space provided. Notice that some verbs are correct.

1. Joe Lloyd, the new pitcher for the Methodist Church team, throw a wicked curve ball.

    Correct form of the verb: _____

2. Although little Junior eats crayons, he never mark on the wall with them.

    Correct form of the first verb: _____

    Correct form of the second verb: _____

3. Bob and Larry was the best of friends until Larry left Bob's radio on the patio during a rainstorm.

Correct form of the first verb: _____

4. Several people rides to work every morning with our chef Bob Johnston.

Correct form of the verb: _____

5. Everybody who was still in line at noon were told to come back at 2:00 P.M.

Correct form of the first verb: _____

Correct form of the second verb: _____

6. There was too many selections on the menu for me to make up my mind quickly.

Correct form of the first verb: _____

7. One of my daughter's most upsetting habits are leaving the television on when she goes to bed.

Correct form of the first verb: _____

Correct form of the second verb: _____

8. Wine and cheese is always safe bets for an informal get-together.

Correct form of the verb: _____

9. After they heard the news, John and Penny was looking for a new place to live.

Correct form of the second verb: _____

10. Everyone of us were ready for the test at the same time.

Correct form of the verb: _____

VERB TENSE

Keep your verb tense consistent. If you begin an essay in the present tense, check to see that all subsequent verbs are present-tense verbs. If you are writing about something that happened in the past, you may want to use past tense; if you do so, you should remain in past tense throughout your essay. The same rule holds for future tense. The key word is *consistency.* Consistent verb tense is important because it avoids confusing your reader. If you switch from present to past tense, for example, the reader may have trouble understanding whether what you are talking about is something happening right now (present tense) or something that already happened (past tense).

The following sentences are excerpted from a student's essay about a job he once had. The opening paragraph is written in past tense. The reader understands at this point that the writer is writing about past experiences. In the second paragraph, however, the writer changes tense, which causes confusion. Read the selection, and notice the changes in tense as you read.

Example   MOBILE-HOME WORKER

After graduating from high school, I went to work. My first job was at a place called Mobility, Inc., which was a mobile-home construction factory. After working there for about seven months, I quit and went to work at Liberty Mobile Homes, Inc., in Huntsville, Alabama. This job was the worst job I have ever had because I was underpaid, and the tools I had to work with were inappropriate.

My job title was "decker." This means that I place plywood on the floor joists of the trailer and staple it down. My starting salary was $5.25 per hour. This would have been satisfactory if all I had to do was deck the houses.

From reading the first paragraph, the reader can assume that the writer has left the job at Mobile Homes, Inc. In the second paragraph, however, in defining the term *decker,* the writer switches to present-tense verbs: *means, place,* and *staple.* Then the writer informs us of what his starting salary *was,* using past tense again. Unnecessary shifting from past to present to past tense creates confusion for the reader. Such shifts should be avoided.

Methods of Finding Errors in Tense   Two approaches are useful for uncovering verb-tense errors:

■ Read through your writing paying special attention to verbs. Usually, the first verb establishes the tense you will use for the rest of the writing. If you begin with present tense, check your writing to see that all verbs are within the present tense time frame and that there are no unnecessary shifts in tense.

■ Again, it is useful to have someone else read your writing to look for any confusing shifts in tense.

Methods of Correcting Errors in Tense   The best way to handle verb-tense errors is simply to change verbs that contain unnecessary shifts in tense back to the tense you used at the beginning of your sentence or paragraph. Thus, the preceding sample paragraphs could be rewritten as follows.

Example   MOBILE-HOME WORKER [revised]

After graduating from high school, I went to work. My first job was at a place called Mobility, Inc., which was a mobile-home construction factory. After working there for about seven months, I quit and went to work at Liberty Mobile Homes, Inc., in Huntsville, Alabama. This job was the worst job I have ever had because I was underpaid and the tools I had to work with were inappropriate.

My job title was "decker." As a decker, I placed plywood on the floor joists of the trailer and stapled it down. My starting salary was $5.25 per hour. This would have been satisfactory if my only responsibility had been to deck the houses.

PRACTICE   The following paragraphs excerpted from student essays contain unnecessary shifts in tense. Find and cross out the mistakes in tense, and write the correct form of the verb above the crossed-out word(s).

GOOD JOB

An ideal job would have many desirable characteristics. Supervision would practice an open-door policy, allowing workers to feel that they could talk freely about job-related issues. Management would use the golden rule, "Do unto others as you would have them do unto you," when dealing with personnel. The work would always be challenging. The employee feels that she is learning and refining new skills. Co-workers would be friendly, caring, and helpful. There is no jealousy or envy among fellow workers.

RESISTORS

Carbon-slug resistors, the most common type, are a low-cost general-purpose variety used in low-power circuits when the value of resistance does not have to be exact. The resistance element is a cylindrical slug molded from a mixture of powdered or granulated carbon, which is a fairly good conductor in pure form, and powdered insulating material. The resistance value is determined by the ratio of carbon to insulator and by the length and diameter of the slug. The slug was encased in a cylinder of nonconducting rigid plastic, which may be from one-quarter inch to one inch long and up to one-quarter inch in diameter, depending on the resistor's power-dissipation capability, which was usually limited to two watts or less.

REVIEW OF PRONOUNS

Before working through the activities on pronouns, you may find the following brief review of pronouns helpful. This review will help you avoid mistakes in pronoun agreement, reference, and point of view.

In the section on subject–verb agreement, you reviewed the definition of pronouns: they are words that take the place of nouns. In the following sentence, the noun *students* is used and then replaced by the pronoun *they*:

Example   When the students planned the Spring Festival, they overlooked the possibility of a downpour.

This sentence would be confusing without the pronoun *they*. The reader would probably assume that the writer was referring to separate groups of students:

Example   When the students planned the Spring Festival, the students overlooked the possibility of a downpour.

Pronouns simplify and clarify writing. In the first sentence, *they* clearly refers to the *students*. *Students* is the antecedent—the word that the writer is referring to by use of the pronoun. Most pronoun mistakes occur in one of the following situations:

■ The pronoun does not agree in number with the word or words it replaces:

Example   The line of students made their way down the hall.

■ It is not clear which word the pronoun refers to:

Example   I always hated my English classes because they made so many writing assignments.

■ The writer has shifted point of view:

Example   One reason I hated English classes was that the teachers made you write so many papers.

Pronoun Agreement   The rule for pronoun agreement is similar to the rule for subject–verb agreement: the pronoun must agree in number with the word or words it replaces. Therefore, if the word a pronoun replaces is singular, the pronoun must also be singular. Conversely, if the word the pronoun replaces is plural, the pronoun must be plural.

In the first preceding sample sentence, the antecedent of *their* is *line*, not *students*. Since *line* is singular a singular pronoun must be used. The sentence should be rewritten as follows:

Example   The line of students made its way down the hall.

The following indefinite pronouns always take a singular verb:

one	nobody	nothing	none
anyone	anybody	anything	each
everyone	everybody	everything	either
someone	somebody	something	neither

These pronouns should also be considered singular when used with other pronouns.

Now let's look at another example:

Example   One of the men on the train left his luggage at the last stop.

In this sentence, *one*, as indefinite pronoun, takes the singular pronoun *his*. The pronoun is always singular when used with an indefinite pronoun such as those in the preceding list. This example is correct if everyone on the train is male. If *one* referred to "one of the women," the proper pronoun would be *her*:

Example   One of the women on the train left her luggage at the last stop.

If the people on the train were a mixed group of women and men, the sentence could be rewritten as follows:

Example   One of the people on the train left his or her luggage at the last stop.

Since the use of "his or her" is somewhat awkward, it is sometimes worthwhile to rewrite a sentence to avoid the use of gender pronouns. For example, we might write the following:

Example   One of the passengers left luggage at the last stop.

PRACTICE   Revise the following sentences so that the pronouns in each agree in number with the nouns they replace. For example, in the sentence, "She carried the basket of apples carefully, but they fell to the floor when the handle broke," you would change the pronoun form *they* to *it*.

1. Everyone on the plane was eating their lunch when the pilot made the announcement.

   Change the pronoun from _____ to _____

2. Someone had left their keys on the counter at the department store.

   Change the pronoun from _____ to _____

3. Bob always has an apple with his lunch for he believes they keep the doctor away.

   Change the pronoun from _____ to _____

4. The reasons people give for one's absences are as varied as their imaginations.

   Change the pronoun from _____ to _____

5. Our friends have a new set of twins, but I haven't seen it yet.

   Change the pronoun from _____ to _____

Pronoun Reference A pronoun must refer clearly to the word it replaces (the antecedent). The word *pronoun* means "for a noun"; consequently, each pronoun must refer to a specific noun. An ambiguous pronoun reference confuses the reader and detracts from the clarity of the writing. Consider the following example:

Example   I always hated my English classes because they made so many writing assignments.

In this sentence, *they* has no antecedent. Even though the reader can figure out that *they* refers to certain previously unnamed teachers, doing so shouldn't be the reader's job. As the writer, you should make the reference clear to the reader by using a noun before you use a pronoun. In this case, the sentence could be rewritten as follows:

Example   I always hated my English classes because the teachers made so many writing assignments.

PRACTICE   Revise the following sentences so that the pronoun references in each are clear.

1. The cowboys shot up the town because they felt they were against them.

    _____

    _____

2. Each of my friends has wrecked their car at least once.

    _____

    _____

3. I got a haircut yesterday, and it looks much better now.

    _____

    _____

4. Each of my teachers has had to see their psychologist at least once while I was in their room.

    _____

    _____

5. We hurried to the theater, but they didn't start selling tickets until eight o'clock.

    _____

    _____

Pronoun Point of View *Point of view* refers to the writer's relationship to his or her audience and to the material being presented. You may write in first person, in which case you will use the pronoun *I* to refer to yourself. Or you may choose to write in second person, *you*. This is particularly appropriate for "how to" essays, but it should generally be avoided in other kinds of writing. Finally, you may write in third person, in which case you use *he, she, it,* or *they.*

Unnecessary shifts in point of view should be avoided because they confuse the reader. Like consistent verb tense, consistent point of view makes your writing clearer and easier to follow. If you begin writing in first person, don't shift to second or third person.

Consider the following example:

Example One reason I hated English classes was that the teachers made you write so many papers.

In this sentence, the writer has shifted from first person to second person. As the sentence is written, it is the writer who hated English classes but the reader who got the writing assignments. The writer has shifted point of view and now includes the reader in his feeling toward English classes. The sentence could be rewritten as follows:

Example One reason I hated English classes was that the teachers made me write so many papers.

The following chart will help you avoid unnecessary shifts in pronoun point of view.

Type of Pronoun	Singular	Plural
first-person	I (my, mine, me)	we (our, us)
second-person	you (your)	you (your)
third-person	he (his, him)	they (their, them)
	she (her)	
	it (its)	

PRACTICE Review the following sentences so that the point of view in each is clear. Cross out unclear pronouns, and write corrections above the crossed-out material. Here is an example of what to do:

Example Jerome didn't go to the math class because he thought the teachers didn't care about ~~you~~ *him.*

Now complete the practice exercise for the following sentences.

1. When I take the dog to the veterinarian, you know that it is going to cost a lot.

2. If a customer wants good service in a restaurant, they should act politely toward the waitress.

3. While we waited for the answer, you could hear a pin drop.

4. When a person buys a new car, they should expect to have some minor problems with it.

5. If a person organizes his time, they can really accomplish a lot more work.

PRACTICE Edit a piece of writing you have recently done to make sure that it maintains a consistent point of view. To begin, determine which point of view the writing is written in. Then decide if it is an appropriate point of view for this particular type of writing. Finally, make any necessary changes to ensure that this point of view remains consistent throughout the writing.

EDITING DICTION

Editing diction involves correcting problems with the choice of words in your writing. At this point in the editing process, you are concerned with making sure that the words you use say what you want them to say—that their meanings are neither unintended nor vague. As you work through the explanations and practices in this section, bear in mind the audience and purpose issues, as discussed in Chapter 1. Audience (whom you are writing for) and purpose (why you are writing) are important considerations in evaluating diction. For example, if you are writing an informal letter to a good friend, the use of slang is certainly permissible. On the other hand, slang is usually quite inappropriate in a literary essay or in a cover letter for a job application.

The ensuing section on editing diction applies to writing that demands a more formal style than may be used in friendly letter writing. Vocabulary, details, and sentence structure—all levels of usage—vary widely, depending on whether your writing is formal (the style used for important documents and many speeches), informal (the style used in most college writing and some professional writing, such as business letters), or colloquial (the style used in friendly letter writing and other kinds of casual writing).

To help improve your skills in editing diction, this section will focus on diction problems in the following areas:

- Word choice
      Connotation
      Slang
      Clichés
      Pretentious language
      Vague terms
      Sexist language
- Appropriate point of view
- Wordiness

CONNOTATION

Words have both connotative and denotative meanings. Dictionaries give denotative (or literal) meanings, which is why dictionary definitions are neutral and have little, if any, emotional impact. But words also have connotative (or implied) meanings. The connotative meaning of a word has an emotional impact that, depending on the reader, may involve either negative or positive associations. The underlined words in the following examples have various connotations—that is, implied meanings. As you read these sentences, notice which underlined words have negative connotations, which have positive connotations, and which have neutral connotations. Then list these words in the appropriate spaces following the sentences.

Examples   Do you mean the <u>fat</u> boy running down the street?

Do you mean the <u>pudgy</u> boy running down the street?

Do you mean the <u>obese</u> boy running down the street?

Do you mean the <u>big</u> boy running down the street?

You mean the <u>overweight</u> boy running down the street?

Which underlined word or words have negative connotations?

_____

Which underlined word or words have positive connotations?

_____

Which underlined word or words have neutral connotations?

All of the underlined words in the preceding questions are roughly synonymous; but depending on how you feel about the synonyms, your responses to the questions can differ considerably from your classmates' responses. For most people, *overweight* is the most neutral term, *obese* is a negative term, and *pudgy* can have various connotations. Your choice of words has a tremendous impact on your writing and helps to shape your readers' understanding and reaction to what you are communicating. Your job as a writer is to make sure that your word choice accurately reflects what you want to say. In Chapter 3, you were encouraged to use lively, descriptive words in your writing. This is desirable, of course, but remember to review the connotative meanings of words as you edit your writing.

SLANG

Slang expressions are unacceptable in many writing assignments because they can be limiting and confusing to your reader. They can be limiting simply because they go out of date so quickly. Yesterday's popular slang expressions may now sound old, boring, and out of step. In fact, slang expressions change so quickly that it is best to avoid them in formal writing. Fifteen years ago, it was hip to say "hip"; today, some people might respond to that term with disdain. Slang expressions are often confusing because not everyone interprets their meaning in the same way. Meanings of slang expressions often vary from group to group. Therefore, except in informal and colloquial writing, it is a good idea to avoid slang.

CLICHÉS

A cliché is an expression that has been overused to the point that it no longer has any significant meaning. For example, the phrase, "it was raining cats and dogs," means that it was raining very hard. But very few people bother to think about that when they hear the phrase because it has been overworked and overused. If you want to convey the description of a hard rain to your reader, try using an original phrase instead of relying on one you have heard before. Even if it isn't as catchy or clever as the first one was, it will probably be more effective simply because it is new.

Not only are clichés boring, they are frequently imprecise, vague, and even untrue. "Meek as a lamb" is a cliché that may conjure up the idea of docility to some people, but sheep farmers may laugh at the idea of meekness in lambs. And how comfortable is a "bed of roses"? Have you ever stopped to think about how a bed of roses might actually feel?

The following brief list of chichés will help you begin to recognize and avoid clichés in writing. Read this list and learn to listen for phrases that are frequently used. To keep your writing fresh and original, stay away from clichés such as these:

one in a million	to make a long story short
proud as a peacock	happy as a lark
sick as a dog	a sight for sore eyes
pain in the neck	wake up and smell the coffee
busy as a bee	slow as molasses
pretty as a picture	slow as Christmas
jump to a conclusion	hot as fire
blind as a bat	cold as ice
first and foremost	soft as silk
few and far between	white as snow

You can probably think of many clichés that are not included in this list. In the space that follows, write down some other clichés. You may want to do this exercise as a group, to get the benefit of everyone's ideas.

_____   _____

_____   _____

_____   _____

_____   _____

PRETENTIOUS WORDS

Many student writers feel that good writing, particularly academic writing, must contain numerous multisyllable words and must be written in a grand, formal tone in order to sound either "educated" or "professional." This is not true. Good writing does not have to be either fancy or elevated in style; neither does it have to rely on multisyllable words. You may certainly use multisyllable words; indeed, one way to increase your vocabulary is to use new words in your writing and in your speech. Just make sure that you understand the word and its proper use before you use it.

The following sentence is an example of pretentious writing:

Example I acquired a camera during the past holiday season.

Here is a revised form of the sentence, stripped of pretentiousness:

Example I received a camera at Christmas.

While the original sentence is grammatically correct, its formal tone and its use of the word *acquired* and the phrase *past holiday season* are so grand that they are almost funny—even though this writer did not intend to be humorous. (The rest of this student's essay explained the proper way to load film into a camera.) Moreover, the word *acquired* connotes something quite different from gift-giving. People acquire an education, a taste for good wine, a power-hitting third baseman, or their grandfather's tendency to a bad temper.

Here is another example of pretentious wording:

Example She manifested exemplary fortitude during the final days of her illness.

And here is a revised form of the sentence, with more natural-sounding words:

Example She remained courageous during the final days of her illness.

Euphemisms People often tend to write in eloquent terms when describing death or death-related subjects. One particular kind of pretentious language uses *euphemisms*—words or phrases that describe distasteful subjects in ways that make them seem less distasteful. Our society has many euphemisms for death, for example. Euphemisms for the word *died* include *passed away, passed on, departed, went to heaven, went to live with the angels, entered the eternal kingdom,* and *entered the larger life.* It is best to avoid euphemisms because they rarely contribute to clear, straightforward writing. In addition, euphemisms may strike the reader as expressing a false sensitivity or refinement, and they are often simply misunderstood.

Here is an example of a euphemism-filled sentence:

Example He sought the solace of oblivion when his beloved companion ascended the golden stair.

And here is a noneuphemistic version of the same sentence:

Example He drank too much after his wife died.

Jargon   Jargon, another form of pretentious language, is inappropriately used technical terminology. Highly technical terminology is appropriate to use if the writing is for a technical audience. But if the writing is directed at a general audience, the use of unnecessary technical words and phrases is misleading, abstract, and often humorous. Jargon tends to come from specialized areas such as electronics (*input, interface*), social work (*support group, share your feelings, meaningful relationships*), and education (*articulate, assessment, evaluation instrument*). All of these words and phrases are perfectly acceptable if used in the proper contexts. But if used out of the proper contexts, they are misleading, annoying, or even funny. If you are a member of a specialized group, use jargon with caution. And if you are writing to a general audience, use specialized vocabulary only when you are certain that your readers will understand the term or when you include a brief explanation of the term.

Here is an example of a sentence riddled with jargon:

Example   After interfacing with his support group, he felt that his input about his wife's childish behavior would convince the others that he was on target.

And here is a revised version of the same sentence, jargon-free:

Example   After talking with his friends, he felt that his ideas about his wife's childish behavior would convince the others that he was right and she was wrong.

VAGUE WORDS

Edit your writing for any vague, nonspecific words that might limit your reader's understanding of your writing. You may have a very clear idea of what constitutes "a lot of studying," for example, but your reader will have no way of sharing that specific idea. Readers tend to glide over such nonspecific phrases; they may fail even to try to form an idea of what you mean by "a lot." Here is an example of a vague sentence:

Example   Last night, I did a lot of studying for my history test.

Here is a rewrite, in three sentences, of the same idea:

Example   To get ready for my history test, I studied for two hours before dinner. Then I went to supper with my roommate but took my notes so she could call things out while we ate. Finally, I went back to my room and studied until I fell asleep at 1:30 A.M.

SEXIST LANGUAGE

Edit your writing to eliminate any nouns or pronouns that suggest either a particular bias or stereotype. In order to avoid the use of sexist language, use the following three guidelines. First, use plural nouns instead of singular ones. Here is an example of a sentence that could be corrected through the use of plural nouns:

Example A good secretary must know a lot about grammar and punctuation in order to present a good letter for her employer to sign.

And here is a corrected version of the same sentence:

Example Good secretaries must know a lot about grammar and punctuation in order to present good letters for their employers to sign.

Second, many occupational titles ending in *–man* or *–woman* can be replaced with nonsexist titles. Some examples are the following:

| fireman | firefighter | saleslady | salesperson |
| chairman | chairperson | policeman | police officer |

Third, you can omit unnecessary pronouns, or you can use a gender-neutral pronoun, such as *you, we,* or *one.* Here are two examples (with accompanying revisions) of sentences where sexist language can be avoided:

Example Each student is responsible for turning his papers in on time.
      Each student is responsible for turning papers in on time.

Example Whenever possible, a person should avoid using sexist terms in her writing.
      Whenever possible, one [or *you,* or *we*] should avoid using sexist terms in one's [or *your,* or *our*] writing.

PRACTICE The following sentences contain examples of poor word choice, including inappropriate connotation, slang, clichés, pretentious wording, euphemisms, jargon, vague terms, and sexist language. To practice identifying and removing these kinds of words and phrases from your writing, rewrite each sentence in the space provided, using the style required in most academic writing. Here is an example of a faulty sentence:

Example The <u>head count</u> at the festival was much higher than anticipated.

And here is a revision that corrects the problem:

Example   The number of people attending the festival was much higher than anticipated.

Now correct the following sentences:

1. From the very first day of school, the child will meet people he just can't stand.

  _____

  _____

  _____

  _____

2. I feel at a loss for words when I try to say how much I care for him. To make a long story short, he really turns me on.

  _____

  _____

  _____

  _____

3. The idea that there could be life on other planets is phenomenologically unsubstantiated.

  _____

  _____

  _____

  _____

4. In conclusion, net sales for the month are reported to be a whopping $150,000.

  _____

  _____

_____

_____

5. Many people dislike watching the nightly news while they eat because the cameras always focus on <u>bodies of deceased individuals</u>.

_____

_____

_____

6. It's a <u>dysfunctional ratiocination</u> to think that you can graduate on schedule at this point in the semester.

_____

_____

_____

7. Before you begin the meeting, inform the participants that the men's restroom is on the left across from the lounge and the <u>ladies'</u> restroom is around the corner on the right.

_____

_____

_____

8. One of the issues <u>mothers</u> have to face every working day is the lack of good day care for their children.

_____

_____

_____

_____

9. One section of the form concerns the breadwinner of the family
and requires the applicant to list the breadwinner's occupation
and <u>his</u> average annual income.

_____

_____

_____

_____

10. I don't <u>hang out with</u> that group of people anymore, because
they're <u>messing around</u> with drugs.

_____

_____

_____

_____

POINT OF VIEW

Consistent pronoun point of view was discussed in the previous section.
But in addition to maintaining a consistent point of view, you may also
want to edit your paper for appropriate point of view. This means
avoiding, in certain kinds of writing, the frequent use of the first-person
pronouns _I_ and _we_ and the second-person pronoun _you_.

First-person pronouns give your writing a chatty, informal tone, which
may be appropriate for some kinds of writing but generally should be
avoided in academic writing. In addition, using these pronouns tends to
emphasize the writer's attitudes toward the topic rather than providing
understanding of the topic. Here is an example of a paragraph that
contains intrusive first-person pronouns:

Example   I think that one solution to the country's drug problem is to forget
about prosecuting people who possess small amounts of relatively

harmless drugs and concentrate on prosecuting the people who have large amounts of dangerous drugs, such as cocaine and heroin. We will never have the prison space to contain everyone who uses drugs, but I think we can accomplish more if we forget the small drug users and take more action against the ones who use or possess large amounts of dangerous drugs.

Here is the same paragraph, edited to avoid the use of first-person pronouns:

Example   One solution to the country's drug problem is to forget about prosecuting people who possess small amounts of relatively harmless drugs and concentrate on prosecuting the people who have large amounts of dangerous drugs, such as cocaine and heroin. The country will never have the prison space to contain everyone who uses drugs, but more can be accomplished if the small drug users are ignored and more action is taken against the ones who use or possess large amounts of dangerous drugs.

Another frequent problem with point of view is the inappropriate use of the second-person pronoun *you,* as in the following paragraph:

Example   The College Work-Study Program provides jobs for undergraduate and graduate students who need financial aid. College Work-Study gives students a chance to earn a part of their educational expenses. The amount that College Work-Study awards depends on your need and the amount of money the school has for this program. In arranging a job and assigning a work schedule, the financial aid administrator at the school will consider the student's need for financial assistance as well as your class schedule, your health, and your academic progress.

Not only has the writer shifted point of view—from the student (third person) to you (second person)—but the use of second-person *you* is too informal and conversational for the more formal tone this writer wanted. The paragraph could be rewritten as follows:

Example   The College Work-Study Program provides jobs for undergraduate and graduate students who need financial aid. College Work-Study gives students a chance to earn a part of their educational expenses.

The amount that College Work-Study awards depends on the student's need and the amount of money the school has for this program. In arranging a job and assigning a work schedule, the financial aid administrator at the school will consider the student's need for financial assistance as well as the student's class schedule, health, and academic progress.

PRACTICE   Rewrite the following sentences, eliminating inappropriate first-person and second-person pronouns. One sentence is informal in tone and therefore does not need to be rewritten.

1. The part of my job I hated most was collection of overdue payments. You had to go to the house and knock on the door, knowing that the people inside did not want to see or talk to you.

_____

_____

_____

_____

2. I think that the threat of nuclear war is one of the things that today's children worry most about, and we should try to do something to alleviate this fear.

_____

_____

_____

_____

3. While the movie certainly had many weak scenes, I was so impressed with the strongly developed characters that I paid little attention to what would have otherwise been a boring movie.

_____

_____

_____

_____

4. I really disliked my fifth-grade teacher because, whenever I misbe-
haved, she would make you call your parents and tell them what
you had done.

_____

_____

_____

5. I think that the best way I had fun as a child was playing dress-up
with my cousins.

_____

_____

_____

_____

WORDINESS

At some point in the editing process, you need to check your writing for
wordiness. This means reading for compactness of expression. Your
reader wants to read what you have written—especially if you have fairly
represented your subject in your contract idea (discussed in Chapter 2)—
but does not care to read unnecessary words or phrases. Indeed, the
reader is not likely to finish an excessively wordy piece of writing.
Although your composition teacher may finish reading what you have
written in order to give you a grade, he or she may develop a negative
attitude toward wordiness in your writing.

Most drafts are wordy; and many writers report that, if they go back
to a piece of writing that is several weeks old, they find many unnecessary
words, phrases, and even sentences in the work. In fact, one good way to
eliminate wordiness is to write and then put the writing away for several

hours or several days. Then go back to the writing, and edit it for wordiness.

PRACTICE Find a term paper, essay, or essay exam that you wrote last semester or last year. Carefully reread the writing, and mark any unnecessary words, phrases, and paragraphs.

Think of wordiness as fat. Your sentences should be lean and concise instead of fat and verbose. Commercials are good examples of lean, concise writing. Advertising writers must make a point, support the point, and convince a listener, reader, or viewer to buy a specific product— all in one to three minutes. While your writing should not be reduced to this extreme point, you can appreciate commercial writing as a type that attempts to communicate without boring or confusing viewers or readers.

Following are several pairs of phrases or sentences. The first sentence in each pair contains fat—unnecessary words or phrases. The second sentence in each group has been reduced; that is, unnecessary words have been trimmed from the sentence.

Example **a.** Due to the fact that post office regulations have changed....

b. Because post office regulations have changed....

"Due to the fact that" is a wordy phrase that means *because*. This one-word phrase is leaner and faster-moving than the five-word phrase. Other examples of phrases that clog the flow of written work when a simple *because* would do the job are "for reasons that," "on the condition that," and "in view of the fact that."

Example **a.** I arrived at the office at 7 A.M. in the morning, only to find my office door open, my desk ransacked, and my file cabinet overturned.

b. I arrived at the office at 7 A.M., only to find my office door open, my desk ransacked, and my file cabinet overturned.

It is unnecessary to include *in the morning* in this sentence, because A.M. means morning.

Example **a.** I think that the death penalty should be abolished.

b. The death penalty should be abolished.

It is generally unnecessary for you to add *I think that* to sentences, because the reader understands that such statements are your opinion.

PRACTICE   The following sentences contain mixed constructions and wordy, awkward phrases. Rewrite each so that it is clear and succinct. You may delete words or make two or more sentences out of a single sentence. We begin with an example of a wordy sentence:

Example   There are several reasons, maybe six or seven or even more, why I chose to go to Western Community College.

And here is a possible revision of the faulty sentence:

Example   There are at least six reasons for my choosing to attend Western Community College.

Now complete the practice exercises that follow.

1. Playing by ear, which to me means hearing and matching a note, is a more creative way to make music than is the traditional method of reading music and playing the notes, although this is helpful in some situations no doubt.

   _____

   _____

   _____

   _____

2. My father, who was a very hard man to please, although not all the time, was also very understanding and willing to help.

   _____

   _____

   _____

3. I enjoyed my summer job at Fastfills Quickstop, which is not a completely true statement, although it didn't pay as much as I would have liked.

   _____

_____

_____

_____

4. I enjoy running and walking, but I prefer swimming to both of these.

_____

_____

_____

_____

5. In my opinion, planning a trip is worrying in advance, according to my brother.

_____

_____

_____

_____

6. Although believing it was helpful, I didn't take anything too seriously.

_____

_____

_____

_____

7. Money not being a problem for me, I went on the trip anyway.

_____

_____

_____

_____

8. He said, "You're lost," and then showed me how to get back to Interstate 25.

_____

_____

_____

_____

9. Betty promised to help me, but I'm sure she forgot, since she didn't show up at the park, and even though I called her house I didn't get an answer.

_____

_____

_____

_____

10. She and Rob trained the dog, but they had some help from a friend of theirs who was once a veterinarian's assistant in another city before moving here to work for an ad agency.

_____

_____

_____

_____

EDITING PUNCTUATION AND MECHANICS

Appropriate punctuation and accurate mechanics are necessary to make your sentences clear and easy to comprehend. *Mechanics* refers to the surface features of written expression and includes such things as knowing when to capitalize and how to abbreviate.

punctuation consists of a number of universally recognized symbols that tell the reader what to do or how to interpret what you have written think of punctuation and mechanics as road markers or signs whereas our road system uses an eight sided sign to signal a driver to stop standard written english uses a period there are driving signs for other kinds of stops such as the yield sign swe uses signs such as semicolons colons commas and dashes as with road signs if everyone understands and uses the appropriate symbols punctuation will make writing much clearer for both the writer and the reader.

If you are like most readers, you had a lot of trouble reading and comprehending the preceding paragraph. You probably had to spend some time figuring out where one thought ended and another began. That is because all punctuation and mechanics were omitted. Here is the same paragraph with the appropriate punctuation:

Punctuation consists of a number of universally recognized symbols that "tell" the reader what to do or how to interpret what you have written. Think of punctuation and mechanics as road markers or signs. Whereas our road system uses an eight-sided sign to signal the driver to stop, Standard Written English uses a period. There are driving signs for other kinds of stops, such as the yield sign; SWE uses signs such as semicolons, colons, commas, and dashes. As with road signs, if everyone understands and uses the appropriate symbols, punctuation will make writing much clearer for both the writer and the reader.

You will need to pay special attention to the following areas:

- End punctuation
    Period
    Question mark
    Exclamation point

- Other punctuation
  - Colon
  - Semicolon
  - Comma
  - Dash
  - Hyphen
  - Ellipsis points
  - Parentheses
  - Apostrophe
  - Quotation marks
- Mechanics
  - Capitalization
  - Abbreviation
  - Numbers

END PUNCTUATION (., ?, !)

The strongest punctuation is the kind that marks the end of a complete sentence. There are three kinds of end punctuation: the period (.), the question mark (?), and the exclamation point (!).

Most sentences end with a period, because most sentences (such as this one) are statements. If you are making a statement, use a period to mark the end of the statement.

Are you asking a question? If so, use a question mark to end the sentence.

To make a strong, forceful statement, use an exclamation point! This symbol should be used far less frequently than the other two; if you overuse it (and beginning writers frequently do), the symbol loses its effect on the reader. Every sentence cannot be strongly worded. If you attempt to make every sentence an exclamation, you will simply lose the power to call your reader's attention to any exceptionally strong, forceful statement.

PRACTICE   Punctuate each of the following sentences, using a period, a question mark, or an exclamation point. Because exclamations are so infrequent, only one of the following sentences needs an exclamation point.

1. If it is raining, the wedding will be inside the chapel rather than in the chapel gardens

2. Do you prefer chocolate syrup or strawberry syrup on your pancakes

3. If it is raining, where will the wedding take place

4. Although I see very little of him anymore, I think about him often

5. She is spending six weeks in the U.K

6. I can't believe you're asking me to do that

7. Tom wants to know when the party begins

8. What should I tell him when he calls

9. ZIP is an acronym for what

10. He wondered how he would make up the test, since the teacher had taken a new job

COLON (:)

Colons serve several purposes. First, use a colon to introduce a long or formal list. Here is an example:

Example   Costs of tuition for part-time students per credit hour are as follows: 0–5 hours, $51.00; 6–7 hours, $103.00; 8 hours, $339.00; 9–11 hours, $390.75.

Second, use a colon to introduce a long quotation, as in the following example:

Example   When the school board members were asked by reporters what they considered the most pressing issues for public school teachers, one replied: "The most pressing issue is the feeling of unprofessionalism. We must provide offices and secretarial help, so teachers can feel pride in the teaching profession."

Third, use a colon to introduce an explanation, particularly if you want to provide emphasis. Again, here is an example:

Example   I have always liked Robert Frost's definition of freedom: "moving easy in harness."

SEMICOLON (;)

Semicolons were briefly discussed in the subsection on run-on sentences and comma splices in the "Editing Sentence Structure and Grammar" section of this chapter. At least three purposes are served by semicolons. First, use a semicolon to mark the break between two complete, independent thoughts that are part of the same sentence.

Example   Alison was terribly afraid of teenagers when she was little; she called them "teen angels" and thought they were ghosts.

Second, use a semicolon to punctuate the connection between two independent clauses that are joined by a subordinating conjunction, such as the following:

however

moreover

thus

therefore

consequently

Use a comma after the joining word. For more detailed information about this use of semicolons, see the review of commas later in this section.

Example   Her sentence consisted of two independent clauses; therefore, she used a semicolon, a joining word, and a comma to connect the clauses.

Third, use a semicolon to punctuate items in a series when the individual items themselves contain commas.

Example   The following people have overdue books and must pay the charges listed before graduation: Billy Ray, $.25; Bobby Jones, $.75; Anna Stevens, $1.25; and Ginger Phillips, $.25.

PRACTICE   Punctuate the following sentences, using colons or semicolons where needed.

   1.   The major topics of inquiry in this analysis are as follows cost of obtaining the four-year degree from various institutions, courses of study to follow at these institutions, and comparisons of the institutions.

2. Lest we lose sight of what's important, I close with this reflection we will need to set priorities that reflect our by-laws because those by-laws are our original plan of action.

3. He hated to miss the party on Friday therefore, he worked a double shift on Thursday so that he could be off.

4. His invention emphasized three concepts information, explanation, and demonstration.

5. The following were my best subjects in high-school extracurricular activities, study hall, and lunch.

6. She heard it through the office grapevine she considered it to be good information anyway.

7. I had a high-school math teacher who was fond of saying to talkative students "It's the empty wagon that makes the most noise!"

8. My favorite poems include "Ode to a Nightingale," by Keats "After Apple-Picking," by Frost and "Leaves of Grass," by Whitman.

9. The data-processing field is one of the fastest-growing industries in the world consequently, it is a field a high-school graduate should seriously consider.

10. My husband thinks that there are two levels for running appliances off and high.

COMMA (,)

Many punctuation errors involve the misuse of commas. The five most common comma errors are related to the following:

- Independent clauses joined by a coordinating conjunction
- Items in a series
- Sentence interrupters
- Introductory material
- Direct quotations

Properly applying the rules for these uses of commas will improve the appearance and readability of your writing.

First, always place a comma before a coordinating conjunction (*and, or, but, for, nor, yet, so*) that joins two independent clauses. Here is an example of this use:

Example   My mother and father came to the wedding, but my brother was unable to attend.

Second, use commas to separate items in a series (a collection of three or more similar units), as in the following example:

Example   I painted the stairway, cleaned out the refrigerator, and played Night Crawler on my computer during my vacation.

Third, use commas before and after a word or phrase that interrupts the flow of thought in a sentence. Here is an illustration:

Example   I failed physics, although not out of laziness, and will have to repeat it next semester.

Fourth, use a comma to separate introductory material from the remainder of the sentence:

Example   Even though the instructor missed several classes, I'm convinced that I learned all I need to know about sociology.

Fifth, use commas with direct quotations:

Example   "Fortunately for you," she announced, "I've decided to stay with you this summer."

PRACTICE   The following sentences contain comma errors. Review each sentence, marking out unnecessary commas and inserting missing commas.

1.   Working at Taco Bell although the hours were bad provided the money I needed to pay my car insurance.

2.   My parents particularly my dad are convinced that I should spend every weekend doing chores around the house.

3.   "When I met, Harry I was just getting over George and I wasn't ready for another heavy-duty relationship" she explained.

4.   Tammy who spends a lot of time on the phone with Chad would really rather be talking to Bill.

5.   Giving my two-year-old a bath, and trimming her fingernails is a job for three people.

6.   I fell down the stairs, and reinjured my back during the recent Christmas holidays.

7.   Living in a small town, like Mapleville, has its advantages.

8. During our summer vacation we visited Denver Taos and Cheyenne.

9. Alison who is our youngest daughter played a Scott Joplin number for her piano recital this past spring.

10. Uncle Vernon cooked the Thanksgiving turkey and, Aunt Roxan made cranberry sauce cream corn biscuits and baked potatoes.

DASH (—)

To form a dash on a typewriter, strike the hyphen key twice. To form a dash if you are writing, make a horizontal mark as long as two letters. A dash is used to indicate a dramatic or sudden shift in thought. A dash creates a pause—a dramatic one—that is longer than the pause created by a comma but not as long as the one created by end punctuation. Here are two examples of sentences using dashes:

Example   I didn't try the caviar—it wasn't offered to me anyway.

Example   Yes, I will be there—with bells on!

HYPHEN (-)

Hyphens serve a number of punctuating purposes. First, use a hyphen to join two words that describe a noun when the two words act as a single word. Here are some phrases that use hyphens in this way:

slow-moving train
blue-gray gnatcatcher
seven-year-old child
wild-eyed look
one-syllable words

Second, use a hyphen to divide a word at the end of a line of typing. Do not divide one-syllable words. Consult a dictionary about the proper way to divide a word if you have doubts about how the word should be divided. Most dictionaries use dots to mark divisions between syllables. Here is an example of a hyphen used as a sign of word division at the end of a line:

Example   Genealogy, the study of a family's ancestry, has become a popular hobby.

Third, use a hyphen with some compound words and with some words that include a prefix; check a dictionary if you have doubts. Here are some compound words and prefix-bearing words that contain hyphens:

sister-in-law
thirty-four
ex-wife
un-American

ELLIPSIS POINTS (. . .)

Ellipsis points are used to signify that material has been omitted from a quoted passage. To make the ellipsis points for omitted material within a sentence, use three periods with spaces before and after each one. For example, suppose that you started with the following quotation:

Example   "And it came to pass in those days, that there went out a decree
from Caesar Augustus that all the world should be taxed."

You could reproduce the sentence, using ellipsis points in place of the words "from Caesar Augustus," as follows:

Example   "And it came to pass in those days, that there went out a decree ...
that all the world should be taxed."

If the omitted material comes at the end of the sentence, use four periods with spaces between each one but no space before the first:

Example   "And it came to pass...."

You may also use ellipsis points if you want to write an incomplete sentence to achieve a certain effect. Here is an example of such a use:

Example   I never watch sports on TV, but my husband ...

If you are ending a sentence with ellipsis points, followed by a parenthetical reference, use three periods with spaces between the parenthetical reference and a final period.

Example   One of the most famous American documents begins, "When in the
Course of human events ..." (Jefferson, 425).

For more information about parenthetical references, see Chapter 13, "Incorporating Sources," page 400.

PARENTHESES ( )

Use parentheses to enclose information that is extra or incidental to the rest of the sentence. Here is an example:

Example   One of the boys (I won't name names) went into our cabin and put shaving cream in the toothpaste tubes.

If the parenthetical information is a complete sentence, a period goes inside the parentheses:

Example   The boundaries of the small country have changed frequently during the past ten years. (See map on page 22.)

If the parenthetical information is part of the sentence and comes at the end of the sentence, the period comes after the parenthesis:

Example   Tuition for full-time students is $441.00 (excluding room and board).

PRACTICE   Add dashes, hyphens, and parentheses as needed to the following sentences. Be aware that, generally, except in the case of words that act as a unit to describe a noun (for example, *one-syllable word*), you should be careful to avoid overusing these marks of punctuation. If you are confused about when to use which punctuation marks, remember that the dash signals an emphatic or sudden shift in thought, while parentheses indicate the setting off of information that is related to the main sentence but does not need emphasis. In some of these sentences, more than one of these types of punctuation will work.

1. He got an A on his last essay breaking his C − record.

2. All of the girls with the exception of Jean and Jane got A's on their essays.

3. She said goodbye to her school forever.

4. The smooth talking salesman had me signing a contract before I realized what was happening.

5. Yes, I've seen her out jogging several times while watching her jog, I've managed to clean out the ditches of the street with my car.

6. Although my car looks old it has several rusted spots and a faded paint job it runs quite well.

7. One thing that really makes me angry is slow moving vehicles hogging the fast lane on the expressway.

8. Another pet peeve is sweet talking salespeople who insist on calling me "honey," or "dear."

9. Did you know that he recently got married for the fourth time?

10. I grew up in a small town population 1,000, and I have always wanted to experience the excitement of living in a large city.

APOSTROPHE (')

Apostrophes are used in three basic ways. First use an apostrophe in words that have been contracted—that is, when two words have been joined to make one word and letters have been omitted in forming the contraction. Here are several contractions:

I + am = I'm   did + not = didn't
it + is = it's   will + not = won't

Second, use an apostrophe plus the letter *s* with nouns that show ownership or possession. With a singular subject, the apostrophe precedes the *s*:

Jennifer's tennis racket

the horse's stall

a cat's meow

With a plural noun ending in *s*, the apostrophe follows the *s*:

the girls' tennis rackets

the horses' stalls

the cats' meows

Never use an apostrophe with a possessive pronoun (*his, hers, ours, yours, its, theirs*). The spelling of these possessive pronouns signifies ownership, without requiring apostrophes. Hence, you might write the following:

Example   The red jacket is mine; the blue denim is hers.

Third, use an apostrophe with the plural form of certain abbreviations or numbers used as words, especially if the use of *s* alone would create confusion. Here are some examples of this situation:

Examples   Mind your p's and q's.

He made four C's and an A.

He had two M.A.'s and a Ph.D.

PRACTICE   Use apostrophes where needed in the following sentences. In the space provided, rewrite the words that need to be changed. Some of the following sentences are correct and need no changes.

1.   Her mothers summer house is my favorite vacation spot.

   _____

2.   San Franciscos airport is easier to get to than Sacramentos.

   _____

3.   Have you ever had an invitation to eat Petes egg rolls?

   _____

4.   His egg rolls are delicious, even though hes not Chinese.

   _____

5.   A secretarys duties are very stressful and demanding.

   _____

6.   The average supervisor doesnt realize how many duties a secretary performs in a day.

   _____

7.   The lecturer discussed television violence and its effects on young children.

   _____

8.   Theres going to be a big party after graduation.

   _____

9.   His eyes wandered during the final examination, causing the teacher to wonder if he cheated.

   _____

10.   Many people misspell my daughters name by using two ls instead of just one.

   _____

QUOTATION MARKS (" ")

Use quotation marks to enclose the exact words of a speaker or writer. Exact words from a quoted source are called a *direct quotation*. An indirect quotation is a rewording of the speaker's words, rather than an exact reproduction of what the person said. Consider the following sentences.

Examples

Indirect quotation

She said she couldn't possibly take the job because she had made too many other commitments.

Direct quotation

"I can't possibly take the job, since I have already made so many other commitments," she replied.

Indirect quotation

She reminded him that he could still do a little housework every now and then, even though he was now attending college.

Direct quotation

"Just because you are going to college doesn't mean you can't do a little work around the house every now and then," she informed him.

Direct quotations add forcefulness to certain kinds of writing. The preceding indirect quotation about housework just doesn't have the power of the direct quotation.

You must follow some special rules when punctuating direct quotations. In particular, these rules involve the correct way to capitalize direct quotations and the correct way to use commas and end punctuation. Consider the following example:

Example

The funniest excuse I ever read was, "Please excuse Johnny from exams. He has to take his grandpa to the doctor's office to get his pacemaker batteries recharged."

Notice that the exact words of the writer are enclosed in quotation marks. Here is another example:

Example

"Please believe me," she begged.

In this case, a comma is placed inside the last set of quotation marks, and a period completes the sentence.

Here is a third instance:

Example

"Please believe me," she begged. "I have no reason to lie to you. I love you!"

In this case, two sets of quotation marks are needed, since words that are not part of the quotation interrupt the quotation. However, no words interrupt the exact words of the last two sentences, so no new quotation marks are needed for the last sentence. As long as no newly introduced words interrupt the exact quotation, you should not use a new set of quotation marks for each new sentence.

Again, here is a different instance:

Example   "Why should I believe you," he snarled, "when you've lied so many times before?"

In this case, a comma follows the word *snarled,* because the sentence is not completed.

Here is a fifth situation:

Example   As he turned away, she said softly, "But this time is different."

In this case, end punctuation comes inside the quotation mark, since the last word of the sentence is part of the direct quotation.

Here is a sixth situation:

Example   "Do you really expect me to buy the line that 'this time will be different,' when I've heard it a thousand times before?"

In this case, the quotation within the larger quotation is enclosed in single quotation marks.

Here is a seventh situation:

Example   Did she really say, "This time will be different"?

In this case, the quotation is part of a larger sentence that is a question. Therefore, the question mark goes outside the quotation marks.

PRACTICE   With one other person in your class, write a short conversation between two or more people. Vary your quotations so that you try several of the methods described in the preceding examples. In other words, don't begin or end every sentence with "He said." Use lively synonyms for the word *said* as you write.

You should also use quotation marks to enclose titles of short works such as essays, articles, chapters in books, short stories, short poems, and songs. Here are some examples:

Examples	"How to Paint Exterior Woodwork"	magazine article
	"The Raven"	poem
	"White Christmas"	song
	"Fourth of July Feasts"	newspaper article
	"Hills Like White Elephants"	short story
	"The Plight of the Homeless"	essay

Do not, however, put quotation marks around your essay's title on either the title page or the first page of the paper.

The titles of books, newspapers, magazines, plays, movies, record albums, and television shows are printed in italics. We, however, underline them. Again, here are some examples:

Examples	"When I'm Sixty-Four"	song from the album *Sergeant Pepper's Lonely Heart's Club Band*
	"The Man with the Twisted Lip"	short story from the book *The Adventures of Sherlock Holmes*

Finally, you should use quotation marks around special words, phrases, or letters in a sentence. Here are two examples:

Examples   The teacher commented that most of the "research" for my research paper had apparently been done in front of a TV set.

Her nickname is "Cinnamon," but everyone calls her "V-8" because of her red hair.

PRACTICE   Insert quotation marks where needed in the sentences that follow.

1. One of my favorite expressions is, Be careful what you ask for; you might get it.

2. Have you ever read The Gold Bug by Edgar Allan Poe?

3. You can tell he's a two-year-old; his favorite word is no.

4. Write an X in all blanks that are not applicable to your situation.

5. Why don't you use your left arm for the backhand? she asked. You'll develop strength in that arm if you use it.

6. My granddaughter likes any bedtime story that begins with the words, once upon a time.

7. If you really want to know, she replied, I've got $10.00 to last the rest of the quarter.

8. The best essay I wrote in freshman composition class was an essay entitled, How I Stopped Smoking.

9. The first sentence of her essay was, General Hospital is my favorite daytime soap opera.

10. The Yiddish word tsuris is a good example of a word that can't be easily translated into a single English word.

CAPITALIZATION

The rules of capitalization can be stated in ten parts. First, capitalize the first word of a sentence or of a direct quotation, as in the following two examples:

Examples   He ran faster and longer than anyone.

He ran up to her and shouted, "Give me a sip of water—fast!"

Second, capitalize the names of days of the week, the months, and holidays. Again, here are two examples:

Examples   I usually get depressed on Sunday evenings.

During the month of December, little work gets done in the office because of all the Christmas parties.

Third, capitalize titles of books, magazines, newspapers, articles, plays, stories, movies, poems, songs, television shows, and papers that you write. Capitalize only the principal words in these titles, leaving prepositions, articles, conjunctions, and words containing fewer than four letters uncapitalized, unless these words begin the title. For example, *for* in *For Whom the Bell Tolls* is capitalized; *the*, however, is not capitalized. Here are several such titles:

The Old Man and the Sea
U.S. News and World Report
The Wall Street Journal
A Chorus Line
Star Wars

Fourth, capitalize the opening and closing of a letter:

Dear Sir: Sincerely yours,
Dear John,   Love always,

Fifth, capitalize proper names of people:

Nick Henderson   Maya Angelou
Rebecca Henderson   Milton Little

Sixth, capitalize the pronoun *I*, as in the following example:

Example   Last night, I spanked my son for the first time.

Seventh, capitalize names that show family relationships and titles that refer to a particular person. But do not capitalize the word if it does not designate a name. Here are six examples, for comparison:

Examples   Before I spanked him, I called Mother to ask her advice.

Before I spanked him, I called my mother to ask her advice.

Most of us who remember 1963 can recall what we were doing when the president's assassination was announced.

I always felt closer to Aunt Ruby and Aunt Dene than to any of my other aunts.

When I was growing up, I was very close to my grandpa.

The way Grandpa helped me most was by just letting me be with him.

Eighth, capitalize titles if they are used with proper names, as in the following examples:

Examples   If John Doe ran for president, he might get elected because everyone knows his name.

I think that President John Doe has a nice, familiar ring to it.

Ninth, capitalize proper names of organizations such as religious or political groups, races, nations, and nationalities. Here are some proper names of this type:

Democratic Party
Spain
Episcopalians
French
Actors' Guild

Tenth, capitalize the names of particular places, historical events, and historical periods:

Amherst, Massachusetts
the Big Apple

War Between the States
University of North Carolina at Chapel Hill
the Roaring Twenties

Do not capitalize the words *east, west, north,* and *south,* unless they refer to particular sections of the country. Here are two examples:

Examples

During the War Between the States, the South lost control of valuable harbors.

When my family and I visited the West last summer, we took the southern route across the United States on the trip out and a northern route on the trip home.

PRACTICE

In the following paragraphs, some capital letters should be added and some should be deleted. Make the necessary changes by crossing out the errors and writing in the corrections.

wilma shumaker opens beauty salon in hayward

a new Beauty Salon recently opened in hayward. wilma's hair-styling Salon is located on rock mountain road two-and-one-half miles north of northwestern high school. the hours are from 9 A.M. to 5 P.M. monday through friday and 9 A.M. to 1 P.M. on saturday. the beauty salon will be closed on independence day and labor day this summer.

wilma's hair-styling salon offers a variety of services. these Services include facials, make-overs, haircuts, hair coloring, hair frosting, manicures, pedicures, shampoos, styling, perms, and hair-care advice.

the Shop is owned and operated by wilma shumaker. mrs. shumaker is a Graduate of western beauty college. Mrs. Shumaker specializes in Hair-cuts and Facials.

religion in the united states

many things influence the way we live. religion, which significantly influences many american lives, is a major guiding force in our society. the united states constitution gives Americans religious freedom, and the variety of religions gives us a choice. three of the more popular religions are the jewish Religion, the catholic religion, and the protestant religion.

dear susan,

You'll never guess what we did yesterday. after we finished the meeting, it was still very early in the day, so we decided to drive to boston. we stopped by the Library on our way out of town, and photocopied a map and some parking information from *a tourist's guide to boston.* then we headed our car north toward boston. we had a great day. we saw a Movie and then had lunch at a terrific little french restaurant on the waterfront. we even got our picture made to send to mom so she will believe that we did this! it was still early afternoon, so i suggested that we have a beer in a little bar that looks exactly like the bar on the TV program *cheers.*

It was almost 4:30 A.M. when we got back to our hotel room, but i was thrilled that we got to spend the day in boston.

sincerely,

Joey

ABBREVIATIONS

Abbreviations are very useful; however, some abbreviations are inappropriate to use in formal writing. The following explanations will serve as a guide to abbreviations that you may use in most kinds of writing.

You may abbreviate titles and degrees, such as *Mr., Mrs., Ms., Dr., Jr., Sr., Ph.D., D.D.S.,* and *St.*:

Mr. Taylor Evans
Ms. Jane Tyler
Dr. Beth Morgan
Anthony Tinsley, Jr.
St. Francis
Vernon Daughtridge, Ph.D.

You may abbreviate the first or middle name in a signature:

Mary S. Morgan
Adam E. Limehouse
Dorothy L. Sayers

You may abbreviate certain references to time:

A.M. or a.m.
P.M. or p.m.

B.C. (before Christ)
A.D. (Anno Domini, *or in the year of our Lord*)

You may abbreviate certain organizations, technical words, and names that are known primarily by their abbreviation. These often are abbreviated without use of periods:

CIA
PBS
RCA

In formal writing, certain abbreviations should not be used, including abbreviations for the names of days, months, states, and countries. Thus the following abbreviations are unacceptable in formal writing:

Sat. (for Saturday)
Dec. (for December)
N.C. (for North Carolina)
lb. (for pound)
ch. (for chapter)
p. (for page)

The last two abbreviations on the preceding list should not be used in the body of a formal paper. In footnotes and bibliographies, however, such abbreviations may be used. Consult the style guide you are following for information on how to use these abbreviations.

NUMBERS

Three general guidelines apply to the use of numbers in writing. First, use numbers for dates, times, addresses, telephone numbers, and parts of a book:

April 23, 1988
12:09
10 Downing Street
667-2981
page 73

If you are using *o'clock* in your writing, spell out the number, but if you are using A.M. or P.M., use numbers:

12:00 A.M.
twelve o'clock

Second, spell out any number that begins a sentence:

Example   Forty-five people were late for registration because of traffic jams.

Third, most authorities agree that, if a number consists of more than two words, you can use the number rather than spelling it. If it can be expressed in two or fewer words, spell it:

350
three
thirteen
thirty-five
300

Remember to be consistent in using numbers. If you are using a series of numbers, either spell them all out or use the numbers in each case. If one of the numbers requires more than two words, use the numbers themselves throughout the section. Here are two examples of this rule:

Examples   For the party, we ordered twelve cases of beer, fifteen bags of pretzels, and two cans of roasted peanuts.

During the past month, I have spent $350 on car repairs, $150 on new rugs for my house, $75 on dental checkups for my children, and $2 on sugarless gum.

PRACTICE   Correct the errors in abbreviations and numbers in the following sentences by writing in the corrections. Some abbreviations and numbers are used correctly.

1. $5.00 movie tickets make home video rental attractive.

2. There are 3 types of fixed-value resistors: carbon-slug, wire wound, & deposited-film resistors.

3. My boyfriend bought my little brother two ice cream cones, three hot dogs, and 1 Coke for lunch; consequently, my brother spent the afternoon on the sofa with a stomachache.

4. Last summer we visited North Carolina, Florida, Georgia, and S.C.

5. I got up at 10 o'clock and went swimming with my cousins.

6. You can find explanations of the greenhouse effect on pages sixty-two, sixty-three, and sixty-four.

7. My favorite soap operas are all on NBC.

8. Final exams begin on Thurs., May 25, 1991.

9. I have a one P.M. appointment with my lawyer & then I will know what to expect.

10. You know that it's a college town, because most everyone in the ph. book has PhD after her name.

JOURNAL SUGGESTIONS

Temporarily focus your journal writing on the subject of editing your writing. Issues that you might write about in your journal include the following:

■ This text asserts that revising and editing are two separate processes. How do they differ? How do you revise and edit your writing?

■ What editing comments or markings have you seen on your papers during your writing career? Have you repeatedly encountered problems over the years, such as run-ons, fragments, or mistakes in subject–verb agreement? Are you aware of a particular problem area in your writing that you now feel you could begin to correct?

■ How valuable do you think the material in this chapter will be in helping you correct editing mistakes in your writing?

PART TWO

MODELS

CHAPTER SEVEN

DESCRIPTION

Effective descriptive writing, often associated with creative writing, is not limited to novels and poems. In fact, description is an effective tool that all writers can use to help their readers experience reality more intensely. Travel brochures full of enticing descriptions of exotic places make us want to pack our bags. Good descriptive copy in a mail-order catalog can convince us that life is not worth living without the latest gadget. Likewise, we are often deeply touched by descriptions of special people and their accomplishments.

Most communication is to some extent descriptive. Much of the time that we devote to communicating is spent describing feelings, people, places, and objects. These descriptions elucidate and enliven both our speaking and our writing. In oral communication, we rely on feedback from our listener(s) in assessing whether our descriptions are sufficiently clear and detailed. When we write, however, we do not always have the benefit of immediate feedback from our readers. Consequently, we have to be very careful and methodical when we write in the descriptive rhetorical pattern.

✎ JOURNAL SUGGESTIONS

Temporarily focus your journal writing on the strategy of thinking and communicating called *description*. Description issues that you might write about in your journal include the following:

- Can written description (books, magazines, poetry) be as powerful as visual description (TV, movies)?
- What visual, auditory, or written description comes to mind as you begin to think about description? Is it a particular place you enjoy, such as a park, a room of your house, your backyard? When you think about this place, what do you see, hear, taste, smell, and feel?
- Do you remember a paragraph from a book you have read or are reading that contains a particularly vivid description? Perhaps you can recall a vivid scene from a movie you have seen. Write about any of these that come to mind.
- Observe the palm of the hand you don't write with. Describe what you see. Include such details as shading, texture, life lines, scars, nicks, scratches, and so on. What is it about the palm of your hand that makes it unique?
- Recall and describe a specific person, place, or object from your childhood.

Finally, try to develop your own ideas and topics for journal entries. What is it about the thinking strategy called *description* that interests you? Remember to refer to these journal entries when you begin work on the writing assignment at the end of this chapter. You may be able to develop one or more of the ideas in your journal into an essay for this assignment.

The following journal entry was written in response to this journal suggestion.

Example   TUESDAY, 28TH

Events from my childhood ... people from my childhood ... places from my childhood ... what will I choose? what comes to my mind? I remember my big bicycle wreck, when I was saved from riding off a steep embankment into a freeway by a light pole. I couldn't remember how to brake the darn thing. I remember dinners at Grandma's ... kids all sat at a big table in the den and the grownups got the dining room. We ate fast so we could play with cousins we hadn't seen in a while ... my grandpa ... riding around the countryside where I grew up with him in his pick-up. I don't know which one to choose ... I guess I'll just choose one and begin writing ...

I grew up in a small, rural Baptist church ... every fourth week of August there was a revival ... you had to go to church every single night for one week and listen to a lot of singing and lo-o-o-o-ng sermons in a sweltering, unairconditioned sanctuary, and worst of all, you had to dress up in Sunday clothes. It was awful, but I couldn't breathe those words to anyone except my best friend. My mom and grandma would have made my life even more miserable if they had heard me express that opinion.

I always knew it was time for revival by two events ... the first was the return of the katydids. Every night at dark the katydids (dry flies, we called them) sang outside the window. Their song was loud and it seemed to get progressively louder as the night went on. How to describe the song? Song is too kind ... it was an awful noise. It sounded like, like, I don't know; I'll have to come back to that one. Anyway, they started singing about the last week in July, and I would think, oh boy, I know what's coming up.

The other sure reminder that revival was beginning was the beginning of school. School always began the last week in August. Hot, unairconditioned rooms, the smell of sweat, the sound of chalk on clean blackboards. School usually began on Thursday, and the following Sunday—just to make my depression and misery complete—revival began.

GUIDELINES

Using the following guidelines will enable you to write more easily in the descriptive rhetorical pattern. It will also ensure that your descriptive writing is both clear and accurate and that your reader can "see" your subject. Here are the guidelines:

- Identify and restrict your topic.
- Observe the predominant characteristics and features of your subject.
- Develop a focus for the description.
- Include the focus of the description in either a general thesis statement or a focused thesis statement about the topic.
- Support the thesis with adequate and detailed specifics.

TOPIC

Descriptive writing requires that you have a thorough knowledge of your subject. Therefore, it is important that you select a topic you are familiar with. Although you could, for example, write an essay in which you described a man you saw at the airport, you might find it a lot easier to write a similar essay in which you describe your kid sister or your grandfather—simply because you have more knowledge of these people.

Make sure that you sufficiently restrict the topic, too. It would be difficult, for example, to write an essay in which you clearly and accurately describe Rocky Mountain National Park. However, you could adequately describe your favorite view in Rocky Mountain National Park in an essay.

PRACTICE   Develop a more restricted, specific topic for an essay on each of the following general topics. Write your restricted topic in the space provided. For example, in place of the general topic "A Favorite Relative," you might develop the specific topic "Uncle Harry."

1. *General topic:* Favorite Pastime

    Restricted topic: _____

2. *General topic:* Most Relaxing Place I Know

    Restricted topic: _____

3. *General topic:* Favorite Restaurant

    Restricted topic: _____

4. *General topic:* The Perfect Vacation Spot

    Restricted topic: _____

5. *General topic:* An Embarrassing Moment

    Restricted topic: _____

6. *General topic:* A Good Teacher

    Restricted topic: _____

7. *General topic:* A Boring Section of the Daily Newspaper

    Restricted topic: _____

8. *General topic:* My Least Favorite Meal

    Restricted topic: _____

9. *General topic:*   A Good Painting

   Restricted topic: _____

10. *General topic:*   An Exciting Personality from U.S. History

   Restricted topic: _____

OBSERVATION

Good descriptive writing depends on careful, detailed observation. Such observation may make use of all five senses. The information and perceptions you collect then become material for your description of the subject. As you observe, do so systematically:

■ First, note the subject's most obvious and predominant features.
■ Second, observe the more subtle characteristics of the subject.

All such data, of course, will be helpful in preparing an accurate and detailed description of the subject.

PRACTICE   The following exercises will help improve your powers of observation and will also give you some practice in recording what you observe.

1.   Select a small, common object to observe. You might, for example, observe a pinto bean, an apple, a marshmallow, the face of a watch, a coffee mug, an orange, or the palm of your hand. Before beginning the observation, set aside a specific amount of time for conducting the observation. Three to five minutes is probably adequate for observing one of these small, simple objects. As you observe, record the data on a scratch piece of paper. Keep your written notes in a brief but specific form. Do not, for example, make notes like the following: "The orange I am observing is round in shape." Rather, write this: "Shape—round," or "Shape—baseball-like." Carry out your observation of the object systematically. Begin by noting overall size, shape, and predominant color. Also note any openings, appendages, or major variations in size, shape, or color. Next, make more detailed observations. As you do so, record less prominent features of the object, such as minor variations in color, the presence of indentations, and, if appropriate, the texture, smell, taste, and sound of the object.

2. Observe a person. As you do so, record the data. Begin by observing the most obvious characteristic of the individual (for example, over six feet tall, slim, red hair). Then focus on less obvious but distinctive features (for example, mole on cheek below left eye, uneven bottom teeth, pierced ears, short scar on top of forearm just above wrist).

3. Observe a place. Begin by selecting an area to observe and defining its boundaries. You might do an observation of your room, the view from the deck in your backyard, your favorite picnic spot, or even a classroom. Again, record your observations in a brief, specific manner. Notice the shape of the area you are observing, openings such as doors and windows, and objects within the area. Be sure to record textures and smells that are associated with the area.

After you complete this exercise, share your observations with other classmates. Working in groups of three to five, exchange papers so that someone else is reading your writing. As your classmate reads your observation to the group, listen to how your writing sounds. Encourage your classmates to comment on your observation, too. Is it detailed? If you rewrote this piece, where might you include more detail? What particular details are interesting as written?

FOCUS

Having identified and restricted your topic and completed your observation, you next need to develop a focus for describing your subject. The focus of the description is simply some aspect or quality of the subject that you select to center the description on. It may not be the predominant or most striking feature of the subject; however, it will be the central idea of the description and thus will serve to unify the description.

If, for example, you're describing your kid sister, you might choose to focus your description on her facial features. On the other hand, if you're writing about your favorite place to relax, you might elect to focus on the quiet, tranquil atmosphere of that place. In either case, your description of the subject will emphasize particular features and characteristics that collectively support the focus of the description.

Your next step is to express the focus in a thesis statement. The thesis statement for a descriptive essay may be either a general thesis statement or a focused thesis statement. A general thesis statement simply presents the dominant impression of the observation. A focused thesis statement, however, contains both the dominant impression of the observation and a plan of development for presenting the description. The following example of general and focused thesis statements about the same topic should make this distinction clear:

Example

Topic   My Kid Sister

General thesis statement   Penny, my kid sister, has a face that clearly expresses her feelings.

Focused thesis statement   Penny, my kid sister, has a face that clearly expresses her feelings of anger, surprise, and even indecision.

The general thesis statement identifies what is to be the dominant idea of this descriptive essay, but it does not suggest how the essay will be developed. The focused thesis statement contains a plan of development, in addition to identifying the dominant idea of this descriptive essay. The plan of development in this focused thesis statement clearly indicates what the content and structure of the essay will be.

PRACTICE

Following are topics for descriptive essays. Working with one other person in the class, write both general and focused thesis statements for essays on two of these topics. Before you write the thesis statements, you may have to make observations of each subject in order to collect data about them. Then you can decide on a descriptive focus (thesis statement) for an essay on each topic. Here is the list of topics:

A favorite restaurant

The perfect day

Your car

The reading room of the local public library

Your favorite teacher

An important element or part of your hobby, such as your camera lens, your favorite stamp in your stamp collection, or the best piece of needlework that you have cross-stitched

Your favorite painting

Best-ever Christmas present

Your pet (dog, cat, goldfish)

A concert you attended

SUPPORT

Once you have selected and narrowed your topic, developed a focus for the topic, and written a thesis statement, you are ready to provide support for the thesis. You do this in the body of the essay, marshaling some or all of the data you collected from your observation of the subject. Remember to be specific. Include details about your subject that will enable your reader to "see" it. Vivid accurate specifics help your reader picture the subject. Such details make your writing come alive for your reader.

PRACTICE   The following sentences lack vivid, accurate details. Rewrite each sentence in the space provided so that it contains from two to four additional descriptive details. We start with an example:

Example   A McDonald's Big Mac has two hamburger patties, cheese, and special sauce.

This can be rewritten more vividly as follows:

Example   A McDonald's Big Mac has two plump, juicy hamburger patties; melted cheese; and a deliciously tangy special sauce that enhances the flavor of the beef.

1.   My history textbook looks rather worn.

    _____

    _____

    _____

2.   I opened several exciting presents on Christmas day.

    _____

    _____

    _____

3.   My father, a machinist, has scarred hands.

    _____

_____

_____

4.   My old car has quite a few dents in it.

_____

_____

5.   The volunteer firemen were dressed rather haphazardly when
they arrived on the fire scene.

_____

_____

_____

6.   The brook made nice sounds as it flowed by our picnic table.

_____

_____

_____

7.   Some of the seventh-graders outdid themselves on Costume Day
during Sixties week.

_____

_____

_____

8.   My boyfriend and I dressed very lavishly for our senior prom.

_____

_____

_____

9. The last German chocolate cake I made didn't turn out as well as I hoped it would.

_____

_____

_____

10. It was a glorious fall day.

_____

_____

_____

READINGS

The following readings are student and professional essays. Read them carefully, and look for their use of the guidelines for descriptive writing presented in this chapter.

STUDENT ESSAY

A BUSY ROOM   Anne Conner

Teenagers, we're told by those who are supposed to know, need a place of their own. Consequently, my husband and I tried to do this for our children. The result, it seems to me, is rather remarkable. A stranger to my house, in fact, would have no difficulty in locating my teenage daughters' bedroom. To begin with, there are two posters taped to the outside of the door. The top poster is a picture of Chicago Bears' football star Jim McMahon, and the bottom poster is a picture of Spuds McKenzie. While this may seem rather orderly, in reality chaos waits just beyond the posters.

Inside the room to the left is "central control," which in this case is really a cosmetics table. There are two small, white stools in front of the table, and a long, lighted wall mirror spans the entire width of the tabletop. The mirror, however, has very little space where reflection is possible because it has been covered with pictures, phone numbers, and banners. Somehow, in spite of all this, the girls apparently manage to see themselves. The

A BUSY ROOM, continued

clutter on the table makes it obvious that they spend many hours here drying hair, painting nails, and applying makeup. The table top is a mad assortment of hair curlers, hair dryers, combs, brushes, and curiously shaped bottles holding fingernail polish, blush, eye shadow, lipstick, mousse, hair spray, and suntan lotion. Interspersed among these items are assorted earrings, bracelets, empty Coke cans, and crumpled chewing gum wrappers.

To the right of this table are the barracks, so to speak. Here are two unmade beds, with nightgowns and teddy bears peeping out from the tumble of blankets and bedspreads. One pillow lies on the floor next to an empty take-home pizza box. The second bed is covered in papers from a draft of some assignment. Sticking out from under the papers are two books, several note cards, a calculator, and a pen.

Perhaps the contents of the beds explain the lack of clutter on the desk. It is on the right side of the room, opposite the cosmetics table, where apparently it was abandoned. The desktop is curiously clean and orderly, with only an empty Coke can beside a neat stack of *Seventeen* magazines and an address book.

Next to the desk is more chaos. A large, yellow bean bag slumps in the corner. It is covered with two jean jackets, several shirts, jeans, a pink-and-white-striped towel, a pair of gray sweatpants, and two unmatched socks.

To describe this room as interesting is certainly an understatement. My daughters, surprisingly, seem to love it, and they don't want me to bother a thing in it. Apparently, what is chaos for me is home for them. I can live with that.

PROFESSIONAL ESSAY

CHINA STILL LIFES

William Gass

If you are a visitor in Beijing, a bus will take you to the Great Wall where the people clambering about on it will likely outnumber the stones. However, not everyone in China is standing inside the circle of the buses, breathing his last, or pushing his way up that ancient barrier's many steps and steel slopes, although it may seem so; nor is the Great Wall this incredible country's only dragon-shaped defender, because

a billion people require the comfort of at least a million walls: walls concealing houses, safeguarding factories, lending themselves to banks and office buildings, hotels and new construction, defining villages, compounds, parks, and squares, protecting pagodas, temples, shrines, and palaces; and along the top of many of these walls a snakelike creature made of slate and tile and stucco seems to crawl, its odd

SOURCE: *House & Garden* magazine. Copyright © 1985 by William Gass.

CHINA STILL LIFES, continued

equine head bearing a dog's teeth, with thin wire flames, like antennae, breathing from its nose. For all their apparent ferocity, the intentions of these monsters are pacific, as are the quiet courses of fired clay they serpentine upon. The city streets themselves appear to pass between walls and beneath trees as if they were enclosed, and the shops open out into them as open doors pour into halls.

In Beijing, alongside even the immediate edge of an avenue, rank after rank of potted flowers have been brought to attention—thousands of salvias, for instance, clearly a favorite—as if a pot had to be put out for every cyclist who might possibly pass. These are protected by low wire loops or sometimes by an iron fence of impeccable design when it is not displaying panda-covered kitsch. Success is hit or miss. For the cyclists, too, collisions are not infrequent. I saw a small truck run over a wheel and a leg as though they were bumps in the road. The wheel bent like soft tin and the cyclist's mouth went "O!" Cyclists *are* the street as water is the river, and you can walk across in safety only if your movements are slow and deliberate and resemble a stone's. The bikes sail down the dark streets at night and show no lights, though the buses like to flare theirs. The Chinese say they do it for safety's sake, but each burst is blinding. In their own much narrower lanes, which in intersections they cannot keep to, trucks and buses honk and growl; you will hear occasionally a hawker's cry; otherwise the city is silent except for the continuous ching-a-chang of the bicycle bells. Serenity is always startling. You take close hold of yourself as if your spirit were about to float away, and you say, "Perhaps it's true, and I

have a soul after all, other than the one emitted by the exhaust pipe of the motorcar."

Near the long red line of blooming plants, as if to root them for as many seasons as the trees shall persevere, there is a grand row or two of weeping birch or sycamore, then a handsome wide walk—crowded of course—and finally the rich red or yellow plastered wall of a public garden or royal house, the whitewashed wall of a simple shop, or often, in the poorer quarters, one of loosely stacked brick in both alternating and parallel courses, in chevrons, on edge, at length, sometimes like a pattern book they lie so side by side in every posture, frequently free of mortar too, the builder expressing his mastery of economics, gravity, and tradition in the humblest stretch of work. These are walls against which the spangled shadows of the trees fall like a celebration, and through which the light runs like driven rain.

In China, to understand some of its most appealing aspects, Necessity should be the first stop for the mind. The comparative freedom of the streets from cars, the sidewalks from dogs, drunks, and vandals, the gutters from trash: these are a few of the slim benefits of poverty and a socialist state. The brooms of the sweepers pass beneath the feet of shoppers as if the shoppers' shoes were simply leaves. Pets compete for a desperately outstretched food supply, and are therefore only surreptitiously kept. And if an improving economy fills these beautiful streets with automobiles, it will be a calamity. But Necessity is never to be admired; it is, at best, only the stepmother of invention; and in China, as elsewhere, it is the cause (or rather, the excuse) for hurried, cheap, high-rise build-

CHINA STILL LIFES, continued

ings, which appear to repeat every greedy callous Western gesture.

One should not sentimentalize (at least not overly much) about the rich street-and-alley culture of the slums, yet the cities of China are made of streets made of people—walking, biking, working, hanging out. In the paths between buildings there is a world of narrow outdoor rooms; along the walks of wider streets, goods are set out for display and sale; in the open doorways workers enjoy the air and light and sun while they repair shoes, sew, shave a round of wood for chopsticks, clean chickens, and wash pans. The edges of the street are lined with barrows, the center is filled with pedestrians, and out over everyone, from both sides, waves the household wash, hung from bamboo poles propped out of second-story windows and held firmly by a slammed sash. Hong Kong is a world away, but the poles still bristle from the windows of the high rises there: a bit of wash can flutter away in the wind like a kite ten floors from the street; the sanitation is superior; water rises magically in hidden pipes; there is more than the personal forty square feet of living space which is Shanghai's average; and you can no longer see your neighbor, smell his fires—a situation which many planners and politicians approve. As a visitor, a Westerner, a tourist, unburdened by the local "necessities," I say, "Let the rich rot in their concrete trees like unpicked fruit, and leave the earth to the people."

For the curious passing eye, of course, these open doors and drawn shades, these tiny passageways and little courtyards, including every inadvertent jiggle in the course of the street, afford, literally, a sudden "insight." Chinese gardens, with their doorless doors, round as the eye says the world is, their Gibson girl and keyhole shaped gates, their doors framed like paintings or sometimes like windows, as well as every other kind of intermission in a wall that they delight in—punched, screened, glazed, shuttered, beaded, barred—have established the motif of the maze, that arena for interacting forms which seems endless in its arbitrary variety yet one which does not entirely conceal its underlying plans, as zigzag bridges, covered paths, and pools of multiplying water make a small space large, and negligently wandering walls and their surprising openings constantly offer charmingly contorted eye lines, while contributing, along with the swooping roofs and undulating levels of the ground, to the ambiguity of every dimension, especially those of out and in, whose mixture is also the experience provided by the city streets.

The big cities now have vast blank squares like Tian Anmen in Beijing—they are people pastures, really—fit mainly for mass meetings, hysteria, and hypnotism, while the new wide and always wounding central avenues are suitable for totalitarian parades and military reviews, although it was no different in the old days, since some of the courtyards in the Imperial Palace can hold a hundred thousand heads together in a state of nodding dunder. This is one reason why it is comforting to find these streets, yards, and squares, filled with running children, strollers, and bicycles, because they are such splendid examples of free movement—of being "under one's own power." Walking, running, swimming, skating, cycling, support the moral realm, as sailing does, inasmuch as each seeks to understand and enjoy ener-

CHINA STILL LIFES, continued

gies already present and often self-made, whereas the horse, train, rocket, car, and plane require and encourage the skills of domination on the one hand, and passivity on the other. The pedicab, alas, is coming back. And one sees people still pulling heavy loads like beasts. In such cases, the load is truly Lord and Master. But the present regime has lifted many a beastly burden from many a human back. I like to imagine that the warm blue autumn skies I enjoyed during most of my stay in China were the radiant reflection of the faces of the people.

That word, and the familiar image I have called back again into service—"a stream of people"—would not seem farfetched or even hackneyed if you were to look down into Guangzhou's Renmin Road (or "street of the people") where a glut of pedestrians slowly moves, not impatiently, though shoulder to shoulder, but reflectively, as a crowd leaves after a splendid concert. It is not New Year's; it is not an occasion of any kind; it is simply midmorning, and the people twine through the streets, living as closely as fibers in cloth. In this crowded world the wall is like one of those inner skins that keeps organs from intervening in the actions of others; they corner chaos like an unruly dog and command its obedience. I saw in a park a pair of lovers fondling one another while lying perilously in the thick fork of a tree. Couples go to such places to quarrel, too, or work out their incompatibilities with one another's relatives, to play with the baby by themselves, or simply to have an unobstructed view of their spouse's face. It is that difficult to be alone.

Nor normally is the eye left empty. The tourist will have to look high and low for the fierce stone lion behind the stiff grins and adopted postures of the Chinese, one hundred of whom are having their pictures taken in the lap of a seated Buddha, on the back of a bronze ox, in front of a garden of rock, beside a still and helpless pool: by whatever seems majestical, ancient, and handy. The photographers thrust the camera toward the ground until it hangs from their arms like the seat of a swing. Taking aim from below their knees, they stare down at the viewfinder as though peering into a well. Whatever their reasons (perhaps, like me, they are waiting for a clear shot), they take their time, so poses are held like bouquets.

That is, they try to stand as still as the burnished brass bowl or stone lamp or painted door they are leaning against. But their lips quiver and their eyes shift and the heart beats high up in their chests. Bystanders fidget and giggle. Movement, not fixity, neither of photograph or statue, is the essence of life. It is an ancient tenet. These walls that I have made the symbolic center of this piece might be thought to be in opposition to mutability and alteration, but in China this is not so. The Great Wall rolls over the mountain ridges like a coaster.

And within the walls, the walls walk; not slowly, according to some customary means of reckoning, but swiftly, each step of brick marking a year as sand does seconds sliding the sides of its glass; and it is perhaps this paradox we understand least when we try to understand China: how calm, how still, and how steadfastly sustaining change in China is; how quickly, like the expression on a face, even bronze can alter; how smartly the same state can come about like a sailboat in the wind; yet

CHINA STILL LIFES, continued

the bronze endures and maintains its vigil; the ship, the water, and the wind remain themselves while disappearing into their actions; so that now, as this great nation opens itself to the West and selects some Western ways to welcome, in nearly every chest, as though it shaped a soft cage for the soul, the revolution still holds its breath, while the breath itself goes in and out of its jar as anciently and as rhythmically, almost, as moods move through a man, and men move from one place to another like vagabonds.

The Great Wall rolls over its ridges, I dared to say, yet the Great Wall stands. The Great Wall draws only tourists now who sometimes steal its stones, not invaders or brigands. Still the Great Wall stands for the past. So it is the past that rolls over the hills here; it is the past which stands, the past which lures the tourist; and the past, when it speaks, speaks obsessively of the present.

In China, the long dispute between tradition and revolution, rest and motion, action and contemplation, openness and secrecy, commitment and withdrawal, politics and art, the individual and the mass, the family and the state, the convoluted and the simple continues with voices raised and much at stake. That's why, perhaps, amid the crush and the closeness, the delighted yet frantic building and trading and making, I was struck by slower times and more wall-like movements.

On a busy Shanghai street, I am brought face to face, not with faces for a change, but with a weather-beaten wooden box, a bowl, a simple pile of goods, all stacked so as to still life, and my sleeping sensuality is shaken awake as it might be by an appealing nakedness.

Or perhaps I notice two women in the act of hanging out a bright banner of wash, arrested for a moment by a thought; or I see on the sidewalk by my feet a display of fruit or school of glistening silver fish or a spread of dried mulberries in the center of which a butterfly has lit and now folds its black-and-white wings.

Or it is a set of tools resting against a garden wall in such a way their energies seem harmonized inside them; another time it is a group of whitewash pots, jugs of wine, or sacks of grain, or an alley empty of everything but chickens, or a stretch of silent street with freshly washed honey pots, their lids ajar to breathe, sunning themselves in the doorways. Chairs draped with bedding may be taking the air; a brush has been thrust between a drainpipe and its building to dry, an ooze of color down the wall like a drip of egg. Shadows of trees, wires, wash, the tassels of lanterns: these further animate even the busiest lanes. I fancy I see in them operatic masks, kites, the ghosts of released balloons. Or you discover your own shadow cast across a golden sheet of drying rice, and you realize that you are still at home in Missouri and that this is your shade, loose in the midst of China's life.

The sill may rot, the bowl fall, but nothing is more ageless and enduring than the simple act of sitting—simply being here or there. The alleys of every city are creased by ledges, crannies, corners, cracks where a rag is wedged, a pot of paint rests, or a basket hangs, a broom leans, a basin waits; and where a plant, placed out of the way like a locked bike, is not a plant now, but will resume its native movements later.

Down a whitewashed little lane in Su-zhou, you may find white bread and flour

CHINA STILL LIFES, continued

for sale on a white box beneath a white sheet stretched out like an awning, and casting a shadow so pale it seems white as well. Through an open window with blowing white curtains you will be handed your change in the soiled palm of a white glove.

In the same lane is a teahouse where a Vermeer may be found: benches, table, tray, row of glasses, teapot just so, all right there—all composed and rendered by the master. On top of the teahouse stove, the tools of the cook's trade lie in a sensuous confusion akin to bedclothes. Even the steam holds its shape and station like a spoon. In front of a few chairs, on a small stage, a lectern for the storyteller has been placed. There is one chair on either side of it, both draped with cloths. I make up an artificial audience, sitting there, looking at the wooden figures where the old tales are spoken, and I am truly overcome by the richness of this world: its care for the small things; this tidiness that transcends need and becomes art; the presence of the past in even the most impoverished places and simplest things, for the act of recitation, too, is as importantly immortal as the lean of a spade or pot's rest.

China seems today in glorious and healthy tumult, but the visitor, charmed by the plenitude or patient genius of the people, the vast landscape and exotic monuments, should not neglect the corners of quiet—the resting bamboo boats or idle ladders, the humblest honey pot or plastic purse or rouged wall—for these things and spaces are everywhere as well, and they are easily as ancient, fully as lively in their own interior way, and certainly as honestly and openly sensual as any rice-ripe, yellow, autumn landscape or langorous stretch of back or thigh.

So it is not by one of the many Buddhas one may see in China that I am reminded of Rilke's poem about that figure,

As if he listened. Silence: depth . . .
And we hold back our breath.

nor is it while I am bemused by the admittedly similar grandeur of the burnished bronze bowl that stands, in company with a carefully regulated tree, in front of a bit of royal wall in the Imperial Palace Garden,

Oh, he is fat. Do we suppose
he'll see us? He has need of that?

but during another kind of encounter entirely, in a commonplace Shanghai street, with a bunch of baskets hung above a stone sink. There is a lame straw fan nearby, and on the sink a blushing cup from which a watercolor brush has been allowed to stick. What hidden field of force has drawn these objects into their conjunction? A wooden bowl leans at the sink's feet, its rosy basin open to the sun. Beside the sink sits a teapot, while behind it rises a pipe where a washrag, dark still from its own dampness, dangles as though done for. There is also a brazier by the sink's side like a sullen brother, a handled pot perched uneasily on its head where a shiny tin lid similarly slides. On top of the sink, again, an enameled saucer waits on a drainboard of worn wood. It contains another jutting brush—a nice touch. It is by these plain things that the lines about the Buddha were returned to my mind, for I was looking at the altar of a way of life. The simple items of this precise and impertinent collection had been arranged by circumstances so complex, historical, and social, so vagarious and yet determined, that I felt

CHINA STILL LIFES, continued

obliged to believe an entire culture—a whole people—had composed it. Vermeer indeed, or some solemn Buddha, could only hold a candle, as though they were another witness, to this peaceful and ardent gathering of things.

For that which lures us to his feet has circled in him now a million years.
He has forgotten all we must endure, encloses all we would escape.

Rhetoric

1. The introduction to "China Still Lifes" doesn't seem to introduce the essay. Rather, as we begin reading the essay, it's as if we are joining an event already in progress. Is this an effective beginning for this essay? In what way or ways is this beginning in character with the tone and structure of the essay?

2. The essay is descriptive. Read the essay again and select three sentences or phrases that you think contain particularly good descriptions. Analyze these to determine what specific words, examples, or phrases make them outstanding descriptions.

3. Analyze sentence length in this essay. Notice that many sentences are quite lengthy. Do these long sentences complicate or weaken the writing? Why or why not?

Ideas

1. In the fourth paragraph of the essay, the author asserts that to understand China, "Necessity should be the first stop for the mind." Based on your reading of the essay, how is an understanding of necessity helpful in understanding the portrait the author paints of contemporary China?

2. The essay contains many images of China and life in China. No single image, of course, can capture the whole of this great country and its people. But select what you think is the one most powerful, informative image in the essay. Then, in a few brief sentences, say what it is about this "picture" that you find particularly impressive or insightful.

3. The essay ends with the author painting a still life of a scene along a Shanghai street. It's as if he has reduced all of China to this single picture. Is it effective? Do you think that it broadens or deepens your understanding of China? In a few sentences, state what you think is the essence of this last "photograph" in the essay.

Response

1. Write a paragraph-length description of a small, restricted area that you are very familiar with, such as the inside of your car or the den of your house. Single out some feature of the area to serve as the focus of your writing.

2. Observe a painting, perhaps a still life, and list as many details about the painting as possible. Allow yourself no more than ten minutes to make your observation and compile your list. After you finish the observation, turn the details on your list into a long paragraph or short essay describing the painting. Remember to develop a focus (dominant impression) for the writing and to use the details selectively to support the focus you developed.

3. Rewrite the observation activity you completed at the beginning of this chapter. For this rewriting, add a focused thesis statement. You may want to look over the discussion of focus at the beginning of this chapter to help you get started with this. After you develop a focused thesis statement, recall or look over the comments your classmates made about details in your observation of a person, place, or object. You may want to incorporate some of their suggestions as you rewrite. Reflect on how the writing sounded to you as you heard it being read aloud by one of your classmates. What gaps do you remember in the description? How might you rewrite particular parts of your description to make them more detailed?

PROFESSIONAL ESSAY

MY FATHER, THE PRINCE   Phyllis Theroux

Fathers. They say that a woman seeks—in love, marriage, or any male-female relationship of real heft—to approximate the father she had, the father she didn't have but wanted, or the father minus the attributes that caused her mother to leave him for good and sufficient reason. In the winnowing-out process that precedes deep commitment to a new man, the daughter subconsciously throws up the wheat of her father's virtues along with the chaff of his faults, and her decision to commit is strongly influenced by that first experience of male companionship.

I think they're right.

We all know that men consider their mothers when they choose a woman for themselves, but fathers have traditionally

MY FATHER, THE PRINCE, continued

been considered mere linkage in the rosary of wombs that produce progeny from one decade to the next. Accessories to the fact, off-campus providers, fathers are six o'clock visitors to the nursery tended by all-powerful mothers.

One can scarcely overestimate the influence that mothers have upon their sons. But fathers have yet to be properly weighed in as determinative factors in the lives of their daughters. To my way of thinking, this is a terrible oversight.

In a grayer, more small-minded period of my life, I used to inwardly gripe at the inaccuracy of the Cinderella story. Cinderella does not go from ashes to amethysts. In real life the brooms and the dustpans materialize after the wedding, whereupon she spends forever after staring out the window wondering where her father—the real prince in her life—has gone.

Of course, women are now rewriting that old script, and this is an age in which we are forming piano-moving companies, hiking up telephone poles, and swimming along with Jacques Cousteau. But I live with a little woman, aged seven, who recently gave me to understand that liberation is an acquired taste and no substitute for gut feeling.

"What's this?" I asked as she handed me a crayon drawing of a little girl next to what looked like a giant lollipop.

"Me," she answered. (There was a crown drawn on the little girl's head.)

"And what are you doing?" I pursued, searching the drawing for some evidence of a plot line.

"Nothing," she said matter-of-factly. "Just standing by the bus stop waiting for the prince."

I put the drawing aside, looked at my matter-of-fact daughter, and thought with chagrin, "Aren't we all!" Spoiled or despoiled by the first prince in our life, we understand, either way, what it means to be born to the purple. No, Cinderella did not accidentally fall for royalty. Her dear departed father had given her an early taste for it. My father did the same.

He was a tall, crooked-toothed, curly-haired man, who smelled of Lucky Strikes and St. Johns Bay Rum shaving lotion. He was the only father who wore penny loafers on business trips, a Mouseketeer hat to pick up my brother on his first movie date, and had the delicious gall to invite the richest girl in my class (she had her own pool but an exclusive number of invitations) to come on over to the house ("When you're free, of course") and watch our lawn sprinklers.

"Sometimes we get them going in opposite directions to each other," he said dryly, "and it's terribly amusing."

The richest girl in the class laughed nervously, I choked back my borrowed triumph, and savored the fact that once again my father had effectively punched out the opposition on my behalf. He had a gift for it.

Yet, unlike other men blessed with a quick wit and a rare natural electricity of being, my father was oddly incapable of parlaying his gifts to his own long-range advantage.

As I grew older and more able to observe him objectively in group situations, I noticed that in a room full of peers he would usually back up against the mantel and go into a sort of social receivership that did not jibe with my understanding of him. It

MY FATHER, THE PRINCE, continued

made me impatient. He was far and away the largest talent in the room, and it seemed a terrible waste to give over the floor to anyone else. Yet he consistently passed up opportunities to reveal himself in public, and it was many years before I realized that my wonderful father was *shy*.

I was thunderstruck. Is Douglas Fairbanks, Jr., shy? Does Cary Grant falter? Should my father have anything in the world to hesitate over?

It was one thing to be a pudgy, preadolescent girl trying to make it in a class full of gazelles, but quite another thing to be that little girl's handsome father, who at various crucial junctures had told her that all she had to do in order to succeed was to take this step, or that action, and—for heaven's sake—was the world such a difficult nut to crack after all? Of course not!

If there was any one thing that my father did for me when I was growing up it was to give me the promise that ahead of me was dry land—a bright, marshless territory, without chuckholes or traps, where one day I would walk easily and as befitting my talents. The fact that I didn't know what my talents were did not put my father off in the slightest. He knew potential when he saw it.

Thus it was, when he came upon me one afternoon sobbing out my unsuccesses into a wet pillow, that he sat down on the bed and, like a strong, omniscient archangel, assured me that my grief was only a temporary setback.

Oh, very temporary! Why he couldn't think of any other little girl who was so talented, so predestined to succeed in every department as I was. "And don't forget," he added with a smile, "that we can trace our ancestry right back to Pepin the Stupid!"

The last piece of news turned out to be true, but whether he believed the rest of his words or not I don't know. He was, after all, gazing down upon a disheveled ten-year-old who was too embarrassed to shift her gum from one cheek to the other.

But I listened to him carefully, and by the time he had finished talking I really did understand that someday I would live among rational beings, and walk with kind, unvindictive people who, by virtue of their maturity and mine, would take no pleasure in cruelty and would welcome my presence among them as an asset. It was only a question of time before I came ripping out of my cocoon, a free-flying butterfly that would skim triumphantly over the meadow of my choice. I cannot say that my father was completely wrong.

Time has passed. Choices have been made. I am no longer a preteen in a net formal who secretly hoped that all the other girls at the Father-Daughter Dance were eating their hearts out. My father's crooked front tooth was replaced several years ago by a nice, straight, shiny one. He passed through the hospital several times. There are grandchildren. I sometimes think that it is not the same between us, or perhaps it never was what I thought.

One's memory is selective, and I admit that it's to my advantage to recall only those moments when my father rose to the occasion and parted another Red Sea of Impossibility and elbowed me across. Yet these moments really did happen and I am not the same because of them.

There are some people, my father is one of them, who carry the flint that lights

MY FATHER, THE PRINCE, continued

other people's torches. They get them all excited about the possibilities of an idea, the "can-do" potential of one's own being.

That was my father's gift to me, and whatever psychic wounds remain to be thrashed out between us are still lying on the floor of my unconscious, waiting for deep therapy to uncover. The fact is that I am closer to my mother. But they say that a daughter carries around the infection of her father for life.

They are right.

Rhetoric

1. The author of "My Father, the Prince" delays describing her father until several paragraphs into the essay. What might be her purpose in doing this? Might the essay have been more effective if her description of her father had begun in the second paragraph?

2. In the first paragraph, Ms. Theroux contends that a woman's decision to commit to a man "is strongly influenced by that first experience of male companionship." Identify material in the body of the essay that seems to support this thesis, at least in the author's case.

3. Evaluate the quality of the details in the essay. Are they specific? concrete? Do they allow the reader to create sharp mental images of the subject matter of the writing? Underline two or three phrases or sentences that you think are particularly detailed and specific.

Ideas

1. Perhaps it is too simplistic to say that the author is describing her father. What other levels of intent and meaning are contained in this essay?

2. In the fourth paragraph of the essay, Ms. Theroux asserts that "fathers have yet to be properly weighed in as determinative factors in the lives of their daughters." Do you agree or disagree? Explain your response in a paragraph.

3. In the paragraph that begins, "But I listened to him carefully . . ." the author describes the self-assurance she gained from a conversation with her father. In your opinion, did her father handle this situation correctly? Do you think his reassurances had a long-term effect on the author's life? Why is it important that we all receive such support from the authority figures in our lives?

Response

1. Analyze the essay closely, and write a brief paragraph in which you summarize "her father's virtues" that strongly influenced her life.

2. Write an essay in which you describe a relative or an acquaintance who you are convinced played a key role in molding your personality and shaping your view of the world.

PROFESSIONAL ESSAY

TWENTY-SEVEN-TWENTY-TWO   Bob Greene

Bexley, Ohio—It was a vacation of sorts, perhaps the strangest I have ever taken. And, although it had none of the glamour of a flight to Mexico or Europe, it turned out to be one of the most satisfying few days I have had in years.

Of all the places I have dreamed of visiting, I have been lucky enough to visit most. And yet the place that is always most on my mind always seemed an impossible destination. Not because it is remote; it is not that far a journey from Chicago to central Ohio. Not because it is expensive, either; money is not even a factor.

But it remained unlikely because people just don't do things like this. What I wanted to do was go back to the house in which I grew up; not just look at it from a car driving by, but spend time there, visit it, remember it as it was. Several families have lived there since my own family moved away; often I have thought about what the reaction would be if I just showed up unannounced someday, but I always rejected that as a fantasy.

This time, though, I did it. I hadn't the nerve to simply knock on the door. But I found out the names of the people who now live in the house—Stanley and Elaine Shayne and their children—and I wrote them a letter asking if they'd mind. Mrs.

Shayne called me and said it would be fine with them.

So I found myself on Bryden Road in Bexley, Ohio, again. The street is still made of red bricks, and when I walked up to the front door, I had a feeling of anticipation that couldn't be equalled at Buckingham Palace or the Ritz Hotel in Paris. To be granted leisurely time again in the most important place in one's memory—that is a true luxury, and I was prepared to savor it.

The Shayne family couldn't have been more understanding; they let me know that it was okay for me to be there (they even put a "Welcome Home" sign on the big tree in the front yard), and yet they realized that it was not them I had come to visit, but the house. They went about their daily business and let me wander. For the better part of three days, I lived at 2722 Bryden Road again.

It was jarring, moving, weird. Think about what it would be like if you were turned loose in the house where you grew up. You would find that it had been redecorated several times as families had moved in and out; you would find strangers living in the rooms you always associated with your parents and brothers and sisters. Everything would be different, yet everything would be the same. One moment you

TWENTY-SEVEN-TWENTY-TWO, continued

would feel a thousand miles away, the next you would feel as if you had never left. It would be confusing and exhilarating and happy and sad, all at the same time.

My visit was all of those things. I found myself climbing the front stairs countless times, looking into bedrooms, sitting on the front stoop waiting for the paper boy to arrive. The Shaynes got used to me soon enough; they had their meals, and talked in the living room or the back yard, and just allowed me to have the run of the place.

It was like being in a movie you half-remember; it was like you had seen it a long time ago, and now you weren't really seeing it, you were inside of it. You recognized the set precisely, but you didn't know the actors, and even as you moved among them they couldn't really see you.

So I went to my old room, and the boy who lives there now was lying on his bed listening to music. What a feeling. That might have been me in there when I was his age, but now I was standing in the doorway, an observer, almost afraid to step inside.

In the upstairs hallway was a little cranny built into the wall to hold a telephone. I had forgotten about it completely, but seeing it again took me back to all the nights I had pulled the cord into my own room and locked the door for privacy. And sure enough, on this evening the phone had been pulled away, and was locked in one of the children's bedrooms.

The interior of the house looked completely different, but every few minutes I would come across a touch that almost made me shiver. The front door, for example; it had been painted and refinished, but when I went to open it, the knob and latch felt so familiar in my hand; I looked at them, and although I hadn't thought about

them in years, I knew immediately that they were the same ones. When you spend all of your growing-up years coming through the same door, you don't forget something like that so quickly.

And the wooden bannister that runs up the stairway and then curves around next to the bedrooms—as I walked I found myself letting my hand glide across the top of it, and I realized that this was a habit I had ever since I was a child. Everywhere I turned there was something like that; the bathrooms had been refurbished and decorated, but in the children's bathroom the old-fashioned heater was still built into the wall beneath the window; you wouldn't imagine that something like that would affect you, but believe me, it does.

The house seemed very small to me. Which is inevitable, I guess; when you are growing up, your house is your whole world, and once your world becomes the real world itself, one building can never seem quite so imposing again. As I stood at the top of the stairs I realized that, of course, there was nothing inherently romantic in this structure; it was just one house on one block in one small city.

Still, when the three days were over, I had a feeling of satisfaction that is hard to describe. I hope, someday, the people in the Shayne family will look back on their years at 2722 Bryden Road with the same warmth and joy that I do; and I hope, if they ever get the urge to come back, they won't be too shy to ask, and that the people who live there in that future summer will not be too protective of their privacy to say yes.

Because I can promise them this: it may not be the most lavish vacation they will ever spend, but it will surely be one of the best.

Rhetoric

1. Does this description essay contain adequate and appropriately detailed specifics? Highlight some details that you think are particularly vivid.

2. "Twenty-seven-twenty-two" was written as a newspaper article. Do you think that accounts for the short, staccato-like paragraphs that make up the essay? Explain your reasoning.

3. The last paragraph of the essay is hardly a paragraph. Is it effective as it is? Why? Would it have been more effective as part of the preceding paragraph?

Ideas

1. Greene observes that "to be granted leisurely time again in the most important place in one's memory . . . is a true luxury." Do you agree? If so, why? Organize and present your reasons in a brief, simple paragraph.

2. Of the places you lived as a child, which one is most important to you? Why?

3. Accept the author's challenge to "think about what it would be like if you were turned loose in the house where you grew up." List some things in this house that you would want to check on, such as the telephone in "a little cranny built into the wall" and the "knob and latch" on the front door. Decide which room you would like to visit first and where in the house you would like to spend most of your visit.

Response

1. Single out some place from your childhood that is particularly important to you, such as your room or a tree in the backyard or a closet in the basement. Describe this place and try to make your reader understand why it means so much to you.

2. Write an essay similar to "Twenty-seven-twenty-two," in which you describe the most important place where you lived during your childhood.

3. Readers of this essay sometimes complain that the Shaynes' ready acceptance of the author into their home is a little unbelievable. However, it is important to remember that the author is telling the story from his point of view and is unconcerned with the Shaynes' reaction to his request for a visit or to his visit. Write a reaction to the author's visit from the point of view of one of the members of the Shayne family. You might "become" the boy in the family,

reacting to the visit from his perspective. Imagine that you are the boy, and observe this stranger observing you in your own house, in your bedroom, in your backyard, and so on. Follow the author through the house, and react to his presence there.

WRITING ASSIGNMENTS

You may select a topic for this writing assignment from one of the following lists, or you may develop a topic of your own. Once you have selected a topic, complete one or more of the specified prewriting activities. After sufficient prewriting, write a draft of an essay on the topic you selected. Finally, revise and edit your essay.

General Writing Assignments

- Your grandmother or grandfather
- The most memorable person you've ever known
- Your favorite painting
- A memorable event
- Your favorite vacation spot
- A favorite relative
- Your house or apartment

Specific Writing Assignments

- Assume that you want to sell your car. Write a rather detailed classified ad, to run in the local newspaper, offering your car for sale. Be sure to describe the car accurately and thoroughly.
- Suppose that your uncle is compiling a genealogy of his side of your family. He has asked you to write a one-page portrait of your mother for inclusion in the book he is putting together. Be sure to limit your description of her to one typed page, or about 250 words.
- Imagine that your history instructor has assigned an essay as part of the course requirements. You are to select one event in American history and write a description of that occurrence, including individual people involved, location, date, and significance. Suggested topics for the essay include battles, natural disasters, enactment of important legislation, and speeches. Your essay does not need to contain documentation or a list of works cited.

If you decide to develop your own topic, you may want to look through your journal for ideas. What topics that you have addressed in your journal lend themselves to this particular strategy of thinking and communicating? You might also look carefully at the focused journal entries you wrote at the beginning of this chapter. Is one of these topics of interest to you? Is it a topic with which you have some experience? With some revision work, could your journal entry on this topic become an essay?

Finally, look back through this chapter at some of the exercises you have done individually and with classmates. Are any of these topics of interest to you? Recall conversations with your classmates. Have they given you ideas for topics? Perhaps interesting topics emerged from the group discussions that followed some of the practices in the chapter. You may want to spend some time discussing these exercises with classmates to help you decide what to write about. Or you may want to do some listing, brainstorming, or freewriting to help you discover a suitable topic.

PREWRITING

After selecting a topic as the subject for a description essay, complete one or more of the following prewriting activities:

■ *Journal*–Journal keeping can be a valuable source of ideas and material for descriptive writing. Journal entries lend themselves to the recording of our impressions of people, places, events, and objects. For this writing assignment, make it a point to write in your journal for at least three days about the topic you have selected. After making the last entry, read through all of the entries on your topic, and look for a dominant impression—a recurring theme or observation—that can serve as the focus for the description essay. Then highlight other information in the journal entries that is related to and supports the dominant impression. These data can serve as details to include in the essay in support of your thesis.

■ *Looping*–Begin this prewriting activity by writing freely and rapidly on the subject of the description essay you are preparing to write. Write for a specified period of time—at least five minutes. After writing for at least five minutes, read what you have written, and underline the central or best idea contained in this piece of writing. Using this central idea as a beginning point, write for another five minutes. Again, review what you have written, and underline the dominant statement or main idea in this piece of writing. You may be able to use this dominant statement as the thesis for your essay. If it's not suitable, complete another loop. As you go through the looping process, you will develop a focus for your description essay. In addition, many details that appear in the loops can be used in the body of the essay to support the thesis statement.

REVISING

In revising your essay, follow these seven steps:

1. Ask a friend, a roommate, or a writing colleague (or colleagues) to listen to or read your writing and then to comment on what you have written. Specifically, are the subject and the purpose of the essay clear? Does the body of the essay make and support points that achieve the purpose of the writing? Do any sentences, passages, or sections of the paper seem either unrelated to or contradictory to the purpose of the writing?

2. Check the introduction and thesis statement of the essay. Have you introduced your reader to the topic you plan to describe? Have you adequately restricted the topic? Does your introductory paragraph include a thesis that makes clear what you plan to say about your topic? Have you developed a focus in the thesis for the description? In what ways do you need to rewrite the introduction in order to engage the reader's interest and clarify your purpose?

3. Check the thesis support in the main body of the essay. Is the material in the body of the essay organized so that it supports the point (thesis) of the writing? Do the details in your description support your particular descriptive focus on the topic?

4. Check the paragraph support throughout the essay. Is each paragraph well written, with clear and specific details to support your thesis? Have you clearly recorded your observations of the predominant characteristics and features of your subject?

5. Check for coherence and unity. As a whole, does the essay make sense? Does it contain any irrelevant material?

6. Check for closure. Is there closure at the end of the essay in either a concluding sentence or a concluding (or summarizing) paragraph?

7. Review the Revision Checklist at the end of Chapter 5. Use the checklist to make sure that you have completed a thorough revision of your essay.

EXAMPLE

Examples are valuable techniques for clarifying and supporting ideas. In fact, we often use examples in ordinary, everyday conversation to enable our listeners to understand what we are trying to convey. Most of us like using examples (or, as they are also known, illustrations), for several reasons. Examples often serve to make ideas and concepts less abstract and more concrete. For instance, by talking about the meaning and importance of justice, we can gain some understanding of what it is. But when we go to court to pay a traffic ticket, we gain an entirely different perspective on the meaning of justice. It suddenly becomes a concrete, tangible force in our lives. In that situation, we develop a profound and sincere hope that justice will be done—that is, that we will be treated fairly under the law. Justice, at this point, has ceased to be merely a concept and has become real for us in an entirely new way.

Examples are also important in rhetorical expression. As we talk and write, we often encounter instances where the use of a specific, relevant example can help us make a point, clarify our position, or simply enhance the listener/reader's comprehension of the material we're presenting.

The use of one or more examples in clarifying and supporting points is an important expository strategy. It appeals to the reader, it makes abstract ideas more concrete, and it provides important support for the point of the communication transaction.

We're all familiar with the use of examples in communication transactions. In fact, we have various ways of cuing readers and listeners when we intend to use examples to support a point. Conversely, listeners have various ways of requesting an example to clarify or support an idea. Here are some of both of these:

Examples

"Let me give you an example of what I'm talking about."

"It sounds good. Has it ever really worked? Give me a for-instance."

"This idea can best be understood if we look at an example of its application."

"Such as?"

"Here's an illustration of what I mean."

"Ideas are one thing. Name someone who's really done it."

Most, if not all, of these cues for example and illustrations are familiar to us. They constitute an important part of our communication activity, both written and oral. Using examples to support our thesis and to clarify the points we make in essay writing is an effective technique.

JOURNAL SUGGESTIONS

We use examples daily in our reading, speaking, and writing. Listen to any conversation or read any magazine article and you're likely to encounter expressions such as "Let me give you an example," or "To illustrate this. . . . " This strategy for thinking and expressing ourselves is vital to the communication process.

Temporarily focus your journal writing on the strategy of thinking called *example*. Example issues that you might write about in your journal include the following:

■ Look through the pages of any chapter in this textbook, and observe the use of the word *example* in the explanations and the practice exercises. Do they help you understand the points being made? Would the explanation of new ideas or of how to do a practice exercise be just as clear without the examples?

■ What adjective would you use to describe yourself—generous? friendly? tense? busy? happy-go-lucky? What specific example(s) would you use to support that opinion of yourself?

■ Think of a current social, political, or environmental issue that you feel strongly about. Begin a journal entry by making a general statement about some aspect of the issue you selected, and then illustrate your point with an example.

■ What adjective would you use to characterize someone you know well, such as your spouse, a good friend, or an employer? What specific example(s) would you use to demonstrate this particular characteristic of this person?

Finally, try to develop your own ideas and topics for journal entries. What is it about the thinking strategy called *example* that interests you? How is it important in your life? Remember to refer to these journal entries when you begin working on the writing assignment at the end of this chapter. You may be able to develop some of the ideas in your journal into an essay for this assignment.

The following journal entry was written in response to this journal suggestion.

Example   WEDNESDAY, 31ST

Well, it's easy to think of a complaint about a person I know. My boss, Mr. Thompkin. He is so argumentative. If somebody said "it's a pretty day, isn't it?" to him, he would argue the point. And he doesn't just disagree and go on. Oh, no; then he stands there and practically lectures about it for a few minutes. I can think of two times he really got me with his arguing. He had done something that was really going to benefit me personally. It came up in a conversation he and some other people were having before a sales meeting one morning. When I walked up to the group and heard what they were talking about, I said, "And I really want to thank you for doing that!" He just barely looked at me and basically without giving it any thought at all quickly said, "Well, thanks is not the issue here..." and just kept talking. I didn't hear anything else the man had to say to me and the group. I was just so stunned. I mean, have you ever had anyone argue with you when you said thanks before?

And then the other time he was so argumentative was at lunch one day. We were talking about romance writers and how quickly they churned out books and what a killing they must make. I said to the group—not just to him—but everyone, "I sure would like to write like that!" Mr. Thompkin "corrected" me by practically shouting, "No, what you mean is that you would like to make that kind of money—not write like that!" Well, I didn't need him to tell me what I meant. Boy, that burned me up. But I didn't argue with him. I just shut up. You can't win an argument with a jerk like him; why bother trying?

GUIDELINES

Using the following guidelines will enable you to write more easily in the example rhetorical pattern:

- Make sure that your topic lends itself to support by an example or examples.
- Organize and develop your essay by using either an extended example or multiple examples.
- Support the point of the writing by making the extended example or multiple examples specific, detailed, and concrete.
- Develop either a general thesis statement or a focused thesis statement.

PRACTICE   Read the student essay in this chapter entitled, "Freedom of Speech: Another Look," by Gordon Chatterton. After reading the essay, answer the following questions related to the guidelines for writing example essays. You may want to work with a small group of your classmates to complete this exercise.

1. Identify the thesis statement of the essay.

    _____

    Is it a general or focused thesis statement?

    _____

2. Does the topic lend itself to support by the use of an example or examples? Explain your response.

    _____

    _____

    _____

3. Does the writer use an extended example or multiple examples?

    _____

    Identify the example or examples the writer uses.

    _____

4. Has the writer adequately supported the point? Are the examples specific, detailed, and concrete? Identify specifics that you especially like.

5. Are there any places in the essay where the example could have been made more specific? Identify these, and explain your response.

TOPIC

The use of an example or examples to make a point or to support a thesis statement has wide application. In fact, almost any persuasive or informative piece of writing can be strengthened by the use of an example or examples.

Some topics, however, are more suitable than others to development through the use of examples. Examples are particularly useful for explaining abstractions.

You might, for instance, want to present your idea of what would constitute a perfect community. In doing so, you could argue that such a community would practice a fair division of labor. This idea, though a good one, is rather vague and nonspecific. An example would certainly help to clarify it. To do so, you might suggest that all community members would share equally in domestic tasks, including food preparation, cleaning, and child care. You could extend this example by explaining how a fair division of labor might be achieved.

Examples are also helpful for expressing experience-based events and occurrences. Let's say, for instance, that you came away from the last family dinner at your house feeling bothered by some things that happened there. If you want to communicate that experience to someone else, you will almost certainly have to use an example or examples to do so. You might do so by relating an event or a conversation that seemed to you to be particularly insensitive or even intentionally hurtful. Perhaps your father reminded you that you need to start looking for a summer job right away. His sarcastic tone, particularly when he said, "Don't forget—life's no picnic," really irked you. In fact, you recalled that the two of you had had this same conversation just the day before and that you had told him then that you had already filled out three job applications.

It is important to remember that examples can be used to support and clarify points you might make about a variety of topics. Following are some thesis statements that could be supported by an example or examples.

Example   Environmental pollution is not a distant or remote problem; it exists in every community, large and small, in our nation.

This thesis could be supported by using an example of a typical community and an environmental pollution problem that exists in that community. Daily newspapers regularly report such instances.

Example   Good nutrition, essential to good health, is so easy to achieve that almost any meal can be made more nutritious with little effort and only minor adjustments.

An example would work well here. Just select a typical meal and make simple, easy-to-follow suggestions for improving its nutritional content.

Example   Good teaching, though difficult to define, is easy to recognize.

This thesis statement could be supported by the use of one or more descriptive examples of a good teacher or good teachers you have known.

ORGANIZATION AND DEVELOPMENT

Having selected a suitable topic for an example essay, you must decide how to organize the body of the essay. Example essays may be developed either through the use of a single example or through the use of multiple examples. Both of these methods of organization and development work equally well for most example essays.

EXTENDED EXAMPLE

You can organize and develop an example essay through the use of a single example. This method of development requires that the example be extended to support the thesis statement fully, since it constitutes the only element of support in the essay. Supporting the thesis of an essay with a single example necessitates presenting the example in a very detailed, specific manner.

You might, for example, elect to use one example to support this thesis: "Good teaching, though difficult to define, is easy to recognize." Perhaps you could select one teacher you've had who was particularly good and use this person as an example to support your thesis. To do so, you would need to write several paragraphs about the teaching style and methods that, in your opinion made the teacher outstanding.

MULTIPLE EXAMPLES

Unlike organization and development through a single extended example, organization and development through multiple examples depends on the use of several different examples to support the thesis. Each example may be presented in one or two paragraphs, and each should contain just enough specifics to provide partial support for the thesis of the essay. Collectively, however, the examples included in the essay should provide full support for the point of the writing. Multiple examples, though not inherently better than a single extended example, may provide a broader base of support for a thesis. Generally, we perceive several instances of a phenomenon to be more trustworthy than a single occurrence. Therefore, you may find that your thesis is more convincing to your reader if it includes several examples rather than only one in support of the thesis.

The preceding thesis statement about good teaching could also be adequately and effectively supported by the use of several examples of good teachers you have known. Of course, you would not be able to provide the same level of detail about three or four teachers that you are able to provide about just one. On the other hand, support for the thesis may be strengthened by including more examples of good teaching.

SUPPORT

Using examples to develop a thesis requires supporting each example with adequate, detailed specifics. It is not enough simply to identify the example. The supporting details enable the reader to relate the example to the thesis of the essay and to be convinced that the thesis has merit. To accomplish this, you must provide enough details in connection with each example to make it meaningful for the reader. As you learned in Chapter 2, readers rely on details to form clear, specific images related to the messages writers are attempting to communicate.

The following example paragraphs illustrate this point. The first paragraph contains vague, ineffective specifics. The second, more effective paragraph contains interesting, concrete specifics that enable the reader to form sharp, detailed mental images of the message the writer is attempting to communicate.

Examples

A GOOD TEACHER

Mr. Daughtridge, my high-school shop teacher, was a particularly good instructor. For one thing, he had a way of making every class very interesting. He also seemed to care about each student. And last, but not least, he was an excellent craftsman.

A GOOD TEACHER

Mr. Daughtridge, my high-school shop teacher, was the instructor I'll always remember. To begin with, he had a way of making every class lively. Although he rarely told funny stories or jokes, he did begin each class with a five-minute discussion of an important current event. We discussed everything from a news report about bribery in the local sheriff's department, to a current court case that concerned euthanasia. In addition to being an interesting teacher, Mr. Daughtridge was also a caring instructor. My best friend Wesley wrecked his Honda and spent a couple of days in Merced County Hospital. To our surprise, Mr. Daughtridge visited him in the hospital and, as a joke, gave him a copy of *Road and Track* magazine. Finally, Mr. Daughtridge was an excellent craftsman. His specialty was gun racks, and he added complex, intricate trim to these creations that looked almost impossible to us novices.

THESIS

Develop either a general or a focused thesis statement for the example essay. A general thesis statement for an example essay contains only the point you intend to make in the essay. A focused thesis statement contains the point of the essay and also identifies the example or examples you intend to use to support your thesis.

The following sentences are general and focused thesis statements for example essays:

Example

Topic The Battle of Hastings

General thesis statement Most historians agree that King Harold exhibited poor judgment in his conduct of the Battle of Hastings.

Focused thesis statement Most historians agree that King Harold exhibited poor judgment in his conduct of the Battle of Hastings, as exemplified by his failure to attack as well as his failure to retreat.

The plan of development in a focused thesis statement specifies the example or examples that will be used to develop the example essay. If you include an example or examples in your thesis statement, you have a focused thesis statement. If you do not include these, you have a general thesis statement.

PRACTICE Working alone or in small groups, develop both general and focused thesis statements for example essays on the following topics. Write your thesis statements in the spaces provided.

1. *Topic:* A Christmas I'll Never Forget
   General thesis statement:

   _____

   _____

   _____

   _____

   Focused thesis statement:

   _____

   _____

_____

_____

2. *Topic:* Favorite Hiking Trails/Picnic Spots
General thesis statement:

_____

_____

_____

_____

_____

Focused thesis statement:

_____

_____

_____

_____

3. *Topic:* Music That Moves Me
General thesis statement:

_____

_____

_____

_____

Focused thesis statement:

_____

_____

_____

_____

4. *Topic:* Gadgets I Have Loved
General thesis statement:

_____

_____

_____

Focused thesis statement:

_____

_____

_____

5. *Topic:* Qualities a Political Leader Should Possess
General thesis statement:

_____

_____

_____

Focused thesis statement:

_____

_____

_____

READINGS

The following readings are student and professional essays. Read them carefully, and look for their use of examples as described in this chapter.

FREEDOM OF SPEECH: ANOTHER LOOK

Gordon Chatterton

The First Amendment to the United States Constitution deals with, in addition to freedom of religion, assembly, and petition, the freedom of speech and press. "Congress shall make no law . . . abridging the freedom of speech, or of the press," it reads in part. Nearly 200 years after the ratification in 1791 of this section of the Bill of Rights, these basic freedoms, speech and press, are still part of the essence of a working and successful democracy. In 200 years, though, conditions change. In these particular 200 years, the explosive changes, such as moon-landings and heart-transplants, are almost beyond belief. Billowing out of those explosions are clear indications, supported by myriad forceful examples, that the language of Article I of the Bill of Rights is too general; that the freedom of speech and press, as envisioned by our forefathers, does not consider the sophisticated tools of rhetoric that have evolved since their time; and that the freedom of speech and the freedom of press guaranteed by the Bill of Rights need to be re-evaluated, bringing them into concert with today's conditions.

Since the days when "speech" meant the human voice and "press" meant the print-ing press, two examples of explosive changes involving rhetorical tools have been the invention and development of the "printed voice" in the form of recording devices and the development of photographic processes in, for instance, the birth and growth of television. These two, thrown together in the Eden of Technological Miracles where micro-circuitry, satellite transmission, and memory banks grow, inevitably produced from their union a whole new concept and a whole new word: "media." The differentiation between "press" and "speech" was eliminated. They became one and the same thing. Prior to the birth of media, there had been an historically distinct difference between libel (a printed defamatory lie) and slander (a spoken defamatory lie). Under Roman law, "abusive chants" was a capital crime; in early English and Germanic law, insults were punishable by cutting out the tongue. With the advent of printing, slander was made a less serious crime, as the printed word evidently was more valuable and forceful than the spoken word. Our ancestors, too, were faced with new conditions and new technology. They recognized the inadequacies of existing laws and mores and changed them.

FREEDOM OF SPEECH: ANOTHER LOOK, continued

Under existing laws, defamation is criminal only when it "provokes a breech of the peace or . . . directly prejudices the public interest." In 1791, the impact of defamation was primarily local in nature. There were notable exceptions. For instance, "God! Save the Queen," shouted by an ancestor of the late Truman Capote during a hotel fire, today can be heard 'round the world. With the advanced technology of mass-distribution and the near-immediate worldwide circulation that now exists, the impact of libel/slander can be enormous. For instance, in its January 12, 1978, issue, *The National Enquirer,* a sensation-packed tabloid, printed a story stating that Carol Burnett, an internationally known entertainment personality, had been "drunk, disorderly, loud, rowdy, and crude," plus some other odious adverbs and adjectives, "in a public place." Ms. Burnett, fit to be tied, sued *The National Enquirer* for libel. Four-plus years later, she was "victorious" in court with actual and punitive damage awards from the court, which are now under appeal. The libelous editorial policy of *The National Enquirer* is a calculated adventure in abuse of the freedom of the press. It is not a criminal adventure; it is a civil adventure. Its rewards can be great in the form of increased circulation and revenue and apparently are. Further, for the occasional "Carol Burnett" who decides to sue, there are many "Johnny Carsons," "Henry Kissingers," and the like, who choose to do nothing about the libel because of the time, expense, and aggravation of ongoing involvement. Clearly, the example of Carol Burnett versus *The National Enquirer* demonstrates a condition not existing when the Bill of Rights was created.

As our bureaucratic government has grown to massive proportions, along with it has grown the tendency to release to the media only such information deemed (by someone) proper and in the best interests of the government. Obviously, the decision as to what is proper and in the government's best interest is an arbitrary one. The policy can cover, literally, a multitude of sins. Thus, the "leak" was born. The "leak" as used here is an unauthorized release of news, usually by an anonymous informant, to the media. By its nature, the information is difficult or impossible to substantiate. The examples abound, but some of the most spectacular, familiar to all of us, came during the Nixon administration, exposed as a by-product of "Watergate." Both the "true leak" and the "false leak" were freely used during this time to mold public opinion and attitudes. The result, of course, is a clear and frighteningly forceful example of government interference with the freedom of the press by the use of sophisticated manipulative techniques of communication, not contemplated at the creation of the Bill of Rights.

The indications that changing conditions, technologies, and attitudes have invalidated at least some of the general language of Article I of the Bill of Rights are there for all of us to see. It is clear, also, that the results of unchecked abuses of the freedom of speech and press are potentially dangerous in ways our forefathers could not even imagine. The loss of these two freedoms is not an acceptable option. The repair of the machinery necessary for the freedoms' survival is mandatory. Just how this repair can be done and how the modifications can be formed and implemented are mind-boggling problems.

FREEDOM OF SPEECH: ANOTHER LOOK, continued

There is, however, more than enough evidence supported by forceful examples to tell us that our democracy has a cancer and that we should treat that cancer with the same concern, the same urgency, and the same intensity as if each of us had it in his own body.

PROFESSIONAL ESSAY

THE PETER PRINCIPLE

Laurence J. Peter and Raymond Hull

When I was a boy I was taught that the men upstairs knew what they were doing. I was told, "Peter, the more you know, the further you go." So I stayed in school until I graduated from college and then went forth into the world clutching firmly these ideas and my new teaching certificate. During the first year of teaching I was upset to find that a number of teachers, school principals, supervisors and superintendents appeared to be unaware of their professional responsibilities and incompetent in executing their duties. For example my principal's main concerns were that all window shades be at the same level, that classrooms should be quiet and that no one step on or near the rose beds. The superintendent's main concerns were that no minority group, no matter how fanatical, should ever be offended and that all official forms be submitted on time. The children's education appeared farthest from the administrator's mind.

At first I thought this was a special weakness of the school system in which I taught so I applied for certification in another province. I filled out the special forms, enclosed the required documents and complied willingly with all the red tape. Several weeks later, back came my application and all the documents!

No, there was nothing wrong with my credentials; the forms were correctly filled out; an official departmental stamp showed that they had been received in good order. But an accompanying letter said, "The new regulations require that such forms cannot be accepted by the Department of Education unless they have been registered at the Post Office to ensure safe delivery. Will you please remail the forms to the Department, making sure to register them this time?"

I began to suspect that the local school system did not have a monopoly on incompetence.

THE PETER PRINCIPLE, continued

As I looked further afield, I saw that every organization contained a number of persons who could not do their jobs.

A UNIVERSAL PHENOMENON

Occupational incompetence is everywhere. Have you noticed it? Probably we all have noticed it.

We see indecisive politicians posing as resolute statesmen and the "authoritative source" who blames his misinformation on "situational imponderables." Limitless are the public servants who are indolent and insolent; military commanders whose behavioral timidity belies their dreadnought rhetoric, and governors whose innate servility prevents their actually governing. In our sophistication, we virtually shrug aside the immoral cleric, corrupt judge, incoherent attorney, author who cannot write and English teacher who cannot spell. At universities we see proclamations authored by administrators whose own office communications are hopelessly muddled, and droning lectures from inaudible or incomprehensible instructors.

Seeing incompetence at all levels of every hierarchy—political, legal, educational and industrial—I hypothesized that the cause was some inherent feature of the rules governing the placement of employees. Thus began my serious study of the ways in which employees move upward through a hierarchy, and of what happens to them after promotion.

For my scientific data hundreds of case histories were collected. Here are three typical examples.

Municipal Government File, Case No. 17. J. S. Minion[1] was a maintenance foreman in the public works department of Excelsior City. He was a favorite of the senior officials at City Hall. They all praised his unfailing affability.

"I like Minion," said the superintendent of works. "He has good judgment and is always pleasant and agreeable."

This behavior was appropriate for Minion's position: he was not supposed to make policy, so he had no need to disagree with his superiors.

The superintendent of works retired and Minion succeeded him. Minion continued to agree with everyone. He passed to his foreman every suggestion that came from above. The resulting conflicts in policy, and the continual changing of plans, soon demoralized the department. Complaints poured in from the Mayor and other officials, from taxpayers and from the maintenance-workers' union.

Minion still says "Yes" to everyone, and carries messages briskly back and forth between his superiors and his subordinates. Nominally a superintendent, he actually does the work of a messenger. The maintenance department regularly exceeds its budget, yet fails to fulfill its program of work. In short, Minion, a competent foreman, became an incompetent superintendent.

Service Industries File, Case No. 3. E. Tinker was exceptionally zealous and intelligent as an apprentice at G. Reece

[1] Some names have been changed, in order to protect the guilty.

THE PETER PRINCIPLE, continued

Auto Repair Inc., and soon rose to journey-man mechanic. In this job he showed outstanding ability in diagnosing obscure faults, and endless patience in correcting them. He was promoted to foreman of the repair shop.

But here his love of things mechanical and his perfectionism became liabilities. He will undertake any job that he thinks looks interesting, no matter how busy the shop may be. "We'll work it in somehow," he says.

He will not let a job go until he is fully satisfied with it.

He meddles constantly. He is seldom to be found at his desk. He is usually up to his elbows in a dismantled motor and while the man who should be doing the work stands watching, other workmen sit around waiting to be assigned new tasks. As a result the shop is always overcrowded with work, always in a muddle, and delivery times are often missed.

Tinker cannot understand that the average customer cares little about perfection—he wants his car back on time! He cannot understand that most of his men are less interested in motors than in their pay checks. So Tinker cannot get on with his customers or with his subordinates. He was a competent mechanic, but is now an incompetent foreman.

Military File, Case No. 8. Consider the case of the late renowned General A. Goodwin. His hearty, informal manner, his racy style of speech, his scorn for petty regulations and his undoubted personal bravery made him the idol of his men. He led them to many well-deserved victories.

When Goodwin was promoted to field marshal he had to deal, not with ordinary soldiers, but with politicians and allied generalissimos.

He would not conform to the necessary protocol. He could not turn his tongue to the conventional courtesies and flatteries. He quarreled with all the dignitaries and took to lying for days at a time, drunk and sulking, in his trailer. The conduct of the war slipped out of his hands into those of his subordinates. He had been promoted to a position that he was incompetent to fill.

AN IMPORTANT CLUE!

In time I saw that all such cases had a common feature. The employee had been promoted from a position of competence to a position of incompetence. I saw that, sooner or later, this could happen to every employee in every hierarchy.

Hypothetical Case File, Case No. 1.

Suppose you own a pill-rolling factory, Perfect Pill Incorporated. Your foreman pill roller dies of a perforated ulcer. You need a replacement. You naturally look among your rank-and-file pill rollers.

Miss Oval, Mrs. Cylinder, Mr. Ellipse and Mr. Cube all show various degrees of incompetence. They will naturally be ineligible for promotion. You will choose—other things being equal—your most competent pill roller, Mr. Sphere, and promote him to foreman.

Now suppose Mr. Sphere proves competent as foreman. Later, when your general

THE PETER PRINCIPLE, continued

foreman, Legree, moves up to Works Manager, Sphere will be eligible to take his place.

If, on the other hand, Sphere is an incompetent foreman, he will get no more promotion. He has reached what I call his "level of incompetence." He will stay there till the end of his career.

Some employees, like Ellipse and Cube, reach a level of incompetence in the lowest grade and are never promoted. Some, like Sphere (assuming he is not a satisfactory foreman), reach it after one promotion.

E. Tinker, the automobile repair-shop foreman, reached his level of incompetence on the third stage of the hierarchy. General Goodwin reached his level of incompetence at the very top of the hierarchy.

So my analysis of hundreds of cases of occupational incompetence led me on to formulate *The Peter Principle:*

In a Hierarchy Every Employee Tends to Rise to His Level of Incompetence

A NEW SCIENCE!

Having formulated the Principle, I discovered that I had inadvertently founded a new science, hierarchiology, the study of hierarchies.

The term "hierarchy" was originally used to describe the system of church government by priests graded into ranks. The contemporary meaning includes any organization whose members or employees are arranged in order of rank, grade or class.

Hierarchiology, although a relatively recent discipline, appears to have great applicability to the fields of public and private administration.

THIS MEANS YOU!

My Principle is the key to an understanding of all hierarchal systems, and therefore to an understanding of the whole structure of civilization. A few eccentrics try to avoid getting involved with hierarchies, but everyone in business, industry, trade-unionism, politics, government, the armed forces, religion and education is so involved. All of them are controlled by the Peter Principle.

Many of them, to be sure, may win a promotion or two, moving from one level of competence to a higher level of competence. But competence in that new position qualifies them for still another promotion. For each individual, for *you*, for *me*, the final promotion is from a level of competence to a level of incompetence.[2]

So, given enough time—and assuming the existence of enough ranks in the hierarchy—each employee rises to, and remains at, his level of incompetence. Peter's Corollary states:

In time, every post tends to be occupied by an employee who is incompetent to carry out its duties.

[2]The phenomena of "percussive sublimation" (commonly referred to as "being kicked upstairs") and of "the lateral arabesque" are not, as the casual observer might think, exceptions to the Principle. They are only pseudo-promotions. . . .

THE PETER PRINCIPLE, continued

WHO TURNS THE WHEELS?

You will rarely find, of course, a system in which *every* employee has reached his level of incompetence. In most instances, something is being done to further the ostensible purposes for which the hierarchy exists.

Work is accomplished by those employees who have not yet reached their level of incompetence.

Rhetoric

1. Look closely at the structure of "The Peter Principle," and try to identify its components. For example, does the essay contain an introduction? If so, where does it end? What part of the writing constitutes the body of the essay? Where does the conclusion begin?

2. Now that you have identified the introduction, analyze it. What kind of introduction is it? Is this an effective introduction for this essay?

3. Analyze the conclusion. Is it effective? Why or why not?

4. Finally, determine which method of development (extended example or multiple examples) is used in this essay.

Ideas

1. Perhaps you disagree with the Peter Principle. If so, explain why.

2. The author begins the essay by noting various discoveries that led him to the conclusion that "every organization contained a number of persons who could not do their jobs." What additional conclusion did he make that enabled him to formulate the Peter Principle?

3. Can the Peter Principle be neutralized, or are we bound to be victimized by it? If you think we can limit its effect, make some suggestions about how we might do so.

Response

1. Write a one-paragraph case history that could be added to this essay to further support the validity of the Peter Principle. Single out someone you know who, in your opinion, has been promoted to his or her level of incompetence. Your case history should be about the same length as those contained in the essay.

2. You may disagree with the Peter Principle. If so, write an essay in which you try to show that the Peter Principle is invalid. You may use examples of individuals you know who, in your opinion, defy the Peter Principle.

PROFESSIONAL ESSAY

ELVIRA'S STORY

Flora Mancuso Edwards

Over 150 years ago the English historian Thomas Carlyle had this to say about Victorian society:

> It is not to die, or even to die of hunger, that makes a man wretched; many men have died; all men must die. . . . But it is to live miserable we know not why; to work sore and yet gain nothing; to be heartworn, weary, yet isolated, unrelated, girt in with a cold, universal Laissez-faire.[1]

There are over 4 million people in the United States today who still live miserable and know not why, who still "work sore and yet gain nothing." They are our laboring poor.

Elvira Ramirez is just one example of those who must sell their labor so cheaply that the necessities of life are just barely met. Elvira is a soft-spoken, cheerful, well-mannered woman who works in a luxurious East Side beauty salon doing shampoos and manicures. Her average day is filled by serving New York's well-to-do matrons who spend spring in New York, winter in Miami, and summer on Cape Cod. Elvira listens sympathetically to their problems in getting "reliable help" or to their last-minute preparations for a child's wedding in Switzerland.

For her services and good company she receives $0.25 to $0.50 from each one and

occasionally $1.00 from a more generous customer. These tips bring up her total salary of $90.00 to approximately $110.00 a week. On this salary, Elvira supports herself, her son, a teen-age daughter, and her mother in a one-bedroom apartment in the Nathan Strauss Housing Projects in the Chelsea section on Manhattan's West Side.

Her apartment is on the third floor of a building whose elevators are as offensive as they are nonfunctioning. Elvira, her mother, her daughter, and her son all used to sleep in one room, but now the boy is older and has inherited the sofa in the living room, which doubles as his bedroom. The apartment has no closets, and there is little room even for the metal Woolworth's wardrobes. The kitchen is so small that there is no place for a table, so when the family must eat together, the sofa is moved and a table set up in the living room.

Elvira receives no health insurance from her job, nor does she receive a vacation or overtime pay. Her mother is only sixty and neither blind nor technically disabled, so she receives no social security or public assistance. Elvira's income—marginal as it may be—is too high for Medicaid, so Elvira works fourteen to sixteen hours a day, six days a week, and prays that no one will get sick. But, because the windows of the third-floor apartment keep getting broken, New York's winter always seems to take its toll in doctor bills, which each year are increasingly hard to pay.

[1]Quoted in Robert Hunter, *Poverty*, ed. Peter d'A. Jones (New York: Macmillan, 1904; Harper & Row, 1965), p. 1.

SOURCE: *The City Today*, edited by George L. Groman. Copyright © 1978 by Harper & Row. Reprinted by permission of the publisher.

ELVIRA'S STORY, continued

When Elvira was hospitalized several years ago, the Department of Social Services came to her rescue. But it did not take long for Elvira to realize that the benefits came at a high price.

No, the welfare is all waiting with the children crying, waiting outside the office for hours in the freezing cold, sick hungry waiting all day in the clinic, waiting to be looked down on, insulted, and humiliated. No, I'm not earning much more— but it's better than waiting.

God willing, I don't get sick again.[2]

Elvira has no savings and therefore cannot move to larger quarters. As it is, rent is her biggest expenditure. Her hopes?

Maybe I go back to the Island when Michele finish school. You know, I guess I didn't do so bad after all. Michele finish fourth in her class. Now she goes to Harpur College. She got a scholarship, you know. I thought when she finish high school she would get a job and help out, but maybe it's better like this. Now she'll be somebody. . . . You know, like a

[2]Personal interviews conducted between May and December 1973.

teacher or a nurse or something. That's the most important thing—the kids. Sure I work hard—but the kids—they're going to be something.

Am I poor? No, not really. Really poor people take the welfare. Most of the time we manage to get by.

Elvira receives no benefits, no medical coverage, no public assistance. She earns $6,000 a year before taxes. She works harder and longer than most people and earns considerably less. She eats little meat and indulges herself in no luxuries. She does not own a car, goes on no vacations, eats in few restaurants, and buys a minimum of clothing.

Elvira's job is similar to almost one-third of all the jobs in New York, and Elvira is one of 600,000 New Yorkers who live below the poverty line and struggle on day by day, eking out a marginal existence in New York, one of the richest cities in the world.

On a national level, over 415 million people (not counting rural sharecroppers) are employed full time and are still poor. In almost half of these families, two people work full time in order to reap the bitter rewards of poverty and want.

Rhetoric

1. Does the essay contain an obvious, clearly stated thesis statement? If so, what is it?

2. How is the essay developed—by multiple examples or by an extended example? Is this method of development effective for the point that this essay is trying to make? If so, why?

3. The conclusion of the essay consists of the last two paragraphs and moves from the particular, Elvira, to the general, the nation's

working poor. Is this an acceptable conclusion for this essay? Does it strengthen or weaken the author's effort to make her point?

Ideas

1. The author informs us that "Elvira Ramirez is just one example of those who must sell their labor so cheaply that the necessities of life are just barely met." In your opinion, must Elvira do this? If not, what options do you think are available to her?

2. Has the U.S. government let Elvira down? If so, how? What might our government do to improve Elvira's economic situation and thus the quality of her (and her family's) life?

Response

1. Write a letter to your representative in the U.S. Congress, expressing your concerns about the working poor in America. Use at least two examples of such people to support your point that our government needs to find more effective means to alleviate the poverty these people live in.

2. Working with two or three of your classmates, compose a letter to your representative in the U.S. Congress, expressing your group's concerns about the working poor in America. The point of your letter might be that our government needs to find more effective means to alleviate the poverty such people live in. Support your recommendation with examples of ways the government could do this.

3. Some people argue that a poor working class is essential to the economic well-being of a capitalistic state. Assume that you agree. Write an essay for your economics or sociology class in which you present and argue for this position. Use an extended example or multiple examples to support your position (thesis).

PROFESSIONAL ESSAY

COURTSHIP THROUGH THE AGES   James Thurber

Surely nothing in the astonishing scheme of life can have nonplussed Nature so much as the fact that none of the females of any of the species she created really cared very much for the male, as such. For the past ten million years Nature has been

COURTSHIP THROUGH THE AGES, continued

busily inventing ways to make the male attractive to the female, but the whole business of courtship, from the marine annelids up to man, still lumbers heavily along, like a complicated musical comedy. I have been reading the sad and absorbing story in Volume 6 (Cole to Dama) of the *Encyclopaedia Britannica*. In this volume you can learn all about cricket, cotton, costume designing, crocodiles, crown jewels, and Coleridge, but none of these subjects is so interesting as the Courtship of Animals, which recounts the sorrowful lengths to which all males must go to arouse the interest of a lady.

We all know, I think, that Nature gave man whiskers and a mustache with the quaint idea in mind that these would prove attractive to the female. We all know that, far from attracting her, whiskers and mustaches only made her nervous and gloomy, so that man had to go in for somersaults, tilting with lances, and performing feats of parlor magic to win her attention; he also had to bring her candy, flowers, and the furs of animals. It is common knowledge that in spite of all these "love displays" the male is constantly being turned down, insulted, or thrown out of the house. It is rather comforting, then, to discover that the peacock, for all his gorgeous plumage, does not have a particularly easy time in courtship; none of the males in the world do. The first peahen, it turned out, was only faintly stirred by her suitor's beautiful train. She would often go quietly to sleep while he was whisking it around. The *Britannica* tells us that the peacock actually had to learn a certain little trick to wake her up and revive her interest: he had to learn to vibrate his quills so as to make

a rustling sound. In ancient times man himself, observing the ways of the peacock, probably tried vibrating his whiskers to make a rustling sound; if so, it didn't get him anywhere. He had to go in for something else; so, among other things, he went in for gifts. It is not unlikely that he got this idea from certain flies and birds who were making no headway at all with rustling sounds.

One of the flies of the family Empidae, who had tried everything, finally hit on something pretty special. He contrived to make a glistening transparent balloon which was even larger than himself. Into this he would put sweetmeats and tidbits and he would carry the whole elaborate envelope through the air to the lady of his choice. This amused her for a time, but she finally got bored with it. She demanded silly little colorful presents, something that you couldn't eat but that would look nice around the house. So the male Empis had to go around gathering flower petals and pieces of bright paper to put into his balloon. On a courtship flight a male Empis cuts quite a figure now, but he can hardly be said to be happy. He never knows how soon the female will demand heavier presents, such as Roman coins and gold collar buttons. It seems probable that one day the courtship of the Empidae will fall down, as man's occasionally does, of its own weight.

The bowerbird is another creature that spends so much time courting the female that he never gets any work done. If all the male bowerbirds became nervous wrecks within the next ten or fifteen years, it would not surprise me. The female bowerbird insists that a playground be built for

COURTSHIP THROUGH THE AGES, continued

her with a specially constructed bower at the entrance. This bower is much more elaborate than an ordinary nest and is harder to build; it costs a lot more, too. The female will not come to the playground until the male has filled it up with a great many gifts: silvery leaves, red leaves, rose petals, shells, beads, berries, bones, dice, buttons, cigar bands, Christmas seals, and the Lord knows what else. When the female finally condescends to visit the playground, she is in a coy and silly mood and has to be chased in and out of the bower and up and down the playground before she will quit giggling and stand still long enough even to shake hands. The male bird is, of course, pretty well done in before the chase starts, because he has worn himself out hunting for eyeglass lenses and begonia blossoms. I imagine that many a bowerbird, after chasing a female for two or three hours, says the hell with it and goes home to bed. Next day, of course, he telephones someone else and the same trying ritual is gone through with again. A male bowerbird is as exhausted as a night-club habitué before he is out of his twenties.

The male fiddler crab has a somewhat easier time, but it can hardly be said that he is sitting pretty. He has one enormously large and powerful claw, usually brilliantly colored, and you might suppose that all he had to do was reach out and grab some passing cutie. The very earliest fiddler crabs may have tried this, but, if so, they got slapped for their pains. A female fiddler crab will not tolerate any caveman stuff; she never has and she doesn't intend to start now. To attract a female, a fiddler crab has to stand on tiptoe and brandish

his claw in the air. If any female in the neighborhood is interested—and you'd be surprised how many are not—she comes over and engages him in light badinage, for which he is not in the mood. As many as a hundred females may pass the time of day with him and go on about their business. By nightfall of an average courting day, a fiddler crab who has been standing on tiptoe for eight or ten hours waving a heavy claw in the air is in pretty sad shape. As in the case of the males of all species, however, he gets out of bed next morning, dashes some water on his face, and tries again.

The next time you encounter a male web-spinning spider, stop and reflect that he is too busy worrying about his love life to have any desire to bite you. Male web-spinning spiders have a tougher life than any other males in the animal kingdom. This is because the female web-spinning spiders have very poor eyesight. If a male lands on a female's web, she kills him before he has time to lay down his cane and gloves, mistaking him for a fly or a bumblebee who has tumbled into her trap. Before the species figured out what to do about this, millions of males were murdered by ladies they called on. It is the nature of spiders to perform a little dance in front of the female, but before a male spinner could get near enough for the female to see who he was and what he was up to, she would lash out at him with a flat-iron or a pair of garden shears. One night, nobody knows when, a very bright male spinner lay awake worrying about calling on a lady who had been killing suitors right and left. It came to him that this business of dancing as a love display

COURTSHIP THROUGH THE AGES, continued

wasn't getting anybody anywhere except the grave. He decided to go in for web-twitching, or strand-vibrating. The next day he tried it on one of the nearsighted girls. Instead of dropping in on her suddenly, he stayed outside the web and began monkeying with one of its strands. He twitched it up and down and in and out with such a lilting rhythm that the female was charmed. The serenade worked beautifully; the female let him live. The *Britannica's* spider-watchers, however, report that his system is not always successful. Once in a while, even now, a female will fire three bullets into a suitor or run him through with a kitchen knife. She keeps threatening him from the moment he strikes the first low notes on the outside strings, but usually by the time he has got up to the high notes played around the center of the web, he is going to town and she spares his life.

Even the butterfly, as handsome a fellow as he is, can't always win a mate merely by fluttering around and showing off. Many butterflies have to have scent scales on their wings. Hepialus carries a powder puff in a perfumed pouch. He throws perfume at the ladies when they pass. The male tree cricket, Oecanthus, goes Hepialus one better by carrying a tiny bottle of wine with him and giving drinks to such doxies as he has designs on. One of the male snails throws darts to entertain the girls. So it goes, through the long list of animals, from the bristle worm and his rudimentary dance steps to man and his gift of diamonds and sapphires. The golden-eye drake raises a jet of water with his feet as he flies over a lake; Hepialus has his powder puff, Oecanthus his wine bot-

tle, man his etchings. It is a bright and melancholy story, the age-old desire of the male for the female, the age-old desire of the female to be amused and entertained. Of all the creatures on earth, the only males who could be figured as putting any irony into their courtship are the grebes and certain other diving birds. Every now and then a courting grebe slips quietly down to the bottom of a lake and then, with a mighty "Whoosh!," pops out suddenly a few feet from his girl friend, splashing water all over her. She seems to be persuaded that this is a purely loving display, but I like to think that the grebe always has a faint hope of drowning her or scaring her to death.

I will close this investigation into the mournful burdens of the male with the *Britannica's* story about a certain Argus pheasant. It appears that the Argus displays himself in front of a female who stands perfectly still without moving a feather. . . . The male Argus the *Britannica* tells about was confined in a cage with a female of another species, a female who kept moving around, emptying ashtrays and fussing with lampshades all the time the male was showing off his talents. Finally, in disgust, he stalked away and began displaying in front of his water trough. He reminds me of a certain male (*Homo sapiens*) of my acquaintance who one night after dinner asked his wife to put down her detective magazine so that he could read a poem of which he was very fond. She sat quietly enough until he was well into the middle of the thing, intoning with great ardor and intensity. Then suddenly there came a sharp, disconcerting *slap*! It turned out that all during the male's display, the

COURTSHIP THROUGH THE AGES, continued

female had been intent on a circling mosquito and had finally trapped it between the palms of her hands. The male in this case did not stalk away and display in front of a water trough; he went over to Tim's and had a flock of drinks and recited the poem to the fellas. I am sure they all told bitter stories of their own about how their displays had been interrupted by females. I am also sure that they all ended up singing "Honey, Honey, Bless Your Heart."

Rhetoric

1. Read the first paragraph of the essay closely, and underline the sentence that you think contains the point or thesis of this piece of writing.

2. Based on what you believe to be the thesis of the essay, what sort of examples must the author select in order to support his point?

3. Most paragraphs in the body of the essay present one example in support of the thesis statement. At least one paragraph, however, contains several examples, all of which support the thesis. Locate this paragraph and count the number of examples it contains. Does this paragraph provide effective support for the thesis?

Ideas

1. Critique Thurber's essay by responding to the following questions:
   A. Is his thesis fair—both to males and to females? Why or why not?
   B. Have the rules for the courtship of humans changed significantly since Thurber wrote this essay in 1939? Explain your response.

2. Is the author's attitude toward women, as expressed in the poetry reading in the last paragraph, too stereotypical? If you think that it is, write a few sentences that explain how it is unfair and inaccurate.

Response

1. Scan the essay and note some of the courtesies Thurber mentions that men extend to women. Then make a brief comparable list of up-to-date courtesies that men offer women. Match your list with a comparable list made by one of your classmates. Working with your classmate on the combined lists, turn them into a short paragraph that enumerates and explains these modern courtship rituals.

2. Assume that, in light of the women's movement, you think that Thurber has a flawed view of male–female relations. Write a brief

essay in which you challenge his assertions about "the sorrowful lengths to which all men must go to arouse the interest of a lady."

WRITING ASSIGNMENTS

You may select a topic for this writing assignment from one of the following lists, or you may develop a topic of your own. Once you have selected a topic, complete one or more of the specified prewriting activities. After sufficient prewriting, write a draft of an essay on the topic you selected. Finally, revise and edit your essay.

General Writing Assignments
- The benefits of population control
- Honesty is not always the best policy
- My senior English teacher did/did not help me get ready for college composition
- Three interests make my life worth living
- A vacation at the beach has its drawbacks
- Three habits I wish I could break
- Some diets are simply not good for you
- Some experiences can be life-changing
- Driving habits that drive me crazy
- Some teachers/courses are better than others

Specific Writing Assignments
- Imagine that you're concerned about the quality of some of the TV programs that are being aired on your local station. Write a letter asking the local station manager to consider eliminating shows that contain what you consider to be objectionable content. Single out three or four specific programs to serve as examples of the kinds of programs you find offensive.
- Assume that you have just completed registering for college courses for the first time and that you found the process trying. Write an article for the student paper in which you give examples of frustrating parts of the registration process and suggest that these be modified or eliminated.
- Assume that your psychology instructor has asked each member of the class to write a brief essay informing the instructor of some things he or she hopes will be covered in the class. As you write this essay,

remember to limit your requests and to explain why each request you make is important to you.

If you decide to develop your own topic, you may want to look through your journal for ideas. What topic that you have addressed in your journal lends itself most readily to this particular strategy of thinking and communicating? You might also look carefully at the focused journal entries you wrote at the beginning of this chapter. Is one of these topics of interest to you? Is it a topic with which you have some experience? With some revision work, could your journal entry on this topic become an essay?

Finally, look back through this chapter at some of the exercises you have done. Are any of these topics of interest to you? Recall conversations with your classmates. Have they given you ideas for topics? Perhaps interesting topics emerged from the group discussions that followed some of the practices in the chapter. You may want to spend some time discussing these exercises with classmates to help you decide what to write about. Or you may want to do some listing on paper to help you discover a suitable topic.

PREWRITING

After selecting a topic as the subject for an example essay, complete one or more of the following prewriting activities:

- *Brainstorming*–Write the topic at the top of a blank sheet of paper. Then jot down every example that comes to mind that is either directly or indirectly related to the topic and to the point you want to make about the topic. As you do so, remember that you are not to qualify or pass judgment on your ideas. You're simply to write them down as they come to mind. Give yourself a time limit of no more than three minutes for this activity. When you finish, look over the list you have compiled, noting the key examples you might use to develop and support your thesis.
- *Journal*–If time permits, use your journal as a source of ideas for an example essay. Begin by selecting a topic for an example essay. Then write about this topic in your journal for at least three consecutive days for at least ten minutes per day. As you do so, record your thoughts, ideas, and feelings about the topic. After your final journal-writing session on this topic, review what you have written and look for an idea that can be developed into a thesis statement for an example essay. Then look for one or more examples that you can use to support your thesis and develop your essay.

REVISING

In revising your essay, follow these seven steps:

1. Ask a friend, a roommate, or a writing colleague (or colleagues) to listen to or read your writing and then to comment on what you have written. Specifically, are the subject and the purpose of the essay clear? Does the body of the essay make and support points that achieve the purpose of the writing? Do any sentences, passages, or sections of the paper seem either unrelated to or contradictory to the purpose of the writing?

2. Check the introduction and thesis statement of the essay. Have you introduced your reader to the topic you plan to support with examples? Have you chosen a topic that lends itself to support with examples? Does your introductory paragraph include a thesis that makes clear what you plan to say about your topic? Is the introduction interesting? clear?

3. Check the thesis support in the main body of the essay. Is the material in the body of the essay organized so that it supports the point (thesis) of the writing? Do you use multiple examples or an extended example?

4. Check the paragraph support throughout the essay. Is each paragraph well written, and does each paragraph include clear and specific details? Do you provide specific, detailed support for your extended or multiple examples?

5. Check for coherence and unity. As a whole, does the essay make sense? Does it contain any irrelevant words, sentences, or paragraphs?

6. Check for closure. Is there closure at the end of the essay in either a concluding (or summarizing) paragraph or a concluding sentence?

7. Review the Revision Checklist at the end of Chapter 5. Use the checklist to make sure that you have completed a thorough revision of your essay.

PROCESS ANALYSIS

Process fills our lives. Trivial and mundane tasks such as pumping gas and brushing teeth involve processes. These and similar processes surround us and both simplify and complicate our lives. The engines in the cars we drive function according to complex, intricate processes. But tying one's shoes is also a process, although a rather simple one, as is studying for a test or baking a birthday cake.

We are always engaged in acquiring new skills, which often involves learning new processes. Getting a college degree, for example, is a process; and the college catalog is a guide for students to follow in order to complete this process. This technological age in which we live requires that we learn new skills almost daily in order to perform such routine tasks as dialing a long-distance number using a credit card, getting a Coke from a talking vending machine, and withdrawing money from a bank account via an ATM. If you have ever stood in front of an automatic teller machine on a stormy, windy night, trying to read the directions in order to withdraw money from your account, you are already aware of the importance of learning and following processes.

Often, a process involves performing a series of steps in a specific order. You may, for example, have either overheard or been involved in an argument about the "right way" to catch a fish, make homemade biscuits, or carve the Thanksgiving turkey. True, almost anyone can bake biscuits using a basic recipe and following a basic set of directions. But if your grandmother taught you a certain way to bake bread, that is the "right way" and you'll probably follow her recipe, regardless of what anyone says.

It's difficult, if not impossible, to imagine carrying on our lives without the benefit of process. Process enables us to identify, establish, and adhere to procedures; and adherence to established procedures enables us to function with a degree of ease and predictability that is unobtainable otherwise.

Process analysis is the step-by-step description and explanation of a systematic procedure. Generally, process analysis takes one of two forms: directional and informative.

A directional process analysis explains how to do something. The reader or listener is informed of how to perform a task or produce a product: examples include "How to Get the Job You Want" and "How to Bake a German Chocolate Cake." Here is a representative directional process analysis:

Example   Removing a stamp from a cover, known to noncollectors as an envelope, is not particularly difficult if you follow the correct procedure. Begin by cutting out the section of the envelope that holds the stamp. It is not necessary to cut the envelope away closely along the edge of the stamp. In fact, most collectors won't cut within more than one-half inch of the stamp in order to lower the risk of accidentally cutting into the stamp itself. Next, soak the stamp on the cover for three to five minutes in about a half-inch of water in a cup. Don't soak the stamp longer than is necessary to remove it from the cover. When it has soaked for a sufficient period of time, you will be able to slide the stamp off the cover by pressing on it gently with your thumb. Once it's off the cover, allow it to dry at room temperature. You may want to dry it under pressure, such as a book, to ensure that it dries smoothly and free of wrinkles. If you do this, be sure to use clean, white blotter paper on each side of the stamp to protect its coloration. Once dry, the stamp is ready to mount.

An informative process analysis describes how something is or was done. The reader or listener is told how something is or was accomplished or attained; examples include "How Glass Is Made" and "How the Oceans Were Formed." Here is a representative informative process analysis:

Example   For most of human history, people have been enthralled, mystified, perplexed, and intrigued by the phenomenon known as fire. Only recently, relatively speaking, have scientists come to understand the process by which fire is produced. This process, of course, is referred to as *combustion* and takes place every time the criteria for the process are met. To begin with, there are three essential components of the process. These are fuel, air, and heat. Secondly, these three components must exist in proper relationship to each other and in appropriate quantities. When they so exist, combustion takes place.

JOURNAL SUGGESTIONS

Reflect for a moment on processes that are important in your life. We all breathe, for example, which is a rather complicated and essential process for sustaining life. We also engage in and benefit from other important processes. If you prepare meals, you follow specific processes called *recipes* for all of the dishes you cook.

Over the next few days, focus your journal writing on analyzing and describing some specific processes. Begin by selecting a simple "how to" process that you perform frequently. Write about this process in your journal. As you do so, remember that you want to make your analysis of the process clear, logical, and detailed.

Selecting topics for these journal entries should not be difficult. Just remember to write about processes with which you are familiar. You might, for example, detail the process for one or more of the following:

- Buying an airline ticket
- Making a hotel reservation
- Opening a bottle of champagne
- Relaxing after a tiring day
- Preparing your favorite dish
- Dribbling a basketball
- Buying a present for someone special
- Doing something else that is important to you

When you begin to work on the writing assignment at the end of this chapter, remember to review these journal entries. You may find a topic and/or ideas that you can develop into an essay for this writing assignment.

The following journal entry was written in response to this journal suggestion.

Example   MONDAY, 14TH

Right now, I wish I knew more about the process of filling out income tax forms. What a dull way to spend time! I'd much rather go skiing again this weekend instead of sitting at my desk going through medical bills and phone bills that are a year old. Skiing is so much fun. I never knew it would be so much fun. All these years, I didn't think I would like it at all. I just wish I was better at it. Maybe I can write about learning to ski. Ski . . . me . . . Ski . . .

Anyway, I'm maybe going to write about that. How to ski. Who knows—maybe if I write it down *logically*, I can remember it better and I won't look so clumsy on the slopes next Wednesday.

Well, in the first place, I've only skied about three times. So I still don't know much about it—except that I love it! But I know that the first thing to do is to get ready. Be well equipped with a ski bib, boots, gloves, poles, skis, and chapstick. If the sun is really bright, take sun block. To put on your skis, you must first have your boots on and fastened. Put the toe of one boot into the front part of the ski opening (I guess that's what you call it). Then press down the heel of your boot into the ski. This locks your foot into place. Do the same with the other foot.

When you get to the top of the slope, you should watch others for a few minutes to get the basic idea. Hold your poles firmly and push off . . . As you're going down the mountain, you lean from side to side in order to turn. Whatever side you lean on turns you in the opposite direction. Some people use snow plowing as a means for stopping or slowing down. This is done by pointing the tops of your skis inward— but not too much! or the skis will cross each other and you'll bust! Lean forward and bend your knees as you go down the mountain. I just wish I could remember and do all these things together the next time I get to ski.

GUIDELINES

Writing in the process analysis rhetorical pattern entails following some rather specific guidelines. Adherence to these guidelines will ensure that the analyses you develop will be accurate, logical, and effective. Using the following guidelines will enable you to write more easily in the process analysis rhetorical pattern:

■ Identify and restrict your topic.

■ Assume, unless you know otherwise, that your reader has little (if any) understanding of the process you are describing.

■ Determine what you know about the process you have chosen to write about.

■ Identify the supporting information associated with each major step of the process.

■ Organize the major steps of the process in performance and/or chronological order.

■ Develop either a general thesis statement or a focused thesis statement for your process analysis essay.

TOPIC

Carefully selecting and adequately restricting a topic for process writing are very important. Keep the following advice in mind as you determine what you will write about:

■ If possible, select a topic that you know something about.

■ If possible, select a topic that you have learned about at least partly through personal experience.

■ Narrow the topic to the point where you can write about all the essential steps of the process in sufficient detail.

PRACTICE   Review the following topics for process analysis essays. Notice that these topics are too broad to be covered in a single, short essay. Restrict and narrow each topic so that it could adequately be written about in a short essay. Write the revised topic in the space provided. After you complete this exercise, discuss your revised topics with a classmate. Is each revised topic now restricted enough to be a suitable topic for a short essay? Further revise any topics that need more restrictions. We begin with an example:

Example   *Topic:*   How to Make Good Grades

Restricted topic: How to Study for Tests

1.   *Topic:*   Guidelines for Parenting
        Restricted topic:

_____

_____

2. *Topic:* Basketball Made Easy
Restricted topic:

_____

_____

3. *Topic:* How to Grow Vegetables
Restricted topic:

_____

_____

4. *Topic:* How to Get a Job
Restricted topic:

_____

_____

5. *Topic:* How to Make Extra Money
Restricted topic:

_____

_____

6. *Topic:* How to Be Healthy
Restricted topic:

_____

_____

7. *Topic:* Preparing Thanksgiving Dinner
Restricted topic:

_____

_____

8. *Topic:* How to Use a Computer
Restricted topic:

_____

_____

9.   *Topic:*   Simple Steps for Breaking Bad Habits
        Restricted topic:

_____

_____

10.   *Topic:*   How a House Is Built
        Restricted topic:

_____

_____

SUPPORT

After you have restricted your topic, your next step in writing the process analysis essay is to gather information in support of the topic. As you gather information, assume that your reader knows little if anything about the process you are explaining. You must be sure to include minor details and specifics, since you can't assume that such material is unneeded by your reader.

Most parents of young children have experienced the frustration of trying to assemble a child's toy, such as a bicycle or playhouse, with poor instructions as their only guide. Such instructions usually go something like this: "Using pliers, attach Part A to Part C at Tab B." Hours later, it becomes obvious that the instructions simply left out the fact that the assembler was supposed to attach Part A to Part B before attaching it to Part C.

As the above example suggests, adequate support and clarity are crucial in process analysis writing, whether the writing is a simple set of instructions or a lengthy essay. We've all had the experience of attempting to follow directions only to find that some vital information has been omitted. Perhaps the author assumed that we knew something we didn't or perhaps he or she just forgot to include it. Regardless, omission of details—even seemingly minor ones—can make it difficult or even impossible to understand a particular process.

There are two sources of information for process analysis essays. The first and more important of these is your own knowledge of the subject. It is essential to assess your knowledge of the subject at this point in writing the process analysis essay. One way to do this is to use the prewriting technique called *inventory.* Allow yourself a specified amount of time during which to complete this activity (three minutes is probably sufficient). During the timed period, write down in succinct, abbreviated form every bit of information that you can think of about the topic. This will provide you with an inventory of your knowledge of the subject and a working basis for organizing and writing the essay.

The second source of information for writing process analysis essays is external authorities. These might include books, other people, magazines, manuals, and video cassettes. Use these sources to fill in the gaps in your own knowledge of the subject, based on the recorded results of the inventory. Perhaps, for example, you're writing about how to roast a turkey. You recorded in the inventory that it should bake for fifteen minutes per pound. However, you cannot remember the temperature setting for the oven. Now is the time to check a cookbook and note the proper temperature setting. Then add this information to the inventory.

Once you have assessed your knowledge of the subject and filled in any gaps by consulting outside sources, you're ready to begin the next part of writing a process analysis essay.

ORGANIZATION

A process analysis essay is usually organized according to the major steps of the process being described. If, for example, you're writing about how to bake a German chocolate cake, you might organize the essay around these major steps of this process:

1. Assemble the ingredients and the utensils.

2. Mix the ingredients.

3. Bake.

This essay, then, identifies three major steps in the process of baking a German chocolate cake. These three steps are the organizational framework of the essay.

Perhaps the easiest and most effective way to identify the major steps of a process is to review and analyze the information contained in the completed inventory. As you review this information, try to group or categorize the various facts included in the list. If you do this carefully, you will soon find yourself dealing with information rather than isolated facts. Gradually, the information contained in the list will be distributed into two, three, or more major categories or steps. These steps can then serve as the organizational scheme for the essay.

PRACTICE   Here are some simple, routine process-oriented activities. Working with a small group of classmates, select two of these and make a list of the steps necessary for accomplishing each activity. When you complete the list of steps, review them to make sure that they are in the proper order for completion. If some steps seem out of order, reorganize them into their proper order. We begin with an example:

Example

Activity   Washing a Car

Steps   1. Assemble implements, including hose, nozzle, bucket, brush, cloths, detergent, and tire cleaner.

2. Prepare wash water.

3. Rinse car.

4. Scrub car, starting at the top.

5. Rinse frequently.

6. Soak tires with cleaner; then scrub and rinse.

7. Wipe car dry.

1.   *Activity:*   Washing Dishes
         Steps:

_____

_____

_____

_____

_____

_____

2.   *Activity:*   Birdwatching
         Steps:

_____

_____

_____

_____

_____

_____

_____

3. *Activity:*   Studying for a Test
Steps:

_____

_____

_____

_____

_____

_____

4. *Activity:*   Proofreading a Paper You Have Written
Steps:

_____

_____

_____

_____

5. *Activity:*   Painting a Room
   Steps:

   _____

   _____

   _____

   _____

   _____

6. *Activity:*   Making a Grilled Cheese Sandwich
   Steps:

   _____

   _____

   _____

   _____

   _____

   _____

7. *Activity:*   Washing Your Hair
   Steps:

   _____

   _____

   _____

   _____

   _____

8.   *Activity:*   How to Relax
      Steps:

_____

_____

_____

_____

_____

9.   *Activity:*   Making Coffee
      Steps:

_____

_____

_____

_____

_____

10.   *Activity:*   Writing a Process Analysis Essay
      Steps:

_____

_____

_____

_____

_____

THESIS

A process analysis essay, whether informative or directional, may contain either a general thesis statement or a focused thesis statement. A general thesis statement for a process analysis essay does not identify the major steps in the process that will be discussed in the essay. Instead, it simply informs the reader of the overall process that will be discussed in the body of the essay.

The following general thesis statement is from a process essay on how to study for a test:

Example   Preparing for a test is as easy as following these simple steps.

Unlike a general thesis statement, a focused thesis statement for a process analysis essay does not identify the steps in the process that will be discussed in the body of the essay. The following focused thesis statement is from an essay on how to study for a test:

Example   Preparing for a test should include a review of class notes, a quick scan of assigned reading, and the use of flash cards to ensure recall of essential facts, definitions, and concepts.

Again, notice that either of these types of thesis statements, general or focused, will work well for process analysis essays.

PRACTICE   Working on your own or with a classmate, develop both general and focused thesis statements for process anlaysis essays on the following topics. Write your general and focused thesis statements in the space provided.

1. *Topic:* Answering an Essay Question on an Exam
General thesis statement:

_____

_____

Focused thesis statement:

_____

_____

_____

2. *Topic:* How to Use Coupons to Lower Your Grocery Bill
General thesis statement:

_____

_____

Focused thesis statement:

_____

_____

_____

3. *Topic:* How to Give a Party
General thesis statement:

_____

_____

Focused thesis statement:

_____

_____

_____

_____

4. *Topic:* How to Conquer a Cold
General thesis statement:

_____

_____

Focused thesis statement:

_____

_____

_____

5. *Topic:*   How Something (such as snow, plywood, aluminum, or cake icing) Is Made
   General thesis statement:

   _____

   _____

   Focused thesis statement:

   _____

   _____

   _____

READINGS

The following readings are student and professional essays. Read them carefully and look for their use of the process analysis guidelines presented in this chapter.

STUDENT ESSAY

HOW TO START AN INTRAVENOUS INFUSION   Judith Heck

Most people are hospitalized for one reason or another at some time in their lives. Certain illnesses, scheduled operations, and medical emergencies are the primary reasons for hospitalizations. During many of these hospitalizations, the doctor will order an intravenous infusion. She will also state the type of fluid she wants to be infused. The nurse will then check the doctor's orders and carry them out. Starting an intravenous infusion, when ordered, consists of several steps.

First, the nurse must gather all the necessay equipment before going to the pa-

tient's room. She must get a bag or bottle of the ordered solution and a box of tubing to run from the bag or bottle at the injection site. She must then insert the tubing into the bag or bottle and prime the line by opening the regulator clamp to allow fluid to run through to the end of the tubing. This will remove any air in the tube so that it does not go into the patient's vein. The air could cause an air embolism that might be fatal if not caught in time. She will then take this setup; an intravenous infusion pole to attach to the end of the bed for hanging the fluids; and a tray con-

HOW TO START AN INTRAVENOUS INFUSION, continued

taining needles, tape, alcohol swabs, antibiotic cream, and tourniquet to the patient's room.

Next, the nurse will explain to the patient the procedure she is going to perform. This is necessary because many people are afraid of the unknown, while others are frightened at being stuck with a needle. She will also explain to the patient why the doctor ordered the intravenous infusion and the effect it will have. She is now ready to begin the most delicate step of the procedure.

The nurse must now inspect the patient's arms and hands to locate a good vein. This is one that can be readily seen. She will then make sure, if at all possible, that the vein is not at an area that has to bend, such as the wrist or the anterior elbow area. The best place to start is with the veins of the hand. She must then choose the appropriate needle for the patient's vein structure and the fluid to be infused. Next, she will apply the tourniquet about halfway up the lower part of the arm. The tourniquet should be tightened only enough to raise the vein but not so tight as to occlude the flow of blood. She will then wipe the vein area from the inside to the outside in a circular motion, using an alcohol swab. The needle is then carefully inserted into the skin. This part of the procedure usually hurts the patient most. The wall of the vein can be felt at this time because of some resistance. With some slight pressure, the needle will pierce the vein. As the needle pierces the vein, some blood will return to the end of the needle. The tourniquet is then removed and the nurse will connect the tubing to the opening and set the flow rate for the infusion. She will then apply some antibiotic cream to the infusion site and tape the needle and tubing into place so that the needle cannot move back out of the vein with movement of the extremity.

From this time on, the nurse must monitor the infusion site frequently for redness and swelling. She must also check the amount of fluid in the bag or bottle so that it does not run dry. An empty air line could cause air embolism. New fluid must be hung before this happens. This completes the process for starting and maintaining an intravenous infusion.

PROFESSIONAL ESSAY

HOW TO COOK DRIED PASTA SO YOU CAN TASTE IT

Corby Kummer

Italian brands of dried pasta, whatever they cost, taste better, I think, than most American ones—they have a clean, slightly nutty flavor and above all a texture that stays firm until you finish eating. Taste and texture make all the difference in pasta,

HOW TO COOK DRIED PASTA SO YOU CAN TASTE IT, continued

but judging by what most American restaurants and home cooks serve, they are unknown attributes of pasta in this country. Many people are surprised to learn that dried pasta can have any flavor at all, let alone stay firm and taste lighter than what they are used to. I recently advised a woman who regularly served truffled omelets and caviar and blinis to her children while they were growing up to buy an imported Italian pasta, something she had never done. The brand she found at her supermarket was Spigadoro, a commonly distributed import whose quality Italians rank solidly in the middle. "I was so knocked out by the difference that I kept cooking a little more until the box was gone in one night," she reported.

Italians criticize Americans for adding soft flour to pasta, and with reason. One American manufacturer boasts in block letters on its packages, "SEMOLINA *plus* FARINA" (farina is a blend of common wheat flours). This, as one importer of Italian pasta put it, is like boasting about mixing diamonds with rocks. Pasta made with common flour, which is less expensive than semolina, leaves the cooking water white with starch, and quickly turns soggy on the plate, even if it is drained when it seems to be what Italians call *al dente*—literally "to the tooth." Italian manufacturers almost never add common flour to pasta: the practice is illegal and a company must go out of its way to cheat. American manufacturers can add flour or not as they please, because there are no laws restricting them to semolina. Even so, many American manufacturers, such as Prince, Ronzoni, and Hershey Foods, which markets six brands of pasta, use only semolina.

You can't tell from looking through the cellophane much about how dried pasta will cook or taste. It should have an even buff color; gray could mean the presence of soft flour. Don't be alarmed if you see tiny black spots. Semolina is milled much more coarsely than ordinary flour, and flecks of bran usually show. A finely pitted, dull surface is far preferable to a glossy one. It suggests that the pasta was made with a bronze die and will hold sauce better.

The regions in Italy famous for the quality of their dried pasta are Campania and Abruzzo. Two of the best brands, Del Verde and De Cecco, are made in Abruzzo. Fortunately, these are also the two most widely distributed imports. Other good brands include La Molisana (from Molise), Braibanti, most of which is marketed as Sidari (from Emilia), and Colavita (from Molise). Gerardo di Nola, made in Campania, is a cult brand that I've never been able to find. You should buy or order Martelli at least once, if only to have a standard against which to judge other dried pasta. If you can't find any of these brands locally, try any Italian brand available. Besides Spigadoro, made in Umbria, a widely distributed standard Italian brand is Barilla, made in Emilia; Barilla is the world's largest pasta manufacturer.

Gauging portion sizes trips up nearly everyone. The standard portion in Italy, and the size recommended on packages, is two ounces. This is fine for the first course to cut the appetite without killing it. I find three ounces an ideal portion for a main course, but hungry people might prefer four. I use a scale, because I cannot judge by eye, and the trick of putting my thumb to my index finger doesn't work when measuring short pasta. Neither does using

HOW TO COOK DRIED PASTA SO YOU CAN TASTE IT, continued

liquid measures. A half-cup of farfalle, or bows (*farfalle* means "butterflies"), is not the same as a half cup of ziti, or ridged tubes (*ziti* means "bridegrooms" in southern Italy; the shape was traditionally served at weddings in Sicily). "Portion measurers" for long pasta, usually flat wooden oblongs with holes, are useless, because the size of the portion will vary with the thickness of the pasta.

To cook pasta you need a lot of water, so that it will come back to the boil soon after you add the pasta, so that there will be more than enough water for the pasta to absorb (pasta usually doubles in volume when cooked), and so that the pasta will keep moving as it cooks and not stick together. Start with a gallon for the first quarter pound and add one quart for each additional quarter pound. When the water reaches a rolling boil, add a tablespoon of salt for each gallon of water, which will season the pasta (you can add lemon juice if you prefer to avoid salt). Cooks differ on whether or not to add oil to the water to prevent sticking. Italians think that it makes pasta absorb water unevenly. Harold McGee, the author of *On Food and Cooking: The Science and Lore of the Kitchen*, finds this unlikely, and also thinks that oil won't keep pasta from sticking unless you add it to cooked pasta. But he does say that oil reduces the foam on the surface and helps prevent water from boiling over. Barbara Kafka suggests in her book *Food for Friends* that you put several tablespoons of oil into the pot just before you drain it; this will discourage sticking without making the pasta so oily that the sauce slides off.

Add the pasta all at once. Bend long pasta into water with a two-pronged cook-ing fork or a wooden spoon. Separate any kind of pasta, so that it doesn't stick, before the water comes back to the boil, and keep it moving as it cooks. The water should be at an active, if not passionate, boil. Don't leave the room.

(Italians say never break the long pasta as you add it—you should learn to eat it like a man. This means not twirling it against a spoon, a practice fit only for milquetoasts, but instead securing two or three strands with a fork and twirling them against the edge of a plate. This is accomplished more easily in the wide, shallow soup bowls in which Italians serve pasta, but it is quite possible to do on a flat plate. There will be dangling ends. Accept them.)

Start timing when the water comes back to the boil. Test after three minutes for dried pasta with egg or five minutes for dried pasta without. The only sure way to test is by biting into a piece. If you wait until it sticks when thrown against a wall—a custom I had always assumed was Italian but can find no Italian to own up to—it will probably be overdone. Breaking a piece apart to examine the interior is also chancy. Pasta is done when the color is uniform, but since it continues to cook after you drain it, you need to know exactly how tiny a dot of uncooked dough should remain in the center before you drain. I have never seen an Italian cook hold a piece of broken pasta up to the light. Everyone tastes the pasta he is making until it is slightly firmer than he wants it to be, and then drains it.

Rather than drain pasta in a colander, Italian cooks usually lift it out of the pot with tongs or a strainer. In this way the pasta stays wet, so that as it finishes cooking out of the pot, it has water to absorb;

HOW TO COOK DRIED PASTA SO YOU CAN TASTE IT, continued

otherwise it would stick to itself immediately. If you intend to make pasta with any frequency, look for a pot with a colander insert, which will enable you to lift all the pasta out at once. Ignore instructions to add cold water to the pot to stop cooking, because the water left on the drained pasta won't be hot enough to evaporate and will make the pasta slimy. For the same reason it is a bad idea to rinse the pasta after it is cooked—a cardinal sin in Italy. If you use a colander, be sure it is solidly placed in the sink, that there is nothing in the sink that you don't want bobbing near your pasta, and that you take your glasses off first.

After cooking, good pasta should look moist rather than gummy. All the pieces should be separate and have a uniform texture, but they won't if you undercook the pasta. The water should be clear. If it is floury, there was ordinary flour in the pasta. Save some of the water the pasta was cooked in. Even if it looks clear it will have some starch, which can be useful for thinning a sauce and binding it at the same time. The cooking water can also be useful for adding to the pasta as it finishes cooking, in case you drained too much.

However you drain cooked pasta, transfer it right away to a warm bowl. The plates should be hot too. Now is the time to add some oil or butter if you're afraid that the pasta will be sticky. This is also the time to add hard grated cheese if you are using it, because it will melt evenly. Don't use too much—a teaspoon or two per portion should suffice—and think twice before using any. Cheese is contraindicated for many sauces. When it is used, it is as a seasoning. The best is Parmesan, and the best Parmesan is Parmigiano-Reggiano. Some cheese stores try to pass off Argentine cheese as the real thing, but it is salty and flat by comparison with the nutty, dry, mellow original. (American Parmesan does not bear even a passing resemblance to Italian.) Look for "Parmigiano-Reggiano" on the rind: it is stamped on every square centimeter. Buy small pieces with rind on—they will keep better—and grate only as much as you need. It is difficult to find a good version of the other common grating cheese—pecorino Romano, which is made of sheep's milk.

Add about two thirds of the sauce you intend to use and gently stir it in. Don't lift the pasta two feet over the bowl as you stir, or it will cool off. And don't add too much sauce. It should just coat the pasta, with no excess at all. Pasta doused in sauce revolts Italians, who when they see it suddenly understand why Americans say that pasta is fattening. (A recipe for baked ziti in *Pastahhh,* an NPA newsletter, calls for one and a half pounds of meat, one pound of ricotta, a half pound of mozzarella, and two cups of white sauce for one pound of pasta—American abundance carried to a perilous extreme.) Two tablespoons of a thick sauce or a quarter to a third of a cup of liquid one should suffice per portion. Put the last spoonful on top of each serving, so that the diner can see what the sauce looks like and have something to do.

Another way to mix sauce and pasta is to drain the pasta when it is harder than *al dente* and heat it for no more than a minute with the sauce. This is helpful for fish-and-wine or stock-based sauces, which do not coat pasta readily: the pasta will absorb sauce as it finishes cooking.

Don't waste a second trying to make the plate look any better. Pasta dishes should be served immediately and thus do not

HOW TO COOK DRIED PASTA SO YOU CAN TASTE IT, continued

lend themselves to presentation, which may be one reason why the French came only recently to pasta. For example, when you see a photograph like one that appears in *The Joy of Pasta*, showing spaghetti surrounded by a neat circle of carrot batons and slices of artichoke sprinkled with red pepper flakes, you can be sure that the dish tasted terrible. It took too long to arrange.

Gourmet, which recently ran a picture of a plate of homemade pasta on its cover for a story called "Pasta à la Française," resorted to pretty china and carefully strewn sprigs of dill to make it look nice. You need never worry about serving a beautifully composed plate of pasta—only about being served one.

Rhetoric

1. The introductory paragraphs of "How to Cook Dried Pasta So You Can Taste It" contain considerable information about the ingredients and processes used in the manufacture of dried pasta. Is this background information necessary or even helpful for understanding the author's instructions for cooking dried pasta? Explain your answer.

2. The author uses an anecdote in the introductory paragraph of the essay. What, if any, contribution does this personal story make to the rest of the essay?

3. Based on a close reading of the essay, list the major steps involved in cooking pasta.

Ideas

1. Obviously, the author prefers Italian pasta to American pasta. Do you think he made a solid case for his preference?

2. Is there any food item you feel strongly enough about to discuss as Kummer does pasta? If so, what and why?

3. Pretend that Kummer has agreed to speak to the International Club at your school about how to cook pasta. You have been asked to introduce him, and this essay is your only source of information about him. Prepare a brief introduction of Kummer.

Response

1. Based on the major steps for cooking dried pasta presented in the essay, write a cookbook-style recipe for cooking pasta.

2. Select some food item, preferably a simple one such as pasta, and write an essay telling how to prepare it. Then ask a classmate to turn the steps of your recipe essay into a cookbook-style recipe.

PROFESSIONAL ESSAY

ODE TO MAKEUP

Irene Egan

Some people like to make a statement with a naked face. Not me. I *love* makeup. I like to line it up and look at it. I like to smell it. Once in a while, I even like to taste it (remember Peppermint Pink lipstick?). I've been wearing makeup for almost as long as I can remember, and I'll be wearing it when that old bronze lid closes over my carefully made-up face. My passion for paint is rooted in my having been born with your basic, you-seen-one-you-seen-'em-all kind of face, which is fine, except that I have never been content with your basic anything. I wanted to look like me. Only, jazzier. Thank God, whoever She is, for peach powder blush and cover sticks of every shade.

David, who shares my life but not my Madeira Wine lipstick, tells me I look the same, with or without makeup. "Okay," I tell him, "then I'll wear it, if it's all the same to you." He sighs real loud and shakes his head, because he can't possibly understand. Man's best friend may be Dog; woman's is, without a doubt, Paint.

I get up two hours before I have to be at school every morning (at 6 A.M., the only person I would wish my face on is Norman Mailer), just so I'll have plenty of time to put on my face. Applying makeup is like meditating. My mantra just happens to be "Maybelline." I like to do it real slow. I line up all my stuff on the kitchen table, just so. I prop my broken mirror against the fruit basket that has everything but fruit in it, lay out my cotton balls, sponges, wands, and brushes, and then I

put the coffee on. Four cups of Colombian Supremo is part of my ritual. One cup to wake up, two cups to makeup, and the last to get me out the door.

I start with astringent. Which at 13 bucks a bottle and rising, I use just the teeniest bit of on a cotton ball. When my face feels like it's been dunked into a bucket of ice cubes, I know it's time to move on to my oil-free foundation. I have Irish-white skin, so I use Ivory foundation. The saleslady with the silverflash hair and the Max Factor eyes always tries to talk me into the Beige or Barely Rose, because she has to order the Ivory special. No way, I tell her, it's Ivory or zip. I can tell she'd like to put out my eye when I say that. But hey—an orange line on the jawbone hasn't been in vogue since I was 15, and I'm not about to start any born-again trends.

A sea sponge gave up its life for me to apply my foundation. And I am truly grateful, because nothing beats a real sponge for the even application of makeup. With foundation smeared carefully over every inch of my face, including lips, I look like one of the undead. A hasty brush of blush on both cheeks brings the life back to my face. Then I painstakingly apply lip liner with a wee sable brush that cost about 25 bucks. The lipstick I use for this purpose has been in my possession for so long, it no longer stands at attention. The good news is, the more I dig, the more there seems to be. This is fortunate because I have no idea what brand or even what shade it is—the little round gizmo

SOURCE: From *Ms.* magazine.

ODE TO MAKEUP, continued

with that information has long since peeled off the bottom of the tube.

With lip liner in place, I fill in with my frosty Madeira Wine lipstick, then practice pouting my lips like I'm about to be soul-kissed by Richard Gere. I always wonder what Sister Regina would say if she could see me. Girls who wore makeup in Sister's class were condemned as "bold, brazen baggage." Those were the days when I wore pancake makeup that turned orange by noon, and pale, pink lipstick that made my mouth look like it had been chalked on. I guess I was just about the boldest, most brazen baggage that Sister and St. Mary's ever saw. In a Catholic school so rigid it required all girls to wear uniforms that pressed us breastless, my first makeup ritual was born in retaliation.

In the beginning there was light. And the light was good—I saw to that by taking the shade off my bedroom lamp. I didn't want to miss any "flaws" that needed covering. At 14, my flaws were few, and mostly imagined. But since I hadn't been born airbrushed, I thought I had a million of them. Besides, I wanted to wear makeup! "C'mon, Ma," I pleaded, "I *gotta* wear makeup—if I don't I'll be lucky if Godzilla asks me out."

Saturday night was slated for new makeup tryouts. With a stack of Major Lance albums hovering over the turntable, I turned to the task of examining and logging my new treasures. While Major sang, I glued eyelashes on and tried my hand at Cleopatra eyes. The kid from the suburbs ceased to exist. In her place, a wanton woman danced, cast sexy looks at strange men, and made her catlike way across the smoky dance floor of a sleazy bistro. Men fell at her feet like tenpins; the world was her willing oyster. On Saturday night the world was mine. On Sunday morning I was just another naked-faced Irish kid on her way to Mass.

Over the years, the ritual has changed. Sometime during the 1970s, I traded Major Lance for Ravel, and gave up false eyelashes entirely. I stopped wearing pancake makeup, and discovered the ecstasy of whipped-to-a-frenzy foundation that went on like beige shaving cream, with a two-week supply costing 30 bucks or your firstborn child, whichever you could come up with first. Cost, of course, has never been an object—can anyone put a price on her best friend?

Makeup has always been there for me. When Freddie LaBel broke up with me in the eighth grade, I put on my face four times in a row, and cried it off every time. When I was fired from my first writing job two years ago, I decided that the sleep I lost wondering where I was going to find another job would be my secret. So the first thing I did was buy a tube of Estée Lauder under-the-eye-concealer, and not a dark shadow showed.

Enough nostalgia; back to my morning ritual. The last thing I put on is my eye makeup. Without it, I lool like a fetal pig. David thinks he has seen me without all my makeup. He's wrong. I wouldn't be caught, awake or asleep (or dead even), without eyeliner. I use a dark-brown eyeliner pencil first. Anyone who has ever used one knows how tricky this can be. The pencil can't be dull. However, when sharpened properly and dragged across the eye without care, the pain is second

ODE TO MAKEUP, continued

only to giving birth the Lamaze way. To avoid pain, the trick is to apply it softly, with featherlike strokes. Once over that hump, eye shadow in shades of pink and brown follow, and finally, the blackest mascara money can buy. And then I sit back and admire my handiwork. Am I beautiful? No, not really. But, boy, do I have a good time.

Rhetoric

1. With ample supporting detail, Egan wittily convinces her readers of her passion for makeup. List the five supporting details that you found most entertaining and convincing.

2. Locate the transitional words, phrases, and sentences that Egan uses to describe the process she follows each morning when putting on makeup. Make a list of these transitions.

Ideas

1. Certain parts of the process of applying makeup are described in more detail than are others. For example, the last paragraph contains a long description of applying eye makeup. Why do you think Egan lengthened that particular part of the explanation of the process? What is the tone of this section as compared to the tone of the preceding paragraph?

2. Several times, Egan makes the point that she is not beautiful, but makeup makes her feel beautiful. Find two examples of this in the essay.

Response

1. How does Egan's use of nostalgia support her declaration of her passion for makeup? Does the use of nostalgic recollection enhance or detract from the description of the process of applying makeup? In a paragraph, analyze the function of nostalgia as Egan uses it.

2. Writing about something for which you have a strong passion is often easier than writing about subjects that don't matter to you. In an essay, write about a passion you have. This could be a relatively light, trivial subject such as that of Egan's essay; a political or social issue; or a hobby you enjoy. Use adequate supporting details to convince your reader both that you are knowledgeable about your subject and that you feel strongly about it.

PROFESSIONAL ESSAY

THE MAKER'S EYE: REVISING YOUR OWN MANUSCRIPTS

Donald M. Murray

When students complete a first draft, they consider the job of writing done—and their teachers too often agree. When professional writers complete a first draft, they usually feel that they are at the start of the writing process. When a draft is completed, the job of writing can begin.

That difference in attitude is the difference between amateur and professional, inexperience and experience, journeyman and craftsman. Peter F. Drucker, the prolific business writer, calls his first draft "the zero draft"—after that he can start counting. Most writers share the feeling that the first draft, and all of those which follow, are opportunities to discover what they have to say and how best they can say it.

To produce a progression of drafts, each of which says more and says it more clearly, the writer has to develop a special kind of reading skill. In school we are taught to decode what appears on the page as finished writing. Writers, however, face a different category of possibility and responsibility when they read their own drafts. To them the words on the page are never finished. Each can be changed and rearranged, can set off a chain reaction of confusion or clarified meaning. This is a different kind of reading, which is possibly more difficult and certainly more exciting.

Writers must learn to be their own best enemy. They must accept the criticism of others and be suspicious of it; they must accept the praise of others and be even more suspicious of it. Writers cannot depend on others. They must detach themselves from their own pages so that they can apply both their caring and their craft to their own work.

Such detachment is not easy. Science fiction writer Ray Bradbury supposedly puts each manuscript away for a year to the day and then rereads it as a stranger. Not many writers have the discipline or the time to do this. We must read when our judgment may be at its worst, when we are close to the euphoric moment of creation.

Then the writer, counsels novelist Nancy Hale, "should be critical of everything that seems to him most delightful in his style. He should excise what he most admires, because he wouldn't thus admire it if he weren't . . . in a sense protecting it from criticism." John Ciardi, the poet, adds, "The last act of the writing must be to become one's own reader. It is, I suppose a schizophrenic process, to begin passionately and to end critically, to begin hot and to end cold; and, more important, to be passion-hot and critic-cold at the same time."

Most people think that the principal problem is that writers are too proud of what they have written. Actually, a greater problem for most professional writers is one shared by the majority of students. They are overly critical, think

THE MAKER'S EYE: REVISING YOUR OWN MANUSCRIPTS, continued

everything is dreadful, tear up page after page, never complete a draft, see the task as hopeless.

The writer must learn to read critically but constructively, to cut what is bad, to reveal what is good. Eleanor Estes, the children's book author, explains: "The writer must survey his work critically, coolly, as though he were a stranger to it. He must be willing to prune, expertly and hard-heartedly. At the end of each revision, a manuscript may look . . . worked over, torn apart, pinned together, added to, deleted from, words changed and words changed back. Yet the book must maintain its original freshness and spontaneity."

Most readers underestimate the amount of rewriting it usually takes to produce spontaneous reading. This is a great disadvantage to the student writer, who sees only a finished product and never watches the craftsman who takes the necessary step back, studies the work carefully, returns to the task, steps back, returns, steps back, again and again. Anthony Burgess, one of the most prolific writers in the English-speaking world, admits, "I might revise a page twenty times." Roald Dahl, the popular children's writer, states, "By the time I'm nearing the end of the story, the first part will have been reread and altered and corrected at least 150 times. . . . Good writing is essentially rewriting. I am positive of this."

Rewriting isn't virtuous. It isn't something that ought to be done. It is simply something that most writers find they have to do to discover what they have to say and how to say it. It is a condition of the writer's life.

There are, however, a few writers who do little formal rewriting, primarily because they have the capacity and experience to create and review a large number of invisible drafts in their minds before they approach the page. And some writers slowly produce finished pages, performing all the tasks of revision simultaneously, page by page, rather than draft by draft. But it is still possible to see the sequence followed by most writers most of the time in rereading their own work.

Most writers scan their drafts first, reading as quickly as possible to catch the larger problems of subject and form, then move in closer and closer as they read and write, reread and rewrite.

The first thing writers look for in their drafts is *information*. They know that a good piece of writing is built from specific, accurate, and interesting information. The writer must have an abundance of information from which to construct a readable piece of writing.

Next writers look for *meaning* in the information. The specifics must build to a pattern of significance. Each piece of specific information must carry the reader toward meaning.

Writers reading their own drafts are aware of *audience*. They put themselves in the reader's situation and make sure that they deliver information which a reader wants to know or needs to know in a manner which is easily digested. Writers try to be sure that they anticipate and answer the questions a critical reader will ask when reading the piece of writing.

Writers make sure that the *form* is appropriate to the subject and the audience. Form, or genre, is the vehicle which car-

THE MAKER'S EYE: REVISING YOUR OWN MANUSCRIPTS, continued

ries meaning to the reader, but form cannot be selected until the writer has adequate information to discover its significance and an audience which needs or wants that meaning.

Once writers are sure the form is appropriate, they must then look at the *structure*, the order of what they have written. Good writing is built on a solid framework of logic, argument, narrative, or motivation which runs through the entire piece of writing and holds it together. This is the time when many writers find it most effective to outline as a way of visualizing the hidden spine by which the piece of writing is supported.

The element on which writers may spend a majority of their time is *development*. Each section of a piece of writing must be adequately developed. It must give readers enough information so that they are satisfied. How much information is enough? That's as difficult as asking how much garlic belongs in a salad. It must be done to taste, but most beginning writers underdevelop, underestimating the reader's hunger for information.

As writers solve development problems, they often have to consider questions of *dimension*. There must be a pleasing and effective proportion among all the parts of the piece of writing. There is a continual process of subtracting and adding to keep the piece of writing in balance.

Finally, writers have to listen to their own voices. *Voice* is the force which drives a piece of writing forward. It is an expression of the writer's authority and concern. It is what is between the words on the page, what glues the piece of writing together. A good piece of writing is always marked by a consistent, individual voice.

As writers read and reread, write and rewrite, they move closer and closer to the page until they are doing line-by-line editing. Writers read their own pages with infinite care. Each sentence, each line, each clause, each phrase, each word, each mark of punctuation, each section of white space between the type has to contribute to the clarification of meaning.

Slowly the writer moves from word to word, looking through language to see the subject. As a word is changed, cut, or added, as a construction is rearranged, all the words used before that moment and all those that follow that moment must be considered and reconsidered.

Writers often read aloud at this stage of the editing process, muttering or whispering to themselves, calling on the ear's experience with language. Does this sound right—or that? Writers edit, shifting back and forth from eye to page to ear to page. I find I must do this careful editing in short runs, no more than fifteen or twenty minutes at a stretch, or I become too kind with myself. I begin to see what I hope is on the page, not what actually is on the page.

This sounds tedious if you haven't done it, but actually it is fun. Making something right is immensely satisfying, for writers begin to learn what they are writing about by writing. Language leads them to meaning, and there is the joy of discovery, of understanding, of making meaning clear as the writer employs the technical skills of language.

Words have double meanings, even triple and quadruple meanings. Each word has its own potential for connotation and denotation. And when writers rub one word against the other, they are often rewarded

THE MAKER'S EYE: REVISING YOUR OWN MANUSCRIPTS, continued

with a sudden insight, and unexpected clarification.

The maker's eye moves back and forth from word to phrase to sentence to paragraph to sentence to phrase to word. The maker's eye sees the need for variety and balance, for a firmer structure, for a more appropriate form. It peers into the interior of the paragraph, looking for coherence, unity, and emphasis, which make meaning clear.

I learned something about this process when my first bifocals were prescribed. I had ordered a larger section of the reading portion of the glass because of my work, but even so, I could not contain my eyes within this new limit of vision. And I still find myself taking off my glasses and bending my nose towards the page, for my eyes unconsciously flick back and forth across the page, back to another page, forward to still another, as I try to see each evolving line in relation to every other line.

When does this process end? Most writers agree with the great Russian writer Tolstoy, who said, "I scarcely ever reread my published writings, if by chance I come across a page, it always strikes me: all this must be rewritten; this is how I should have written it."

The maker's eye is never satisfied, for each word has the potential to ignite new meaning. This article has been twice written all the way through the writing process, and it was published four years ago. Now it is to be republished in a book. The editors make a few small suggestions, and then I read it with my maker's eye. Now it has been re-edited, re-revised, re-read, re-re-edited, for each piece of writing to the writer is full of potential and alternatives.

A piece of writing is never finished. It is delivered to a deadline, torn out of the typewriter on demand, sent off with a sense of accomplishment and shame and pride and frustration. If only there were a couple more days, time for just another run at it, perhaps then . . .

Rhetoric

1. What is Murray's purpose in writing "The Maker's Eye?" Is it primarily to inform, persuade, or entertain? Explain your response.

2. In which paragraph does Murray actually begin his explanation of the revision process?

3. How many steps are given? List these steps.

Ideas

1. Murray ends his essay in the middle of a sentence. Why is this an effective way to end this essay?

2. Murray asserts that both professional and student writers tend to be critical of their writing. Based on your writing experience, do you agree or disagree? How do you feel about your writing when it is ready to be submitted to the instructor (confident, optimistic,

pessimistic, hopeful, doubtful)? How do you feel when that writing is returned to you?

3. Murray uses several terms and phrases that may or may not be familiar to you to explain the writing process. Each term is explained in the text. Find and explain the following terms:

zero draft
detachment from your writing
audience
form
structure
voice

Response

1. Murray quotes many professional writers and is a professional writer himself. Do you think his views about rewriting apply only to professional writing or should his views apply to student writing as well? In a short essay, state and defend your opinion about student rewriting.

2. Assume the role of a news reporter for your college newspaper. Your assignment is to interview Donald Murray and ask him questions about his essay and about professional writing. Carefully formulate three questions you might ask him. The questions should be created with a general audience in mind—an audience that knows how to write but perhaps knows little about professional writing and rewriting.

3. To be done well, many processes require practice, just as good writing requires rewriting. One can, for example, learn the basics of cabinet making in a classroom; but to be a good cabinetmaker, one must practice the craft. In doing so, a cabinetmaker goes beyond the basics and learns to improve, embellish, and finally perfect the craft. Write an essay in which you describe a process that you know well. Assume that the reader knows the basics of the process. Focus your essay on describing the process as you have improved and enhanced it.

WRITING ASSIGNMENT

You may select a topic for this writing assignment from one of the following lists, or you may develop a topic of your own. Once you have selected a topic, complete one or more of the specified prewriting activities. After sufficient prewriting, write a draft of an essay on the topic you selected. Finally, revise and edit your essay.

General Writing Assignments

- How to buy a house
- How to research your family tree
- Selecting a vocation
- Finding the perfect summer job
- How to maintain healthy relationships
- Preparing for a special event such as a wedding, confirmation, family reunion, or party
- Beginning a hobby (stamp collecting, stargazing, knitting, or the like)

Specific Writing Assignments

- The editor of the local newspaper who knows that you are reasonably accomplished at a particular hobby (such as coin collecting, gun collecting, gardening, beekeeping, hiking, or needlepoint), asks you to write an article for the leisure section of the paper about how to get started in your hobby.
- You and your cousin, who lives in another state, have decided to organize a family reunion. Write a letter to your cousin in which you give your views about how the family get-together should be arranged.

If you decide to develop your own topic, you may want to look through your journal for ideas. What topics that you have addressed in your journal lend themselves to this particular strategy of thinking and communicating? You might also look carefully at the focused journal entries you wrote at the beginning of this chapter. Is one of these topics of interest to you? Is it a topic with which you have some experience? With some revision, could this journal entry become an essay?

Finally, look back through this chapter at some of the exercises you have done. Are any of these topics of interest to you? Have classmates given you ideas for topics? You may want to spend some time discussing topics with classmates to help you discover what you want to write about. Or you may want to do some focused freewriting on the subject of an interesting and suitable topic for this essay.

PREWRITING

After selecting a topic as the subject for a process analysis essay, complete one or more of the following prewriting activities:

- *Brainstorming*—Write the topic you selected at the top of a blank sheet of paper. Then, in a list format, write down all the ideas, words, and phrases that come to mind as you think about the subject. Try to record as many different words or phrases as you can. When you finish, review the list, looking for main ideas and supporting details to use in organizing and writing a process analysis essay.

■ *Looping*–Begin the looping exercise by writing for a set period of time on the topic you chose for your process analysis essay. Write freely, rapidly, and without stopping. Just concentrate on getting your thoughts on paper. After writing for the allotted time, read what you have written, and underline what you believe to be the central or best idea contained in the writing. Then, at the top of a clean sheet of paper, write a sentence that summarizes the dominant idea or statement from your first loop. Then perform another loop for a set period of time—this time writing about the summary statement. Repeat this process until you have developed a central idea that you can use to focus and organize a process analysis essay on the topic you selected.

REVISING

In revising your essay, follow these seven steps:

1. Ask a friend, a roommate, or a writing colleague (or colleagues) to listen to or read your writing and then to comment on what you have written. Are the subject and the purpose of the essay clear? Does the body of the essay make and support points that achieve the purpose of the writing? Do any sentences, passages, or sections of the paper seem either unrelated to or contradictory to the purpose of the writing? In a process analysis essay, the purpose of the essay should be very clear. Are you writing this essay for readers who have some understanding of your topic? Or are you writing it for readers who know nothing about the topic?

2. Check the introduction and thesis statement of the essay. Have you introduced your reader to the process you plan to analyze? Is the topic clearly identified and restricted? Have you used a general thesis statement or a focused thesis statement? Does the introduction need any revision to make it clearer or more interesting?

3. Check the thesis support in the body of the essay. Is the material in the body of the essay organized so that the major steps of the process you are describing are clear? Are the steps of the process organized appropriately in either performance order or chronological order?

4. Check the paragraph support throughout the essay. Is each paragraph well written, with plentiful supporting information for each step of the process?

5. Check for coherence and unity. As a whole, does the essay make sense? Does it contain any irrelevant material? Have you left any gaps in the process you are analyzing that might make the essay hard to follow and understand? As you reread the essay, ask yourself whether you could follow the logic of the process analysis if you were unfamiliar with the process.

6. Check for closure. Is there closure at the end of the essay in either a concluding (or summarizing) paragraph or a concluding sentence?

7. Finally, review the Revision Checklist at the end of Chapter 5. Use the checklist to make sure that you have completed a thorough revision of your essay.

CLASSIFICATION

Classification is the grouping of ideas, objects, events, and people on the basis of a common characteristic or a set of common characteristics. Our ability to classify enables us to make sense out of much of our environment. A simple trip to the grocery store is made easier by the fact that the items for sale there are classified or grouped in particular sections of the store. But even as we classify much of the world around us, we are classified ourselves. For example, all of us have spent many years in educational institutions where we were classified by grade (fourth grade, tenth grade, and so on), based on our age and academic accomplishments.

It's hard to imagine relating to our environment without being able to classify. We often depend on our ability to classify to help us select our friends, choose our vocations, and even decide whom we will marry. We may also use the rhetorical pattern of classification to make sense of more complex, even abstract information and concepts.

For example, if you want to think logically and clearly about the topic "American Wars," you might find the subject very confusing and difficult to comprehend. If you choose to classify the wars America has fought in, however, you have a handle on the subject—or more precisely, a logical way to comprehend and organize this rather extensive body of information. In fact, you might be able to say something seemingly simple about this complex subject, such as, "America, throughout her long history, has fought in only three kinds of wars."

JOURNAL SUGGESTIONS

Grouping things, ideas, and people is something all of us do regularly. For example, Part Two of this textbook is classified according to strategies of thinking you can use in your writing. In fact, the classes you're currently enrolled in are classified according to the subject matter covered in each course. This is why we generally refer to academic courses as *classes*.

Temporarily focus your journal writing on the strategy of thinking called *classification*. Classification issues that you might write about in your journal include the following:

- Is the ability to classify important? Why?
- What if humans didn't have the ability to classify? Wouldn't the world be a kinder place?
- Classify the objects in your bedroom into three or four categories.
- Reflect on the courses you are currently enrolled in. Can you divide these courses into two or more groups? Explain this division in an entry in your journal.
- Some musicologists think that popular music in America today is very fragmented. If you agree, try to classify current pop music into three or more types.

Finally, try to develop your own ideas and topics for journal entries. What is it about the thinking strategy called *classification* that interests you? How is it important in your life? Remember to refer to these journal entries when you begin work on the writing assignment at the end of this chapter. You may be able to develop some of the ideas in your journal into an essay for this assignment.

The following journal entry was written in response to this journal suggestion.

Example   FRIDAY, 21ST

I didn't realize until class yesterday that I use classification a lot. I got to thinking that I classify my friends—me, the great humanist, the great believer in equality! But yes, loyal fans of mine, it's true . . . I do classify you . . . Sorry.

But almost as soon as I realized this, it occurred to me that my classification of my friends is not really permanent (static? fixed? what's the word I want here?). In fact, I'm continually classifying and reclassifying them, depending upon circumstances, needs, situations, etc.

If I want someone to go to a movie with, then I quickly classify my friends to determine who would be good to go to a movie with and who wouldn't. On the other hand, if I need someone to give me a ride to the mall, then I classify my friends differently—who has a car? Who doesn't?

GUIDELINES

In order to write in the classification rhetorical pattern, you must follow some rather specific guidelines. Adhering to them will ensure that the classification systems you develop are accurate and meaningful. The following guidelines will enable you to write more easily in the classification rhetorical pattern:

- Identify and restrict your topic.
- Select a single principle of classification.
- Include all members of the universe.
- Specify the distinguishing characteristics of the members of each class.
- Maintain balance among the various parts of the essay.
- Develop either a general thesis statement or a focused thesis statement.

TOPIC

Select a topic that you are interested in and knowledgeable about. You might, for example, decide to classify parents. Or you might classify teachers. Finally, you might even classify the jobs that interest you most.

Once you have selected a topic for classification, you must carefully define and restrict the topic. In doing so, you might find it helpful to think of your topic as a universe.

For example, if you decide to classify parents, your topic is the universe "parents," and all parents are members of this universe. You could restrict this topic by limiting your subject to "American parents." No longer would this universe consist of all parents; henceforth, it would consist of all American parents.

This process of defining and restricting the universe you're writing about will work with any topic. It is an effective way to restrict the subject of a classification essay.

PRACTICE   Working either in small groups or in some other way (as your teacher directs), suggest two restricted universes for each of the following topics. We begin with an example:

Example   *Topic:* Cars
Restricted universe: American Cars
Restricted universe: Luxury Cars

Now complete the following practice exercises:

1. *Topic:* Houses

    Restricted universe: _____

    Restricted universe: _____

2. *Topic:* Movies

    Restricted universe: _____

    Restricted universe: _____

3. *Topic:* Dreams

    Restricted universe: _____

    Restricted universe: _____

4. *Topic:* Food

    Restricted universe: _____

    Restricted universe: _____

5. *Topic:* Music

    Restricted universe: _____

    Restricted universe: _____

6. *Topic:* Drug Stores

    Restricted universe: _____

    Restricted universe: _____

7. *Topic:* Baseball Players

Restricted universe: _____

Restricted universe: _____

8. *Topic:* Dates

Restricted universe: _____

Restricted universe: _____

9. *Topic:* Baby-sitters

Restricted universe: _____

Restricted universe: _____

10. *Topic:* Part-time Jobs

Restricted universe: _____

Restricted universe: _____

When you finish this exercise, compare the work of your group with that of other small groups in the class. Are their restricted universes similar to yours? different? Discuss these as a group.

PRINCIPLE OF CLASSIFICATION

In any classification paper, you must select an appropriate method for classifying the members of the universe that you are writing about. The rhetorical term for this method or device is "principle of classification."

You may think of classification as an exercise in division. Anytime you classify, you are actually dividing the members of a universe into classes. In order to do that, you must have a divisor—namely, a principle of classification. If, for example, you are classifying American parents, you must decide how to classify them. You could classify American parents according to the methods of discipline they use, according to the number of children they have, or even according to their incomes.

PRACTICE   Working with one other person from your class, suggest a principle of classification for each of the following topics. Then briefly explain why you selected this principle of classification. We begin with an example:

Example   *Topic:* Teachers

Principle of classification: Teaching methods

Explanation: Teachers may be classified according to the teaching methods they use: some are primarily lecturers; others depend heavily on class discussion. Therefore, "teaching methods" is a way (principle of classification) to classify teachers.

Now complete the following practice exercises:

1. *Topic:* Pets

Principle of classification: _____

Explanation: _____

_____

_____

2. *Topic:* Diets

Principle of classification: _____

Explanation: _____

_____

_____

3. *Topic:* Relatives

Principle of classification: _____

Explanation: _____

_____

_____

4.   *Topic:*   Department Store Clerks

Principle of classification: _____

Explanation: _____

_____

5.   *Topic:*   Rock Musicians

Principle of classification: _____

Explanation: _____

_____

6.   *Topic:*   Parties

Principle of classification: _____

Explanation: _____

_____

7.   *Topic:*   Shakespeare's Plays

Principle of classification: _____

Explanation: _____

_____

8.   *Topic:*   Politicians

Principle of classification: _____

Explanation: _____

_____

_____

9. *Topic:* Insurance

Principle of classification: _____

Explanation: _____

_____

_____

10. *Topic:* Books

Principle of classification: _____

Explanation: _____

_____

_____

11. *Topic:* [one of your own choosing]

Principle of classification: _____

Explanation: _____

_____

_____

SPECIAL FEATURES OF CLASSIFICATION ESSAYS

Classification essays have many features in common with essays based on other strategies of thinking, but they also involve some special features. Three of these can be considered under the general headings *classes*, *characteristics*, and *balance*.

CLASSES

Once you have restricted your topic and decided on a principle of classification, you must identify the classes. It is important to establish clear, distinct classes. You'll know that the classes are distinct if each member of the universe you are classifying fits into only one of the classes you created. If, for example, you classify American parents according to methods of discipline, you must ascertain that each American parent will fit into only one of the classes (methods of discipline) that you created.

CHARACTERISTICS

The members of each class or group within your classification system will share unique characteristics that distinguish them from members of the other classes. As you describe each class, it is important to identify these distinctive characteristics. In fact, the specifics that make up the paragraphs of the body of your classification essay will consist primarily of descriptions of these distinctive characteristics.

BALANCE

Maintain a balance of information presented for each class in your classification essay. Write approximately equal-length paragraphs about each class. Each class in the classification essay should receive approximately equal coverage in the body of the essay.

THESIS

You may use a general thesis statement or a focused thesis statement for the classification essay. The following general and focused thesis statements could be used for the same classification essay:

Example   *Topic:*   American cars

General thesis statement: There are basically three types of American automobiles.

Focused thesis statement: Most new American cars are available in a base model with no options, a standard model with limited options, or a luxury model with full options.

As you can see, the plan of development in a focused thesis statement for a classification essay identifies the classes into which you have divided the topic. If you include the classes in the thesis statement, you have a focused thesis statement. If you do not include the classes, you have a general thesis statement.

PRACTICE Working with one or two people from your class, develop both general and focused thesis statements for classification essays on the following topics. Write your thesis statements in the spaces provided.

1. *Topic:* Enemies

General thesis statement: _____

_____

Focused thesis statement: _____

_____

2. *Topic:* TV Game Shows

General thesis statement: _____

_____

Focused thesis statement: _____

_____

3. *Topic:* College Textbooks

General thesis statement: _____

_____

Focused thesis statement: _____

_____

4. *Topic:* Supervisors

General thesis statement: _____

_____

Focused thesis statement: _____

_____

5. _Topic:_   Fish

General thesis statement: _____

_____

Focused thesis statement: _____

_____

6. _Topic:_   Desserts

General thesis statement: _____

_____

Focused thesis statement: _____

_____

7. _Topic:_   Christmas Presents

General thesis statement: _____

_____

Focused thesis statement: _____

_____

8. _Topic:_   Hobbies

General thesis statement: _____

_____

Focused thesis statement: _____

_____

9. *Topic:* Drivers

General thesis statement: _____

_____

Focused thesis statement: _____

_____

10. *Topic:* Church Members

General thesis statement: _____

_____

Focused thesis statement: _____

_____

11. *Topic:* The topic you selected in the previous practice exercise (page 266).
General thesis statement: _____

_____

Focused thesis statement: _____

_____

After you have finished the preceding exercise, look over your work. Can you visualize how any of these topics (or any of the topics in the previous exercises) might be developed into a complete essay? Which of them have the most interest or the most potential for development? Select one of the focused thesis statements you created, and brainstorm briefly (two to four minutes) to discover information relevant to this topic.

Here is an example of one person's thesis statements on the topic "Supervisors," together with the results of subsequent brainstorming on these thesis statements.

Example   *Topic:* Supervisors

General thesis statement: Over the years that I've held jobs, I've had several different kinds of supervisors.

Focused thesis statement: I have had three different jobs with three very different supervisors: the first supervisor was a personification of the Peter Principle; the second supervisor was an autocrat; and the supervisor I have now is an intelligent, caring friend as well as a supervisor.

Brainstorming:

Mr. Salt — eighth-grade education . . . couldn't read or spell very well . . . sexist, socially promoted, very prejudiced against females and other minorities, drank coffee and talked on the telephone with his poker buddies and his girlfriend most of the day.

Mr. Myerson — not very bright either . . . a dictator . . . stood by the door looking at his watch to make sure employees were back from breaks on time . . . ran an auditor out of his office one day . . . got very angry if an employee disagreed with or questioned him about anything . . . would raise his voice and invite the person to go somewhere else to work . . . made all decisions himself . . . changed rules when he needed to, without letting all employees know.

Mr. Litmaye — my current supervisor . . . bright, politically active, concerned about environment, the homeless, and other causes . . . keeps all employees informed about decisions made by the management . . . a good listener . . . asks frequently how things are going, and really listens to your answer . . . offers challenging special assignments occasionally, but in a way that you don't feel they are forced down your throat . . . easy to talk to about the job as well as other issues . . . is proud of the fact that I'm taking college courses after work and has let me leave early both semesters when the finals were scheduled at other times than regular class meetings . . . helped me work out a plan to make up the missed work time.

PRACTICE The following thesis statements are attempts to classify the stated subjects. Read each statement and decide whether or not it is a valid classification of the topic. Record your "yes" or "no" answer in the space following each sentence. Then briefly explain your response in the remaining space. You may want to work in a small group on this exercise.

We begin with an example, to familiarize you with the layout of the exercise:

Example   *Topic:* Jobs
Thesis: Jobs may be classified as either interesting, boring, or financially rewarding.

_____ yes   __X__ no

Explanation: This is not an appropriate classification of jobs, since a job may be interesting and financially rewarding or boring and financially rewarding. Therefore, the answer is "no."

Now complete the six practice exercises that follow.

1. *Topic:* Teaching Methods
    Thesis: Teachers may present material in lectures, through class discussions, and by demonstration.

    _____ yes   _____ no

    Explanation: _____

    _____

    _____

2. *Topic:* Pizza
    Thesis: Most people select pizza according to the type of crust it has, choosing either thin-crust pizza, thick-crust pizza, or cheese pizza.

    _____ yes   _____ no

    Explanation: _____

    _____

    _____

3. *Topic:* Restaurants

Thesis: Restaurants provide various levels of service, including full table service, self-service, and carry-out service only.

_____ yes   _____ no

Explanation: _____

_____

_____

4. *Topic:*   New Cars
Thesis: Most new cars are available in a base model with no options, a standard model with limited options, or a luxury model with full options.

_____ yes   _____ no

Explanation: _____

_____

_____

5. *Topic:*   Loans
Thesis: Consumer loans available today may be grouped according to interest schedules as variable-rate-interest loans, fixed-rate-interest loans, and easy-payment loans.

_____ yes   _____ no

Explanation: _____

_____

_____

6. *Topic:*   Friends
Thesis: Friends, so important to all of us, are generally of three types: forever-there friends, fairweather friends, and rich friends.

_____ yes   _____ no

Explanation: _____

_____

_____

READINGS

The following readings are student and professional essays. Read them carefully, and look for their use of the classification guidelines presented in this chapter.

STUDENT ESSAY

MY THREE ROLES   Martha Howard

People generally fill several roles in their daily lives. Of these, work may occupy a key position for women, and motherhood may be a starring part for many years. A person may also become a sports addict, hobby craftsman, gardener, or culture devotee. Many roles may be juggled by those fascinated by life and unwilling to forgo beckoning experiences. However, through the years, one activity may be substituted for another, and the number may dwindle. I spend my present life filling three main roles: housekeeper, student, and companion.

I deliberately titled my first role *housekeeper*, rather than *homemaker*, to accentuate the physical tasks involved rather than any labor of love accompanying it. I no longer have to prove myself by upholding such standards as, "every square inch of walls, woodwork, floors, and furniture

shall be scrubbed and polished each spring and fall." I no longer pore over color spreads of appetizing concoctions and trendy interiors in *Better Homes and Gardens*. Instead, I routinely bend and stretch to reach each dusty surface with a flick and the promise of another flick next week. My knees protest the unyielding bathroom tiles, and my arms complain of the cramped movements necessary to scour the tub. I pull and tug at recalcitrant blankets that seem to have an affinity for the floor. And, once more, the soapy water gurgles down the sink, and the dishes sparkle in the drainer. I accept these duties with good grace, but my time schedule is built around my new interest—school.

The novelty of being a full-time student is still with me, although the daily routine is set. I trot from class to class, drinking in new knowledge. School means sitting still

MY THREE ROLES, continued

while my mind races; it means sharing ideas and answers with new friends. Then, as evening falls, I settle down to homework. I attempt to parrot each assigned chapter in preparation for the inevitable test. Often, after working for an hour on an obstinate accounting problem, I discover I've miscopied numbers from the book. Essay writing frequently results in a lost weekend. As the pile of finished assignments grows and my attention flags, it is a pleasure to shift to my third and most sustaining role.

The paradox of being a companion is that I get back more than I give. After school, my husband and I spend an hour or more sharing the day's experiences. Later,

a TV news broadcast spawns lively arguments over our differing opinions and viewpoints. If one has a craving to eat pizza or to see *Platoon*, he knows he has a willing partner. What interests one automatically is of interest to the other. It is a mutual sharing and reinforcement without which my life would indeed be dreary.

The full days slide by, and I've never been happier than in my three present roles, which satisfy the physical, mental, and emotional sides of my nature. I feel complete because I am serving and also being self-indulgent. However, that doesn't mean that I'm not looking forward to life and its changes. After all, there are a lot more roles to try on for size.

PROFESSIONAL ESSAY

FRIENDS, GOOD FRIENDS— AND SUCH GOOD FRIENDS

Judith Viorst

Women are friends, I once would have said, when they totally love and support and trust each other, and bare to each other the secrets of their souls, and run—no questions asked—to help each other, and tell harsh truths to each other (no, you can't wear that dress unless you lose ten pounds first) when harsh truths must be told.

Women are friends, I once would have said, when they share the same affection for Ingmar Bergman, plus train rides, cats, warm rain, charades, Camus, and hate

with equal ardor Newark and Brussels sprouts and Lawrence Welk and camping.

In other words, I once would have said that a friend is a friend all the way, but now I believe that's a narrow point of view. For the friendships I have and the friendships I see are conducted at many levels of intensity, serve many different functions, meet different needs and range from those as all-the-way as the friendship of the soul sisters mentioned above to that of the most nonchalant and casual playmates.

FRIENDS, GOOD FRIENDS—AND SUCH GOOD FRIENDS, continued

Consider these varieties of friendship:

1. Convenience friends. These are the women with whom, if our paths weren't crossing all the time, we'd have no particular reason to be friends: a next-door neighbor, a woman in our car pool, the mother of one of our children's closest friends or maybe some mommy with whom we serve juice and cookies each week at the Glenwood Co-op Nursery.

Convenience friends are convenient indeed. They'll lend us their cups and silverware for a party. They'll drive our kids to soccer when we're sick. They'll take us to pick up our car when we need a lift to the garage. They'll even take our cats when we go on vacation. As we will for them.

But we don't, with convenience friends, ever come too close or tell too much; we maintain our public face and emotional distance. "Which means," says Elaine, "that I'll talk about being overweight but not about being depressed. Which means I'll admit being mad but not blind with rage. Which means that I might say that we're pinched this month but never that I'm worried sick over money."

But which doesn't mean that there isn't sufficient value to be found in these friendships of mutual aid, in convenience friends.

2. Special-interest friends. These friendships aren't intimate, and they needn't involve kids or silverware or cats. Their value lies in some interest jointly shared. And so we may have an office friend or a yoga friend or a tennis friend or a friend from the Women's Democratic Club.

"I've got one woman friend," says Joyce, "who likes, as I do, to take psychology courses. Which makes it nice for me—and

nice for her. It's fun to go with someone you know and it's fun to discuss what you've learned, driving back from the classes." And for the most part, she says, that's all they discuss.

"I'd say that what we're doing is *doing* together, not being together," Suzanne says of her Tuesday-doubles friends. "It's mainly a tennis relationship, but we play together well. And I guess we all need to have a couple of playmates."

I agree.

My playmate is a shopping friend, a woman of marvelous taste, a woman who knows exactly *where* to buy *what*, and furthermore is a woman who always knows beyond a doubt what one ought to be buying. I don't have the time to keep up with what's new in eyeshadow, hemlines and shoes and whether the smock look is in or finished already. But since (oh, shame!) I care a lot about eyeshadow, hemlines and shoes, and since I don't *want* to wear smocks if the smock look is finished, I'm very glad to have a shopping friend.

3. Historical friends. We all have a friend who knew us when . . . maybe way back in Miss Meltzer's second grade, when our family lived in that three-room flat in Brooklyn, when our dad was out of work for seven months, when our brother Allie got in that fight where they had to call the police, when our sister married the endodontist from Yonkers and when, the morning after we lost our virginity, she was the first, the only, friend we told.

The years have gone by and we've gone separate ways and we've little in common now, but we're still an intimate part of each other's past. And so whenever we go to Detroit we always go to visit this friend

FRIENDS, GOOD FRIENDS—AND SUCH GOOD FRIENDS, continued

of our girlhood. Who knows how we looked before our teeth were straightened. Who knows how we talked before our voice got un-Brooklyned. Who knows what we ate before we learned about artichokes. And who, by her presence, puts us in touch with an earlier part of ourself, a part of ourself it's important never to lose.

"What this friend means to me and what I mean to her," says Grace, "is having a sister without sibling rivalry. We know the texture of each other's lives. She remembers my grandmother's cabbage soup. I remember the way her uncle played the piano. There's simply no other friend who remembers those things."

4. Crossroads friends. Like historical friends, our crossroads friends are important for *what was*—for the friendship we shared at a crucial, now past, time of life. A time, perhaps, when we roomed in college together; or worked as eager young singles in the Big City together; or went together, as my friend Elizabeth and I did, through pregnancy, birth and that scary first year of new motherhood.

Crossroads friends forge powerful links, links strong enough to endure with not much more contact than once-a-year letters at Christmas. And out of respect for those crossroads years, for those dramas and dreams we once shared, we will always be friends.

5. Cross-generational friends. Historical friends and crossroads friends seem to maintain a special kind of intimacy—dormant but always ready to be revived—and though we may rarely meet, whenever we do connect, it's personal and intense. Another kind of intimacy exists in the friendships that form across generations in what

one woman calls her daughter-mother and her mother-daughter relationships.

Evelyn's friend is her mother's age—"but I share so much more than I ever could with my mother"—a woman she talks to of music, of books and of life. "What I get from her is the benefit of her experience. What she gets—and enjoys—from me is a youthful perspective. It's pleasure for both of us."

I have in my own life a precious friend, a woman of 65 who has lived very hard, who is wise, who listens well; who has been where I am and can help me understand it; and who represents not only an ultimate ideal mother to me but also the person I'd like to be when I grow up.

In our daughter role we tend to do more than our share of self-revelation; in our mother role we tend to receive what's revealed. It's another kind of pleasure—playing wise mother to a questing younger person. It's another very lovely kind of friendship.

6. Part-of-a-couple friends. Some of the women we call our friends we never see alone—we see them as part of a couple at couples' parties. And though we share interests in many things and respect each other's views, we aren't moved to deepen the relationship. Whatever the reason, a lack of time or—and this is more likely—a lack of chemistry, our friendship remains in the context of a group. But the fact that our feeling on seeing each other is always, "I'm *so* glad she's here" and the fact that we spend half the evening talking together says that this too, in its own way, counts as a friendship.

(Other part-of-a-couple friends are the friends that came with the marriage, and

FRIENDS, GOOD FRIENDS—AND SUCH GOOD FRIENDS, continued

some of these are friends we could live without. But sometimes, alas, she *is* our husband's best friend. And so we find ourself dealing with her, somewhat against our will, in a spirit of what I'll call *reluctant* friendship.)

7. Men who are friends. I wanted to write just of women friends, but the women I've talked to won't let me—they say I must mention man-woman friendships too. For those friendships can be just as close and as dear as those that we form with women. Listen to Lucy's description of one such friendship:

"We've found we have things to talk about that are different from what he talks about with my husband and different from what I talk about with his wife. So sometimes we call on the phone or meet for lunch. There are similar intellectual interests—we always pass on to each other the books that we love—but there's also something tender and caring too."

In a couple of crises, Lucy says, "he offered himself, for talking and for helping. And when someone died in his family he wanted me there. The sexual, flirty part of our friendship is very small, but *some*—just enough to make it fun and different." She thinks—and I agree—that the sexual part, though small, is always *some*, is always there when a man and a woman are friends.

It's only in the past few years that I've made friends with men, in the sense of a friendship that's *mine*, not just part of two couples. And achieving with them the ease and the trust I've found with women friends has value indeed. Under the dryer at home last week, putting on mascara and rouge, I comfortably sat and talked with a fellow named Peter. Peter, I finally decided, could handle the shock of me minus mascara under the dryer. Because we care for each other. Because we're friends.

8. There are medium friends, and pretty good friends, and very good friends indeed, and these friendships are defined by their level of intimacy. And what we'll reveal at each of these levels of intimacy is calibrated with care. We might tell a medium friend, for example, that yesterday we had a fight with our husband. And we might tell a pretty good friend that this fight with our husband made us so mad that we slept on the couch. And we might tell a very good friend that the reason we got so mad in that fight that we slept on the couch had something to do with that girl who works in his office. But it's only to our very best friends that we're willing to tell all, to tell what's going on with that girl in his office.

The best of friends, I still believe, totally love and support and trust each other, and bare to each other the secrets of their souls, and run—no questions asked—to help each other, and tell harsh truths to each other when they must be told.

But we needn't agree about everything (only 12-year-old girl friends agree about *everything*) to tolerate each other's point of view. To accept without judgment. To give and to take without ever keeping score. And to *be* there, as I am for them and as they are for me, to comfort our sorrows, to celebrate our joys.

Rhetoric

1. "Friends, Good Friends—and Such Good Friends" contains several paragraphs of introductory material. Is this effective? Why?

2. What rhetorical device or pattern does the author use to develop her explanation of "special-interest friends"?

3. The conclusion of the essay is rather short. Is it effective? Write two to four additional sentences to expand the conclusion and make it less abrupt.

Ideas

1. Although the author focuses on types of friendship, she also provides some of the elements of a definition of friendship. Locate these parts of the definition of friendship, and use them to write a one-paragraph definition of friendship.

2. The author identifies eight types of friends. Is this a complete classification of friends? Can you think of other types not included here?

Response

1. Write a paragraph about one of your friends who is an example of one of the types of friends identified by the author. The topic sentence for your paragraph might be similar to this one: "Mary's unique interests make her one of my special-interest friends."

2. Write an essay in which you classify your friends. You may structure your essay similarly to the author's, or you may devise your own categories.

PROFESSIONAL ESSAY

BUYING A PICKUP TRUCK   Noel Perrin

One of the ways a newcomer to the country knows he's getting acclimated is when he begins to notice trucks. (I say "he" strictly through obedience to grammar. The phenomenon happens to women almost as much as to men. Under age 25, I'd say just as much.)

Back in his other life, back when he was urban or suburban, it may have been sports cars that caught the newcomer's

SOURCE: From *First Person Rural* by Noel Perrin. Copyright © 1978 by Noel Perrin. Reprinted by permission of David R. Godine, Publisher.

BUYING A PICKUP TRUCK, continued

eye. Or maybe a showroom full of compacts, fresh and glittering from the factory. Now he finds himself eyeing some neighbor's sturdy green pickup with a big load of brush in the back and wondering how much one like it would cost. Welcome to the club.

Pickups aren't necessary in the country, but they are certainly handy. Any rural family that can afford two vehicles should probably make one of them a truck. And it is quite possible to have a truck as a family's sole transportation. It is also quite economical, since pickups begin almost as cheap as the cheapest cars, and go up in price, size, and quality at the same rate cars do—except that about halfway up the car price range, you have reached the most expensive pickups there are.

What's handiest about pickups is their versatility. First, obviously, in load. Because of that big open space in back, you can carry almost anything. Two beef cattle. Two full-length sofas that you're donating to the rummage. All the apples in a small orchard. With the tailgate down, a load of sixteen-foot boards. About 40 bales of hay. A full cord of firewood (provided its dry). All your fence posts, your wire, and your tools, when you're building a fence. It's possible to get a little drunk with power, just thinking what a pickup can do.

Second, in range. Even without four-wheel drive, a pickup is a great deal freer than most cars to leave roads and drive over fields. Picking up hay bales, for example. Or to squeeze along homemade woods roads. This freedom comes partly because pickups are designed to have fairly high road clearance, even when loaded. Partly because they can take tires that will walk

you right through a wet spot or over a (not-too-big) rock. Most pickup owners in rural New England keep a pair of oversize snow tires mounted on the rear wheels all year round. And partly because you can shift weight around in a truck to get maximum traction in a way that would cause the average car to collapse on its fat Detroit springs.

Third, a pickup is versatile in function. Besides its truck role, a pickup can do anything a car can do, with one exception—about which, more later. It can drive you to work, for example, using no more gas than a car, and when you arrive, it will not only park in the regular lot, it will do so in a smaller space than a Cadillac or an Oldsmobile.

Nor are you going to complain on the way that it drives like a truck, because it doesn't. It drives like a car. The ride is reasonably smooth, the surreptitious U-turn reasonably easy. Drivers of big highway trucks have ten gears to shift, and air brakes to worry about. Drivers of pickups have a standard shift and regular car brakes. And if they hate shifting, most pickups can be had with automatic transmission. For that matter, most can be equipped with a stereo tape deck, so that you barrel out to the woods playing Beethoven. I admit that a fully loaded pickup—say, a Chevrolet C-10 with a ton of rocks in the back or a six-barrel gathering tank full of maple sap—doesn't corner quite so neatly as an MG, but it still drives essentially like a car.

The one exception is that a pickup is not much good for carrying a big load of people. At least, not in the winter or in wet weather. On a sunny summer day, its ca-

BUYING A PICKUP TRUCK, continued

pacity is something else. Giving hayrides at our local fair, I once had fifteen children and two mothers back there in the hay, plus myself and a friend in the cab. I make that eighteen passengers.

Even if two couples are going out for dinner, a pickup is not handy. Four adults will fit not too uncomfortably in the cab of an American (though not a Japanese) pickup—but the law says three. The other husband may or may not want to crouch in back. Furthermore, it doesn't take many bags of groceries to produce a sense of claustrophobia in a pickup cab. A mother taking two children shopping on a rainy day in a pickup generally wishes she had a car.

There *is* a solution, to be sure. People who go out to dinner a lot, or mothers with four children, can get a crew-cab pickup. This is not what you'd call a glamour vehicle. It has two cabs, one behind the other, and looks something like a centipede dragging a large box. But it does seat six people. The only problem is that you now have a truck not only so ugly but so big that it is no longer versatile in the woods. I do not recommend it.

One last advantage of pickups should be mentioned. They never make hideous noises or refuse to start because you haven't fastened the seat belt. Like other trucks, they are exempt from that law. You can use the belts when you're roaring down the highway and skip them when you're going one mile an hour in the woods. Handy.

So much for pickups and their virtues. The time has now come to discuss the art of buying one. It *is* an art, incidentally, unlike car buying. A few wrong decisions

on options can cut a farm pickup's usefulness by 50%.

The first decision, of course, is new or used. A really old pickup, small and square and no-nonsense, is about the most charming vehicle there is. Also one of the cheapest. You can get one for $200. Any children you know will adore the running boards and—if you have an old enough one—the windshield that pushes open for ventilation.

On the other hand, old pickups tend to have unreliable brakes and not notably reliable anything else. The 1947 Dodge I once owned—from its nineteenth to its twenty-first years—couldn't be counted on to start at any temperature much below freezing. That meant a long period of parking on hills and losing my temper, each October and November, until I finally gave up and put it in the barn until spring. One year I waited a week too late and had it frozen in the barnyard, in the way of practically everything, for three and a half months.

Even much newer pickups have generally led hard lives. (Little old ladies seldom own pickups.) Furthermore, it's difficult and expensive to have heavy-duty springs and other desirable country equipment installed in an existing truck. Probably only people with real mechanical ability should consider getting one.

But one last word. If you do get one, take a nice winter vacation and get it in some place like South Carolina. South Carolina pickups have never experienced road salt. At least the body won't rust out on you in a few years.

Now let's turn to new pickups. They come, basically, in three sizes and three styles. The sizes are called half-ton, three-

BUYING A PICKUP TRUCK, continued

quarter-ton, and one-ton. Not one of these names means what it says. Which is a good thing, because a bunch of trucks that could carry only 1,000 to 2,000 pounds wouldn't be worth much.

Let me define the three. A half-ton is the basic pickup: what you find at a car dealer, what people mean when they speak of a pickup. At the moment it comes in two avatars. It is a small Japanese-made truck that can carry almost a ton of cargo. Or it is a somewhat larger American-made truck that, with proper springs and tires, can manage a ton and a half.

A three-quarter ton looks much the same, but has a much larger, truck-type rear axle. It costs more, gives a rougher ride, and carries loads of up to about three tons. People with campers put them on three-quarter-ton pickups—and then usually get about six miles to the gallon.

A one-ton has an even bigger rear axle. With dual rear wheels, it can carry up to near five tons. Neither it nor a three-quarter is what most people need for use on a country place. Not unless they plan to get into the lumber-delivery business, or maybe have always wanted, since they were kids, to have their own personal dump truck. (No fooling. There are truck shops in every New England state that will put a dump body on a three-quarter or a one-ton. The cost runs around $1,200. I have sometimes played with the notion.) But for general country use a half-ton is right; and for the rest of this article I shall talk about half-tons only.

Of the three styles, one can be dismissed right off. This is the tarted-up and chromed-up half-ton which attempts to pass itself off as a car. Chevrolet calls its

El Camino; other makes have equally foolish names.

For families that are sincerely embarrassed at having to own a truck and that really think it would be preferable to drive something that looks like a scooped-out car, spending the extra money for an El Camino may make sense. Especially in those flat and treeless parts of the country where taking your truck out to the back forty must be something like driving across a very large football field. But to get one as a working truck on a rocky, hilly, wooded New England farm would be an act of insanity.

The other two styles are narrow-bed and wide-bed. Just as the half-ton is the classic American pickup, the narrow-bed is the classic half-ton. The design has been stable for 50 years now. Behind the cab you have—in most makes— a wooden-floored metal box four feet wide and six or eight feet long. (You get to pick.) This sits inside the rear wheels. Because it doesn't rust and because it gives surer footing to any livestock you happen to be transporting, the wooden floor is a considerable advantage.

Until a few years ago, the narrow-bed was the cheapest of all pickups; now it costs exactly the same as a wide-bed. It retains two other advantages. Since the rear wheels don't stick up into the bed, you can slide slidable cargo in and out with great ease. And because this is the classic model, the tailgate in most makes is still the traditional kind that you hook with a chain on each side. That matters. You are able either to put such a tailgate down level, as an extension of the bed, if you are carrying a load of long boards, or to let it

BUYING A PICKUP TRUCK, continued

drop all the way down for ease in loading. Now that I no longer have one, I miss it.

All the Japanese-made pickups and most of the current American ones are wide-bed. These have a cargo space five and a half feet wide (American) or four and a half feet (Japanese). Obviously you can carry a lot more cargo. On the other hand, the rear wheel housings stick in on each side, which is sometimes inconvenient. (I will say they are handy for children to sit on.) And on many wide-beds you get a fancy one-handled tailgate, like a station wagon's, which won't drop down unless you disconnect the hinges. It's not difficult, it's just tedious. And when you want to close the tailgate, you have to reconnect them.

Which style is better? Myself, I used to have a narrow-bed and now have a wide-bed. I think the advantages and disadvantages of the two models just about balance. So on my current truck, I made the choice on esthetic grounds. The narrow-bed lost. Properly designed, it is the truest of trucks, the very platonic essence of a truck. But in the last five years Ford, Dodge, Chevrolet, Jeep, and International Harvester (a GMC pickup is just a relabeled Chevrolet)—all have moved to such enormously wide cabs that a new narrow-bed looks hydrocephalic. Wide-bed is now the handsomer truck.

As to whether Toyota, Datsun, LUV, or an American make, the decision really rests on how much highway driving you're going to do. The Japanese trucks, with four-cylinder engines, get far better gas mileage. According to *Consumer Reports*, they average about twenty mpg, while American half-tons average fifteen. My own experience suggests that Japanese pickups do a

little better than twenty, and American pickups a little worse than fifteen. For a vehicle that I was going to commute to work in, and just use as a truck on the occasional weekend, I would probably choose to save gas (plus about $300 in purchase price) and get a Japanese.

But for a truck that was to be mainly or even considerably a working farm vehicle, I still prefer the larger and more versatile American pickup. It's not just that you can carry more weight, it's that you can get a specially adapted country model. The Japanese trucks tend to be unadaptable, the same for an appliance dealer in New York City as for a family with 60 acres of woods in Colebrook, Connecticut.

The man delivering refrigerators in the Bronx doesn't need any special traction. He never leaves the pavement. But the family in Colebrook does. And one of the most humiliating things that can happen is to get stuck in your own truck on your own place. Especially since you're so unlikely to be able to jack, or rock, or bull your way out.

The trick is not to get stuck. Which means that you may want the four-wheel drive available as an option (a very expensive one) on all the American but none of the little Japanese trucks. Otherwise, you will certainly want limited-slip differential. This inexpensive ($75 to $100) option means a special rear axle designed so that when one rear wheel starts to spin, all the power goes to the other wheel. Normally when one wheel starts to spin, all the power goes to *it*, and that's why you get stuck. Limited-slip differential is said to have its dangers, especially in very fast highway driving, where you may fishtail in

BUYING A PICKUP TRUCK, continued

a skid, but it is highly desirable in a farm pickup. I would rate it, quite impressionistically, as making about a third of the difference between regular two-wheel drive and four-wheel drive. You can get it on American pickups, but not Japanese. It's only fair to add that I know farmers with Datsun pickups who say they have no trouble at all zipping up and down their rolling fields, even on dewy mornings, but I still commend limited-slip differential.

If you decide on a Japanese truck anyway, about all you have to do is go get it. Maybe settle whether or not you want a radio. But if you opt for an American truck, you still have to pick your engine, with at least six more country options to consider.

The engine is easy. Get a six-cylinder. Almost all pickups—including three-quarter and one-tons—can be had either six or eight cylinders. A six has all the power you will ever need, and wastes less gas. As to options, the first and most important is to specify heavy-duty springs in the rear, and heavy-duty shock absorbers front and rear. All this costs about $40; its value in increased usefulness must be about 50 times that much.

Second, for any pickup that's going to leave roads, either a four-speed shift or automatic transmission is a great asset. Why? Because going through a field with long grass (and hidden rocks), or up into the woods, you need to be able to creep along, almost literally feeling your way, and still not lose momentum. Low speed in a three-speed shift will not let you go slowly enough.

Here the Japanese trucks have an advantage, since all of them come with a four-speed shift. It costs an extra $125 on an American pickup. But even better than four-speed is an automatic transmission. You can creep with astonishing slowness, and still have power. I have never owned a car with automatic transmission and never plan to, but on my sturdy green pickup I find it marvelous. It does, of course, use too much gas, and my next truck will be four-speed manual.

Third, you ought to get a step-and-tow bumper. Unlike cars, trucks are sold with no rear bumper at all. (How much rear bumper have you ever seen on a tractor-trailer or on a gasoline truck?) But a step-and-tow—which is a broad bumper covered with sheet steel—really is handy for pulling, and as a rear step. The ones you get factory installed, for about $50, are not nearly as sturdy as they look, but are still worth having. The ideal is to have one made by a local welder. Rodney Palmer, the man who owns the garage in Thetford Center, is a superb welder; and for $101.50 I have a rear bumper that will fend off anything short of a Centurion tank, that is heavy enough to give me good traction with no load in the truck, and that will last for a hundred years. (Rodney designed it so that I can move it from pickup to pickup for the rest of my life. Then I'll will it to my daughters.) Incidentally, if you don't get a bumper like that, you should plan to keep a couple of large flat rocks or about four cement blocks in the back each winter. Way back. Otherwise you'll find yourself spinning to a halt halfway up icy hills. Better anchor them too, so that if you have to slam the brakes on hard they won't come hurtling through the back of the cab and kill you.

Fourth, for a family truck it is worth getting extra padding in the seat. A pickup

BUYING A PICKUP TRUCK, continued

has a reasonably smooth ride, but not so smooth that additional cushioning won't be pleasing to visiting grandparents, people with bad backs, and so on. If you're going to get stereo tapes, you might even want to pad the whole cab, so as to reduce road noise.

Fifth, if you can talk the dealer into it, get him to remove the four automobile tires the truck comes equipped with, and have him put on four truck tires. They should be not merely heavier ply, but if possible an inch larger in diameter. And as I said earlier, the rear ones should probably be snow tires, even if you get the truck in May. (Come winter, put snow tires on the front, too. They won't improve traction unless you have four-wheel drive, but they will help astonishingly in preventing sideslipping.)

If you can't talk the dealer into it, you're no horsetrader. In that case, resign yourself to your helpless condition, and pay extra for big tires. Or go to another dealer. Or hurry home and read Faulkner's *The Hamlet*. Then you will learn—from a master—how to trade.

Sixth, get the truck undercoated. Presumably any New Englander knows about undercoating anyway—but it's even more important on pickups than cars, since people usually keep pickups longer. The process called Ziebarting is probably the best and certainly the most expensive. If you can stand having your truck smell like fish oil for a month or so, I recommend it. If not, a grease undercoating is said to be adequate. But the full mysteries of Duracoat (acrylic resin), asphalt, and all the other undercoatings, I do not pretend to be a master of.

There are all sorts of other machismo things one can get with a pickup. You can have a snowplow mounted—in which case be sure to get four-wheel drive. Plan also to have the front end realigned frequently, because plowing will spoil the wheel alignment with surprising speed. You can have an electric winch put on the front, and thus be sure of freeing yourself 99% of the time when you get stuck. (Though a two-ton manual winch of the kind called a come-along will do nearly as well. You can get one for about $45, and keep it under the seat.) You can have a power take-off on most larger pickups, and run your own sawmill. You can merely buy a logging chain, keep that under the seat, too, and then when you find eight-foot poplars growing in the corners of your best field, you can hook the chain on your step-and-tow bumper and pull them out by the roots. They don't grow back next year *that* way.

But just a basic pickup is machismo (or feminismo) enough. In fact, I can think of just one problem. Someday when you're going past the post office with a big load of brush, you'll glance up and see a whole row of summer people staring at you. With naked envy in their eyes.

Rhetoric

1. Early in this essay, the author lets us know that he will use the pronoun *he* to refer to nouns of common gender. Do you think that his use of *he* is sexist? Suggest two alternatives to using *he* to refer to nouns of common gender.

2. Plentiful graphic details help make this essay very effective. Select a representative paragraph, and make a list of the details in that paragraph.

3. Although this essay is considered a classification essay, only the central section of the essay actually classifies pickup trucks. What functions do the first and last sections of the essay serve?

Ideas

1. Perrin's respect for pickup trucks is an acquired one. Would he feel differently about these vehicles if he had always been around them or if he depended on them to make a living? If so, how?

2. Can you make any inferences about the author's personality on the basis of his preference for a particular style or type of pickup truck? If so, what?

3. Many of us stereotype people who drive pickup trucks. Describe this stereotype. Does the author fit this stereotype? Why or why not?

Response

1. Which type of pickup discussed in the essay do you prefer? Write a paragraph in which you explain why you like this particular type of pickup and how you think it complements your personality. Your topic sentence for this paragraph might be similar to this one: "I particularly like a three-quarter-ton pickup, since it, like me, is strong and rugged."

2. Write an essay in which you classify family cars. You may want to structure your essay similarly to the author's.

PROFESSIONAL ESSAY

CINEMATYPES   Susan Allen Toth

Aaron takes me only to art films. That's what I call them, anyway: strange movies with vague poetic images I don't always understand, long dreamy movies about a distant Technicolor past, even longer black-and-white movies about the general meaninglessness of life. We do not go unless at least one reputable critic has found the cinematography superb. We went to *The Devil's Eye*, and Aaron turned to me in the middle and said, "My God, this is *funny*." I do not think he was pleased.

CINEMATYPES, continued

When Aaron and I go to the movies, we drive our cars separately and meet by the box office. Inside the theater he sits tentatively in his seat, ready to move if he can't see well, poised to leave if the film is disappointing. He leans away from me, careful not to touch the bare flesh of his arm against the bare flesh of mine. Sometimes he leans so far I am afraid he may be touching the woman on his other side. If the movie is very good, he leans forward, too, peering between the heads of the couple in front of us. The light from the screen bounces off his glasses; he gleams with intensity, sitting there on the edge of his seat, watching the screen. Once I tapped him on the arm so I could whisper a comment in his ear. He jumped.

After *Belle de Jour* Aaron said he wanted to ask me if he could stay overnight. "But I can't," he shook his head mournfully before I had a chance to answer, "because I know I never sleep in strange beds." Then he apologized for asking. "It's just that after a film like that," he said, "I feel the need to assert myself."

Pete takes me only to movies that he thinks have redeeming social value. He doesn't call them "films." They tend to be about poverty, war, injustice, political corruption, struggling unions in the 1930s, and the military-industrial complex. Pete doesn't like propaganda movies, though, and he doesn't like to be too depressed, either. We stayed away from *The Sorrow and the Pity;* it would be, he said, just too much. Besides, he assured me, things are never that hopeless. So most of the movies we see are made in Hollywood. Because they are always topical, these movies offer what Pete calls "food for thought." When

we saw *Coming Home,* Pete's jaw set so firmly with the first half-hour that I knew we would end up at Poppin' Fresh Pies afterward.

When Pete and I go to the movies, we take turns driving so no one owes anyone else anything. We leave the car far from the theater so we don't have to pay for a parking space. If it's raining or snowing, Pete offers to let me off at the door, but I can tell he'll feel better if I go with him while he finds a spot, so we share the walk too. Inside the theater Pete will hold my hand when I get scared if I ask him. He puts my hand firmly on his knee and covers it completely with his own hand. His knee never twitches. After a while, when the scary part is past, he loosens his hand slightly and I know that is a signal to take mine away. He sits companionably close, letting his jacket just touch my sweater, but he does not infringe. He thinks I ought to know he is there if I need him.

One night, after *The China Syndrome,* I asked Pete if he wouldn't like to stay for a second drink, even though it was past midnight. He thought a while about that, considering my offer from all possible angles, but finally he said no. Relationships today, he said, have a tendency to move too quickly.

Sam likes movies that are entertaining. By that he means movies that Will Jones in the *Minneapolis Tribune* loved and either *Time* or *Newsweek* rather liked; also movies that do not have sappy love stories, are not musicals, do not have subtitles, and will not force him to think. He does not go to movies to think. He liked *California Suite* and *The Seduction of Joe Tynan,* though the plots, he said, could

CINEMATYPES, continued

have been zippier. He saw it all coming too far in advance, and that took the fun out. He doesn't like to know what is going to happen. "I just want my brain to be tickled," he says. It is very hard for me to pick out movies for Sam.

When Sam takes me to the movies, he pays for everything. He thinks that's what a man ought to do. But I buy my own popcorn, because he doesn't approve of it; the grease might smear his flannel slacks. Inside the theater, Sam makes himself comfortable. He takes off his jacket, puts one arm around me, and all during the movie he plays with my hand, stroking my palm, beating a small tattoo on my wrist. Although he watches the movie intently, his body operates on instinct. Once I inclined my head and kissed him lightly just behind the ear. He beat a faster tattoo on my wrist, quick and musical, but he didn't look away from the screen.

When Sam takes me home from the movies, he stands outside my door and kisses me long and hard. He would like to come in, he says regretfully, but his steady girlfriend in Duluth wouldn't like it. When the *Tribune* gives a movie four stars, he has to save it to see with her. Otherwise her feelings might be hurt.

I go to some movies by myself. On rainy Sunday afternoons I often sneak into a revival house or a college auditorium for old Technicolor musicals, *Kiss Me Kate*, *Seven Brides for Seven Brothers*, *Calamity Jane*, even once, *The Sound of Music*. Wearing saggy jeans so I can prop my feet on the seat in front, I sit toward the rear where no one can see me. I eat large handfuls of popcorn with double butter. Once the movie starts, I feel completely at home. Howard Keel and I are old friends; I grin back at him on the screen. I know the sound tracks by heart. Sometimes when I get really carried away I hum along with Kathryn Grayson, remembering how I once thought I would fill out a formal like that. I am rather glad now I never did. Skirts whirl, feet tap, acrobatic young men perform impossible feats, and then the camera dissolves into a dream sequence I know I can comfortably follow. It is not, thank God, Bergman.

If I can't find an old musical, I settle for Hepburn and Tracy, vintage Grant or Gable, on adventurous days Claudette Colbert or James Stewart. Before I buy my ticket I make sure it will all end happily. If necessary, I ask the girl at the box office. I have never seen *Stella Dallas* or *Intermezzo*. Over the years I have developed other peccadilloes: I will, for example, see anything that is redeemed by Thelma Ritter. At the end of *Daddy Long Legs* I wait happily for the scene when Fred Clark, no longer angry, at last pours Thelma a convivial drink. They smile at each other, I smile at them, I feel they are smiling at me. In the movies I go to by myself, the men and women always like each other.

Rhetoric

1. The author discusses three distinct types of film buffs. She does not, however, name these types. Working with a small group of classmates, create short labels (names) for each of the types of moviegoers the author discusses.

2. Does the author's classification of cinema buffs include all movie-goers? If not, can you think of other types of movie viewers? Working with the writing group you joined for the previous exercise, create a list of other types of movie viewers.

Ideas

1. Pete prefers movies that he thinks have redeeming social value. Is this the best criterion for judging a movie? What other reasons might there be for seeing a particular movie?

2. The essay is not just about types of movie buffs but also about types of men. Write a brief summary statement that describes each type of man the author presents. When you finish this, compare your list of types with lists made by some of your classmates.

Response

1. Assume that the essay needs an introduction; with another class-mate, write a brief introduction for it.

2. Decide which type of movie buff you are, and write about this in an essay.

WRITING ASSIGNMENT

You may select a topic for this writing assignment from one of the following lists, or you may develop a topic of your own. Once you have selected a topic, complete one or more of the specified prewriting activities. After sufficient prewriting, write a draft of an essay on the topic you selected. Finally, revise and edit your essay.

General Writing Assignments

■ In a lighthearted essay, classify your friends *or* your enemies.
■ People react differently to good news. Some celebrate; others look for the black lining behind the silver cloud. Write an essay in which you classify the types of reactions people have to good news.
■ You will receive numerous writing assignments in your college courses. Classify these assignments. As you prepare this classification scheme, you might consider length, format requirements, subject, and style. Present the results in an essay.
■ Choice of vocation is important to all of us. Generally, we consider several types of work before finally selecting a specific field. Discuss the types of vocations you are currently considering or have considered.

Specific Writing Assignments

■ As a college freshman, you are very concerned about declaring a major and selecting a vocation. The college's career placement counselor has helped you narrow your choices. The placement counselor has also recommended that you write an essay in your journal or diary in which you classify the fields you are interested in.

■ As the arts editor of your college newspaper, you review a movie or a book each week for the paper. For your review for the next issue, recall the major characters in a movie you saw or a novel you read recently. Write a review of this novel or movie, focusing on a classification of the major characters according to their different personalities.

If you decide to develop your own topic, you may want to look through your journal for topic ideas. What topics that you have addressed in your journal lend themselves to this particular thinking strategy? You might also look carefully at the focused journal entries you wrote at the beginning of this chapter. Is that particular topic of interest to you? Is it a topic with which you have some experience? With some revision work, could your journal entry on this topic become an essay?

Finally, look back through this chapter at some of the exercises you have done, individually and with others in your class. Are any of these topics of interest to you? Recall conversations with your classmates. Have they given you ideas for topics? Perhaps interesting topics emerged from the group discussions that followed some of the practices in the chapter. You may want to spend some time discussing these exercises with classmates to help you decide what to write about. Or you may want to do some listing on paper to help you discover a suitable topic.

PREWRITING

After selecting a topic as the subject for a classification essay, complete one or more of the following prewriting activities:

■ *Looping*–Write for a specified amount of time, such as six minutes, on the topic you selected. Then read what you have written. Select the most promising idea from this loop, and then write for another limited amount of time on this idea. Again review what you have written, select the best idea, and (if necessary) do another loop. The ideas you generate in each loop can become the main point (thesis) and supporting ideas for your essay.

■ *Journal*–If time permits, write about the topic in your journal over a period of several days. Then review these entries, and select ideas (as single words, as phrases, or as complete sentences) that can become the focus for your essay on this topic.

REVISING

In revising your essay, follow these seven steps:

1. Ask a friend, a roommate, or a writing colleague (or colleagues) to listen to or read and then comment on what you have written. Specifically, are the subject and the purpose of the essay clear? Does the body of the essay make and support points that achieve the purpose of the writing? Do any sentences, passages, or sections of the paper seem either unrelated to or contradictory to the purpose of the writing?

2. Check the introduction and thesis statement of the essay. Have you introduced your reader to the topic you plan to classify? Have you adequately restricted the topic? Does your introductory paragraph have a thesis that makes clear what you plan to say about your topic? Have you developed a focus in the thesis for the classification? Is your introduction interesting? clear? In what ways do you need to rewrite the introduction so that you engage the reader's interest and clarify your purpose?

3. Check the thesis support in the body of the essay. Is the material in the body of the essay organized so that it supports the point (thesis) of the writing? Is the principle of classification maintained in a consistent manner?

4. Check the paragraph support throughout the essay. Is each paragraph well written? Does each paragraph include clear and specific details? Have you adequately specified the distinguishing characteristics of the members of each class, as explained in this chapter? Have you maintained a reasonable balance among the various parts of the essay? Have you maintained distinct classes within the essay?

5. Check for coherence and unity. As a whole, does the essay make sense? Does it contain any irrelevant material?

6. Check for closure. Is there closure at the end of the essay in either a concluding (or summarizing) paragraph or a concluding sentence?

7. Finally, review the Revision Checklist at the end of Chapter 5. Use the checklist to make sure that you have completed a thorough revision of your essay.

COMPARISON AND CONTRAST

Comparison and contrast is a very useful intellectual process for gaining information about many things. If, for example, someone asked you what hate is, you might begin your response by saying, "Well, hate is the opposite of love." This could be the beginning of an explanation of the meaning of the term *hate* based on the comparison and contrast rhetorical pattern.

You might continue the comparison and contrast rhetorical strategy by saying that both love and hate are emotions. Love is a positive, caring emotion. Hate, however, is a negative, hostile emotion. As this comparison and contrast develops, we learn more about hate.

A *comparison* is a showing of how two things are alike *or* of how they are both alike and different. A *contrast* is a showing of how two things are different.

✎ JOURNAL SUGGESTIONS

Temporarily focus your journal writing on the strategy of thinking called *comparison and contrast*. Comparison and contrast issues that you might write about in your journal include the following:

■ In our American consumer-oriented society, how important is it to be able to compare and contrast? How do you employ this thinking strategy when you make routine or special purchases such as toothpaste, a new car, fast food, or magazines? When you walk down the aisle of a grocery store where options are plentiful, how do you make purchase decisions? Do you buy the toothpaste that's on sale? Do you buy the one in a pretty box? Do you buy the one that has attractive TV or magazine advertising? How do you evaluate the item you purchase?

■ Everyone has had good and bad teachers. Write about a good teacher and a bad teacher you have had. What particular characteristics, teaching methods, and personality traits made them different?

■ Compare your daily routine with the imagined daily routine of someone who lives in a third-world country. Based on what you know from your readings and from watching TV about life in such a place, how would the routines be similar and how would they differ?

Finally, try to develop your own ideas and topics for journal entries. What is it about the thinking strategy called *comparison and contrast* that interests you? How is it important in your life? Remember to refer to these journal entries when you begin work on the writing assignment at the end of this chapter. You may be able to develop one or more of the ideas in your journal into an essay for the assignment at the end of this chapter.

The following journal entry was written in response to these journal suggestions.

Example   FRIDAY, 10TH

    Reading these suggestions for journal entries makes me think of last week, when I took Lynn to the dermatologist. She's been having some kind of rash that makes her itch. The dermatologist asked me what kind of laundry detergent we use, and I laughed and told him whatever's on sale.

    I guess that's how I make laundry detergent purchases most of the time. I push my grocery cart down the long detergent and household cleaners aisle, looking for the little yellow tags hanging down from the shelf that mean there's a sale. Sometimes I have coupons. I hate keeping up with coupons. I mean, why don't the manufacturers just give you a few pennies off instead of playing those games? But sometimes if the coupon is really good or there's a double coupon offer at the store, I take them with me and buy that detergent. Of course, if the yellow tagged item is cheaper than the item with the coupon, I usually forget the couponed item and buy the sale item.

    Are there other ways I buy detergent? Well, if I don't have a coupon and there's no sale, I buy the generic brand. And then sometimes there are brands that aren't generic but are not heavily advertised and they're pretty cheap. I sometimes buy those. I guess cost is the big factor for me when it comes to buying laundry detergent. Thank goodness the dermatologist said it didn't matter what I used with her clothes—just to rinse everything twice for a while until her rash clears up.

GUIDELINES

Using the following guidelines will enable you to write more easily in the comparison and contrast rhetorical pattern.

- Select two items to compare or contrast.
- Develop suitable bases of comparison or contrast.
- Select a method of organization for presenting the information.
- Maintain balance among the various parts of the essay.
- Develop either a general thesis statement or a focused thesis statement.

TOPIC

Select two ideas or items to compare and contrast. You might, for example, contrast your father and your mother. Or you might compare two cars you are considering purchasing, such as a Chevrolet GEO and a Toyota Corolla. Finally, you might compare or contrast two ideas, such as justice and fairness.

PRACTICE   The following thesis statements are for use in either comparison essays or contrast essays. Read each thesis statement, and determine whether it is for a comparison essay or for a contrast essay. Use *c* to indicate comparison thesis statements and *cn* to indicate contrast thesis statements. We begin with two examples:

Example   _cn___ Vacationing at Disney World and in New York City are as different as night and day.

_c___ Going to school and working at a job have many things in common.

Now complete the practice exercises that follow.

_____ 1. The way we celebrate Christmas at our house is very different from the way my family celebrated Christmas when I was a child.

_____ 2. When I was considering purchasing a computer, I paid special attention to the basic differences and similarities of the Apple IIe and the IBM PC.

_____ 3. Billy Budd and Captain Vere represent two very different perspectives toward the application of justice in civilized society.

_____ 4. Although I recently got a promotion, my job responsibilities didn't change very much.

_____ 5. My senior English teacher and my college English professor covered very similar material in their courses.

_____ 6. Cats and dogs, both good pets, have different needs and provide different kinds of satisfaction to their owners.

_____ 7. My first car, a used Toyota, gave me better service, lower operating costs, and more interior space than the new Chevrolet Spectrum I recently purchased.

_____ 8. My mother and my father have very different ideas about how I should live my life.

_____ 9. Ignorance and stupidity, though superficially similiar, are actually very different concepts.

_____ 10. My friends Jesse and Brandon are alike in personality, what they do for fun, and the goals they have for their lives.

The distinctions between comparison and contrast, though seemingly minor, are important. If you're instructed to contrast two things, you are to show only how they differ. If, on the other hand, you are to compare two things, you must show how they are alike, although you may also show how they differ.

BASES OF COMPARISON OR CONTRAST

Your next task is to select appropriate bases for the comparison or contrast. Bases are features, characteristics, or qualities that both items have in common. Of course, the quantity or precise nature of the features, characteristics, or qualities the items have in common may differ. It is important to select common or shared bases for comparison or contrast.

Let's say that you're comparing two friends, Bob and Larry. You must decide what characteristics of Bob and Larry you will compare. For example, you could compare their looks, their personalities, their vocations, and their scholastic interests. These, then, would be your bases for comparing Bob and Larry.

As you write the comparison essay, you must also be careful to write only about these bases. Under the circumstances, it would be inappropriate to talk about Larry's athletic accomplishments and Bob's family background, since neither of these were included among your bases for comparing these two friends.

PRACTICE   Following are several topics suitable for comparison or contrast essays. In the spaces provided, list at least two bases of comparison or contrast for each topic. Before listing the bases of comparison or contrast for each topic, you must decide whether you are going to compare or contrast the items contained in each topic. We begin with an example:

Example   *Topic:* Pizza and Spaghetti
Bases of comparison or contrast:

    A. Both are Italian dishes.

    B. Both contain similar ingredients.

Now complete the practice exercises that follow.

1.   *Topic:*   High School and College
Bases of comparison or contrast:

    A. _____

    B. _____

2.   *Topic:*   Dogs and Cats as Pets
Bases of comparison or contrast:

    A. _____

    B. _____

3.   *Topic:*   Radio and Television
Bases of comparison or contrast:

    A. _____

    B. _____

4. *Topic:* Country and Rock Music
   Bases of comparison or contrast:

   A. _____

   B. _____

5. *Topic:* The Civil War and the War of Independence
   Bases of comparison or contrast:

   A. _____

   B. _____

6. *Topic:* Jealousy and Envy
   Bases of comparison or contrast:

   A. _____

   B. _____

7. *Topic:* The Lecture and Discussion Methods of Teaching
   Bases of comparison or contrast:

   A. _____

   B. _____

8. *Topic:* An Orange and an Apple
   Bases of comparison or contrast:

   A. _____

   B. _____

9. *Topic:* Ignorance and Stupidity
   Bases of comparison or contrast:

   A. _____

   B. _____

10. *Topic:* Feminism and Male Chauvinism
    Bases of comparison or contrast:

    A. _____

    B. _____

11.   *Topic:*   [one of your own choosing]
        Bases of comparison or contrast:

A. _____

B. _____

ORGANIZATION

You must present information (support) very clearly and systematically in a comparison or contrast essay. There are two basic methods for doing this: the whole method, and the point-by-point method.

WHOLE METHOD

The whole method of comparison or contrast involves presenting information separately for each item you are comparing or contrasting. You write first about one item and then about the other.

Here is an outline of a comparison essay developed according to the whole method:

Example

Topic	My Friends
Thesis	My friends Bob and Larry are similar in looks, personalities, and scholastic interests.
Body paragraph 1	This paragraph presents information about Bob's looks, personality, and scholastic interests.
Body paragraph 2	This paragraph presents information about Larry's looks, personality, and scholastic interests.
Conclusion	This paragraph makes a summary statement about how Larry and Bob are similar in looks, personalities, and scholastic interests.

If you have too much information for a single paragraph on each item you are comparing, you may develop the whole method with several body paragraphs. The following outline illustrates this alternative form of whole-method development.

Example

Topic	My Friends
Thesis	My friends Bob and Larry are similar in looks, personalities, and scholastic interests.

Body paragraph 1	Bob's looks are described.
Body paragraph 2	Bob's personality is described.
Body paragraph 3	Bob's scholastic interests are described.
Body paragraph 4	Larry's looks are described.
Body paragraph 5	Larry's personality is described.
Body paragraph 6	Larry's scholastic interests are described.
Conclusion	This paragraph makes a summary statement about how Larry and Bob are similar in looks, personalities, and scholastic interests.

POINT-BY-POINT METHOD

The point-by-point method of comparison or contrast involves presenting information about both items at the same time. That is, you make a point about one item, and then you make a point about the other—in the same paragraph.

Here is an outline of the above comparison essay developed according to the point-by-point method.

Example

Topic	My Friends
Thesis	My friends Bob and Larry are similar in looks, personalities, and scholastic interests.
Body paragraph 1	Bob's and Larry's looks are discussed.
Body paragraph 2	Bob's and Larry's personalities are discussed.
Body paragraph 3	Bob's and Larry's scholastic interests are discussed.
Conclusion	This paragraph makes a summary statement about how Larry and Bob are similar in looks, personalities, and scholastic interests.

PRACTICE Read the following essays, and note whether the essays are developed according to the whole method or according to the point-by-point method.

Identify the thesis of the essay, as well as the main points covered in the essay. Write your answers in the space provided. Compare your conclusions with those of a classmate. Discuss any differences in the results.

STUDENT ESSAY

KEEPING UP WITH THE JONESES

Judith Heck

I grew up in a small town in Pennsylvania in a single-parent home. Mother's income was not very much. She worked long, hard hours at a local book-publishing company. We did not have a lot of nice little extras around the house as did some of our friends and neighbors. However, Mother always said that, as long as the things we had were neat and clean, we could be happy with them. When I grew older and got married, my mother's words came back to me, for I found that keeping up with the neighbors was what everybody was trying to do. I have two neighbors who try to outdo each other all of the time. Jo and Ann are very much alike in their tastes for clothing and home furnishings, but one of them always has to go one better than the other.

Jo likes to go shopping in exclusive women's clothing stores. She usually goes once a month and buys expensive, new outfits. Paying eighty dollars for a sweater and one hundred and twenty dollars for a pair of wool slacks doesn't seem to bother her at all. Jo will come home and show her new purchases to Ann. Ann's jealousy to go one better sends her to a bigger and better exclusive women's clothing store to buy a similar outfit. It must, however, cost a little more than Jo's. She then shows her new purchase to Jo to let her know that she did just a little bit better.

Jo recently remodeled her home. She picked out beautiful, plush pile carpeting to cover most of the upstairs living area, the stairs, and the basement. She made arrangements to have two oversized sofas and a chair of contemporary design built and upholstered in a contrasting color to highlight the carpet. It took several months for the project to be completed. Ann made daily inspection visits to check the progress. One could detect the envy and jealousy in Ann's facial expressions and in her voice. It wasn't long after Jo's project was finished that the workers' cars and trucks started turning up daily on the other side of the street. Eventually, Ann's project was also finished, and Jo was invited to come see what Ann had done. Ann's floors were covered in the same type of carpet as Jo's, except that it was just a little bit thicker and a different color. Ann had also had her furniture redone to contrast with her new carpet. This was one time that Jo did not appear to be happy.

Keeping up with the Joneses can have its problems. Friends can become enemies in a big hurry when each tries to outdo the other. I try to remember how things were in my childhood and to make do with what I have. Keeping up with the Joneses, at least for me, is not the answer.

Method of Organization: _____

Thesis: _____

Outline: _____

_____

_____

_____

STUDENT ESSAY _____

PAINT   Dean Bullis

Last Tuesday morning, Tom and Joe went to Sherwin-Williams to buy paint for Joe's father. After spending about thirty minutes in the store, they were totally confused. To put it simply, they didn't know the difference between oil paint and latex paint. Thanks to a helpful salesman, they discovered the differences and similarities of the two paints. As Tom and Joe learned, oil and latex paints differ in composition, uses, and manageability.

Oil paints are made up of a vehicle and many different pigments. The vehicle in oil paint is called linseed oil. Linseed oil is obtained from the seed of the flax plant. The pigments in oil paints are colored powders. These are what give the paint its many colors.

Oil paints have a variety of uses. Oil paints are used as outside paints, metal-protective paints, wall paints, and floor paints. Oil paint is most widely used as a metal-protective paint. For example, it is used for painting bridges, ships, farm and factory machinery, and other metal surfaces. Oil paints are also used by artists.

Oil paints are widely used; however, they can be difficult to work with. Brushes and rollers that have been used to apply oil paints must be washed out in turpentine. Also, oil paints can take from one to twenty-four hours to dry. This is useful to an artist who needs to rewash a specific area on a picture.

In comparison to oil paints, latex paints are similar and different. Latex paints are also made up of a vehicle and pigments. Latex paints have a vehicle known as latex. Latex is suspended resin particles in water, obtained from plants and trees of the sapodilla family. However, the pigments in latex paints are exactly the same pigments as those in oil paints. This is the reason the same shade of color can be found in these two different types of paint.

Latex paints are used as wall paints, masonry paints, and outside paints. Unlike oil paints, latex paints are most widely

PAINT, continued

used as interior paints. For instance, latex paint is used on walls in homes, offices, and schools.

Many people prefer latex paints to oil paints for household painting because they are easier to use. Brushes, rollers, and other painting equipment can easily be cleaned with soap and water after being used to apply latex paints. Latex paints also dry more quickly than do oil paints.

As Tom and Joe left the store, they knew that they had learned something. They knew that there is more to paint than just color. They knew that composition, uses, and manageability play important roles in the world of paint.

Method of Organization: _____

Thesis: _____

Outline: _____

_____

_____

_____

BALANCE

It is important to maintain a balance among the blocks of information presented about each item in your comparison or contrast essay. If you write a lengthy paragraph about one item, do not follow it with a very short paragraph about the next item. Each item in the comparison or contrast essay should receive approximately equal coverage in the body of the essay.

THESIS

You may use either a general thesis statement or a focused thesis statement for the comparison and contrast essay. The following general and focused thesis statements could be used for the same essay.

Example

Topic   My Friends

General
thesis
statement   My friends Larry and Bob are similar in several ways.

Focused
thesis
statement   My friends Larry and Bob are similar in looks, personalities, and scholastic interests.

The plan of development in a focused thesis statement is the basis of comparison or contrast for the essay. If you include the basis, you have a focused thesis statement. If you do not include the basis, you have a general thesis statement.

Remember to use comparison or contrast words and phrases in your thesis statements. These special words signal to your reader that you are comparing or contrasting. The following words are comparison and contrast signal words: *similar, different, alike, unlike, similarly, contrary to, opposite of, also, however, in like manner, nevertheless, but,* and *yet.*

PRACTICE   Working with another classmate, develop both general and focused thesis statements for comparison or contrast essays on the following topics. Write your thesis statements in the spaces provided. You will have to decide whether you are going to compare or contrast the items in each topic.

1. *Topic:* Having Your Own Apartment Versus Living at Home

   General thesis statement: _____

   _____

   _____

   _____

   Focused thesis statement: _____

   _____

   _____

   _____

2. *Topic:* Johnny Carson and David Letterman

General thesis statement: _____

_____

_____

_____

Focused thesis statement: _____

_____

_____

_____

3. *Topic:* Halloween and the Fourth of July

General thesis statement: _____

_____

_____

_____

Focused thesis statement: _____

_____

_____

_____

4. *Topic:* Your Two Favorite Vacation Spots

General thesis statement: _____

_____

_____

_____

Focused thesis statement: _____

_____

_____

_____

5. *Topic:* Baseball and Basketball

General thesis statement: _____

_____

_____

_____

Focused thesis statement: _____

_____

_____

_____

READINGS

The following readings are student and professional essays. Read them carefully, and look for their use of the comparison and contrast guidelines presented in this chapter.

STUDENT ESSAY

HANDS   Lynn Fredericks

At a recent showing of art work by local high-school students, I discovered an interesting piece. Its composition was simply three overlapping red outlines of the artist's hands. These hands had been colored with felt-tip markers; one was checkered

HANDS, continued

black and white, one was colored with waving red and white stripes, and the other was filled with small, irregular, multi-colored spaces, giving a stained glass effect. The three hands that held my attention were structurally the same, yet so different.

After leaving the gallery, I looked at my husband's hands next to mine. Our hands were basically alike. They each had five fingers and nails, each had the same number of joints in the fingers, and each had knuckles that protruded at the base of the fingers when we made fists. But with further observation, I realized that the many small differences between our hands were subtle clues to our heredity, our individual life-styles, and the various things we do with our hands.

Some of the personal characteristics we inherit can be observed in our hands. For example, Dan's fingers and palms are long and wide and in proportion to his tall, large-boned frame. My fingers are as long as Dan's, but much slimmer. And, like my Granddaddy McDaniel, my bony frame is long and slender. Dan and several other members of his family are left-handed. Since the creative processes are centered in the dominant side of the left-hander's brain, one might suspect that Dan has artistic abilities. I am right-handed; the side of my brain that is used most is primarily concerned with logical perception. So it is no surprise that I am the more practical one of the pair.

I also made several observations about our life-styles by noticing the way we present our hands. Dan's fingernails are fairly long, rough, and uneven; he is generally unconcerned about his appearance. My nails are trimmed and rounded; I am usu-

ally a bit neater than he is. Dan's hands are often dingy, with a trace of dirt under his nails. He seems never to have gotten over a little boy's aversion to bath time and puts off bathing as long as possible. But soaking in a hot tub is one of my favorite luxuries, and the cleanliness of my hands and nails reflects this. Dan wears no jewelry on his hands. He also dresses simply, wearing only practical, serviceable clothes. But I wear two rings—a wedding band and a birth stone handed down to me from my aunt. Similarly, I enjoy dressing up, though probably not as extravagantly as someone who wears several flashy rings.

Our hands also give clues to the way we use them. Dan's hands, as mentioned earlier, are dirtier than mine. They often have smudges of oil paint, soot, dirt, and ground-in grease on them. These are all evidence that he spends much time painting, tending the wood stove, working outdoors, and tinkering with his ever-ailing VW. My hands are usually cleaner than his, not only from my love of baths, but because so much of my time is spent in domestic tasks. Washing dishes soaks them clean, cooking and cleaning require continuous trips to the sink to rinse them, and the creative craft I enjoy—basket weaving—involves soaking materials and keeping them wet. The skin on Dan's hands is rough and dry and usually has a few scrapes or scratches. He often works outdoors, exposing his hands to the elements, but, being an artist, he is conscious of the importance of them and rarely hurts them seriously. My hands are smoother and softer, since I regularly use a moisturizing lotion on them. But I am much more careless and often have cuts from a kitchen knife, punctures from my basketry awl,

HANDS, continued

and scrapes on my knuckles from the few times I help gather the firewood. Dan's hands are callused on the palms at the base of each finger, indicating that he often does heavy work with them. My only callus is on my second finger, where I grip my pen, evidence of the long hours that I spend laboring over my English essays.

And finally, the strength of our hands is not the same. In a hand-squeezing contest, my hand always gets crushed. Dan often works with heavy tools that he must hold and guide with his hands, such as a chain saw, skill saw, maul, and a hammer. But

when I lift my forty-five-pound son into a grocery cart, haul a basket full of wet clothes to the clothesline, or drag a bale of hay to the barn, I strengthen my arms and do little to make my hands stronger.

Many clues to a person's character and life-style can be found in his or her hands. The size and shape of one's hands often reflect the nature of the entire body. The attention given to the hands is often an indication of a person's attitudes about his or her body. And the wear on one's hands can tell a lot about how they are used.

PROFESSIONAL ESSAY

THE TRANSACTION: TWO WRITING PROCESSES

William Zinsser

Several years ago a school in Connecticut held "a day devoted to the arts," and I was asked if I would come and talk about writing as a vocation. When I arrived I found that a second speaker had been invited—Dr. Brock (as I'll call him), a surgeon who had recently begun to write and had sold some stories to national magazines. He was going to talk about writing as an avocation. That made us a panel, and we sat down to face a crowd of student newspaper editors and reporters, English teachers and parents, all eager to learn the secrets of our glamorous work.

Dr. Brock was dressed in a bright red jacket, looking vaguely Bohemian, as au-

thors are supposed to look, and the first question went to him. What was it like to be a writer?

He said it was tremendous fun. Coming home from an arduous day at the hospital, he would go straight to his yellow pad and write his tensions away. The words just flowed. It was easy.

I then said that writing wasn't easy and it wasn't fun. It was hard and lonely, and the words seldom just flowed.

Next Dr. Brock was asked if it was important to rewrite. Absolutely not, he said. "Let it all hang out," and whatever form the sentences take will reflect the writer at his most natural.

SOURCE: *On Writing Well* by William K. Zinsser. Copyright © 1980 by William K. Zinsser. Reprinted by permission of the author.

THE TRANSACTION: TWO WRITING PROCESSES, continued

I then said that rewriting is the essence of writing. I pointed out that professional writers rewrite their sentences repeatedly and then rewrite what they have rewritten. I mentioned that E. B. White and James Thurber were known to rewrite their pieces eight or nine times.

"What do you do on days when it isn't going well?" Dr. Brock was asked. He said he just stopped writing and put the work aside for a day when it would go better.

I then said that the professional writer must establish a daily schedule and stick to it. I said that writing is a craft, not an art, and that the man who runs away from his craft because he lacks inspiration is fooling himself. He is also going broke.

"What if you're feeling depressed or unhappy?" a student asked. "Won't that affect your writing?"

Probably it will, Dr. Brock replied. Go fishing. Take a walk.

Probably it won't, I said. If your job is to write every day, you learn to do it like any other job.

A student asked if we found it useful to circulate in the literary world. Dr. Brock said that he was greatly enjoying his new life as a man of letters, and he told several luxurious stories of being taken to lunch by his publisher and his agent at Manhattan restaurants where writers and editors gather. I said that professional writers are solitary drones who seldom see other writers.

"Do you put symbolism in your writing?" a student asked me.

"Not if I can help it," I replied. I have an unbroken record of missing the deeper meaning in any story, play or movie, and as for dance and mime I have never had even a remote notion of what is being conveyed.

"I *love* symbols!" Dr. Brock exclaimed, and he described with gusto the joys of weaving them through his work.

So the morning went, and it was a revelation to all of us. At the end Dr. Brock told me he was enormously interested in my answers—it had never occurred to him that writing could be hard. I told him I was just as interested in *his* answers—it had never occurred to me that writing could be easy. (Maybe I should take up surgery on the side.)

As for the students, anyone might think that we left them bewildered. But in fact we probably gave them a broader glimpse of the writing process than if only one of us had talked. For of course there isn't any "right" way to do such intensely personal work. There are all kinds of writers and all kinds of methods, and any method that helps somebody to say what he wants to say is the right method for him.

Rhetoric

1. The introductory paragraph of "The Transaction: Two Writing Processes" presents the two writers in a debate situation. Why is this an effective introduction for a contrast essay?

2. William Zinsser writes in short, simple, and direct sentences. Do you think this is an effective writing technique? Why or why not?

3. What are the bases of contrast in this essay?

Ideas

1. What is the subject of this article?

2. What basic questions does this essay raise about the practice of writing?

Response

1. Write a paragraph in which you disagree with one of the ideas about the act of writing presented in this article.

2. Write an essay in which you compare or contrast your ideas about the writing process with one of the two positions presented in this selection.

PROFESSIONAL ESSAY

THAT LEAN AND HUNGRY LOOK   Suzanne Britt

Caesar was right. Thin people need watching. I've been watching them for most of my adult life, and I don't like what I see. When these narrow fellows spring at me, I quiver to my toes. Thin people come in all personalities, most of them menacing. You've got your "together" thin person, your mechanical thin person, your condescending thin person, your tsk-tsk thin person, your efficiency-expert thin person. All of them are dangerous.

In the first place, thin people aren't fun. They don't know how to goof off, at least in the best, fat sense of the word. They've always got to be adoing. Give them a coffee break, and they'll jog around the block. Supply them with a quiet evening at home, and they'll fix the screen door and lick S&H green stamps. They say things like "there aren't enough hours in the day." Fat people never say that. Fat people think the day is too damn long already.

Thin people make me tired. They've got speedy little metabolisms that cause them to bustle briskly. They're forever rubbing their bony hands together and eyeing new problems to "tackle." I like to surround myself with sluggish, inert, easygoing fat people, the kind who believe that if you clean it up today, it'll just get dirty again tomorrow.

Some people say the business about the jolly fat person is a myth, that all of us chubbies are neurotic, sick, sad people. I disagree. Fat people may not be chortling all day long, but they're a hell of a lot *nicer* than the wizened and shriveled. Thin people turn surly, mean, and hard at a young age because they never learn the value of a hot-fudge sundae for easing tension. Thin people don't like gooey soft things because they themselves are neither gooey nor soft. They are crunchy and dull, like carrots. They go straight to the

Reprinted by permission of the author.

THAT LEAN AND HUNGRY LOOK, continued

heart of the matter while fat people let things stay all blurry and hazy and vague, the way things actually are. Thin people want to face the truth. Fat people know there is no truth. One of my thin friends is always staring at complex, unsolvable problems and saying, "The key thing is. . . ." Fat people never say that. They know there isn't any such thing as the key thing about anything.

Thin people believe in logic. Fat people see all sides. The sides fat people see are rounded blobs, usually gray, always nebulous and truly not worth worrying about. But the thin person persists. "If you consume more calories than you burn," says one of my thin friends, "you will gain weight. It's that simple." Fat people always grin when they hear statements like that. They know better.

Fat people realize that life is illogical and unfair. They know very well that God is not in his heaven and all is not right with the world. If God was up there, fat people could have two doughnuts and a big orange drink anytime they wanted it.

Thin people have a long list of logical things they are always spouting off to me. They hold up one finger at a time as they reel off these things, so I won't lose track. They speak slowly as if to a young child. The list is long and full of holes. It contains tidbits like "get a grip on yourself," "cigarettes kill," "cholesterol clogs," "fit as a fiddle," "ducks in a row," "organize," and "sound fiscal management." Phrases like that.

They think these 2,000-point plans lead to happiness. Fat people know happiness is elusive at best and even if they could get the kind thin people talk about, they wouldn't want it. Wisely, fat people see that such programs are too dull, too hard, too off the mark. They are never better than a whole cheesecake.

Fat people know all about the mystery of life. They are the ones acquainted with the night, with luck, with fate, with playing it by ear. One thin person I know once suggested that we arrange all the parts of a jigsaw puzzle into groups according to size, shape, and color. He figured this would cut the time needed to complete the puzzle by at least 50 percent. I said I wouldn't do it. One, I like to muddle through. Two, what good would it do to finish early? Three, the jigsaw puzzle isn't the important thing. The important thing is the fun of four people (one thin person included) sitting around a card table, working a jigsaw puzzle. My thin friend had no use for my list. Instead of joining us, he went outside and mulched the boxwoods. The three remaining fat people finished the puzzle and made chocolate, double-fudge brownies to celebrate.

The main problem with thin people is they oppress. Their good intentions, bony torsos, tight ships, neat corners, cerebral machinations, and pat solutions loom like dark clouds over the loose, comfortable, spread-out, soft world of the fat. Long after fat people have removed their coats and shoes and put their feet up on the coffee table, thin people are still sitting on the edge of the sofa, looking neat as a pin, discussing rutabagas. Fat people are heavily into fits of laughter, slapping their thighs and whooping it up, while thin people are still politely waiting for the punch line.

Thin people are downers. They like math and morality and reasoned evaluation of the limitations of human beings.

THAT LEAN AND HUNGRY LOOK, continued

They have their skinny little acts together. They expound, prognose, probe, and prick.

Fat people are convivial. They will like you even if you're irregular and have acne. They will come up with a good reason why you never wrote the great American novel. They will cry in your beer with you. They will put your name in the pot. They will let you off the hook. Fat people will gab, giggle, guffaw, gallumph, gyrate, and gossip. They are generous, giving, and gallant. They are gluttonous and goodly and great. What you want when you're down is soft and jiggly, not muscled and stable. Fat people know this. Fat people have plenty of room. Fat people will take you in.

Rhetoric

1. According to the author's thesis statement, "All of them are dangerous." In what ways are thin people dangerous?

2. List three bases the author uses to contrast thin people and fat people.

Ideas

1. Although the tone of "That Lean and Hungry Look" is amusing, the author makes some important claims about human nature and the nature of reality. Identify two of these.

2. Do you agree with Britt's thesis that, "All of them [meaning thin people] are dangerous?" Why or why not?

Response

1. In parallel columns, list the characteristics of thin people and the contrasting characteristics of fat people.

2. Write an essay in which you disagree with at least three of the author's statements about thin people.

PROFESSIONAL ESSAY

VENEZUELA FOR VISITORS   John Updike

All Venezuela, except for the negligible middle class, is divided between the Indians (*los indios*) and the rich (*los ricos*). The Indians are mostly to be found in the south, amid the muddy tributaries of the Orinoco and the god-haunted *tepuys*

SOURCE: *Hugging the Shore* by John Updike. Copyright © 1983 by John Updike. Reprinted by permission of Alfred A. Knopf, Inc.

VENEZUELA FOR VISITORS, continued

(mesas) that rear their fearsome mile-high crowns above the surrounding jungle, whereas the rich tend to congregate in the north, along the sunny littoral, in the burgeoning metropolis of Caracas, and on the semi-circular shores of Lake Maracaibo, from which their sumptuous black wealth is drawn. The negligible middle class occupies a strip of arid savanna in the center of the nation and a few shunned enclaves on the suburban slopes of Monte Avila.

The Indians, who range in color from mocha to Dentyne, are generally under five feet tall. Their hair style runs to pageboys and severe bangs, with some tonsures in deference to lice. Neither sex is quite naked: the males wear around their waists a thong to which their foreskins are tied, pulling their penises taut upright; the females, once out of infancy, suffer such adornments as three pale sticks symmetrically thrust into their lower faces. The gazes of both sexes are melting, brown, alert, canny. The visitor, standing among them with his Nikon FE and L. L. Bean fannypack, is shy at first, but warms to their inquisitive touches, which patter and rub across his person with a soft, sandy insistence unlike both the fumblings of children and the caresses one Caucasian adult will give another. There is an infectious, wordless ecstasy in their touches, and a blank eagerness with yet some parameters of tact and irony. *These are human presences*, the visitor comes to realize.

The rich, who range in color from porcelain to mocha, are generally under six feet tall. Their hair style runs to chignons and blow-dried trims. Either sex is elegantly clad: the males favor dark suits of medium weight (nights in Caracas can be cool), their close English cut enhanced by a slight Latin flare, and shirts with striped bodies but stark-white collars and French cuffs held by agates and gold; the females appear in a variety of gowns and mock-military pants suits, Dior and de la Renta originals flown in from Paris and New York. The gazes of both sexes are melting, brown, alert, canny. The visitor, standing among them in his funky Brooks Brothers suit and rumpled blue button-down, is shy at first, but warms to their excellent English, acquired at colleges in London or "the States," and to their impeccable manners, which conceal, as their fine clothes conceal their skins, rippling depths of Spanish and those dark thoughts that the mind phrases to itself in its native language. They tell anecdotes culled from their rich international lives; they offer, as the evening deepens, confidences, feelers, troubles. These, too, are human presences.

The Indians live in *shabonos*—roughly circular lean-tos woven beautifully of palm thatch in clearings hacked and burned out of the circumambient rain forest. A *shabono* usually rots and is abandoned within three years. The interiors are smoky, from cooking fires, and eye diseases are common among the Indians. They sleep, rest, and die in hammocks (*cinchorros*) hung as close together as pea pods on a vine. Their technology, involving in its pure state neither iron nor the wheel, is yet highly sophisticated: the chemical intricacies of curare have never been completely plumbed, and with their blowpipes of up to sixteen feet in length the Indians can bring down prey at distances of over thirty meters. They fish without hooks, by employing nets and thrashing the water with poisonous lianas. All this sounds cheerier than it is. It is

VENEZUELA FOR VISITORS, continued

depressing to stand in the gloom of a *sha-bono*, the palm thatch overhead infested with giant insects, the Indians drooping in their hammocks, their eyes diseased, their bellies protuberant, their faces and limbs besmirched with the same gray-brown dirt that composes the floor, their possessions a few brown baskets and monkey skins. Their lives are not paradise but full of anxiety—their religion a matter of fear, their statecraft a matter of constant, nagging war. To themselves, they are "the people" (*Yanomami*); to others, they are "the killers" (*Waikás*).

The rich dwell in *haciendas*—airy long ranch houses whose roofs are of curved tile and, surprisingly, dried sugar-cane stalks. Some *haciendas* surviving in Caracas date from the sixteenth century, when the great valley was all but empty. The interiors are smoky, from candlelit dinners, and contact lenses are common among the rich. The furniture is solid, black, polished by generations of servants. Large paintings by Diebenkorn, Stella, Baziotes, and Botero adorn the white plaster walls, along with lurid religious pictures in the colonial Spanish style. The appliances are all modern and paid for; even if the oil in Lake Maracaibo were to give out, vast deposits of heavy crude have been discovered in the state of Bolívar. All this sounds cheerier than it is. The rich wish they were in Paris, London, New York. Many have condominiums in Miami. *Haute couture* and abstract painting may not prove bulwark enough. Constitutional democracy in Venezuela, though the last dictator fled in 1958, is not so assured as may appear. Turbulence and tyranny are traditional. Che Guevara is still idealized among students. To themselves, the rich

are good, decent, amusing people; to others, they are "*reaccionarios*".

Missionaries, many of them United States citizens, move among the Indians. They claim that since Western civilization, with all its diseases and detritus, must come, it had best come through them. Nevertheless, Marxist anthropologists inveigh against them. Foreign experts, many of them United States citizens, move among the rich. They claim they are just helping out, and that anyway the oil industry was nationalized five years ago. Nevertheless, Marxist anthropologists are not mollified. The feet of the Indians are very broad in front, their toes spread wide for climbing avocado trees. The feet of the rich are very narrow in front, their toes compressed by pointed Italian shoes. The Indians seek relief from tension in the use of *ebene*, or *yopo*, a mind-altering drug distilled from the bark of the *ebene* tree and blown into the user's nose through a hollow cane by a colleague. The rich take cocaine through the nose, and frequent mind-altering discotheques, but more customarily imbibe cognac, *vino blanco*, and Scotch, in association with colleagues.

These and other contrasts and comparisons between the Indians and the rich can perhaps be made more meaningful by the following anecdote: A visitor, after some weeks in Venezuela, was invited to fly to the top of a *tepuy* in a helicopter, which crashed. As stated, the *tepuys* are supposed by the Indians to be the forbidden haunts of the gods; and, indeed, they present an exotic, attenuated vegetation and a craggy geology to the rare intruder. The crash was a minor one, breaking neither bones nor bottles (a lavish picnic, including *mu-*

VENEZUELA FOR VISITORS, continued

cho vino blanco, had been packed). The bottles were consumed, the exotic vegetation was photographed, and a rescue helicopter arrived. In the Cessna back to Caracas, the survivors couldn't get enough of discussing the incident and their survival, and the red-haired woman opposite the visitor said, "I *love* the way you pronounce '*tepuy.*'" She imitated him: *tupooey.* "Real zingy," she said. The visitor slowly realized that he was being flirted with, and that therefore *this woman was middle-class.* In Venezuela, only the negligible middle class flirts. The Indians kidnap or are raped; the rich commandeer, or languorously give themselves in imperious surrender.

The Indians tend to know only three words of Spanish: "¿*Cómo se llama?*"

("What is your name?"). In Indian belief, to give one's name is to place oneself in the other's power. And the rich, when one is introduced, narrow their eyes and file one's name away in their mysterious depths. Power among them flows along lines of kinship and intimacy. After an imperious surrender, a rich female gazes at her visitor with new interest out of her narrowed, brown, melting, kohl-ringed eyes. He has become someone to be reckoned with, if only as a potential source of financial embarrassment. "Again, what is your name?" she asks.

Los indios and *los ricos* rarely achieve contact. When they do, *mestizos* result, and the exploitation of natural resources. In such lies the future of Venezuela.

Rhetoric

1. In "Venezuela for Visitors" the author includes numerous supporting details in every paragraph of the essay. Make a list of the specifics contained in the fourth paragraph of the essay.

2. Is information in the body of the essay presented primarily in the point-by-point method or in the whole method?

3. Identify as specifically as you can the bases of comparison and contrast used in the essay.

Ideas

1. Analyze your response to the information presented in the essay. Do you feel particularly sympathetic toward either the Indians or the rich? Explain your response.

2. The author seems purposefully to minimize the existence as well as the role of the *mestizos* in Venezuela. The essay, however, concludes by focusing on this new class of Venezuelan citizens. Why did the author end the essay in this way? What hint might he be giving the reader about the future of this country?

Response

1. Good essays either directly or indirectly deal with the issues of audience and purpose. Working with a small group of classmates, discuss the audience and purpose of this essay. After discussing these with your classmates, write a brief paragraph in which you identify what you believe are the audience and the purpose of this essay. Give two or more reasons that support your conclusions.

2. Write a paragraph in which you identify and describe the tone of the essay.

3. You are a member of numerous groups, including (perhaps) an athletic team, a dormitory's residents, a church, and various social clubs or organizations. There are, of course, divisions, groups, and cliques within each of these larger groups. Write an essay in which you identify and then compare or contrast two cliques or divisions within a larger group of which you are a member.

WRITING ASSIGNMENT

You may select a topic for this writing assignment from one of the following lists, or you may develop your own topic. Once you have selected a topic, complete one or more of the specified prewriting activities. After sufficient prewriting, write a draft of an essay on the topic you selected. Finally, revise and edit your essay.

General Writing Assignments

- Two teachers you especially liked
- The two places where you would most prefer to live
- Two similar cars
- Two movies you've seen recently
- Two of your relatives or two of your friends
- Apartment living versus owning your own home
- Where you used to live and where you live now

Specific Writing Assignments

- While you were home from college for a visit, your younger brother, a ninth-grader, asked you how college differs from high school. Back in your dorm room, you decide to write a letter to your brother in which you identify and clarify the primary differences between high school and college.

■ Your history instructor has asked selected members of the class, including you, to write essays comparing the structure, content, and merits of objective and essay tests. Based on the persuasiveness of the essays, your instructor will determine which type of test to give your class.

If you decide to develop your own topic, you may want to look through your journal for ideas. What topics that you have addressed in your journal lend themselves to this particular strategy of thinking and communicating? You might also look carefully at the focused journal entries you wrote at the beginning of this chapter. Is one of these topics of interest to you? Is it a topic with which you have some experience? With some revision work, could your journal entry on this topic become an essay?

Finally, look back through this chapter at some of the exercises you have done individually and with classmates. Are any of these topics of interest to you? Recall conversations with your classmates. Have they given you ideas for topics? Perhaps interesting topics emerged from the group discussions that followed some of the practices in the chapter. You may want to spend some time discussing these exercises with classmates to help you decide what to write about. Or you may want to do some listing, brainstorming, or freewriting to help you discover a suitable topic.

PREWRITING

After selecting a topic as the subject for a comparison or contrast essay, complete one or more of the following prewriting activities:

■ *Clustering*—Write the topic in the center of a blank sheet of paper; then draw a box around the topic. Next, write the main ideas you have about the topic at random around the topic and draw a box around each main idea. Connect each main idea to the topic with a straight line. Finally, jot down your ideas about each main idea, and connect each of them with a line to the most appropriate main idea. One or more of these clusters will serve as a focus or direction for an essay on this topic.

■ *Focused freewriting*—Write the topic you selected at the top of a blank sheet of paper. Then write about this topic for six minutes without stopping. After writing, review what you have written, and select the best material there to serve as a focus for an essay on this topic.

REVISING

In revising your essay, follow these seven steps:

1. Ask a friend, a roommate, or a writing colleague (or colleagues) to listen to or read your writing and then to comment on what you have written. Specifically, are the subject and the purpose of the essay clear? Does the body of the essay make and support points that achieve the purpose of the writing? Do any sentences, passages, or sections of the paper seem either unrelated to or contradictory to the purpose of the writing?

2. Check the introduction and thesis statement of the essay. Have you introduced your reader to the topic you plan to compare or contrast? Have you adequately restricted the topic? Does your introductory paragraph have a thesis that makes clear what you plan to say about your topic? Have you developed a focus in the thesis for the comparison or contrast? In what ways do you need to rewrite the introduction so that you engage the reader's interest and clarify your purpose?

3. Check the thesis support in the body of the essay. Is the material in the body of the essay organized so that it supports the point (thesis) of the writing? Are the details in your comparison or contrast organized in one of the ways discussed at the beginning of the chapter—either whole method or point-by-point method?

4. Check the paragraph support throughout the essay. Is each paragraph well written, with clear and specific details to support your thesis? Have you selected suitable bases of comparison or contrast? Have you maintained balance among the various parts of the essay?

5. Check for coherence and unity. As a whole, does the essay make sense? Does it contain any irrelevant or misplaced material?

6. Check for closure. Is there closure at the end of the essay in either a concluding sentence or a concluding (or summarizing) paragraph?

7. Finally, review the Revision Checklist at the end of Chapter 5. Use the checklist to make sure that you have completed a thorough revision of your essay.

DEFINITION

The process of defining is one of the key ways we make sense of the world around us. In fact, we are regularly engaged in the act of creating definitions as we deal with both trivial and important questions and issues. The following conversation represents one such instance:

Example

"How can you say you love me when you do things like you did yesterday? Do you call that love?"

"Of course I love you. You know I love you. I'll say it again—I love you."

"Well, if you call that love, I'd like to know what you mean by love."

Obviously, this is a rather heated, emotional discussion. Nevertheless, it's easy to see where this conversation could be leading. The two parties involved are going to have to talk about what the term *love* means to each of them. By doing so, they will in effect create two different definitions of this concept.

Many other instances illustrate the importance of defining. We all, for example, want to live the "good life," but our individual definitions of what that is will vary considerably. The process of defining is also vitally important in the institutions of society. Our court system is still struggling to define "cruel and unusual punishment" and our government, along with the government of the Soviet Union, is working diligently to define what is meant by "détente" and "verifiable reduction in nuclear weapons."

In academic settings, definitions take on particular and specific significance. What, for example, do historians mean by the word *history*, and does the English instructor's understanding of the term *symbol* vary considerably from the popular understanding of this word? As a member of the academic community, you'll frequently be asked to provide definitions of concepts, terms, and objects. As you engage in the process of defining, remember that it is process-oriented and that how you go about creating a definition has a significant effect on the content of the definition you ultimately produce.

JOURNAL SUGGESTIONS

Temporarily focus your journal writing on the strategy of thinking called *definition*. Definition issues that you might write about in your journal include the following:

- Our culture is fascinated by the concept of romantic love. Think about movies, popular songs, and TV shows you have seen or heard recently. How do they tend to define *love*? In other words, according to popular music (for example), what is love? What characterizes it?
- Have you had the experience of discovering that your concept of something or idea contradicted the concept someone else had? How did your concepts differ? How did you know that your concepts differed? Did you discuss it?
- The issue of human rights is in the news frequently. We as Americans have a definition of "human rights" that we support, although our definition differs from that of other countries. How would you define the American concept of "human rights"?

Finally, try to develop your own ideas and topics for journal entries. What is it about the thinking strategy called *definition* that interests you? How is it important in your life? Remember to refer to these journal entries when you begin work on the writing assignment at the end of this chapter. You may be able to develop some of the ideas in your journal into an essay for the assignment at the end of the chapter.

The following journal entry was written in response to these journal suggestions.

Example   FRIDAY, 10TH

I love to go to the movies. Although I'm not against VCRs, and I check movies out frequently, to me there's nothing like going to the movies, buying that good popcorn and a large Diet Coke, and settling down in a dark theater to watch that wide screen fill up and to be surrounded by the stereo sound.

But movies have become so expensive, I can't go as often as I used to. Even the bargain matinee is not cheap any more! And the price of Diet Coke and popcorn at the movies is laughable. So I have come up with a new way of defining movies to help me decide whether to see them at home or at the theater. I read reviews, watch ads, and talk to my friends to find out about new releases. Then I decide whether the movie is what I call a movie movie or a VCR movie. Movie movies are the ones I'm willing to spend the megabucks on; VCR movies are the ones I check out for a night and make my own popcorn for.

A movie movie is a blockbuster, a big one, a long-awaited event. It may have big stars, actors and actresses who no longer bother with the cheap stuff, who only work in pictures that are worth their time and effort. If the script is worth these actors' and actresses' time and effort, chances are it's also going to be worth my time—but mainly my money.

A movie movie has a plot. It doesn't just show somebody walking around in a big city getting into trouble and getting old ladies and beautiful women out of trouble. It has a story line that enthralls me and makes me think.

A movie movie may have good music. The soundtrack for a movie movie is one I might consider purchasing later on. I go to a movie in the theater if I know that the music is going to be really good, because it sounds so good in a good theater and watching the movie and hearing the accompanying music at the same time increases my understanding of the music and how it relates to the plot.

One of the best things about going to a movie movie is when the scenery is especially beautiful. There are some movies that are just meant to be seen on that wide screen. Watching them on the small screen in the den is just not the same.

If a movie doesn't have any of these characteristics, I define it as a VCR movie. If it has good reviews, I may check it out and watch it at home. If not, I'll read a good book that evening.

WAYS OF DEFINING

Definitions generally are of two types: dictionary definitions and extended definitions.

DICTIONARY DEFINITIONS

The term *dictionary definition* refers, of course, to the type of definition common to dictionaries. Although we sometimes use this term to mean a short definition, it refers to a definition that has a very specific structure and controlled content. The typical dictionary definition is a three-part construction that provides basic and essential information about a particular word. This construction consists of the following parts:

Term	Class	Contrast
The word being defined	The group, class, or category of which the word is a member	Qualities or characteristics the word does not share with other members of its class

Here is how these parts handle a dictionary definition of *love:*

Example

Term	Class	Contrast
love	emotion	affection, attachment, devotion

Definition of *love*

Love is an *emotion* characterized by *affection* or *attachment* or *devotion* to a person, place, or object.

This simple definition contains the elemental meaning of the term *love*. It does not, of course, deal with the complexities and myriad applications of the term. To do so would require a broader and more in-depth treatment of this concept.

EXTENDED DEFINITIONS

Dictionary definitions are adequate in many speaking and writing situations where defining a term is necessary or desirable. In many other instances, lengthy, focused definitions are essential to making a point, classifying one's position toward an issue, or simply eliminating confusion. Such definitions are called *extended definitions*.

Extended definitions are fundamental to academic inquiry and are a part of all academic disciplines. Historians attempt to tell us what the

Great Depression was, literary scholars want us to know what Romantic poetry is, psychologists define and redefine *depression*, and sociologists constantly struggle to create a working, technical definition of the phenomenon called *society*.

Extended definitions are also crucial for understanding abstractions. When we talk about freedom, beauty, love, justice, and similar ideas, we are forced to develop extended, tentative definitions of these concepts. Perhaps, for example, it is impossible to create the perfect definition of *justice;* nevertheless, we regularly face the need to say what is just and what is not. And to do so, we must have a working definition of the term.

As you continue to study and learn as a member of an academic community, you will find that it is frequently necessary to define. Anytime you are confronted with statements and questions like the following, you are being asked to develop a definition:

Examples

- What does _____ mean?
  What does neoclassical mean?
- _____ is _____ .
  Suicide is murder.
- What is the meaning of _____ ?
  What is the meaning of realism?
- What is meant by _____ ?
  What is meant by poverty?
- What differentiates _____ from _____ ?
  What differentiates middle-class society from upper-middle-class society?
- How can _____ be recognized?
  How can botulism be recognized?
- _____ means _____ .
  Courage means bravery.

GUIDELINES

Developing extended definitions is one of the most challenging writing tasks any writer faces. Often, creating a workable extended definition involves using varied expository strategies, including comparison and contrast, process analysis, example, description, and even classification.

Although writing an extended definition is challenging, it need not be intimidating. The following guidelines are well-established, effective strategies that will enable you to create precise and informative extended definitions and to write more easily in the definition rhetorical pattern. As you review these guidelines, consider how you might apply them to specific writing tasks. Here are the guidelines:

- Identify and restrict your topic.
- Obtain a dictionary definition of your topic.
- Determine the purpose of the extended definition.
- Select one or more expository strategies for developing a definition essay.
- Develop either a general or focused thesis statement.

TOPIC

Generally, topics for definition essays will be assigned by instructors. You may receive such an assignment from an instructor in almost any discipline since all academic disciplines rely heavily on specialized vocabularies. *Heat*, for example, does not mean quite the same thing to a physicist that it does to you when your roommate says, "Turn up the heat; it's cold in here."

Once you have received such an assignment, make sure that you fully identify and restrict the topic. For example, if your political science instructor asks you to write a brief essay in which you define *democracy*, be sure to find out whether you're supposed to write the definition from a legal, a political, or an economic perspective—or from two or more of these perspectives. Such clarification can help you develop a sense of direction and scope as you begin the prewriting process.

STANDARD MEANING

A standard meaning—the dictionary definition—of a term such as *democracy* does not go very far toward explaining all aspects of this complex, volatile, and powerful concept. However, a quick look at a dictionary definition of the word will give you some important and helpful information about it. For example, it's easy to see that Americans did not invent the term. Rather, it came from the Greek via Medieval Latin and then French. The source terms in Greek, *demos* and *kratos*, simply mean "the people" and "power." The next part of the standard dictionary definition of *democracy* is "a government in which. . . ." Now we know that *democracy* belongs to the class or category called *govern-*

ment. The next part of the dictionary entry for *democracy* consists of several definitions of the term, all of which attempt to differentiate this form of government from other forms of government. Collectively, of course, these definitions do not provide a full understanding of what we usually mean when we use the term *democracy,* but they do provide a starting point for developing a fuller definition of this concept.

PURPOSE

Once you have identified and restricted your topic and checked its standard dictionary definition, you must be clear about your purpose in writing an extended definition of the term. Do you want to define the term in order to persuade your reader of something? If so, what and why? Or do you want simply to inform your reader of the meaning or meanings of this term? Perhaps doing so will prove to your reader, who might be a teacher, that you understand the concept. Or do you simply feel that your reader will benefit somehow from learning the meaning of the term or developing a more precise understanding of the term?

Once you know what you want to accomplish by writing a definition essay, you are ready to consider strategies for accomplishing your purpose.

STRATEGIES OF DEVELOPMENT

There are numerous ways to extend the definition of a term into a full-length essay or into a response to an essay exam question. These strategies are presented and discussed in the following subsections.

DEVELOPMENT BY EXAMPLES

Often, definitions are extended and clarified through the use of examples. Examples help give the reader a tangible understanding of the term being defined. Here are two examples, one supporting a definition of *fear* and one supporting a definition of *beauty:*

Examples   For example, fear can sometimes be seen in a person's face. When my friend Roy walked within two feet of a copperhead snake, his mouth fell open, his eyes widened, and all the color drained from his face.

Beauty, of course, is also the result of form. Many people, for example, agree that the 1968 Chevrolet Corvette is a truly beautiful car, and most base their opinion simply on the shape—form—of the car. It's sleek, low, and powerful-looking without unattractive bulk and conflicting lines.

DEVELOPMENT BY CONTRAST

Another strategy for extending a definition involves using contrast or differentiation. Often we indicate what something is by saying what it is not. If you wanted to acquaint someone who has never seen an apple, but who is familiar with oranges, with what an apple is, you might begin by saying that an apple, like an orange, is a fruit. You might add that an apple, unlike an orange, has a thin, edible skin; and so forth.

Developing a definition by contrast enables you to emphasize some or even all of the distinctive characteristics of the term you are defining. It also allows you to create a frame of reference for constructing the definition. Once you say, for example, that an apple is like an orange, you have created a framework of reality for your reader to fit the term *apple* into. Your reader then knows some things about the apple, such as the following:

- It must be edible.
- It must be a fruit, or at least fruitlike.
- It is probably about the size of an orange.

The subsequent contrast differentiates an apple from an orange by specifying how an apple differs from an orange.

The following paragraph is from an essay whose purpose is to inform the reader of the meaning of the term *Industrial Age*. This paragraph helps extend the writer's definition of *Industrial Age* by contrasting this period of history with the earlier agrarian period of civilization.

Example   THE INDUSTRIAL AGE

Like the agrarian past in human civilization, the Industrial Age has to do with how most people earn their livings and provide for their needs. In the agrarian past most individuals worked close to the land. They either worked on the land as farmers or worked in enterprises that were closely connected to farming, such as animal husbandry. In the ensuing Industrial Age, however, the majority of people for the first time in the history of the race worked at tasks many times removed from tilling the soil. The typical job became one directly or indirectly related to manufacturing, ranging from providing the raw materials for the manufacturing process to merchandising the finished products to servicing and repairing products in use.

DEVELOPMENT BY FUNCTION

Another important method for extending a definition consists of including the function or functions of the thing being defined. A writer normally begins such an explanation by stating what the thing does. This statement of function or functions may include some or all of the uses of the object or idea being defined. In some cases, of course, it is virtually impossible to include all of the functions of a particular thing.

About the functions of justice, for example, we might say that justice provides for a fair hearing for anyone accused of a crime. While this is a function of justice as we understand it in our society, it is certainly not the only function of justice. In fact, justice has many more functions than would be appropriate to include in a short definition essay on the topic. On the other hand, including all the functions of a pencil, which are rather limited, in such an essay is certainly possible and probably desirable.

Part of the statement of function may include an explanation of how the thing being defined works or how it is used. You might, for example, explain what enables a pencil to function as a writing instrument and then explain how a pencil is used for writing.

Example   Writing with a pencil is a relatively simple process. Begin by trimming (sharpening) one end of the pencil so that the center stick of graphite it contains is exposed. Then, holding the pencil in an upright or nearly upright position, move it across a suitable writing surface so that the graphite center makes contact with the writing surface. When done properly, the graphite will be transferred to the writing surface in the form of a mark or marks.

THESIS

You may use either a general thesis statement or a focused thesis statement for the definition essay. The following general and focused thesis statements could be used for the same definition essay:

Example

Topic	Beauty
General thesis statement	Although beauty may be in the eye of the beholder, there is some agreement on what might be called the essence of beauty.
Focused thesis statement	Although beauty may be in the eye of the beholder, there is some agreement that the essence of beauty is an appropriate mix of color, form, and function.

The plan of development in a focused thesis statement for a definition essay specifies the elements or components of the definition. Including these elements makes the thesis statement a focused thesis statement; without them, the thesis statement is a general thesis statement.

PRACTICE   Working in small groups, as your teacher directs, develop both general and focused thesis statements for definition essays on the following topics. Write your thesis statements in the spaces provided. For focused thesis statements on these topics, include at least two functional components that the definition essay will contain. When you finish this exercise, compare the work of your group with the work of other groups in the class.

1. *Topic:* Good Grades
   General thesis statement:

   _____

   _____

   Focused thesis statement:

   _____

   _____

2. *Topic:* Ignorance
   General thesis statement:

   _____

   _____

Focused thesis statement:

_____

_____

3. *Topic:*   The Good Life
General thesis statement:

_____

_____

Focused thesis statement:

_____

_____

4. *Topic:*   Love
General thesis statement:

_____

_____

Focused thesis statement:

_____

_____

5. *Topic:*   Sportsmanship
General thesis statement:

_____

_____

Focused thesis statement:

_____

_____

_____

6. *Topic:* [one of your own choosing]
   General thesis statement:

   _____

   _____

   Focused thesis statement:

   _____

   _____

READINGS

The following readings are student and professional essays. Read them carefully, and look for their use of the definition guidelines presented in this chapter.

STUDENT ESSAY

FREEDOM   Sandy Faw

Many meanings have been attached to the word *freedom*. Different sources define it in different ways—some good and some not so good. Freedom has been defined by scholars, writers, and musicians; by advertisers, who are notorious abusers of the language; and even by me.

Probably the first place one would look for the definition of freedom is in a dictionary. *Webster's* gives several meanings for the word *freedom*. It defines freedom as "the absence of necessity, coercion, or constraint in choice or action; liberation from slavery or restraint from the power of another; ease or facility; frankness or outspokenness; boldness of conception or execution; and franchise or privilege."

Another popular dictionary says that "freedom is a liberty taken; freedom is the absence of ceremony or reserve; freedom is the power to make one's own choices." In other words, what these dictionaries are really telling us is that freedom is being the person we want to be, and thinking, saying, and doing the things that we want to think, say, and do, with no reservations.

Numerous scholars, poets, and musicians have told us what freedom means. In the song "Me and Bobbi McGee," Kris Kristopherson says that "freedom's just another word for nothing left to lose." This is an intriguing but depressing definition of the word. Charles Pequy says, "Freedom is a system based on courage." In the

FREEDOM, continued

words of Zechariah Chafee, "Freedom is not safety but opportunity." Wendell Lewis Willkie wrote, "Freedom is an indivisible word. If we want to enjoy it and fight for it, we must be prepared to extend it to everyone. . . ." In a poem by John Barbour, freedom is defined as "a noble thing which makes man to have liking and gives him solace." And Thucydides believed that freedom is the secret of happiness. Freedom is also defined in the film *Future Shock* based on the book by the same title by Alvin Toffler. In the film, the narrator states that "freedom is a loss of a sense of belonging." Obviously, these more personal and restricted definitions of freedom are somewhat different from the ones found in dictionaries.

More modern times, it seems, have brought about new, simpler definitions of freedom. These are best seen in advertising. Today, freedom is wearing Bausch and Lomb Softlens contact lenses. Freedom is the feeling achieved by racing down the highway in a Dodge Shadow, or by wearing a Bali bra. Freedom is taking Tylenol instead of aspirin when you have a headache. Freedom is a feminine napkin. From these pop definitions of freedom, it is amazing to see how the word has lost its real meaning and has become cheap, almost meaningless.

Regardless of what meaning others attach to the word *freedom*, I have my own personal definition. To me, freedom is being able to express my thoughts and feelings without shame or fear of being ridiculed. Freedom is having my own little space in the world and spending my time in whatever way I wish. Freedom is going about my own business without being afraid of being attacked or violated. Freedom is enjoying my life. All of these meanings make freedom a very important and meaningful thing for me.

With all the different definitions of the word *freedom*, it is difficult to say what the word really means. Does it have any meaning? Or is it simply an abstraction of the human mind? These are questions that must be answered on an individual basis. The meaning of freedom can't be pulled out of a dictionary, borrowed from a philosopher, or given in a thirty-second commercial between the six o'clock news and the regular weeknight game show. The true meaning of freedom must come from within one's self.

PROFESSIONAL ESSAY

ABOUT MEN   Gretel Ehrlich

When I'm in New York but feeling lonely for Wyoming I look for the Marlboro ads in the subway. What I'm aching to see is horseflesh, the glint of a spur, a line of distant mountains, brimming creeks, and a reminder of the ranchers and cowboys

ABOUT MEN, continued

I've ridden with for the last eight years. But the men I see in those posters with their stern, humorless looks remind me of no one I know here. In our hellbent earnestness to romanticize the cowboy we've ironically disesteemed his true character. If he's "strong and silent" it's because there's probably no one to talk to. If he "rides away into the sunset" it's because he's been on horseback since four in the morning moving cattle and he's trying, fifteen hours later, to get home to his family. If he's "a rugged individualist" he's also part of a team: ranch work is teamwork and even the glorified open-range cowboys of the 1880s rode up and down the Chisholm Trail in the company of twenty or thirty other riders. Instead of the macho, trigger-happy man our culture has perversely wanted him to be, the cowboy is more apt to be convivial, quirky, and softhearted. To be "tough" on a ranch has nothing to do with conquests and displays of power. More often than not, circumstances—like the colt he's riding or an unexpected blizzard—are overpowering him. It's not toughness but "toughing it out" that counts. In other words, this macho, cultural artifact the cowboy has become is simply a man who possesses resilience, patience, and an instinct for survival. "Cowboys are just like a pile of rocks—everything happens to them. They get climbed on, kicked, rained and snowed on, scuffed up by wind. Their job is 'just to take it,' " one old-timer told me.

A cowboy is someone who loves his work. Since the hours are long—ten to fifteen hours a day—and the pay is $30 he has to. What's required of him is an odd mixture of physical vigor and maternalism. His part of the beef-raising industry is to birth and nurture calves and take care of their mothers. For the most part his work is done on horseback and in a lifetime he sees and comes to know more animals than people. The iconic myth surrounding him is built on American notions of heroism: the index of a man's value as measured in physical courage. Such ideas have perverted manliness into a self-absorbed race for cheap thrills. In a rancher's world, courage has less to do with facing danger than with acting spontaneously—usually on behalf of an animal or another rider. If a cow is stuck in a boghole he throws a loop around her neck, takes his dally (a half hitch around the saddle horn), and pulls her out with horsepower. If a calf is born sick, he may take her home, warm her in front of the kitchen fire, and massage her legs until dawn. One friend, whose favorite horse was trying to swim a lake with hobbles on, dove under water and cut her legs loose with a knife then swam her to shore, his arm around her neck lifeguard-style, and saved her from drowning. Because these incidents are usually linked to someone or something outside himself, the westerner's courage is selfless, a form of compassion.

The physical punishment that goes with cowboying is greatly underplayed. Once fear is dispensed with, the threshold of pain rises to meet the demands of the job. When Jane Fonda asked Robert Redford (in the film *Electric Horseman*) if he was sick as he struggled to his feet one morning, he replied, "No, just bent." For once the movies had it right. The cowboys I was sitting with laughed in agreement. Cowboys are rarely complainers; they show their stoicism by laughing at themselves.

If a rancher or cowboy has been thought of as a "man's man"—laconic, hard-drink-

ABOUT MEN, continued

ing, inscrutable—there's almost no place in which the balancing act between male and female, manliness and femininity, can be more natural. If he's gruff, handsome, and physically fit on the outside, he's androgynous at the core. Ranchers are midwives, hunters, nurturers, providers, and conservationists all at once. What we've interpreted as toughness—weathered skin, calloused hands, a squint in the eye and a growl in the voice—only masks the tenderness inside. "Now don't go telling me these lambs are cute," one rancher warned me the first day I walked into the football-field-sized lambing sheds. The next thing I knew he was holding a black lamb. "Ain't this little rat good-lookin'?"

So many of the men who came to the West were southerners—men looking for work and a new life after the Civil War—that chivalrousness and strict codes of honor were soon thought of as western traits. There were very few women in Wyoming during territorial days, so when they did arrive (some as mail-order brides from places like Philadelphia) there was a standoffishness between the sexes and a formality that persists now. Ranchers still tip their hats and say, "Howdy, ma'am" instead of shaking hands with me.

Even young cowboys are often evasive with women. It's not that they're Jekyll and Hyde creatures—gentle with animals and rough on women—but rather, that they don't know how to bring their tenderness into the house and lack the vocabulary to express the complexity of what they feel. Dancing wildly all night becomes a metaphor for the explosive emotions pent up inside, and when these are, on occasion, released, they're so battery-charged and

potent that one caress of the face or one "I love you" will peal for a long while.

The geographical vastness and the social isolation here make emotional evolution seem impossible. Those contradictions of the heart between respectability, logic, and convention on the one hand, and impulse, passion, and intuition on the other, played out wordlessly against the paradisical beauty of the West, give cowboys a wide-eyed but drawn look. Their lips pucker up, not with kisses but with immutability. They may want to break out, staying up all night with a lover just to talk, but they don't know how and can't imagine what the consequences will be. Those rare occasions when they do bare themselves result in confusion. "I feel as if I'd sprained my heart," one friend told me a month after such a meeting.

My friend Ted Hoagland wrote, "No one is as fragile as a woman but no one is as fragile as a man." For all the women here who use "fragileness" to avoid work or as a sexual ploy, there are men who try to hide theirs, all the while clinging to an adolescent dependency on women to cook their meals, wash their clothes, and keep the ranch house warm in winter. But there is true vulnerability in evidence here. Because these men work with animals, not machines or numbers, because they live outside in landscapes of torrential beauty, because they are confined to a place and a routine embellished with awesome variables, because calves die in the arms that pulled others into life, because they go to the mountains as if on a pilgrimage to find out what makes a herd of elk tick, their strength is also a softness, their toughness, a rare delicacy.

Rhetoric

1. "About Men" begins with a contrast introduction. Why is this an effective way to begin an essay about the modern cowboy? Summarize your response in a few sentences.

2. Locate and underline the sentence that you think is the thesis statement of the essay. Then compare your conclusion with a classmate's. If you disagree, reread the introductory paragraph and reevaluate your choice.

3. Read the body paragraphs of the essay carefully, and indicate by underlining and with margin notes the strategies the author used to develop her definition of the cowboy. Such strategies might include contrast, process analysis, examples, and others we discussed.

Ideas

1. The essay is about cowboys. Does it also raise the larger question of male-female relationships? If so, how?

2. The essay gives some information about the type of work that makes up much of a cowboy's life. How might the nature of his work shape his personality and his view of the world? Is the work a cowboy does healthier, more wholesome, and more fulfilling than the work done by the rest of us? If so, how and why?

3. In your opinion, is the myth of the cowboy an important component in how we as Americans see ourselves? If so, are articles such as this one helpful or destructive in shaping our self-conception? Explain your response.

Response

1. Identify and then describe what you felt was the most surprising element in the author's definition of a cowboy. What about it surprised you? Did it alter or expand your concept of the cowboy?

2. Write an essay in which you define or redefine another common American figure who you think is misunderstood and whose public image differs considerably from the way this person really is. A suitable occupation to use for this assignment might be teacher, firefighter, storekeeper, police officer, or lawyer.

PROFESSIONAL ESSAY

THE MAIL OF THE SPECIES

William Swanson

A gentleman from the Midwest writes:

Dear Sir,

What must a fellow do in this day and age to receive a good letter? Time was when it was quite enough to have a handful of literate friends scattered here and there, and to maintain a permanent address. The rest came more or less naturally.

Lamentably,
Waiting for the Post

Dear Waiting,

I know what you mean. I recently received a letter written by—not merely on—a computer. The letter began "Dear Bill" and then attempted to sell me on time-sharing in a Colorado ski-slope condominium. Anybody or anything familiar enough to address me "Dear Bill" would have known not only that I do not ski, but that I dislike hills. The correspondent was clearly an imposter, the correspondence an imposition. If the truth be told, I can't remember when I last received a really good letter.

How would I define a "good" letter? Well, like sex and the backstroke, it is considerably easier to demonstrate than to explain. Suffice it to say that the "good" refers not to the news a letter con-

tains, but to the quality of the letter itself. Some of the best letters I've ever received were full of bad news—news of broken hearts and shattered hips, of wasted lives and squandered fortunes. Some of the best letters I've ever *read*, for that matter, were written by such anguished souls as Wolfgang Amadeus Mozart and included lines like: "Great God! I would not wish my worst enemy to be in my present position," and "Whereas I felt tolerably well yesterday, I am absolutely wretched today."

I would say further that a good letter possesses at least the following attributes (perhaps a great many more), which I'll list not necessarily in the order of their importance:

Personality.   A good letter is addressed to you as a person, by another person, *not* to you as a consumer, customer, subscriber, patron, draftee, by a computer or some other device. The writer should know, if not love, you, and should ask you for money only if he is a blood relative.

Individuality.   A good letter does not begin with "Dear Member of the Class of '63," or "Dear Buick Owner," or even, God knows, "Dear Friend."

"Dear Friend," of course, is the classic salutation of the dreaded Christmas letter.

THE MAIL OF THE SPECIES, continued

As such, it is acceptable only when posted from the mission fields of Tanzania or Upper Volta. Years ago, the dreaded Christmas letter was easily spotted and consigned to the Yuletime fire, owing to the inferior quality of the copy—a watery and all-but-illegible blue, often still damp from the abysmal mimeograph machine whence it came. Nowadays, though, the wordprocessing personal computer makes each dreaded Christmas letter so fresh and sharp and original-looking that the hapless recipient must peruse the first few sentences before he can determine just what it is. The tip-off is the use of the broadest common denominator of news ("Well, it sure seems quiet around here what with the kids off to college . . . "), the repetition of the kids' and pets' names and ages, and the frequent reminders of Dad's and Mom's occupations and health status.

A good letter, by vivid contrast, is a one-on-one proposition. It is rife with gossip, sly reference, and double-entendre intelligible, at best, only to the sender and recipient. A good letter, or series of good letters, produces what John Updike has called "involuntary autobiography." A good letter shares precious secrets and awful truths—and sometimes, for both parties' sake, should be torched immediately upon reading.

Imperishability.   A good letter, though crackling with esoterica, is terrific to read years, even decades, later. That is why, against all better judgment, good letters are in fact so rarely torched. A good letter is, indeed, literature of a sort, with all the color and spunk of, say, one of Mark Twain's sketches.

It helps, of course, if the letter's author is Mark Twain, and it is certainly no accident that some of the greatest letters we read today were written by the likes of James, Flaubert, Joyce, and Waugh. Talk about imperishable! Consider this tantalizing introduction, lifted from a letter written by peripatetic Henry James, in Paris, in 1876:

> *Dear Father,*
>
> *. . . The slender thread of my few personal relations hangs on, without snapping, but it doesn't grow very stout. You crave chiefly news, I suppose, about Ivan Sergeitch [Turgenev!] whom I have lately seen several times. . . .*

Literacy is, of course, a basic requirement of the good-letter writer, which may explain, at least in part, why you, dear Waiting, are waiting. But a person does not have to know a Henry James or an E. B. White to receive a good letter. A person needn't even know a Mozart or a Churchill or a Groucho Marx—although I'd be the first to agree that it would significantly improve one's chance.

Frequency.   More often than not, the good letter will come from someone with whom you correspond fairly often. This tends to rule out the condominium hustler seeking your "once-in-a-lifetime" investment dollar and the fund-raising presidential hopeful groveling for your quadrennial support. It should also rule out the dreaded-Christmas-letter writer, who tends to hoard his epistolary non-news for his year-end extravaganza. On the positive side, frequency encourages in-

THE MAIL OF THE SPECIES, continued

timacy, and intimacy is the well of truth, which is of course indispensable to a good letter and most other good things.

Length.   It is a rare good letter whose contents can be confined to the few square inches of a postcard or a holiday Hallmark. I have nothing against either one of those formats—or, for that matter, against an occasional telegram—but they simply do not allow sufficient room for the detail and development required of a good letter.

There is not, to my knowledge, any strict requirement as to the number of words in a good letter. But there is, in a good letter, a sense of the heft and volume one finds in a good novel—a heft and volume not found even in the best short stories, much less on a post- or greeting card or in the currently very popular "note." Alas, in the past few years the "cute note" has pretty much taken the place of the good letter. YOU, DEAR WAITING, undoubtedly receive your share of these "notes." They are usually personal, individual, and all-too-frequent, but they invariably fall far short of the mark in terms of length and imperishability.

The typical note comes written on smallish, pastel-colored paper that suggests nothing more imperishable than a Kleenex tissue. Sometimes there is a little flower or happy face in an upper corner, or a cute saying ("Help! Send chocolate!") along the upper margin where the name and address of the sender is usually embossed on legitimate stationery. And, though intended for a specific individual, notes are generally begun with the commonplace "Hi! Just thought I'd drop you a note . . ." and displayed, envelopeless, under a strawberry-shaped magnet on a refrigerator door.

People jot notes nowadays because they're "too busy" to write letters. And there is indeed an urgent, stenographic quality to most such notes that bespeaks the mad dash of our times. Futhermore, we have so damn many people to keep in touch with today that we should perhaps be forgiven our shortcomings in matters of length and imperishability. Given the demands on our time and attention, perhaps even a note is a minor miracle—a daisy sprouting from a crack in the parking-lot pavement. We could perhaps take care of *all* of our business over the phone.

A friend of mine (via the phone, as it happens) provides an additional thought on the subject. Perhaps, he suggests, we have grown fearful of expressing ourselves imperishably, on paper, lest we literally stamp ourselves something we ought not be: unfashionable, unhip, unwithit. Perhaps, as far as that goes, we've grown fearful of getting people angry at us. It's one thing, my friend reminds me, to call someone a duplicitous cretin on the telephone, by which medium a hasty qualification or even abject apology can be made, if deemed prudent, right on the spot. It's quite another thing to commit your disparagement to letter, a rather more tangible and permanent medium by which the duplicitous cretin may justify his coming to look for you with a chain saw.

I remain unconvinced. Henry James somehow managed to dash off literally thousands of mostly personal, individual, imperishable, frequent, and lengthy letters in a 50-year span otherwise occupied

THE MAIL OF THE SPECIES, continued

by the writing of some two dozen novels, more than a hundred "tales," a dozen-odd plays, plus countless travel sketches, literary critiques, and more, not to mention his frequent jaunts about the continent and dinner parties with Turgenev, Flaubert, et al. Ernest Hemingway, to use a more recent example, fought Spanish bulls, chased German submarines, and wrote at least a dozen volumes of undying prose, even as he knocked out between 6,000 and 7,000 letters during the 45 years of his writing life. Hemingway was not afraid to speak his mind in his letters either—and there were plenty of duplicitous cretins and chain saws in his day, too. The truth is, I can't imagine a good letter coming from someone who *isn't* up to his eyeballs in the business of a busy life. What on earth would such a person write about?

I don't think it's time or fortitude or literacy that we're lacking nowadays.

What we're lacking, I think, is the will and generosity required to shape our thoughts, feelings, and news into a coherent message every once in a while, and to share that message with another person in the world. A good letter, let's face it, is no longer required of us when we wish or need to communicate—even if our communicant lives an ocean away. Thus, a good letter, in this era of telecommunications satellites and quick, quipping note paper, is something akin to a hand-crocheted afghan or a jar of homemade currant preserves: a small act of grace, a hand-wrought little gift from one human being to another.

But I'm afraid I digress, dear Waiting. In answer to your question, I can only reply with what must by now be obvious. In order to *get* a good letter in this day and age, you're probably first going to have to sit down and *write* one.

Rhetoric

1. What kind of introduction does Swanson use to begin "The Mail of the Species"? Is the introduction too abrupt? Is it effective?

2. Locate what you think is the thesis statement of the essay. Does it appear to be a standard thesis statement? Does it contain the components of a good thesis statement?

3. Swanson defines a "good letter" through the use of differentiation. Explain how he does this, and cite some examples of this in the essay.

Ideas

1. The author offers at least two explanations for the demise of letter writing. According to him, people are too busy to write letters, and, perhaps, people are afraid to express themselves imperishably on paper. In your opinion, does either of these constitute a valid reason for not writing letters? Do these concerns have an effect on your letter-writing habits?

2. Does a phone call from a friend or relative whom you see only rarely mean as much to you as a letter from one of these individuals? Explain your response.

3. Might a return to writing "good letters" improve personal relationships? Why or why not?

Response

1. Write a brief paragraph in which you agree or disagree with the author's definition of a "good letter." If you agree with the author, you might begin by saying: "I agree with Mr. Swanson that a good letter...." If you disagree, you might begin by saying: "Unlike Mr. Swanson, I feel that a good letter...." When you finish, compare your written response to the responses of some of your classmates.

2. Write a letter to a friend or relative in which you incorporate three or more of the qualities that, according to the author, a good letter should possess.

PROFESSIONAL ESSAY

ON BOXING   Joyce Carol Oates

They are young welterweight boxers so evenly matched they might be twins—though one has a redhead's pallor and the other is a dusky-skinned Hispanic. Circling each other in the ring, they try jabs, tentative left hooks, right crosses that dissolve in midair or turn into harmless slaps. The Madison Square Garden crowd is derisive, impatient. "Those two! What'd they do, wake up this morning and decide they were boxers?" a man behind me says contemptuously. (He's dark, nattily dressed, with a neatly trimmed mustache and tinted glasses. A sophisticated fight fan. Two hours later he will be crying, "Tommy! Tommy! Tommy!" over and over in a paroxysm of grief as, on the giant closed-circuit television screen, middleweight champion Marvelous Marvin Hagler batters his challenger, Thomas Hearns, into insensibility.)

The young boxers must be conscious of the jeers and boos in this great cavernous space reaching up into the $20 seats in the balconies amid the constant milling of people in the aisles, the smells of hotdogs, beer, cigarette and cigar smoke, hair oil. But they are locked desperately together, circling, jabbing, slapping, clinching, now a flurry of light blows, clumsy footwork, another sweaty stumbling despairing clinch into the ropes that provokes a fresh wave of derision. Why are they here in the Garden of all places, each fighting what

ON BOXING, continued

looks like his first professional fight? What are they doing? Neither is angry at the other. When the bell sounds at the end of the sixth and final round, the crowd boos a little louder. The Hispanic boy, silky yellow short, damp, frizzy, floating hair, strides about his corner of the ring with his gloved hand aloft—not in defiance of the boos, which increase in response to his gesture, or even in acknowledgment of them. It's just something he has seen older boxers do. He seems to be saying "I'm here, I made it, I did it." When the decision is announced as a draw, the crowd's derision increases in volume. "Get out of the ring!" "Go home!" Contemptuous male laughter follows the boys in their robes, towels about their heads, sweating, breathless. Why had they thought they were boxers?

How can you enjoy so brutal a sport, people ask. Or don't ask.

And it's too complicated to answer. In any case, I don't "enjoy" boxing, and never have; it isn't invariably "brutal"; I don't think of it as a sport.

Nor do I think of it in writerly terms as a metaphor for something else. (For *what* else?): No one whose interest in boxing began in childhood—as mine did as an offshoot of my father's interest—is likely to suppose it is a symbol of something beyond itself, though I can entertain the proposition that life is a metaphor for boxing—for one of those bouts that go on and on, round following round, small victories, small defeats, nothing determined, again the bell and again the bell and you and your opponent so evenly matched it's clear your opponent *is* you and why are the two of you jabbing and punching at each other on an elevated platform enclosed by ropes

as in a pen beneath hot crude all-exposing lights in the presence of an indifferent crowd: that sort of writerly metaphor. But if you have seen five hundred boxing matches, you have seen five hundred boxing matches, and their common denominator, which surely exists, is not of primary interest to you. "If the Host is only a symbol," the Catholic writer Flannery O'Connor said, "I'd say the hell with it."

Each boxing match is a story, a highly condensed, highly dramatic story—even when nothing much happens: then failure is the story. There are two principal characters in the story, overseen by a shadowy third. When the bell rings no one knows what will happen. Much is speculated, nothing known. The boxers bring to the fight everything that is themselves, and everything will be exposed: including secrets about themselves they never knew. There are boxers possessed of such remarkable intuition, such prescience, one would think they had fought this particular fight before. There are boxers who perform brilliantly, but mechanically, who cannot improvise in midfight; there are boxers performing at the height of their skill who cannot quite comprehend that it won't be enough; to my knowledge there was only one boxer who possessed an extraordinary and disquieting awareness, not only of his opponent's every move or anticipated move, but of the audience's keenest shifts in mood as well—Muhammad Ali, of course.

In the ring, death is always a possibility, which is why I prefer to see films or tapes of fights already past—already crystallized into art. In fact, death is a statistically rare possibility of which no one likes to

ON BOXING, continued

think—like your possible death tomorrow morning in an automobile crash, or in next month's airplane crash, or in a freak accident involving a fall on the stairs—a skull fracture, subarachnoid hemorrhage.

A boxing match is a play without words, which doesn't mean that it has no text or no language, only that the text is improvised in action, the language a dialogue between the boxers in a joint response to the mysterious will of the crowd, which is always that the fight be a worthy one so that the crude paraphernalia of the setting—the ring, the lights, the onlookers themselves—be obliterated. To go from an ordinary preliminary match to a "Fight of the Century"—like those between Joe Louis and Billy Conn, Muhammad Ali and Joe Frazier, most recently Marvin Hagler and Thomas Hearns—is to go from listening or half-listening to a guitar being idly plucked to hearing Bach's "Well-Tempered Clavier" being perfectly played, and that too is part of the story. So much is happening so swiftly and so subtly you cannot absorb it except to know that something memorable is happening and it is happening in a place beyond words.

The fighters in the ring are time-bound—is anything so excruciatingly long as a fiercely contested three-minute round?—but the fight itself is timeless. By way of films and tapes, it has become history, art. If boxing is a sport, it is the most tragic of all sports because, more than any human activity, it consumes the very excellence it displays: Its very drama is this consumption. To expend oneself in fighting the greatest fight of one's life is to begin immediately the downward turn that next time may be a plunge, a sudden incomprehensible fall. *I am the greatest*, Muhammad Ali says. *I am the greatest*, Marvin Hagler says. You always think you're going to win, Jack Dempsey wryly observed in his old age, otherwise you can't fight at all. The punishment—to the body, the brain, the spirit—a man must endure to become a great boxer is inconceivable to most of us whose idea of personal risk is largely ego related or emotional. But the punishment, as it begins to show in even a young and vigorous boxer, is closely assessed by his rivals. After junior-welterweight champion Aaron Pryor won a lackluster fight on points a few months ago, a younger boxer in his weight division, interviewed at ringside, said: "My mouth is watering."

So the experience of seeing great fighters of the past—and great sporting events are always *past*—is radically different from having seen them when they were reigning champions. Jack Johnson, Jack Dempsey, Joe Louis, Sugar Ray Robinson, Willie Pep, Rocky Marciano, Muhammad Ali—as spectators we know not only how a fight ends but how a career ends. Boxing is always particulars, second by incalculable second, but in the abstract it suggests these haunting lines by Yeats:

Everything that man esteems
Endures a moment or a day.
Love's pleasure drives his love away,
The painter's brush consumes his dreams;
The herald's cry, the soldier's tread
Exhaust his glory and his might:
Whatever flames upon the night
Man's own resinous heart has fed.
—from "The Resurrection"

The referee, the third character in the story, usually appears to be a mere observer, even an intruder, a near-ghostly

ON BOXING, continued

presence as fluid in motion and quick-footed as the boxers themselves (he is frequently a former boxer). But so central to the drama of boxing is the referee that the spectacle of two men fighting each other unsupervised in an elevated ring would appear hellish, obscene—life rather than art. The referee is our intermediary in the fight. He is our moral conscience, extracted from us as spectators so that, for the duration of the fight, "conscience" is not a factor in our experience; nor is it a factor in the boxers' behavior.

Though the referee's role is a highly demanding one, and it has been estimated that there are perhaps no more than a dozen really skilled referees in the world, it seems to be necessary in the intense dramatic action of the fight that the referee have no dramatic identity. Referees' names are quickly forgotten, even as they are announced over the microphone preceding a fight. Yet, paradoxically, the referee's position is one of crucial significance. The referee cannot control what happens in the ring, but he can frequently control, to a degree, *that* it happens; he is responsible for the fight, if not for the individual fighter's performance. It is the referee solely who holds the power of life and death at certain times; whose decision to terminate a fight, or to allow it to continue, determines a man's fate. (One should recall that a well-aimed punch with a boxer's full weight behind it can have an astonishing impact—a blow that must be absorbed by the brain in its jelly sac.)

In a recent heavyweight fight in Buffalo, 220-pound Tim Witherspoon repeatedly struck his 260-pound opponent, James Broad, caught in the ropes, while the referee looked on without acting—though a number of spectators called for the fight to be stopped. In the infamous Benny Paret–Emile Griffith fight of March 24, 1962, the referee Ruby Goldstein was said to have stood paralyzed as Paret, trapped in the ropes, suffered as many as 18 powerful blows to the head before he fell. (He died ten days later.) Boxers are trained not to quit; if they are knocked down they will try to get up to continue the fight, even if they can hardly defend themselves. The primary rule of the ring—to defend oneself at all times—is both a parody and a distillation of life.

Boxing is a purely masculine world. (Though there are female boxers—the most famous is the black champion Lady Tyger Trimiar with her shaved head and tiger-striped attire—women's role in the sport is extremely marginal.) The vocabulary of boxing is attuned to a quintessentially masculine sensibility in which the role of patriarch/protector can only be assured if there is physical strength underlying it. First comes this strength—"primitive," perhaps; then comes civilization. It should be kept in mind that "boxing" and "fighting," though always combined in the greatest of boxers, can be entirely different and even unrelated activities. If boxing can be, in the lighter weights especially, a highly complex and refined skill belonging solely to civilization, fighting seems to belong to something predating civilization, the instinct not merely to defend oneself—for when has the masculine ego ever been assuaged by so minimal a gesture?—but to attack another and to force him into absolute submission. Hence the electrifying effect upon a typical fight crowd when fighting emerges suddenly out of boxing—

ON BOXING, continued

the excitement when a boxer's face begins to bleed. The flash of red is the visible sign of the fight's authenticity in the eyes of many spectators, and boxers are right to be proud—if they are—of their facial scars.

To the untrained eye, boxers in the ring usually appear to be angry. But, of course, this is "work" to them; emotion has no part in it, or should not. Yet in an important sense—in a symbolic sense—the boxers *are* angry, and boxing is fundamentally about anger. It is the only sport in which anger is accommodated, ennobled. Why are boxers angry? Because, for the most part, they belong to the disenfranchised of our society, to impoverished ghetto neighborhoods in which anger is an appropriate response. ("It's hard being black. You ever been black? I was black once—when I was poor," Larry Holmes has said.) Today, when most boxers—most good boxers—are black or Hispanic, white men begin to look anemic in the ring. Yet after decades of remarkable black boxers—from Jack Johnson to Joe Louis to Muhammad Ali—heavyweight champion Larry Holmes was the object of racist slurs and insults when he defended his title against the over-promoted white challenger Gerry Cooney a few years ago.

Liberals who have no personal or class reason to feel anger tend to disparage, if not condemn, such anger in others. Liberalism is also unfairly harsh in its criticism of all that predates civilization—or "liberalism" itself—without comprehending that civilization is a concept, an idea, perhaps at times hardly more than a fiction, attendant upon, and always subordinate to, physical strength: missiles, nuclear warheads. The terrible and tragic silence dramatized in the boxing ring is the si-

lence of nature before language, when the physical *was* language, a means of communication swift and unmistakable.

The phrase "killer instinct" is said to have been coined in reference to Jack Dempsey in his famous early fights against Jess Willard, Georges Carpentier, Luis Firpo ("The Wild Bull of the Pampas"), and any number of other boxers, less renowned, whom he savagely beat. The ninth of eleven children born to an impoverished Mormon sharecropper and itinerant railroad worker, Dempsey seems to have been, as a young boxer in his prime, the very embodiment of angry hunger; and if he remains the most spectacular heavyweight champion in history, it is partly because he fought when rules governing boxing were somewhat casual by present-day standards. Where aggression must be learned, even cultivated, in some champion boxers (Tunney, Louis, Marciano, Patterson, for example), Dempsey's aggression was direct and natural: Once in the ring he seems to have wanted to kill his opponent.

Dempsey's first title fight in 1919, against the aging champion Jess Willard, was called "pugilistic murder" by some sportswriters and is said to have been one of boxing's all-time blood baths. Today, this famous fight—which brought the nearly unknown twenty-four-year-old Dempsey to national prominence—would certainly have been stopped in the first minute of the first round. Badly out of condition, heavier than Dempsey by almost sixty pounds, the thirty-seven-year-old Willard had virtually no defense against the challenger. By the end of the fight, Willard's jaw was broken, his cheekbone split, nose smashed, six teeth broken off at the gum, an eye was battered shut,

ON BOXING, continued

much further damage was done to his body. Both boxers were covered in Willard's blood. Years later Dempsey's estranged manager Kearns confessed—perhaps falsely—that he had "loaded" Dempsey's gloves—treated his hand tape with a talcum substance that turned concrete-hard when wet.

For the most part, boxing matches today are scrupulously monitored by referees and ring physicians. The devastating knockout blow is frequently the one never thrown. In a recent televised junior-middleweight bout between Don Curry and James Green, the referee stopped the fight because Green seemed momentarily disabled: His logic was that Green had dropped his gloves and was therefore in a position to be hurt. (Green and his furious trainer protested the decision but the referee's word is final: No fight, stopped, can be resumed.) The drama of the ring begins to shift subtly as more and more frequently one sees a referee intervene to embrace a weakened or defenseless man in a gesture of parental solicitude that in itself carries much theatrical power—a gesture not so dramatic as the killing blow but one that suggests that the ethics of the ring are moving toward those that prevail beyond it. As if fighter-brothers whose mysterious animosity has somehow brought them to battle are saved by their father. . . .

In the final moment of the Hagler-Hearns fight, the dazed Hearns—on his feet but clearly not fully conscious, gamely prepared to take Hagler's next assault—was saved by the referee from what might well have been serious injury, if not death, considering the ferocity of Hagler's fighting and the personal anger he seems to have brought to it that night. This eight-minute fight, generally believed to be one of the great fights in boxing history, ends with Hearns in the referee's protective embrace—an image that is haunting, in itself profoundly mysterious, as if an indefinable human drama had been spontaneously created for us, brilliantly improvised, performed one time and one time only, yet permanently ingrained upon our consciousness.

Years ago in the early 1950s, when my father first took me to a Golden Gloves boxing tournament in Buffalo, I asked him why the boys wanted to fight one another, why they were willing to get hurt. My father said, "Boxers don't feel pain quite the way we do."

Gene Tunney's single defeat in an eleven-year career was to a flamboyant and dangerous fighter named Harry Greb ("The Human Windmill"), who seems to have been, judging from boxing literature, the dirtiest fighter in history. Low blows, butting, fouls, holding and hitting, using his laces on an opponent's eyes—Greb was famous for his lack of interest in the rules. He was world middleweight champion for three years, but a presence in the boxing world for a long time. After the first of his several fights with Greb, the twenty-four-year-old Tunney had to spend a week in bed, he was so badly hurt; he'd lost two quarts of blood during the fifteen-round fight. But as Tunney said years afterward: "Greb gave me a terrible whipping. He broke my nose, maybe with a butt. He cut my eyes and ears, perhaps with his laces. . . . My jaw was swollen from the right temple down the cheek, along under

ON BOXING, continued

the chin and part way up the other side. The referee, the ring itself, was full of blood. . . . But it was in that first fight, in which I lost my American light-heavy-weight title, that I knew I had found a way to beat Harry eventually. I was fortunate, really. If boxing in those days had been afflicted with the commission doctors we have today—who are always poking their noses into the ring and examining superficial wounds—the first fight with Greb would have been stopped before I learned how to beat him. It's possible, even probable, that if this had happened I would never have been heard of again."

Tommy Loughran, the light-heavyweight champion from 1927 to 1929, was a master boxer greatly admired by other boxers. He approached boxing literally as a science—as Tunney did—studying his opponents' styles and mapping out ring strategy for each fight. He rigged up mirrors in his basement so that he could see himself as he worked out—for, as Loughran realized, no boxer ever sees himself quite as he appears to his opponent. But the secret of Loughran's career was that he had a right hand that broke so easily he could use it only once in each fight: It had to be the knockout punch or nothing. "I'd get one shot, then the agony of the thing would hurt me if the guy got up. Anybody I ever hit with a left hook, I knocked flat on his face, but I would never take a chance for fear if my left hand goes, I'm done for."

Both Tunney and Loughran, it is instructive to note, retired from boxing before they were forced to retire. Tunney was a highly successful businessman and Loughran a successful sugar broker on the Wall Street commodities market—just to suggest that boxers are not invariably illiterate, stupid, or punch-drunk.

One of the perhaps not entirely acknowledged reasons for the attraction of serious writers to boxing (from Swift, Pope, Johnson to Hazlitt, Lord Byron, Hemingway, and our own Norman Mailer, George Plimpton, Wilfrid Sheed, Daniel Halpern et al.) is the sport's systematic cultivation of pain in the interests of a project, a life-goal: the willed transposing of the sensation called "pain" (whether physical or psychological) into its opposite. If this is masochism—and I doubt that it is, or that it is simply—it is also intelligence, cunning, strategy. It is the active welcoming of that which most living beings try to avoid and to flee. It is the active subsuming of the present moment in terms of the future. Pain now but control (and therefore pleasure) later.

Still, it is the rigorous training period leading up to the public appearance that demands the most discipline. In this, too, the writer senses some kinship, however, oblique and one-sided, with the professional boxer. The brief public spectacle of the boxing match (which could last as little as sixty seconds), like the publication of the writer's book, is but the final, visible stage in a long, arduous, fanatic, and sometimes quixotic, subordination of the self. It was Rocky Marciano who seems to have trained with the most monastic devotion, secluding himself from his wife and family for as long as three months before a fight. Quite apart from the grueling physical training of this period and the constant preoccupation with diet and weight, Marciano concentrated on only the upcoming fight, the opening bell, his opponent. Every

ON BOXING, continued

minute of the boxer's life was planned for one purpose. In the training camp the name of the opponent was never mentioned and Marciano's associates were careful about conversation in his presence: They talked very little about boxing.

In the final month, Marciano would not write a letter. The last ten days before a fight he saw no mail, took no telephone calls, met no new acquaintances. The week before the fight he would not shake hands with anyone. Or go for a ride in a car. No new foods! No envisioning the morning after the fight! All that was not *the fight* was taboo: when Marciano worked out punching the bag he saw his opponent before him, when he jogged early in the morning he saw his opponent close beside him. What could be a more powerful image of discipline—madness?—than this absolute subordination of the self, this celibacy of the fighter-in-training? Instead of focusing his energies and fantasies upon Woman, the boxer focuses them upon the Opponent.

No sport is more physical, more direct, than boxing. No sport appears more powerfully homoerotic: the confrontation in the ring—the disrobing—the sweaty, heated combat that is part dance, courtship, coupling—the frequent urgent pursuit by one boxer of the other in the fight's natural and violent movement toward the "knockout." Surely boxing derives much of its appeal from this mimicry of a species of erotic love in which one man overcomes the other in an exhibition of superior strength.

Most fights, however fought, lead to an embrace between the boxers after the final bell—a gesture of mutual respect and apparent affection that appears to the onlooker to be more than perfunctory. Rocky Graziano, often derided for being a slugger rather than a "classic" boxer, sometimes kissed his opponents out of gratitude for the fight. Does the boxing match, one almost wonders, lead irresistibly to this moment: the public embrace of two men who otherwise, in public or in private, could not approach each other with such passion. Are men privileged to embrace with love only after having fought? A woman is struck by the tenderness men will express for boxers who have been hurt, even if it is only by way of commentary on photographs: the startling picture of Ray (Boom Boom) Mancini after his second losing fight with Livingstone Bramble, for instance, when Mancini's face was hideously battered (photographs in *Sports Illustrated* and elsewhere were gory, near-pornographic); the much-reprinted photograph of the defeated Thomas Hearns being carried to his corner in the arms of an enormous black man in formal attire—the "Hit Man" from Detroit now helpless, only semiconscious, looking precisely like a black Christ taken from the cross. These are powerful, haunting, unsettling images, cruelly beautiful, very much bound up with the primitive appeal of the sport.

Yet to suggest that men might love one another directly without the violent ritual of combat is to misread man's greatest passion—for war, not peace. Love, if there is to be love, comes second.

Boxing is, after all, about lying. It is about cultivating a double personality. As José Torres, the ex-light-heavyweight champion who is now the New York State Boxing Commissioner, says: "We fighters understand lies. What's a feint? What's a left hook off the jab? What's an opening?

ON BOXING, continued

What's thinking one thing and doing another . . . ?"

There is nothing fundamentally playful about boxing, nothing that seems to belong to daylight, to pleasure. At its moments of greatest intensity it seems to contain so complete and so powerful an image of life—life's beauty, vulnerability, despair, incalculable and often reckless courage— that boxing *is* life, and hardly a mere game. During a superior boxing match we are deeply moved by the body's communication with itself by way of another's flesh. The body's dialogue with its shadow-self— or Death. Baseball, football, basketball— these quintessentially American pastimes are recognizably sports because they involve play: They are games. One *plays* football; one doesn't *play* boxing.

Observing team sports, teams of adult men, one sees how men are children in the most felicitous sense of the word. But boxing in its elemental ferocity cannot be assimilated into childhood—though very young men box, even professionally, and numerous world champions began boxing when they were hardly more than children. Spectators at public games derive much of their pleasure from reliving the communal emotions of childhood, but spectators at boxing matches relive the murderous infancy of the race. Hence the notorious cruelty of boxing crowds and the excitement when a man begins to bleed. ("When I see blood," says Marvin Hagler, "I become a bull." He means his own.)

The boxing ring comes to seem an altar of sorts, one of those legendary magical spaces where the laws of a nation are suspended: Inside the ropes, during an officially regulated three-minute round, a man may be killed at his opponent's hands but he cannot be legally murdered. Boxing inhabits a sacred space predating civilization; or, to use D. H. Lawrence's phrase, before God was love. If it suggests a savage ceremony or a rite of atonement, it also suggests the futility of such rites. For what atonement is the fight waged, if it must shortly be waged again . . . ?

All this is to speak of the paradox of boxing—its obsessive appeal for many who find in it not only a spectacle involving sensational feats of physical skill but an emotional experience impossible to convey in words; an art form, as I have suggested, with no natural analogue in the arts. And of course this accounts, too, for the extreme revulsion it arouses in many people. ("Brutal," "disgusting," "barbaric," "inhuman," "a terrible, terrible sport"— typical comments on the subject.)

In December 1984, the American Medical Association passed a resolution calling for the abolition of boxing on the principle that it is the only sport in which the *objective* is to cause injury. This is not surprising. Humanitarians have always wanted to reform boxing—or abolish it altogether. The 1896 heavyweight title match between Ruby Robert Fitzsimmons and Peter Maher was outlawed in many parts of the United States, so canny promoters staged it across the Mexican border four hundred miles from El Paso. (Some three hundred people made the arduous journey to see what must have been one of the most disappointing bouts in boxing history—Fitzsimmons knocked out his opponent in a mere ninety-five seconds.)

During the prime of Jack Dempsey's career in the 1920s, boxing was illegal in many states, like alcohol, and like alcohol, seems to have aroused a hysterical public

ON BOXING, continued

enthusiasm. Photographs of jammed out-door arenas taken in the 1920s with boxing rings like postage-size altars at their centers, the boxers themselves scarcely visible, testify to the extraordinary emotional appeal boxing had at that time, even as reform movements were lobbying against it. When Jack Johnson won the heavy-weight title in 1908 (he had to pursue the white champion Tommy Burns all the way to Australia to confront him), the special "danger" of boxing was also that it might expose and humiliate white men in the ring. After Johnson's victory over the "White Hope" contender Jim Jeffries, there were race riots and lynchings throughout the United States; even films of some of Johnson's fights were outlawed in many states. And because boxing has become a sport in which black and Hispanic men have lately excelled, it is particularly vulnerable to attack by white middle-class reformers, who seem uninterested in lobbying against equally dangerous but "establishment" sports like football, auto racing, and thoroughbred horse racing.

There is something peculiarly American in the fact that, while boxing is our most controversial sport, it is also the sport that pays its top athletes the most money. In spite of the controversy, boxing has never been healthier financially. The three high-est paid athletes in the world in both 1983 and 1984 were boxers; a boxer with a long career like heavyweight champion Larry Holmes—forty-eight fights in thirteen years as a professional—can expect to earn somewhere beyond $50 million. (Holmes said that after retirement what he would miss most about boxing is his million-dol-lar checks.) Dempsey, who said that a man

fights for one thing only—money—made somewhere beyond $3,500,000 in the ring in his long and varied career. Now $1.5 million is a fairly common figure for a single fight. Thomas Hearns made at least $7 million in his fight with Hagler while Hagler made at least $7.5 million. For the first of his highly publicized matches with Roberto Duran in 1980—which he lost on a decision—the popular black welterweight champion Sugar Ray Leonard received a staggering $10 million to Duran's $1.3 mil-lion. And none of these figures takes into account various subsidiary earnings (from television commercials, for instance) which in Leonard's case are probably as high as his income was from boxing.

Money has drawn any number of retired boxers back into the ring, very often with tragic results. The most notorious example is perhaps Joe Louis, who, owing huge sums in back taxes, continued boxing well beyond the point at which he could per-form capably. After a career of seventeen years he was stopped by Rocky Marciano—who was said to have felt as upset by his victory as Louis by the defeat. (Louis then went on to a degrading second career as a professional wrestler. This, too, ended abruptly when 300-pound Rocky Lee stepped on the forty-two-year-old Louis's chest and damaged his heart.) Ezzard Charles, Jersey Joe Walcott, Joe Frazier, Muhammad Ali—each continued fighting when he was no longer in condition to defend himself against young heavyweight boxers on the way up. Of all heavyweight champions, only Rocky Marciano, to whom fame and money were not of paramount significance, was prudent enough to retire before he was defeated. In any case, the prodigious sums of money a few boxers

ON BOXING, continued

earn do not account for the sums the public is willing to pay them.

Though boxing has long been popular in many countries and under many forms of government, its popularity in the United States since the days of John L. Sullivan has a good deal to do with what is felt as the spirit of the individual—his "physical" spirit—in conflict with the constrictions of the state. The rise of boxing in the 1920s in particular might well be seen as a consequence of the diminution of the individual vis-à-vis society; the gradual attrition of personal freedom, will, and strength—whether "masculine" or otherwise. In the Eastern bloc of nations, totalitarianism is a function of the state; in the Western bloc it has come to seem a function of technology, or history—"fate." The individual exists in his physical supremacy, but does the individual matter?

In the magical space of the boxing ring so disquieting a question has no claim. There, as in no other public arena, the individual as a unique physical being asserts himself; there, for a dramatic if fleeting period of time, the great world with its moral and political complexities, its terrifying impersonality, simply ceases to exist. Men fighting one another with only their fists and their cunning are all contemporaries, all brothers, belonging to no historical time. "He can run, but he can't hide"—so said Joe Louis before his famous fight with young Billy Conn in 1941. In the brightly lighted ring, man is *in extremis*, performing an atavistic rite or agon for the mysterious solace of those who can participate only vicariously in such drama: the drama of life in the flesh. Boxing has become America's tragic theater.

Rhetoric

1. "On Boxing" is a long and complex essay. In a single sentence, sum up the point you think the author is trying to make in this piece of writing.

2. What type of introduction does the author use to begin the essay? Write a new introduction for the essay, using a different type of introduction. You may want to review the discussion of types of introductions presented in Chapter 4 of the text.

3. Some paragraphs within the essay contain numerous and particularly detailed specifics (support). Locate a paragraph that, in your judgment, is especially detailed. Count the specifics in that paragraph. Also, observe the quality of the specifics. Are they exact and concrete? Do they help you create mental images of the subject matter of the writing?

Ideas

1. Does Oates take a pro or con position toward the sport of boxing? Explain your response.

2. If you were preparing a case for outlawing boxing, would you use all or part of this essay to help make your point? If so, which part?

3. Is boxing really a sport? Explain your answer.

Response

1. Working with a classmate, single out the statements in the essay that define boxing. Incorporate these into a single paragraph. Your topic sentence might begin as follows: "According to Joyce Carol Oates, boxing . . ."

2. Using "On Boxing" to support your thesis, write an essay in which you argue for or against the continuation of the sport of boxing.

3. Single out some sport (such as basketball, hockey, football, or tennis) that you have an interest in, and write an essay defining that sport. You may or may not choose to model your essay on "On Boxing."

WRITING ASSIGNMENT

You may select a topic for this writing assignment from one of the following lists, or you may develop your own topic. Once you have selected a topic, complete one or more of the specified prewriting activities. After sufficient prewriting, write a draft of an essay on the topic you selected. Finally, revise and edit your essay.

General Writing Assignments
- The spirit of Christmas
- Living the good life
- Freedom
- Perseverance
- Conflict

Specific Writing Assignments
- Your sociology instructor is preparing to lecture on the meaning and importance of the concept of family in American society. Prior to assigning readings and beginning to lecture on this subject, she asks class members to write a short definition essay on the concept of family. As she makes the assignment, she informs the class members that they will be asked to revise their essays following completion of the readings, lectures, and discussions of this issue.

■ Your psychology study group is preparing for the final exam in the course. The members of the group have identified four topics that they feel might turn up as essay questions on the exam. Each group member has offered to prepare a response to one of these hypothetical questions. You have agreed to discuss in some detail what is meant by the term *behavior.*

If you decide to develop your own topic, you may want to look through your journal for ideas. What topics that you have addressed in your journal lend themselves to this particular strategy of thinking and communicating? You might also look carefully at the focused journal entries you wrote at the beginning of this chapter. Is one of these topics of interest to you? Is it a topic with which you have some experience? With some revision work, could your journal entry on this topic become an essay?

Finally, look back through this chapter at some of the exercises you have done individually and with classmates. Are any of these topics of interest to you? Recall conversations with your classmates. Have they given you ideas for topics? Perhaps interesting topics emerged from the group discussions that followed some of the practices in the chapter. You may want to spend some time discussing these exercises with classmates to help you decide what to write about. Or you may want to do some listing, brainstorming, or freewriting to help you discover a suitable topic.

PREWRITING

After selecting a topic as the subject for a definition essay, complete one or more of the following prewriting activities:

■ *Focused freewriting*—This prewriting activity is particularly effective for beginning a definition essay, since it lets you say a lot about what you think a term means, or at least what it means to you, without having to decide in advance which expository strategies you will use to extend the definition. Write the term you want to define at the top of a blank sheet of paper. Then write about this term for six minutes without stopping. Then review what you have written, and select one idea from the writing to use as a focus for your essay. Other ideas in this focused prewriting may serve as starting points for particular expository strategies you may use to extend the definition.

■ *Cubing*—This prewriting strategy will lead you to think about the term you are defining from at least six different perspectives. One of these may serve as a focus for the essay, and one or more of the others may serve as ideas for extending the definition into a full-length essay. Begin by envisioning a cube. On the six surfaces of the cube are six writing assignments asking you to describe, compare, associate, analyze, apply, and argue for or against the term you're defining. As you respond to each miniature writing assignment, you'll get new ideas about what to include in your definition essay.

REVISING

In revising your essay, follow these seven steps:

1. Ask a friend, a roommate, or a writing colleague (or colleagues) to listen to or read your writing and then to comment on what you have written. Specifically, are the subject and the purpose of the essay clear? Does the body of the essay make and support points that achieve the purpose of the writing? Do any sentences, passages, or sections of the paper seem either unrelated to or contradictory to the purpose of the writing?

2. Check the introduction and thesis statement of the essay. Have you introduced your reader to the topic you plan to define? Have you adequately restricted the topic? Does your introductory paragraph have a thesis that makes clear what you plan to say about your topic? Have you developed a focus in the thesis for the definition? In what ways do you need to rewrite the introduction so that you engage the reader's interest and clarify your purpose?

3. Check the thesis support in the body of the essay. Have you determined the purpose of the extended definition essay? Have you obtained a dictionary definition of the topic, as appropriate to your purpose? Is the material in the body of the essay organized so that it supports the point (thesis) of the writing?

4. Check the paragraph support throughout the essay. Is each paragraph well written, with clear and specific details to support your thesis? Have you selected appropriate expository strategies for developing your definition essay?

5. Check for coherence and unity. As a whole, does the essay make sense? Does it contain any irrelevant or misplaced material?

6. Check for closure. Is there closure at the end of the essay in either a concluding sentence or a concluding (or summarizing) paragraph?

7. Finally, review the Revision Checklist at the end of Chapter 5. Use the checklist to make sure that you have completed a thorough revision of your essay.

PART THREE

APPLICATIONS

APPLYING WRITING SKILLS

The writing skills you have learned and practiced in this book can be used in all writing—not just in college English classes. In Part One, you learned some ways to get started, how to develop a thesis, how to support the thesis, and how to revise and edit. In Part Two, you learned some strategies for developing ideas into essays. In Part Three of this text, you will examine other kinds of writing that you may need or want to do. This part of the text also offers analyses of other kinds of college writing that you may be asked to do as well as of some common types of noncollegiate writing.

USING WRITING SKILLS
IN OTHER COLLEGE COURSES

You are probably enrolled in more that one course at the college you are attending. More than likely, at least one of the other classes you are taking involves some writing. In the space provided, make a list of the writing assignments you have received in other classes you are taking. If you are not taking another class now, or if the other class you are taking has no writing assignments, list writing assignments you were given in a class you have already completed.

Class or Subject Area	Writing Assignment
_____	_____
_____	_____
_____	_____
_____	_____
_____	_____

You may have listed writing assignments such as critical reviews, summaries, research papers, essays, essay examinations, and reports. These assignments are frequently made in various subject areas, including math, literature, history, biology, psychology, diesel mechanics, broadcasting, and cosmetology. When a teacher in any subject area requires you to write, your writing will probably be evaluated in two different ways: on the basis of what you say—demonstrated knowledge of content in the subject areas—and on the basis of how you say it— demonstrated knowledge of written communication skills.

This puts two burdens on you, as a writer: you must prove that you have knowledge about your subject, and you must prove that you are capable of communicating that knowledge. In fact, some teachers assign two grades for written work—one for content, and one for the quality of the writing. It is important for you to be able both to communicate knowledge and to demonstrate your competence in a subject area. One of the most frequently used methods of testing for learning is to make writing assignments. Using the skills you have learned in this course to help with your writing in another course enhances your ability to prove your competence in communicating your knowledge of a particular subject.

GETTING STARTED

As in any writing assignment, there are some preliminary activities to consider before you actually begin writing. All of these were discussed in Chapter 1, but they are briefly reviewed here. As you work through this section of the book, keep these prewriting activities in mind for each type of writing assignment discussed. You many want to refer to this page each time you begin a writing assignment. The points discussed here are a good way to focus your thoughts before you write.

If you need further information or explanation about any of the following topics, refer to the appropriate section of Chapter 1.

FOCUSING

To ensure that you have established a clear focus for your essay, you must do the following:

- Identify your audience. Is the writing for personal use or for some other audience? Is the audience clearly defined for you, or is it an invoked audience?
- Determine the purpose of the writing.
- Determine the appropriate tone.
- Decide what point of view you should use.

PREWRITING

Use one or more of the following prewriting strategies to help you get started:

- Journal
- Freewriting
- Focused Freewriting
- Looping
- Cubing
- Inventory
- Clustering

The circumstances under which you carry out college writing tasks can vary a great deal. For example, sometimes you are given a specific topic to write about. Other times you are told to choose any topic related to the course of study. You may be given a period of several weeks during which to complete a writing assignment. Other writing assignments must be completed within a class hour. Still others must be completed in an examination period of two hours.

All of these circumstances influence the amount of time you can spend focusing and prewriting. Indeed, you may have to eliminate some preliminary activities entirely if you are under extreme time constraints. But regular use of these prewriting strategies will sharpen your skills considerably. If you have made a regular practice of considering how to focus your writing and have practiced some prewriting strategies, those skills will be a part of your unconscious preparation for any writing task you undertake.

WRITING TO LEARN

Personal writing is writing that you do in conjunction with your course work. It is for your personal use, however, and not necessarily for any other audience. Note taking is a good example of this kind of personal writing.

TAKING NOTES

Taking lecture notes is a form of personal writing. The notes are an aid you use to help you remember important concepts, facts, and general information about the subject. Once you have taken notes in class, you can use them in several ways to help you complete class assignments and prepare for tests. You may want to try any or all of the following methods. The important thing to remember is that your purpose is to learn the course material. Any aid is simply a device to help you accomplish that goal.

Making a Double-entry Notebook On one side of the notebook, write your classroom notes, leaving the facing page empty. Later, as you review your classroom notes, make personal notes commenting on what you are reading. You might even want to make up questions about your notes—questions that you think might be included on some future test. This is also a good place to record questions that you want to ask the professor before, during, or after the next class period.

The history notes in Figure 13.1 and the reaction in Figure 13.2 are from a double-entry notebook. The notes consist of information written during a classroom lecture; the reactions are comments and questions recorded both during and after the lecture.

PRACTICE Keep a double-entry notebook for one week for this course or for another course you are presently taking. At the end of the week, analyze the value of keeping a double-entry notebook.

Highlighting or Making Special Notations   As you read through your notes, use a highlighter to mark important information and make special notations. Some people overuse highlighter pens; that is, they tend to highlight everything, which negates the value of highlighting. If you find highlighting helpful, try to limit the number of sentences and phrases you highlight. Ask yourself if the sentence or word or phrase you are about to highlight is important. If it is a minor fact or a supporting detail, chances are it should be left as it is. Remember that the purposes of highlighting are to make it easy for you to review important information quickly before a test and to gather material for a paper. If only important information is highlighted, that information will be easier to locate.

Recopying Class Notes   The act of recopying helps you comprehend information in a new way. As you recopy, you may find that you can reorganize the material so that lists are made complete and definitions are arranged in a certain order; or you may compose a separate list of important dates or facts. Another advantage of recopying notes is that it helps you fill in gaps that occurred as you hurriedly took notes in class.

Following are two versions, original and recopied, of the same history notes as taken in class. Here are the original notes:

Example   Declaration of Independence— 18th-century document based on liberal political thought of that cent. Addressed to mankind. not congress not George III Dec. attempts to show the purpose of the revolution. Longest section is list of G's wrong acts. Jeff. wants to justify Am. action of revol.

Jefferson—life, liberty, happiness

Locke—life, liberty, property

Here are the recopied notes:

Example   The Declaration of Independence is an 18th-century document because it is based to a great extent on the liberal political thought of that century.

It is addressed to mankind rather than to the Congress or to George III, the reigning king of England at the time of the writing of the Declaration. Jefferson wanted to present his reasons for the Declaration to the world at large so that everyone would understand the reasons for making such a declaration. Jefferson's goal was to present a logical, rational, yet genuine reason for the Declaration.

FIGURE 13.1 Class notes

The Declaration of Independence
  A document based on the liberal
  political thought of the 18th century.

Thomas Jefferson

Declaration addressed to mankind – not
  congress – not George III.

Attempts to show the purpose of
  revolution.

Jefferson wants to justify revolt
  Jefferson – life, liberty, happiness
  Locke – life, liberty, property

FIGURE 13.2   Reactions to class notes

* Know date of signing, key authors/
  signers — where it was signed.

  Sources of ideas in the Declaration
  Did the public accept it? Who
  read it?

  Is the Declaration like any previous
  documents?
  In America? In England?

  Read section about John Locke, p. 119

Even though the Declaration is not addressed to George III, the largest section of the document concerns him. Jefferson includes a long list of all the wrongdoings of George III. A big reason for including this list is to justify the revolutionary actions of the colonists in support of the Declaration.

Jefferson was influenced by and had great respect for the ideas of John Locke. Locke believed that the citizens of England had a right to life, liberty, and property.

PRACTICE   If you are taking another course, recopy one class period's lecture notes. If you are not taking another course, get notes from a class you have taken in the past and recopy those.

Outlining Your Notes   Outlining can serve as an excellent organizational tool. As you outline your notes, you will also focus on the important information, because an outline reduces a large quantity of information to the main ideas and main details of the writing. By knowing how to outline, you develop the ability to glean the main ideas from what you are reading.

Outlining involves ranking and organizing main ideas and key supporting points. Main ideas of equal rank are given the same level of symbols, such as Roman numerals. Key supporting ideas are also given a consistent level of symbols, such as capital letters. The main ideas and supporting ideas are condensed into a few words that clearly and concisely state the idea presented.

The following outline was written based on the preceding classroom notes about the Declaration of Independence. Notice how many ideas are clearly distinguished from supporting ideas as a result of the way they are organized. Here is the outline:

Example   THE DECLARATION OF INDEPENDENCE

    I. An 18th-century document

       A. Based on liberal political thought of the 18th century

       B. Addressed to mankind rather than to Congress or to George III

II. Reasons for the Declaration

   A. To show the purposes of the revoltion

   B. To justify the action of revolution

      1. The longest section is a list of George's wrong acts.

      2. Today, many people omit reading this section of the Declaration.

III. Jefferson's unalienable rights compared to those of John Locke

   A. Jefferson: life, liberty, happiness

   B. Locke: life, liberty, property

TEXTBOOK OUTLINING

Another useful personal writing aid is textbook outlining. As in outlining notes, key ideas are grouped and organized, and large amounts of information are reduced to these key ideas. Textbook outlines are a very effective way to take notes on large blocks of material. Outlining key ideas, definitions, and examples can help you determine what is important in the text, and it can help you locate this information rapidly.

As you outline a chapter in a textbook, look for definitions, enumerations, and, in some cases, important dates. Usually, some or all of these provide important information that can be included in the outline. Also pay attention to headings and subheadings. Quite often, headings and subheadings serve as a rough outline of the material.

Following is an outline of the material in this chapter up to this point. As you read the outline, notice how main ideas are represented by Roman numerals and how supporting ideas are enumerated by letters. Notice, too, that each idea is presented in a clear, precise manner; main ideas begin at the same point on the left margin, and subordinate ideas of the same rank are indented equally under the main ideas.

Example   <u>APPLICATIONS</u>

    I. Introduction

    II. Using Writing Skills in Other College Courses

    III. Getting Started

       A. Focusing

          1. Identify audience

            a. Personal writing

            b. Invoked audience

> 2. Determine the purpose of the writing
>
> 3. Determine the appropriate tone
>
> 4. Decide what point of view you should use
>
> B. Prewriting Strategies
>
> 1. Journal
>
> 2. Freewriting
>
> 3. Focused freewriting
>
> 4. Looping
>
> 5. Cubing
>
> 6. Inventory
>
> 7. Clustering
>
> IV. Writing to Learn
>
> A. Taking Notes
>
> 1. Double-entry notebook
>
> 2. Highlighting/special notation
>
> 3. Recopying notes
>
> 4. Outlining notes
>
> B. Textbook Outlining

PRACTICE   From any textbook, select one chapter of five to ten pages. Read the chapter and outline it, using the preceding example as a model. Observe these precautions as you work:

1. Remember to title your outline; a title helps you to remember the subject of the chapter.

2. As you read the chapter, look for lists, definitions, headings, and subheadings. These will help you distinguish between significant and minor material in the chapter. Outlines should tend to be brief rather than lengthy; remember that your purpose is to condense material. To achieve brevity, include only the most significant points in your outline.

3. Order your main points by using Roman numerals; use letters, numbers, and lower-case letters for different levels of supporting information. Follow the form used in the preceding example.

4. Keep entries brief. Don't overdevelop outlines through wordiness or the use of too many subheadings.

RESPONDING TO ESSAY QUESTIONS

Teachers in many disciplines frequently use essay questions to test students' knowledge of a particular subject. Essay questions require you to demonstrate knowledge of a subject by writing clearly, logically, and in an informed manner about the material covered.

 Essay questions generally give students some latitude, whereas objective or short-answer questions allow almost no latitude, (since you either know the answer or you don't). While it is true that essay questions give you some freedom of expression, do not make the mistake of thinking that anything you write in answer to an essay question is acceptable. Two essential elements are involved in any satisfactory answer to an essay question: subject knowledge and effective writing.

SUBJECT KNOWLEDGE

First, a thorough knowledge of the subject is necessary before you can answer essay questions effectively. If you are being tested on a list of facts, you will find it much easier, after cramming the night before, to respond to multiple-choice questions than to discuss those facts in an essay. That is because discussion requires knowledge and organization beyond the mere facts; it requires you to marshal support for the points you make in your discussion. To handle this task, you must read the assigned text, study your notes, attend class, and keep up with all assignments on a regular basis, so that you can spend your time before an essay test reviewing the material rather than reading and studying it for the first time.

EFFECTIVE WRITING

Second, responding satisfactorily to an essay question requires clear, coherent, orderly writing. Faced with two separate papers that respond to the same question—one paper that is well written, and one paper that is incoherent, rambling, and full of grammatical errors—a teacher is likely to give a higher grade to the well-written paper, even if the general content of both papers is similar. Remembering and practicing the writing process you have studied in this course will enable you to write good responses to essay questions.

 The remainder of this section identifies several ways of improving your skills in answering essay questions. The suggestions assume that the essay questions are questions you must answer in a testing situation. You may, however, be asked to answer essay questions in other situations, such as in the case of discussion questions that are part of a homework assignment or discussion questions that may be included at the end of a chapter in a textbook. If so, most of these suggestions will still apply, although some of them will not.

ANTICIPATING ESSAY QUESTIONS

One useful strategy is to anticipate essay questions as you study. Of course you can't know what precise questions will be asked, but you can make some educated guesses. What points were emphasized in the textbook? the lectures? class discussions? These will give you some idea of what topics will be addressed. Instructors tend to test on topics they have emphasized, so it is a good idea to look over your notes to see what the instructor emphasized. After you anticipate the topics, make up some essay questions on these topics. This activity will help you begin to focus on answers to potential questions.

Here is an example. Angie reviewed her notes and her textbook and determined that the Industrial Age and the Romantic poets were likely topics for essay questions in her British literature class. After determining the topics, she made up the following hypothetical essay questions about those topics:

Example
- Evaluate the effects the Industrial Age had on the Romantic poets.
- Choose one Romantic poet, and discuss the influence the Industrial Age had on his or her poetry. Be as specific as possible.
- Define Romantic poetry. Support your definition by giving examples from specific poems of the Romantic Period.
- Contrast the satiric nature of Neoclassical poetry in the eighteenth century to the idealistic nature of Romantic poetry in the nineteenth century.

Once you have made up questions for the exam, as Angie did, you may or may not want to answer them. You may simply want to begin directing your thinking along the lines of your questions. On the other hand, you may want to sit down with your notes and textbook and write out detailed repsonses to the questions. Another (and probably more realistic) response is to outline answers. A good outline will enable you to map out a clear and logical response without taking the time to write out all the supporting details.

Of course you may choose the wrong topics, or the questions the instructor asks may be utterly unlike the questions you composed. But this is still a valuable exercise, because it forces you to think about the topic, review your notes, review your textbook, and focus your thinking.

TAKING AN ESSAY EXAM

Once you get to the exam and receive your test questions, read over the questions and budget the time you have to answer them. For example, if you have four questions of equal weight to answer in two hours, you will allot roughly thirty minutes per question. For each question, you should allow approximately five to eight minutes to read and analyze the question and to outline your answer. The next fifteen to twenty minutes can be devoted to answering the question, and the last five to eight minutes should be spent rereading and proofreading your response. At the expiration of that time, you should be prepared to go on to the next question.

Read the essay questions carefully. Don't make the mistake of skimming the question and then blindly rushing into the answer. Take time to determine what the question asks you to do. The verb in the question is extremely important. It is the direction word—the word that tells you what you are supposed to do with the topic. Several direction words are commonly used in essay questions. Become familiar with the following list of direction words and their definitions, and thenceforth you will understand what task each word is asking you to perform:

- *Analyze* – to separate and describe each part of an object or concept, and to show how the separate parts relate to each other or to show what the tendencies of each part are.
- *Classify* – to separate the parts or groups of an object or concept into classes according to some system or principle of classification.
- *Compare* – to describe objects, persons, and ideas in a way that emphasizes their similarities.
- *Contrast* – to describe objects, persons, and ideas in a way that emphasizes their differences.
- *Define* – to identify the distinguishing characteristics of an object, person, or idea; to tell what the object, person, or idea is and/or what it isn't.
- *Describe* – to give a picture in words of a person, object, idea, place, or event.
- *Discuss* – to present a careful examination of persons, objects, or ideas; discussion may also include argumentation and persuasion.
- *Enumerate* – to list, one by one, the main ideas related to the topic.
- *Evaluate* – to examine and assess the worth or value of persons, objects, and ideas; to weigh both their positive and their negative qualities or characteristics.
- *Explain* – to discuss, to analyze, to describe.
- *Illustrate* – to explain by providing examples of the point or topic.
- *Narrate* – to relate the particulars of an event, usually in chronological order.

■ *Outline* – to present (usually in discussion or essay format rather than in outline format) the main points about a subject and the main details about those points.

■ *Summarize* – to present the essential substance of the topic briefly and concisely.

PRACTICE   In a group with two or three other people in your class, read the following essay questions and decide how each question should be answered. In the space that follows each question, state specifically what should be done to answer that question. We begin with an example question and response:

Example

Question   [English] *Evaluate the effects the Industrial Age had on the Romantic poets.*

Response   Define the Industrial Age by listing its characteristics. As each

characteristic is presented, explain how that particular characteris-

tic influenced the Romantic poets. Choose specific poets who were

particularly affected by that characteristic or whose poetry reflects

an impact. Include both the positive and negative effects of the Indus-

trial Age.

Now complete the following practice exercises.

1.   [Sociology]   *What is a social problem? Give examples of social problems.*

_____

_____

_____

_____

_____

_____

2. [Philosophy] *Discuss Stoicism and Skepticism, and enumerate the major tenets of each.*

_____

_____

_____

_____

_____

_____

3. [History] *Describe life on a medieval manor.*

_____

_____

_____

_____

_____

4. [World Religions] *Write a brief biographical essay about Mahavira, the founder of Jainism.*

_____

_____

_____

_____

_____

_____

5. [Political Science] *Show how John Locke's theories shaped to a significant extent the course of politics in 18th-century America.*

_____

_____

_____

_____

_____

_____

PRACTICE   Make up five essay questions on material covered in other courses you are taking. Include a brief statement of how you would answer each question. If you are not taking any other courses, choose two or more of the essays in this text, and make up two essay questions about each of them.

After you have carefully read the essay question on your exam, outline your answer based on what the question asks you to do. At first recoil, you may feel that your time would be better spent answering the question than outlining your answer: after all, the outline is for your own personal use, and it will never be seen by the grader of your essay. But an outline is crucial to a good answer. You would not start on a journey to a specific street in a strange town without either a road map or some specific directions on how to get there. Neither should you begin writing without some direction. Like a road map, an outline provides direction for your efforts. Without it, you will be blindly writing whatever comes into your head about the subject. The result may be a paper with solid content but bad organization, which can result in a poor grade. Once you have outlined your response, refer to the outline as you would refer to a road map, to find out where to turn next.

Your next step is to answer the question. Fifteen to twenty minutes may not seem like much time to spend actually anwering an essay question, but it should be adequate if you have prepared a good working outline. If you are answering the question within a specific time limit, you may need to do some editing as you write. If so, concentrate primarily on the content of your answer and secondarily on editing. Since you have been practicing good writing skills during this course, your writing will already be relatively free of such grammatical errors as fragments and run-ons.

Include a brief introduction and conclusion in your answer. Both the introduction and conclusion can be as brief as one sentence each, but some sort of introductory statement(s) and concluding statement(s) add polish to your essay answer. Follow the guidelines given in Chapter 4 for writing introductions and conclusions. Remember also to include transition words, phrases, and sentences where appropriate. More information about transitions can be found in Chapter 3.

Allow yourself some time to reread and proofread each answer. Again, you may have little time for this, but, if possible, allot a few minutes for this purpose. Most teachers will accept essay answers with corrections written above lines and in the margins of your paper. If you have more time, you may want to recopy your response. Most teachers, however, are reasonable about what they require. For example, if you have two questions to answer in two hours, you can spend more time on editing than if you have to answer four questions in the same time period. Obviously, the more questions you are asked, the less time you will have for proofreading and editing.

PRACTICE   The following unabridged student essay answers are written in response to essay examination questions. Along with other members of your class, read each question; then read the student response. After you and your classmates have read the questions and responses, discuss the effectiveness of the essays. In your discussion, consider the following questions:

- Did the student answer the question asked; that is, did the student adequately follow the direction words in the question?
- Is the answer thorough, or are some parts of the essay inadequately developed?
- Is there an adequate introduction? conclusion? transition words and phrases?
- While there may be some editing problems and problems with poor diction, do you feel that the paper is acceptable or unacceptable? If you feel that the grammar and diction are unacceptable, be prepared to point out specific inadequate places in the essay.

Question   *Write an essay in which you discuss the conflicts between the tenets of Calvinism and the basic positions of Deism.*

Response   CALVINISM VS. DEISM: THE BASIC CONFLICTS

There are several basic conflicts between the tenets of Calvinism and the positions of Deism. Each held contrasting beliefs in God's power and ability, the Bible, and the nature of man.

The Calvinists held that God had all-powerful rule over man, while the Deists felt that man held free will, which limited God's power. The Calvinists also believed that God was active in all aspects of nature. The Deists saw God as a "watchmaker" who had finished with creation and now sat back to watch his work.

The second major conflict concerned the Bible. Calvin held that the Bible was the inspired word of God and the way to knowing God's will. The Deists felt that the Bible was a good book but was uninspired and full of superstition. They could not believe the accounts of miracles or the Trinity.

Another contrast was over the nature of man. Calvin felt man was basically evil and damned; therefore, only the elect could be saved. The Deists saw man as created in the likeness of God. Through a study of nature, man could become perfect.

These basic positions on God, the Bible, and man make up the basic conflicts between Calvinism and Deism.

Question

Response

Describe each of the three levels of the study of history.

The first level is the individual—what happens. What was the outcome.

The second is the comparative. In checking for cycles, or changed under like circumstances.

The third is the theoreticals—or the hand of god intervening. Looking for evidence to back up a theory.

Question

Response

Describe each of the three levels of the study of history.

The first level of the study of history is the study of individual events. Doing this helps the historians understand what actually happened, how it happened, and the causes and effects of the particular historical event. Analyzing each event in history aids historians in better understanding and in putting facts together. This leads to the next level of the study of history.

The second level is the comparative level of study. Two or more events are compared to discover likenesses and similarities. For example, historians study all world wars and find the commonalities. This could prove helpful in preventing future wars. History can be a useful tool to use to help determine the future if it is used correctly and judiciously.

The third level of the study of history is the theoretical level. Many possible causes of events are considered. Many different factors affect history and sometimes, direct relationships can be discerned.

There are many theoretical approaches to the study of history. One theory is theological. Historians who study history from this approach believe that events in history are caused by divine intervention and that everything happens according to God's will. Another theory is the geological theory, the way events are affected by the geographical area in which they take place. For example, the Nile River greatly affected Egyptian civilization. It provided all of the water for human and agricultural needs. It also provided a north/south highway for transportational needs. Furthermore, it was an advantageous location in time of war. Defense was facilitated by forming a blockade at both ends of the river.

Historians are always looking for the key to what makes things happen, and this is an important step in the realization that what once happened could reoccur. Historians use these levels of the study of history to study our past in order to create a better future for humanity.

SUMMARIES, REPORTS, AND REVIEWS

Summaries, reports, and reviews are three other kinds of collegiate writing you may be asked to do. Usually, these writing assignments are generated from a book, magazine, or journal article that you are required to read; they may also be based on a film or TV program that you are instructed to view. The teacher then asks you to write a summary, a review, or a report about the assignment.

Your teachers may also use such terms as *evaluation, abstract, critical review,* and *analysis.* While there may be slight differences in meaning between these words and the words *summary, report,* and *review,* all are tied to writing assignments involving assigned reading or audiovisual material. Most instructors, when making such an assignment, include specific directions covering any special requirements related to the assignment.

Each such writing assignment enables you, the student, to accomplish the following:

- You read material that is supplemental to the course.
- You become acquainted with the experts in the field, by reading books and articles they have written. You also become familiar with scholarly journals related to your course of study.
- By writing about the readings, you learn the material.
- Writing about the readings and audiovisual materials also improves your reading, writing, and study skills.

The remainder of this section provides more detailed discussions of summaries, reviews, and reports. Refer to this material each time you are assigned one of these kinds of writings, regardless of the subject area. The guidelines here will serve as a quick review of what you are expected to do with such an assignment.

SUMMARIES

Summaries are written condensations of the main points and key supporting ideas of a longer article, book, or audiovisual piece. Teachers assign summaries of TV shows, books, videos, and even lectures. One of the most frequently used summary assignments is of a journal or magazine article. Usually, the teacher expects you to go to the library, read an article in a magazine or journal related to a particular field of study, and then write a summary of the article. Completing such an assignment requires practicing various study skills, including library use, reading, and writing.

To write a good summary, you must be thoroughly familiar with the article, book, or film you are writing about. This involves close reading of the article so that you can determine the key points and the subordinate points in the article. After you have read and reread the article, you must employ good writing skills in producing the summary.

The following guidelines for writing a summary of a magazine article can be adapted to help you write good summaries of other articles, books, and films, too:

1. Read the title of the article. Notice the name of the magazine. Read any subtitles, and then quickly thumb through the article. As you do so, read headings, subheadings, and any information accompanying pictures, charts, and graphs. This quick scan gives you a preview of the article.

2. Some scholarly journals and magazines begin each article with a brief summary (often called a *precis* or *abstract*) of its contents. Occasionally, a short summary of each article is included in the table of contents. Don't overlook these important sources of preview information about an article.

3. Now go back to the beginning, and read the article. You don't have to worry about an in-depth reading this time; instead, read the article to get a sense of key points and main ideas. Note these as you go through the article.

4. Go back to the beginning again, and carefully reread the article. This time, read with the goal of understanding what each sentence means and how each sentence relates to the previous and following sentences.

5. Take notes on the article. You may find that the main ideas you noted on your first reading are no longer those you now consider to be the main ideas of the article. After this final careful reading, you should have a good understanding of the article.

6. Now you are ready to begin writing. You may want to begin your first draft by composing a summary statement of the subject of the article. Ask yourself, "What is the most important point of this article?" Turn the answer into an opening sentence. In this opening sentence, you also need to identify the article's title, the author's name, and the name and date of the journal or magazine containing the article. For example, you might open your summary by writing, "In an article entitled 'Checkpoint Hadrian,' in the April 1989 issue of *Natural History*, John J. Wilkes states that Hadrian's Wall was built to serve as a boundary demarcation and a discouragement to surreptitious infiltration from the north, rather than as a defense against invading armies."

7. The remainder of the summary will consist of a paragraph or two (or more, depending on your instructor's particular requirements) in which you state in your own words the main ideas and key supporting points of the article.

8. As you write this draft, keep in mind that you are condensing the article. You don't want to sacrifice any important points, but neither do you want a summary that is longer than the original article! For that reason, observe the following points:
    - Use direct quotations sparingly. Your own words are better in a summary, unless the author uses some particularly unique phrase that needs to be credited to her or him.
    - Use a clear, no-nonsense style of writing. Maintain a tone that is similar to that of the writing you are summarizing. If the tone is formal, use a formal tone; if the tone is light and witty, use a lighter tone.
    - Follow the organizational pattern of the article as much as possible. Don't rearrange the author's points. A summary should

enable another person to get the main ideas of the original article, without having to read it.

9. At this point, you are ready to rewrite and revise the summary until you have completed a satisfactory final draft.

If you are summarizing a book, follow the same guidelines, but use chapter headings and the table of contents as preview material. Include the title of the book and the author's name in the opening sentence of the summary.

If you are summarizing a film or a piece in some other audio or visual medium, include the name of the piece in the opening sentence. You may wish to take notes as you view; if possible and if time permits, try to view the film twice, taking notes during the second viewing.

The following summary was written for an English class in connection with a study of Geoffrey Chaucer's *Canterbury Tales*.

Example   A SUMMARY OF *FROM EVERY SHIRE'S ENDE*

The film *From Every Shire's Ende* is an intriguing glimpse into the world of the pilgrims in Chaucer's *Canterbury Tales*. The film provides a detailed, visual prologue to Chaucer's story of the journey these people made from London to Canterbury to see Becket's shrine. While the "General Prologue" of the *Canterbury Tales* introduces the reader to each of the pilgrims and sets the stage for each character's story, this film enriches that introduction by providing the reader a visual portrait of that long journey.

The film offers a sensual perspective of the long pilgrimage. The sights of the moors and marshes, the rough wayside crosses, the tapestry-lined halls of the castles, and the small cottages are all enriched by the sounds of the rushing streams, the bells attached to the horses' reins, and the songs and prayers of the monks in the monasteries, where the pilgrims might have spent a night or two. Additionally, the viewer receives a vivid reminder of the very quiet, profoundly rural landscape the pilgrim must have enjoyed along the way.

PRACTICE   Use the guidelines in this section to write a one-paragraph summary of the material you just read about how to write a summary. After you finish, compare your summary to those written by other class members. Discuss your summaries with others, looking first at the opening sentence of each summary. Whose first sentence is most concise? Does that sentence include the bibliographical information? Then compare paragraphs, looking at the first point presented after the opening sentence. Does everyone agree on the first point? Why or why not? Discuss as many points as time permits.

PRACTICE Use the guidelines in this section to write a summary of "Ode to Makeup," by Irene Egan (in Chapter 9 of this text). Remember to follow her organizational pattern and to maintain a similar tone.

PRACTICE Choose a topic related to a subject you are currently studying. For example, if you are taking a world history class, you might look for such topics as colonialism, nationalism, civil wars, or eighteenth-century European culture. If you are not taking any other classes, make your topic rhetoric, English grammar, or writing. Use the *Reader's Guide to Periodical Literature* to help you locate an article about the subject you selected. Prepare a summary of the article you found on the topic you selected. Follow the guidelines in this section when reading the article and when writing the summary.

REPORTS

Reports are another form of collegiate writing. Like summaries, most reports are generated from a book, an article, a TV show, or a film that you are instructed to read or view. You may also be required to write lab reports, in which you report or narrate what happened in an experiment.

Most reports consist of two parts: a summary of the book, film, or experiment; and your reaction to it. Of course, if you are assigned to write a report in a class, your instructor may specify the procedures for you to follow. If your instructor assigns a report and makes no further stipulations about specific requirements, however, you may find the following guidelines helpful.

Writing the Summary

1. The first paragraph or two (depending on the length of the article you are summarizing) should be a summary of the article. This summary is also called an *abstract*. Follow the instructions given in

the preceding section about how to read an article or view a film prior to writing a summary.

2. Begin the report with a topic sentence that includes the relevant bibliographical information about the article or book you are summarizing.

3. Remember to summarize by writing about key ideas and key supporting ideas. Keep this part of the report objective and factual; avoid including any personal opinion here.

Writing Your Reaction

1. Begin a new paragraph when you begin this part of the report. If possible and appropriate, use some kind of transition sentence, as discussed in Chapter 3.

2. Develop some method to organize your reaction. For example, you might want to provide a two-paragraph reaction. The first paragraph could focus on how you personally reacted to the work. What emotions did it arouse in you? How did you feel about the author's perspective toward the topic? Did the author change your personal perspective about the topic? If so, how? The second paragraph could focus on what were for you the most significant parts of the article. Remember to justify your opinion by explaining why you feel that way. Don't resummarize the book or article at this point in the report. If you want to discuss the significance of a specific part of the book or article, do so without repeating your summary. If you intend to discuss certain points in this part of the report, refer the reader to the appropriate part of the summary section for a recitation of these points, if necessary.

3. If you use general terms, such as *interesting, helpful,* and *informative,* be sure to follow your general statement with specifics showing how you personally thought it was interesting, helpful, or informative. You might want to consult a thesaurus for less pedestrian synonyms for such general terms. For example, instead of opening with a sentence stating that the book was "interesting," use a word such as *intriguing* or *enlightening.*

4. End the report with a short concluding paragraph or sentence, as appropriate, depending on the length of the report.

5. It is appropriate to use personal pronouns in the reaction section of the report.

PRACTICE   The following report is an altered version of the summary of the film *From Every Shire's Ende,* presented earlier in this chapter. Now it includes the viewer's reactions to the film. Read the report and answer the questions that follow.

Example   A REPORT ON *FROM EVERY SHIRE'S ENDE*

The film *From Every Shire's Ende* is an intriguing glimpse into the world of the pilgrims in Chaucer's *Canterbury Tales*. The film provides a detailed, visual prologue to Chaucer's story of the journey these people made from London to Canterbury to see Becket's shrine. While the "General Prologue" of the *Canterbury Tales* introduces the reader to each of the pilgrims and sets the stage for each character's story, this film enriches that introduction by providing the reader a visual portrait of that long journey.

The film offers a sensual perspective of the long pilgrimage. The sights of the moors and marshes, the rough wayside crosses, the tapestry-lined halls of the castles, and the small cottages are all enriched by the sounds of the rushing streams, the bells attached to the horses' reins, and the songs and prayers of the monks in the monasteries, where the pilgrims might have spent a night or two. Additionally, the viewer receives a vivid reminder of the very quiet, profoundly rural landscape the pilgrim must have enjoyed along the way.

This film gives me a clear perspective on the differences in social classes in Chaucer's day. For example, the harvest time is a time of games for the peasants, while the nobles enjoy jousting. Feasting, however, is a common pleasure for everyone. I am also reminded of how the churches and the clergy emerge as important, integral parts of society. The church is a place of social life as well as prayer; a country fair and Mass are both held in the same rooms of the church.

The film underscores this period of English history as an ostentatious age. This is especially vivid in the film's remarkable telephoto details of the cathedrals. The high arches, stained glass, misericords, and grotesques are carefully depicted in the film. The film's attention to these details of the cathedrals emphasizes the importance of the church for the people of this era.

1. Assuming that the summary section was limited to two paragraphs, does the report adequately summarize the film? Why or why not?

   _____

   _____

   _____

2. Which sentence begins the reaction part of the report? How can you tell that this is where the reaction section begins?

   _____

   _____

   _____

3. What questions does this writer seem to answer in the reaction? In other words, how is the reaction organized?

   _____

   _____

   _____

PRACTICE   Choose one of the summaries you wrote in the preceding section on summaries, and turn it into a report by adding a reaction section to it. Make any necessary changes in the summary before you begin. Follow the guidelines given in this section for writing a reaction.

After you write the reaction, exchange reports with other people in the class. Analyze two or three of your classmates' reactions by checking to see that the reactions sections of their reports correspond to the guidelines given in this section.

PRACTICE Watch a TV show, play, or movie. Prepare a report of the show. Choose one of the following audiences, and write your report with that audience in mind, developing a tone and style appropriate to that audience and to the tone and style of the movie, play, or TV show you watched.

Audiences

- Classmates in your composition class
- A teacher
- The entire student body via the student newspaper
- The local newspaper

PRACTICE Write a one-paragraph reaction to a chapter of a textbook for a course you are currently taking. Follow the guidelines given in this section for writing your reaction.

REVIEWS

Reviews are another common academic task generated from a book, article, or audiovisual assignment. Some reviews are essentially the same as reports, in that the instructor requires you to provide only a summary and your reaction.

Usually, however, reviews contain three components: a summary, a reaction, and an evaluation. Guidelines for writing a summary and a reaction have been given in the previous two sections. The following guidelines are for writing an evaluation:

1. Like a reaction, an evaluation is subjective; that is, it is composed of your thoughts and opinions. For this reason, first-person pronouns are acceptable here, too.

2. Evaluations are composed of your personal response and reaction to what you have read or viewed. In this section, you state what you believe to be the merits and faults of what you have read or viewed; you tell the value of it. You can focus an evaluation by answering any or all of the following questions, as appropriate:
   - How does the required reading or viewing relate to the course of study for which it was assigned? What have you read in your textbook or heard in class that relates to this work?
   - How does the work relate to your experiences or to your ideas about the topic? How can you apply these ideas to the course of study you're invovled in, to your life, or to society?

■ Does the author of the work change your perspective in any way? Does the author alter your viewpoint in any way? If so, does the author do so in a just and fair way, or do you perceive biases on the part of the author? What, if anything, do you know about the author's life or other work that justifies or explains such a bias?

■ What do you think of the organization and physical appearance of the work? What do you think of the writing style, organization, accuracy, or general effectiveness of the work?

3. Write a fair evaluation. Avoid words that might cause your reader to feel that you are being vindictive or unfair. Maintain a balance between personal opinion and unfair or unjust statements.

The essay that follows is a duplication and continuation of the essay presented in the sections on writing summaries and on writing reports. Pay particular attention to the last paragraph, which is the evaluation.

Example   A REVIEW OF *FROM EVERY SHIRE'S ENDE*

The film *From Every Shire's Ende* is an intriguing glimpse into the world of the pilgrims in Chaucer's *Canterbury Tales.* The film provides a detailed, visual prologue to Chaucer's story of the journey these people made from London to Canterbury to see Becket's shrine. While the "General Prologue" of the *Canterbury Tales* introduces the reader to each of the pilgrims and sets the stage for each character's story, this film enriches that introduction by providing the reader a visual portrait of that long journey.

The film offers a sensual perspective of the long pilgrimage. The sights of the moors and marshes, the rough wayside crosses, the tapestry-lined halls of the castles, and the small cottages are all enriched by the sounds of the rushing streams, the bells attached to the horses' reins, and the songs and prayers of the monks in the monasteries, where the pilgrims might have spent a night or two. Additionally, the viewer receives a vivid reminder of the very quiet, profoundly rural landscape the pilgrim must have enjoyed along the way.

This film gives me a clear perspective on the differences in social classes in Chaucer's day. For example, the harvest time is a time of games for the peasants, while the nobles enjoy jousting. Feasting, however, is a common pleasure for everyone. I am also reminded of how the churches and the clergy emerge as important, integral parts of society. The church is a place of social life as well as prayer; a country fair and Mass are both held in the same rooms of the church.

The film underscores this period of English history as an ostentatious age. This is especially vivid in the film's remarkable telephoto details of the cathedrals. The high arches, stained glass, misericords, and grotesques are carefully depicted in the film. The film's attention to these details of the cathedrals emphasizes the importance of the church for the people of this era.

The steps leading into the Canterbury Cathedral were the film's most vivid and stark reminder of the place the church had in the pilgrims' lives. The steps have been worn down by the thousands of pilgrims, who, since Chaucer's age, have walked up the steps to have a glimpse of Becket's shrine. As I viewed the film, it was easy to imagine the miller, the yeoman, the knight, as well as the other pilgrims in Chaucer's story, ascending the steps in this last part of their long journey. The steps helped to provide an historical context for these characters. They are a small group of people doing what thousands of other groups have done before and since—they are making a pilgrimage.

PRACTICE   Now you are ready to turn the report you wrote into a review. Follow the preceding guidelines for writing the evaluation section. Rewrite, as necessary, the sections on summary and reaction.

After you write the review, exchange essays with other people in the class. Analyze two or three of your classmates' reviews, checking to see how well their evaluations satisfy the guidelines for writing evaluations given in this section.

THE RESEARCH PAPER

For most students, the research paper is the most dreaded of high-school and college writing assignments. Most students would react more positively to being asked to finish all requirements for the course in a week than they would to being given a three-week research paper assignment!

In the space below, jot down some of the reactions you have when you are assigned a research paper. What are your first thoughts? What aspects of such an assignment worry or scare you the most?

_____

_____

_____

_____

_____

Perhaps you can't think of a single thing to write on these lines. You dread writing a research paper, but such an assignment is simply awesome and mysterious to you. In fact, you don't know _why_ you dread it, other than that you know it's a big assignment and that other friends have told you how terrible it is.

If you could think of reasons why you dread research assignments, you may have listed such reasons as these:

Examples
- It's a big assignment, and I won't be able to think of enough to say.
- It involves a lot of writing, and I won't be able to think of enough to say to fill the pages.
- I'll have to camp out in the library for the next three weeks.
- I hate doing note cards and bibliography cards, because I don't see the point.
- I always think there will be plenty of time to work on it another day, and before I know it, it's the week before the final paper is due.
- I never know how to use sources, and I'm always afraid I'll accidentally plagiarize something.

This section will not necessarily dispel all of your fears about research paper assignments. After all, they usually _are_ big assignments. But after reading this section, answering the questions, and completing the exercises, you should be able to approach research paper assignments with more confidence and skill.

Research writing differs from other writing. The following scenario illustrates just how this kind of writing differs from essays, reports, paragraphs, and the like.

Example
Catherine has studied the human foot for ten years. She has examined thousands of feet of people of every nationality. After years of observation

and analysis, the most significant new fact in Catherine's many discoveries about the human foot is that 50 percent of the feet she observed had a big toe that was shorter than the toe next to it. After determining this, she is ready to communicate her important discovery to her colleagues. She decides to write a report narrating her experiences, describing her observation techniques, and reporting her findings. She knows that other people who have studied human feet will want to hear about what she has learned.

Three years after Catherine's landmark study and published report, Kevin decides to write a research paper about the human foot for his anatomy class. He goes to the library and reads about feet. Catherine's report is one of the most interesting he finds on this subject. When he writes his paper, he includes a section about the varying length of big toes, in which he uses the discoveries Catherine made about toe length.

This silly story illustrates two important ways that research writing differs from other kinds of writing:

1. Catherine's writing is not based on research from books. It is based on primary research—examining toes! Therefore, her report narrated her observations and experiences.

2. Kevin's paper was based on secondary, not primary research. He did not examine toes; instead, he read what other people reported about their examination of toes. He then incorporated that information into his essay about feet.

You may want to think of a research paper as a research essay. Essentially, you will follow the same guidelines for choosing and narrowing a research topic and writing a research paper that were given for general essays in Part One of this book. The major difference between an essay and a research paper is that the research paper includes research about the topic. The remainder of this section will discuss guidelines for writing a research paper.

CHOOSING A TOPIC

Occasionally, your instructor will assign you a topic for a research paper. More often, however, you will be allowed to choose a topic related to the course of study. Assuming that this is the case, you must first decide on a topic. Use any or all three of the following guidelines to help you choose a topic.

One, choose something that interests you. Have you, for instance, studied some particular person, place, situation, or event that you would like to know more about?

Wanetta, for example, chose the topic of rubella fever for her NUR 201 Infectious Diseases course. She chose that topic because her great grandmother lost two young children to rubella fever. Because of this personal link to the disease, Wanetta decided she would like to know more about it.

Two, choose a topic that addresses a question or problem you have thought about during the course. What questions or problems have interested you in the course? Which of these issues could be more thoroughly explored in a research paper?

Carolyn, for example, is taking a microbiology course. For her research project, she has decided to find out more about how cheese is made, since she hopes to get a job at the local cheese factory when she graduates from college.

John, who has been working at the cheese factory for ten years, is also taking the microbiology class. In his work, he has seen the potential health hazards caused by the presence of certain pathogens in cheese. He wants to find out more about two of these pathogens, and he would like to compare their characteristics to see if he can determine if they are coming from the same sources of milk.

Three, review your journals and notes, looking for interesting ideas or comments that you, your teacher, or a classmate made during the course. These comments might lead you in the direction of a topic for a paper.

Jess, for example, was intrigued by a comment her English professor made about the poet Percy B. Shelley. The professor said that many of Shelley's ideas were radical during his day but had later become reality. She wrote this comment down in her notes and forgot about it until she was trying to choose a topic for a research paper. She reread her notes and found this comment, written during the first week of the semester. Since the assignment was open—choose a topic related to the English Romantic poets—she decided to find out which ideas of Shelley's were radical and how they had come true.

Similarly, in preparation for her world history research paper assignment, Debbie read through her notes and journal. In her double-entry notebook, she found a comment she had made to herself about a book on the Declaration of Independence that she had wanted to read. She didn't know much about the Declaration, but she decided to check the book out of the library, scan it, and see if any ideas for a research paper could be developed from what she read.

PRACTICE   Choose a topic for a research paper for a course you are currently taking or have taken in the past year. (No, you will not be required to write a full research paper on that topic! The purpose of this exercise is to give you some practice in selecting research paper topics—which often is difficult to do.) Assume that the topic can be one of your choosing, subject to instructor approval. The only restriction is that it should be related to the course of study. Use the preceding guidelines for choosing a topic. At this point, you need not be specific about how the topic will be developed. Write the topic you select in the following space.

_____

_____

LIMITING THE TOPIC

After selecting a topic, you may or may not have some idea of what you want to do with it. Most of the research ideas mentioned in the last subsection were developed from topics by students who had specific purposes in mind. But you may be like Debbie, the last research writer, who had no specific purpose in mind. If that is true, you face the added tasks of developing some purpose for writing about the topic you choose and then limiting the topic.

The Declaration of Independence is a broad topic. If you choose it as a topic, without having any specific idea of how to limit the scope of your investigation, the next thing you must do is limit the topic. Here are two suggestions for limiting a topic:

1. You may need to skim through several books and articles, looking for ways to limit your topic. As you read, remember that you want to focus on some aspect of the Declaration that interests you and is of manageable size.

2. Try some of the prewriting exercises discussed in Chapter 1. For example, after you have skimmed several books, sit down and freewrite about the topic for ten minutes. After you finish, read what you have written and circle or underline any interesting points, statements, and phrases you wrote. Freewrite for another ten minutes, using one of the underlined phrases from the first freewriting session as the controlling sentence. If necessary, repeat this process. Remember that writing sometimes helps you discover what you want to say.

It is helpful to have a restricted topic before you go to the library. At this early stage, you may still change your mind about the topic or the focus of the topic, but at least you have something to focus on as you begin to prepare a tentative list of sources to use in your paper.

PREPARING A WORKING BIBLIOGRAPHY

A working bibliography is a list of sources you might use to gather information about your topic. It differs from the final bibliography in that it identifies sources you are considering using in your paper; the final bibliography, on the other hand, is a list of the sources you actually did use in your paper.

The library will be your main source of information about the topic. But before you go to the library, decide on a method of collecting information for your working bibliography.

Most writers of research papers use 3″ × 5″ index cards to record bibliographical information. You may want to do that, too. Another method is to use only one side of sheets of loose-leaf notebook paper. Use only one side, so you don't have to check the back side of each sheet for valuable information you may have copied there. Another effective method is to use slips of paper, perhaps cut to 2″ × 4″.

Before you go to the library, look through your notes and your textbook for the names of any special books you need to check. Don't hesitate to make an appointment with your instructor to talk about your ideas for a paper. He or she may be able to suggest some excellent books or articles for you to check.

Other people besides your instructor might be able to give you information. For example, Debbie might check with her world history professor, but she could also check with instructors of courses in government, political science, and even American literature.

Remember to make up a list of questions for the people you interview, and don't go without a scheduled appointment. Don't go expecting miracles either. This is your research paper, and the most you can expect from other people is educated suggestions.

You will find that it is extremely helpful to have some familiarity with the layout of the library you will be using, before you reach this point in the project. As a result, you will be able to use your library time more effectively. After you get to the library, you may want to check any or all of the following:

- The subject section of the card catalog
- Other subject headings (listed on the subject card) under which the book is cataloged
- General periodical indexes, such as *The Reader's Guide to Periodical Literature* and *The New York Times Index*
- Specialized indexes related to your topic, such as the *Humanities Index* or the *Applied Science and Technology Index*

As you check each source, record the bibliographical information on your index cards, slips of paper, or other paper medium. For a book, record the following:

- Author or authors (last name first; if more than one author, record names in the order in which they appear)
- Title (underline it to emphasize that it is the *exact title*)
- Place of publication
- Publisher
- Date of publication
- Call number for the book

For an article in a periodical, record the following:

- Author or authors (last name first; if more than one author, record names in the order in which they appear)
- Title of the article (use quotation marks)
- Title of the periodical (underlined)
- Volume number, if available
- Page numbers of the article
- Complete date

PRACTICE Frequently, writers do not locate an adequate number of sources for working bibliographies. One reason for this is their failure to think about and check the card catalog for topics related (cross-referenced) to the chosen topic. Working with one or two classmates, list at least three other places you might look for information in the card catalog. We begin with an example:

Example *Topic:* Feminism

Related topics: Women; Gender; History: Twentieth Century; Relationships; Sexual Roles; a name of someone influential from the feminist movement, such as Greer, Germaine; Friedan, Betty; Steinem, Gloria.

Now complete the practice exercises that follow.

1. *Topic:* Alcohol

   Related Topics: _____

   _____

   _____

2. *Topic:* Violence on Television

Related Topics: _____

_____

_____

3. *Topic:* *The Scarlet Letter* by Nathaniel Hawthorne

Related Topics: _____

_____

_____

4. *Topic:* Pablo Picasso

Related Topics: _____

_____

_____

5. *Topic:* Fire Prevention

Related Topics: _____

_____

_____

DEVELOPING A WORKING THESIS

At this point in the project, several things should be beginning to come together for you. From developing a working bibliography, you can develop a purpose for the research paper, if you haven't already done so. You can also begin to develop a working thesis statement for the paper—a statement of opinion about your topic.

The working thesis will guide you as you begin to take notes from the sources you have collected in your working bibliography. It will also help you take such notes selectively. If you don't have a working thesis at this point, the process of taking notes will help you restrict your topic and develop a focus.

A working thesis, of course, is not a refined, polished thesis statement. Rather, it is an unpolished phrase or statement that emerges from your thoughts about the topic, your purpose for choosing the topic, and your attempts to focus the topic.

For example, when Rico was assigned a research paper in English literature, he chose Shakespeare's *Macbeth* as his topic, because he enjoyed the play. After freewriting to focus his topic and compiling a working bibliography, he discovered that his main interest in the play was its supernatural aspects. At this point, his working thesis became a series of questions:

- Why did Shakespeare include witchcraft?
- What was going on in England at the time he wrote the play that would cause him to include witches as characters?
- Did playgoers believe in witches?

Later on in the process, Rico will turn one or more of these questions into a thesis statement. For now, however, the questions serve as a framework for examining the sources listed in the working bibliography.

TAKING NOTES

Before you begin examining the sources in your working bibliography, work out a system for taking notes. Here are some suggestions for taking notes:

1. Use paper that is different from but roughly the same size as the material you used for compiling your working bibliography. For example, if you used 3″ × 5″ index cards for the bibliography, use 4″ × 6″ cards for notes, or use 3″ × 5″ slips of paper or 3″ × 5″ cards of a different color. Then, when you sort through all of these little slips of paper, you will be able to tell quickly whether you are looking at a bibliography (bib) card or at a note card.

2. As you take notes, make sure that you have written up a bib card for each source you are using. In looking through the library shelves for books listed in your working bibliography, don't overlook books close to these on the shelves. You might find one that is both interesting and useful. If you find such a book, make a bib card for it; then you will have the bibliographical information if you decide to use material from the book.

3. Include enough bibliographical information on each note card to ensure that you can match it to the appropriate bib card. It is helpful to include author and page number on the top right-hand

side of each note card. If the author of your source has written other books you will be examining (as is often the case), you should also include the name of the book so that you won't confuse it with other books by that author.

4. Write on one side of the note cards only, so you don't overlook information when you sort back through the cards.

5. Use plenty of note cards. Don't cram all of the information from one book onto one card. If the author has several ideas that you like, make a separate card (including bibliographical information) for each idea. When you begin to write your first draft, you will find this system much more manageable. As you take notes, you will begin to see a system of organization for your paper taking shape; in other words, you should begin to formulate a working outline.

6. As you take notes, make note cards about any thoughts, ideas, or sudden flashes of inspiration that you have. You may want to do this on a separate card; or if you are reading a particular source and an idea pops into your head, record it on the same note card, but use a different color of ink or mark the thought in some other way so that you know it is yours.

7. As you examine sources, you may also want to make informative notes to yourself about them on the bib cards. As you examine each source, make a note at the bottom of the card: "useful," "not helpful," "good information about. . . ."As you go back through the material you can make different stacks of bib cards, based on each source's potential usefulness. Don't throw anything away at this point. If your working thesis is later refocused (as it still may be), you could find those sources useful.

Take notes about ideas you think may be related to your topic. Examine the tables of contents and the indexes of books to find relevant information. Scan chapters or sections of chapters that seem to be related to your topic. Then carefully read any chapters or sections that you are certain you want to use. When you find useful information, take notes on that information, following the preceding guidelines. As you look for information, keep your topic, your purpose, and your working thesis in mind. These things will help you determine what information you should collect.

Let's return to our example of Rico, who is writing a paper on supernatural elements in *Macbeth*. After he compiled a working bibliography and a working thesis, he began checking sources and taking notes about the supernatural occurrences in the play. As he checked sources, he looked for information about this restricted topic. Thanks to his having a restricted topic, he can probably overlook such unrelated topics as Lady Macbeth's ambition, Banquo's relationship to Duncan, and instances of comic relief in the play. But as he scans tables of contents, indexes, and chapters, Rico knows that he will want to read about such topics as blood imagery, setting, atmosphere, and witchcraft, because these topics may include information he could use in his paper.

The notes you take will be in one of the following formats:

- Direct quotation
- Paraphrase
- Summary
- Some combination of these
- Your own ideas

Direct Quotation   Anytime you copy directly from a source and use someone's ideas word for word, you are quoting directly. When you do this, you must give credit to the person who wrote it.

If you want to copy a direct quotation in your notes, put quotation marks around the material being directly quoted so that, when you look at the quote later on, you will know that it is a direct quotation. When you are looking through several sources, it is easy to get confused about what is being directly quoted and what has been paraphrased or summarized. Develop a system to ensure that you can distinguish between them—perhaps by using quotation marks or several colors of ink to color-code your notes. In addition, double-check to make sure that you have copied correctly.

Paraphrase   After reading a chapter or a paragraph, if you want to use the material but you don't want to quote it directly, you can paraphrase it. This means that you put into your own words what someone else has written or said. When you paraphrase in your notes, remember to note that it is a paraphrase. Keep in mind that authors of paraphrased material must be acknowledged.

Summary   Summarized material is a condensation of the original writer's ideas. To summarize, read the source and then, in your own words, identify the main points and key supporting points the author makes. For further information, review the section on summaries from the first part of this chapter. Be sure to acknowledge the author of any summarized material that you include in your notes and in your research paper.

Here are two more guidelines for using sources:

1. Use direct quotations, but don't rely on them as the main source of information for your paper or use them as filler. One way to think

of sources is as supporting points for your thesis. Remember that you are writing a paper based on an assertion or thesis of your own. You must check sources in order to know what others have written about the topic. The thesis, however, is something you assert, so you should use others' ideas merely to support what you think about the topic.

2. A direct quotation is valuable when you feel that the original statement is more effective than a restatement in your words.

Consider the following weather predictions from two different weather forecasters:

Examples 1. "Expect more hot, muggy weather for the next several days, until the high-pressure system moves on out to sea."

2. "The hot, muggy weather we've been having for the past week will continue for the next several days. It sorta reminds me of an armpit!"

The first quotation can easily be summarized without being quoted directly. The second, however, is effective and original; therefore, you might want to use a direct quotation to give credit for this.

Reproduced as illustrations are four note cards written about the same sentence from an essay about *Macbeth* by A. C. Bradley. The first note card (Figure 13.3) is a direct quotation. The second (Figure 13.4) paraphrases the information, and the third card (Figure 13.5) summarizes the material. The fourth card (Figure 13.6) is an example of a combination of direct quotation and paraphrase. Here is the original material on which the note cards are based:

> *Now all these agencies—darkness, the lights and colours that illuminate it, the storm that rushes through it, the violent and gigantic images— conspire with the appearances of the Witches and the Ghost to awaken horror, and in some degree also a supernatural dread.*

The reason you must be so careful in using information from sources is to avoid plagiarism—taking someone else's ideas and using them as if they were your own. The best way to avoid plagiarizing is to be scrupulously precise in copying down information that is directly quoted; in noting page numbers for ideas that are quoted, paraphrased, or summarized; and in developing a system for knowing which is which.

PRACTICE   The following excerpt is from "How to Cook Dried Pasta So You Can Taste It" by Corby Kummer, an essay that appears in Chapter 9. Read the

FIGURE 13.3 Direct quotation

Quote   Bradley, p. 331
"Now all these agencies—darkness, The lights, and colours that illuminate it, The storm that rushes through it, The violent and gigantic images—conspire with the appearances of the Witches and the Ghost to awaken horror, and in some degree also a supernatural dread."

FIGURE 13.4 Paraphrase

Paraphrase   Bradley, p. 331
Darkness and the lights and colors that create the darkness, the storm and the images all work together to create horror when the witches appear.

FIGURE 13.5   Summary

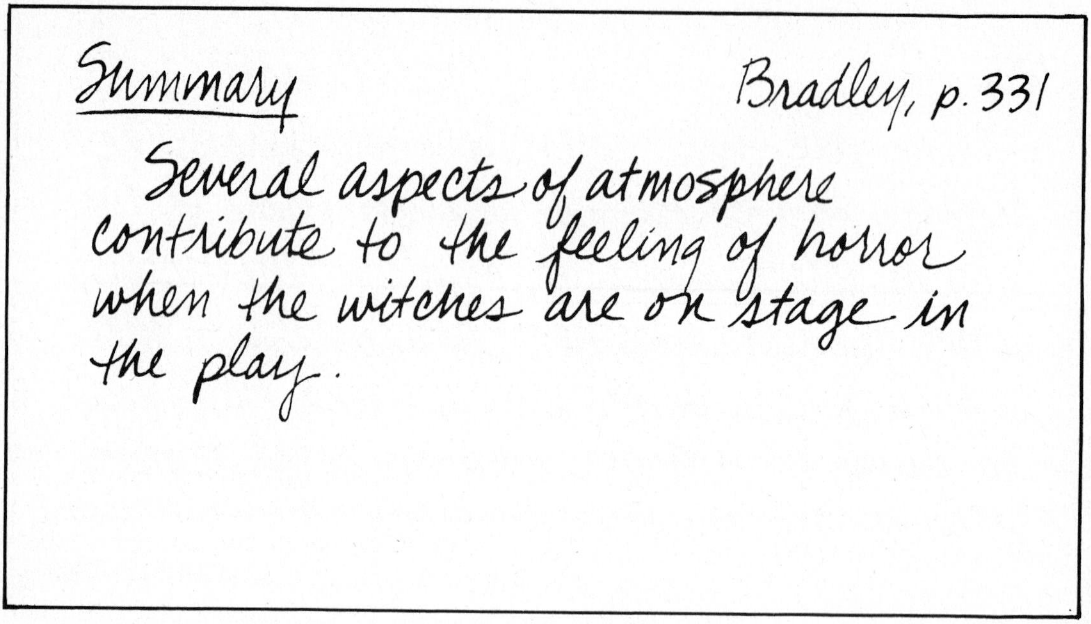

Summary   Bradley, p. 331

    Several aspects of atmosphere contribute to the feeling of horror when the witches are on stage in the play.

FIGURE 13.6   Quotation and paraphrase

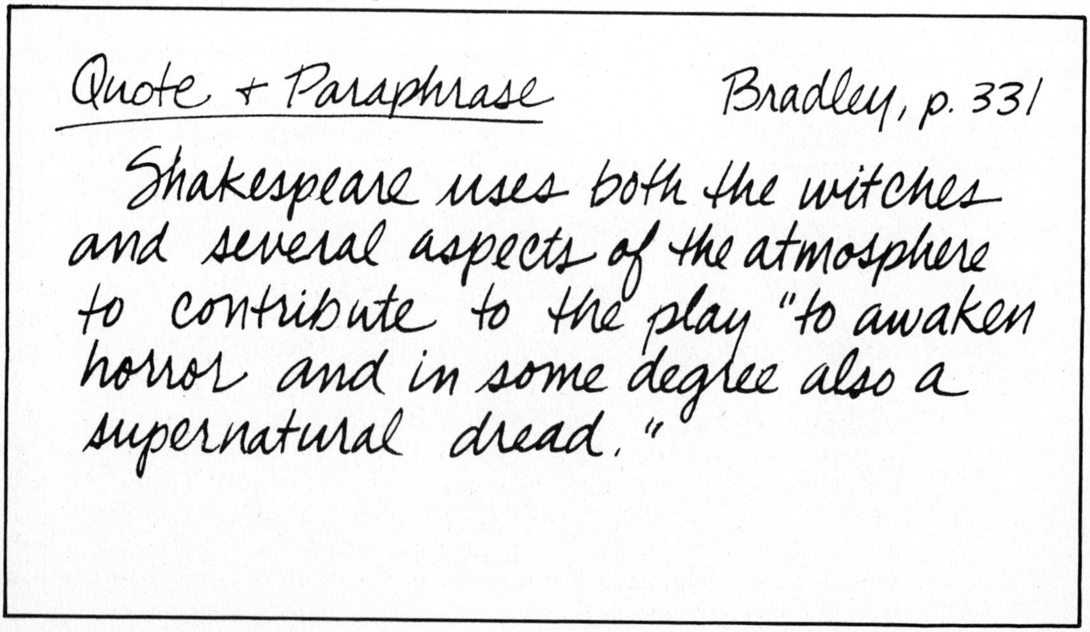

Quote + Paraphrase   Bradley, p. 331

    Shakespeare uses both the witches and several aspects of the atmosphere to contribute to the play "to awaken horror and in some degree also a supernatural dread."

material, and then write a brief paraphrase of its main points. Include at the top of the page the appropriate information about the material, as if you were making a note card. After you finish, prepare a bibliography card on a separate piece of paper, using the bibliographical information in the acknowledgments section at the beginning of this book. Then read one or two of your classmates' paraphrases, and discuss them as a group. Did you include basically the same information?

Italians criticize Americans for adding soft flour to pasta, and with reason. One American manufacturer boasts in block letters on its packages, "SEMOLINA plus FARINA" (farina is a blend of common wheat flours). This, as one importer of Italian pasta put it, is like boasting about mixing diamonds with rocks. Pasta made with common flour, which is less expensive than semolina, leaves the cooking water white with starch, and quickly turns soggy on the plate, even if it is drained when it seems to be what Italians call al dente—literally, "to the tooth." Italian manufacturers almost never add common flour to pasta: the practice is illegal and a company must go out of its way to cheat. American manufacturers can add flour or not as they please, because there are no laws restricting them to semolina. Even so, many American manufacturers, such as Prince, Ronzoni, and Hershey Foods, which markets six brands of pasta, use only semolina.

DEVELOPING AN OUTLINE

As you read sources and take notes, you should formulate a working thesis for your paper, if you haven't already done so. If you developed a working thesis earlier, you may find as you examine sources that you want to modify it. Alternatively, you may stay with your original topic but take a different approach to that topic.

For example, after reviewing several sources for his paper on *Macbeth*, Rico made some additional refinements of his thesis. He decided that there were too many supernatural elements in the play for him to be able to cover them all adequately in one paper. His main interest was in the witches, so he decided to modify his thesis "questions." Instead of writing about all aspects of witchcraft, he decided to focus on how the witches contributed to the evil tone of the play. Consequently, his working thesis is now related to just that aspect of witchcraft in the play, and it reads as follows: "One of the ways Shakespeare sustained a tone of evil and darkness in *Macbeth* was through witchcraft." Later, Rico will modify this thesis again, but for now he has a working thesis from which to develop an outline.

As you examine each source in the working bibliography, you should begin to think about how you are going to support and explain your thesis. The organizational ideas you develop should be hammered into an outline, which is a plan of action. For some people, an outline is a form of prewriting that helps them discover what they want to say about a topic. Once you have developed a working thesis, you must plan an outline in order to know how you are going to proceed.

By this point in the process of writing a research paper, you have developed resources to help you create an informal outline. Here are two methods of developing the outline.

1. Sort through your note cards. You should now be able to separate them into groups of notes that pertain to various aspects of your topic. Sorting through your notes is also an excellent way to begin to make decisions about how you are going to explain and support the thesis of your paper and how you are going to organize and present the ideas it will contain.

2. As you formulate your outline, think about the expository strategies for developing ideas that were discussed in Part Two of this text. To incorporate these strategies into your outline, try freewriting about how you might use them.

Let's check in on Wanetta, who is writing a research paper on rubella. Her working thesis is "Because of the complications and discomfort, rubella is a disease that needs to be eliminated." After developing a working thesis and examining sources, Wanetta did a ten-minute session of freewriting about her topic, with the following question in mind: "What is it I want to do with this thesis?" Here is her freewriting about this:

Example

I don't know what I want to do. I want to talk about my aunts and uncles and how my Grandmother felt about it. That's not ok for a research paper ... its more essay I guess. What I want to do: ok, I have to do something. Let's see. I guess I want to tell what rubella is. I want to define it ... I will define and describe rubella. The characteristics of rubella. Then I will tell how the virus is transmitted and analyze some of the popular theories about how the virus is spread. First I will list the popular theories and tell a little about them. No that's off the subject too much. I'll just list the theories and analyze each as I go. I'll end that section by telling which theory I think is best and why.

I need to describe the symptoms. Sort of how rubella begins and what happens first and then what happens next and so on. How long it lasts. I want to list some of the complications. This is where I will begin to argue that the disease can be eliminated and should be through inoculation. Especially the complications to fetuses. I want to give examples of complications.

How the disease is diagnosed, how it is treated once you get it.

Argue that prevention is the most important key.

Immunize...how easy immunization is...then some kind of conclusion.

From this piece of freewriting, Wanetta was able to develop an outline. She later recalled some things she had forgotten to include in the freewriting, and she eventually concluded that some of the ideas she had included didn't belong. However, it proved to be a good way for her to get started. Keep in mind that freewriting, like any other prewriting activity, can be used at any point in the writing process. For example, Wanetta had a working thesis from which to freewrite for an outline. Had she not had a working thesis at that point in the process, she could have done some freewriting or another prewriting activity to help her develop a thesis.

Here is part of the informal outline Wanetta developed. Remember, an informal outline is not a final product. Outlines can and should be revised as you proceed and as the focus of your writing shifts.

Example   <u>RUBELLA</u>

Thesis   Because of discomfort and possible complications, rubella is a disease that can and should be eliminated.

    I. Define Rubella
        A. Characteristics of the rubella virus
        B. Some theories about how the virus is transmitted
            1. Contact with blood, urine, or secretions
            2. Transplacental transmission
    II. Incubation Period and Symptoms of the Disease

WRITING A DRAFT OF YOUR PAPER

At long last, you are ready to write the first draft of your paper. Find a place to write where you can spread out your sources and your notes;

also assemble plenty of paper and good pencils and pens. Then congratulate yourself for having made it this far and for having done all of the hard preparatory work.

Writing the actual paper is much like writing the essays assigned in this course. You begin with an introductory paragraph in which you introduce your topic and perhaps your thesis. Then, following a plan of development for supporting your thesis, you develop several paragraphs of exposition about the thesis. Finally, you write a concluding paragraph or two. As you write this draft and subsequent drafts of the paper, practice the guidelines for good writing you have learned in this text. Specifically, write and revise with unity, support, and coherence in mind. Then edit and reedit, making sure that each sentence is grammatically correct and rhetorically effective. Ask yourself whether each sentence supports the topic sentence of each paragraph and whether each topic sentence supports the thesis of the paper. Follow the guidelines in Part One for writing effective introductions and conclusions.

The main differences between writing the essays you have been assigned in this course and writing a research paper are as follows:

- A research paper is usually longer than an essay; often there is a specific page-length requirement.
- Generally, college research paper assignments are written for an academic audience, consisting of your colleagues, your instructor, and the academic community. However, you may conduct research and write for other audiences, so analyze your audience and write in the appropriate style and tone.
- A research paper incorporates sources, which means that you must study and follow an approved, accepted format for documenting sources.
- Usually, a title page, a formal outline, and a list of sources used (bibliography) are required as part of the research paper. Your instructor will give you specific information about these components.

For more information about audience and tone, see Chapter 1 of this text. You may also want to review the section on formal and informal diction in Chapter 6.

INCORPORATING SOURCES

As you write the research paper, remember that your purpose is to offer an opinion (thesis) about some topic, and then to support that opinion with your ideas and with other scholars' ideas that you have found in your research. The content of the paper should flow smoothly from the introductory paragraph(s) and thesis statement to subsequent body paragraphs, which smoothly blend your ideas and the ideas of the writers you researched. Here are some guidelines for incorporating source material into your writing:

1. Don't let source material be the main component of your essay. Instead, use this material to support and clarify your thesis. The most important thing to remember as you write is to subordinate other people's ideas to the thesis—your idea. Remember, too, that your readers want to know what you think. Reference material must be included in a research paper to show that you have done other reading about the topic and to ensure you give credit to ideas that are not your own. But the paper should not be a string of quotations, paraphrases, or summaries of other writers' thoughts.

2. Don't overuse direct quotations. Use them when the author of the quote says something in such an impressive, original, or emphatic way that you feel you must use the author's original language.

3. When you do use direct quotations, lead into them by using transition words and phrases and introductory words and phrases. Here are examples of a direct quotation that appears abruptly with no lead-in and a direct quotation that merges smoothly with the content of the paper:

Examples

Storms are always present when the witches are on stage and add to the feeling of horror. "Now all these agencies—darkness, the lights and colours that illuminate it, the storm that rushes through it, the violent and gigantic images—conspire with the appearances of the Witches and the Ghost to awaken horror, and in some degree also a supernatural dread" (Bradley 331).

Storms are always present when the witches are on stage and add to the feeling of horror. A. C. Bradley observes, "Now all these agencies—darkness, the lights and colours that illuminate it, the storm that rushes through it, the violent and gigantic images— conspire with the appearances of the Witches and the Ghost to awaken horror, and in some degree also a supernatural dread" (331).

4. If appropriate, pull from a long quotation only the particular words and phrases that you need to support or clarify your idea. In the preceding example, the entire sentence was used as the direct

quotation, but the part of the quotation that Rico chiefly wanted for his paper is only a small portion of the sentence. Rico could edit the sentence, using only the portion of the sentence he needed, as follows:

Example

> Storms are always present when the witches are on stage and add to the feeling of horror. In fact, A. C. Bradley observes that the storm and the witches help "to awaken horror, and in some degree also a supernatural dread" (331).

5. Vary the lead-ins to your quotations so that you don't repeat the same phrase over and over. Here are three ways to vary the presentation of the preceding quotation:

Examples

> Storms are always present when the witches are on stage and add to the feeling of horror. In fact, A. C. Bradley points out that the storm and the witches help "to awaken horror, and in some degree also a supernatural dread" (331).

> Storms are always present when the witches are on stage and add to the feeling of horror. In fact, the storm and the witches help "to awaken horror, and in some degree also a supernatural dread" (Bradley 331).

> Storms are always present when the witches are on stage and add to the feeling of horror. Perhaps A. C. Bradley expressed the idea best when he wrote that the storm and the witches help "to awaken horror, and in some degree also a supernatural dread" (Bradley 331).

6. Punctuate quotations correctly. Follow the rules for using quotation marks and commas given in Chapter 6.

FORMAT FOR WRITING RESEARCH PAPERS

Format refers to the arrangement of text on a page and also to the arrangement of different parts of the paper: the title page, outline, body of the paper, and bibliography. Format includes everything from the width of margins on a page to the arrangement of outline material. Because research papers are formal papers, they usually must adhere to a standardized format. However, different disciplines within academic and professional communities use different standardized formats. Your teacher will tell you which format to use.

Formats are explained in style manuals. A good style manual should answer all formatting questions for the research writer. The manual should tell you what margins to use, how to arrange outline material, where your name should appear on the title page, and how to handle every other aspect of putting your research paper into final form.

The following explanations about format and the sample research paper included near the end of this chapter use the guidelines of the Modern Language Association (MLA). If you are writing a research paper for any course in the humanities, you will most likely be required to use the MLA format. If you are writing a botany research paper, however, your instructor might want you to use the system recommended by the Council of Biology Editors (CBE); and students in the social sciences are often required to use the American Psychological Association (APA) system. Style guides are usually available in college bookstores, but always check with your teacher to find out which style guide you are expected to follow.

Some general guidelines for writing research papers are true for almost every style guide. For example, a research paper usually must be typed, double-spaced, on only one side of each page. Most style guides require some kind of page numbering system, such as: "Every page numbered consecutively within the paper, excluding the title page." Some guides require that page numbers be situated at the bottom of the page and centered, while most guides suggest placing the numbers at the top, right-hand corner of the paper. Most guides suggest one-inch margins on all four sides of the page.

Two significant events related to writing research papers have occurred in the past few years. Both of these events have greatly simplified the formatting of research papers.

One is the advent of personal computers and word processing. Word-processing programs greatly simplify writing of any sort, but especially the writing of research papers. If your school has a computer writing center, or if you have a personal computer, you may want to invest in a good word-processing program and learn to use it. Of course this takes time, and the night before the paper is due is definitely not the time to learn how to write on a computer!

You should also check with your teacher to find out if computer printouts of research papers are acceptable. Most printers produce dot-matrix characters, and some teachers find dot-matrix printouts unacceptable for formal papers. Even if your teacher will not accept these printouts, you may still find a computer helpful in getting your paper ready for the final draft. Fortunately, most teachers now recognize the time-saving effectiveness of writing on computers and accept research papers written on computers.

The other significant event involves documentation of sources. The *MLA Handbook* and some other style manuals now include two ways of documenting sources: footnotes/endnotes and parenthetical documentation.

When you incorporate source material into your paper, you must let your readers know where the material is located. This is called *documentation*. For years, documentation had to be done in the form of footnotes. If a source was used in the body of the paper, a footnote was included at the bottom of the page the material appeared on, to let the reader know where the idea or quotation came from. At the point in the body of the paper where an idea or quotation was used, the writer placed a number to the right of and slightly above the end of the passage. At the bottom of the page, the writer wrote the same number and then included the author's name, the name of the book or other source, the relevant bibliographic information, and the page number in the source where the idea or quotation could be found. Then, on a separate page (the bibliography) at the end of the paper, the writer listed all the sources used in the paper. Here is an example of how such a research paper would use footnotes. First, in the main body of the paper, a citable quotation arises:

Example   John Gardner's *The Life and Times of Chaucer* is a loving, witty

account of the poet's life. Gardner's affection for the poet is obvious.

For example, he affectionately refers to him as "young Jeff."[1]

Then, at the bottom of the same page, a footnote containing the appropriate information is appended:

Example   [1]John Gardner, *The Life and Times of Chaucer* (New York: Alfred A.

Knopf, 1977) 23.

And at the end of the paper, in the bibliography, an entry for this source is listed:

Example   Gardner, John. *The Life and Times of Chaucer.* New York: Alfred A.

Knopf, 1977.

While footnotes are complicated, some research formats still require them. If you must use footnotes, study the assigned style guide and follow its directions for writing a paper using footnotes.

Another system of documentation uses endnotes. In this system, numbers are used, as in the footnoting system, to mark the occurrence of a citation to an original source; but the footnotes themselves are placed on a separate page at the end of the paper, rather than at the bottom of the page on which the reference occurs. Again, if your teacher requires that you use endnotes, consult the recommended style guide for specific guidelines.

The simple method that has made documenting research writing so much easier is called *parenthetical documentation*. In this system of documentation, you include in parentheses in the body of the paper only enough information to enable the reader to locate your complete source in the bibliography of the paper. Here is how the same citation we just looked at in a footnote citation system would be handled using parenthetical documentation. First, the citable quotation arises:

Example   John Gardner's *The Life and Times of Chaucer* is a loving, witty account of the poet's life. Gardner's affection for the poet is obvious. For example, he affectionately refers to him as "young Jeff" (23).

Then, in the bibliography at the end of the paper, the following entry is listed:

Example   Gardner, John. *The Life and Times of Chaucer*. New York: Alfred A. Knopf, 1977.

Following are some guidelines for using parenthetical references in your paper. Again, for a more detailed explanation of parenthetical documentation, consult the style guide your instructor recommends.

First, if you use an authority in your text but do not refer to the authority by name before using her or his idea, place the authority's last name and the page number of the source in parentheses immediately after the quoted, paraphrased, or summarized material. Here is an example:

Example   Tangible evidence is available for study, which includes physical trace cases of UFO landings and the change of soil condition or plants at the reported UFO site (Story 265).

Parentheses go before the end punctuation, but after the quotation marks, if any, at the end of the sentence. No punctuation marks are placed between the author's name and the page number in the source.

Second, if you use an authority in your text and refer to the authority by name in the lead-in to the quoted, paraphrased, or summarized material, include only the page number in parentheses. Here is an example:

Example   As Story maintains, "Tangible evidence is available for study, which includes physical trace cases of UFO landings and the change of soil condition or plants at the reported UFO site" (265).

Third, when you cite more than one work by the same author, include a short version of the title of the book or article in the parentheses so that the reader will know which book contains the quoted, paraphrased, or summarized material. Here is an example of this form:

Example   (Dickens, *David Copperfield* 35)

Notice that, in this case, a comma is used after the author's name.

Fourth, if you are citing a work that has more than one author, use both authors' last names. Here is an example:

Example   (Comer and Mann 129)

For sources written by more than two authors, use the last name of the first author, followed by the abbreviation "et al." Again, here is an example of the proper form:

Example   (Mann et al. 86)

Fifth, at the end of the paper, include a list of all sources used in the body of the paper. This is commonly called a "Works Cited" page or a "Bibliography." Follow the guidelines in the style manual you are using for citing sources correctly.

SAMPLE RESEARCH PAPER

The following research paper was written for ENG 113: Introduction to Literature. As recommended by the instructor, the student adhered to the format and documentation guidelines of the *MLA Handbook*.

SAMPLE STUDENT PAPER

FAIRY TALES AND
CHILDREN DO MIX

Donna H. Lyall
Dianne Wagner
Eng 113
22 June 1987

"Once upon a time . . ." are the common four words that begin most of the fairy tales we grew up with and loved as children. Fairy tales transcend generations of children, since they "existed originally as folk tales transmitted by word of mouth for many generations until they were finally written down" (Heuscher 5). The use of fairy tales in educating or reading to children is a debated topic among many psychologists, teachers, and parents. Critics argue that fairy tales (especially in their original form) teach children incorrect lessons and are the wrong type of literature for our young (Gibson 95). Realists argue that "although possibly acceptable in earlier times, fairy tales are inconsistent with what modern parents want for their children" (Gibson 95). Another argument against fairy tales is made by professor and psychiatrist Richard Gardner (Barthelme 96). Gardner has rewritten many fairy tales and given them titles such as: "Mack and the Beanstalk," "Cinderlma," and "Hans and Greta" (Barthelme 96). Gardner feels that many fairy tales are "sick and maladaptive," and that they teach violent solutions rather than civilized methods (Barthelme 26). He also feels that the violence of fairy tales teaches that "killing off an adversary is the cleanest and quickest way to solve problems" (Barthelme 26). Another very strong realist view is given by Julius Lester, author of *The Kind of Books We Give Our*

Children (Sadker 2). Lester states this of fairy tales: "In a world in which a child can be dead from an overdose of heroin at age twelve, Snow White is not only inadequate, it is in danger of being vulgar" (Sadker 2). Lester also feels that children's books should contain more realistic views of today's society: "Ghettos, slums, wars, and drunks on the street should be dealt with instead of fantasy, nonsense, and animals" (Sadker 2).

Many disagree with the views of Gardner and Lester and the other critics of fairy tales and stress that the revised or modern fairy tales, which delete violence and other aspects of the original tale, leave the story shallow and with no relevance to the concerns of the child (Gibson 98). As Barthelme maintains, "Safe stories which mention neither death nor aging, the limits of existence, or the wish for eternal life, do not consider the importance of educating, supporting, and liberating the emotions of children" (26). Kay E. Vandergrift wrote the following in her book, *Child and Story:* "The adult who forces his or her judgement on a child denies that child her own critical abilities, her sense of self, and thus her opportunity for growth" (11). Also, getting rid of the violence or censoring other aspects of the story destroys hidden messages of the fairy tale and makes it harder for the child to recognize the special "soul-world language" of the fairy tale and, thereby, leads to confusion (Heuscher 195).

FAIRY TALES AND CHILDREN DO MIX, continued

Julius E. Heuscher argues that the violence of the fairy tale actually helps the child feel that he is not alone with his own sometimes violent fantasies (185). He also feels that "healthy small children tolerate without difficulty the violence and cruelties in the stories, feeling that the fairy tale belongs to a different and special world" (Heuscher 184).

Another renowned advocate of fairy tales is Bruno Bettelheim, author of *The Uses of Enchantment*. This book above all others gives the most convincing argument for the uses and psychology of fairy tales and their special place with children. Bettelheim feels that "fairy tales are unique, not only as a form of literature, but as works of art which are fully comprehensible to the child as no other form of art is" (12). He also feels that today's children now read "prettified and simplified" fairy tales, which rob them of all deeper significance and change the meaning and intent of the story (Bettelheim 24). I also found Bettelheim's theory behind some of the drug problems of children today to be very convincing. He states that many children are deprived of magic and fantasy early in their childhood, and that reality is forced upon them too soon (Bettelheim 51). Later in adolescence these children feel the need to escape the pressures of that reality, and they turn to drugs as a form of magic and fantasy to help relieve the pressures they never learned to handle as small children (Bettelheim 51). This is a very powerful statement, and, in response to the statements of Lester, I wonder if the problem children of our society and the children he refers to have ever read or had someone tell them a fairy tale.

For a parent or an educator, all of these views are very significant and must be carefully considered before forming conclusions. Theories and psychology about fairy tales produce convincing evidence that fairy tales and children do mix. Fairy tales are helpful to children because they teach lessons on the child's own level, offer explanations for the child's emotions, and teach about the world and the people who make up that world.

The first value of the fairy tale is its ability to teach and speak to the child on the child's own level. Parents and teachers can use fairy tales as an important aid for communication with children on a level that is fun for them and taps their fantasy and dream life (Ekstein 9). This is one reason that fairy tales are often read or told at bedtime to ease the child from the real world to his or her dream world (Ekstein 7).

One reason the child understands and enjoys fairy tales is their simple and direct messages. They are written in a simple way that does not put demands on the child, and they never make a child feel inferior in any way (Bettelheim 26). Fairy tales help children understand the people around them because they are able to "describe abstract qualities of people in concrete terms they understand" (Gibson 96). Young children can interpret, in their own way, many of the "secret" messages of fairy tales. Because they are written in the way a child thinks and perceives the world, the child finds fairy tales very convincing and learns from them (Bettelheim 45). Because of the natural, simple way fairy tales convey their messages, they help stimulate the child's imagination (Barry 52). It is the

FAIRY TALES AND CHILDREN DO MIX, continued

very imagination of the child that makes the fairy tales so convincing (Barry 38).

The next reason the child is drawn to the enchantment of the fairy tale is by the author's use of fantasy and magic. Most fairy tales, especially earlier ones, use enchantment and wonder in their tales to convey their messages of wisdom, but with only very little use of magic (Egoff 204). At times, young children feel stupid or weak when compared to their parents or other adults, and this is when fairy tale magic can help them cope with negative feelings about themselves (Gibson 96). As Gibson maintains, "Children are delighted when a good fairy, a magic potion, or a magic sword make the hero, who is always weak in the beginning (just like children), strong and powerful" (96). This identification with the hero allows the child to work through his difficult emotions, and, through fantasy, he can cope with his own feelings of inadequacies (Bettelheim 65). A small child does not care whether a tale is make-believe or reality because he uses and needs both to grow (Barry 36). This is why fairy tales speak so clearly to the child; adults know that animals do not talk and that objects do not suddenly come to life, but children "know" they can (Gibson 96). As children grow older, they eventually learn the difference between fantasy and reality. For a while, however, they find the magic and fantasy of the fairy tale helpful in dealing with the difficulties of growing up (Gibson 98). It is this capability of problem-solving that makes the next aspect of the fairy tale so important.

The next value of the fairy tale is its ability to offer explanations and reassurances for the emotions and inner pressures of the child to help him grow up emotionally fit. Without belittling the struggles of growing up, the fairy tale speaks to the child's unconscious in a way that he understands (Bettelheim 6). This helps to relieve preconscious and unconscious pressures and offers temporary and permanent solutions to these problems. Fairy tales are helpful because they deal with human problems, especially problems the child faces, and these tales speak to his ego and help in his development (Bettelheim 6). They deal with very complex ideas: life, death, time, space, good and evil, and the struggle of the child to understand these concepts (Egoff 80). In fairy tales, problems and virtues, good and bad, are depicted simply in the shape of a hero or villain (Bettelheim 25). This simple, clear presentation makes identification of positive characteristics understandable and easier to absorb, so that the child can apply this information to her or his own life. Fairy tales not only show problems; they also help solve them, even if they have to use very powerful situations and examples to accomplish their goal (Mallet 208).

One positive aspect is the fairy tale's ability to relieve the child's anxieties and, through its messages, help him cope with very strong emotions. Through a thin disguise, fairy tales show difficult problems and emotions so that the child can apply them to his own fears and emotions (Gibson 96). Fairy tales help the child feel that he has choices in his life, and this makes him feel more powerful (Egoff 24). They also give the child a great source of characters to use in play acting; through this form of play, she or he has the chance to experience courage, nobility, and other

FAIRY TALES AND CHLDREN DO MIX, continued

positive emotions (Egoff 24). The child learns to identify with the hero so that she too can have a "happily ever after." Through these emotional experiences, the child obtains the courage to look forward and tackle all challenges successfully (Heuscher 186). Children can grow while experiencing the physical and mental conflicts of the fairy tale, especially if left to interpret it at their own speed and level of development (Ekstein 9). By experiencing the emotions of the characters, the child can explain his own happy and unhappy feelings (Gibson 96).

Another positive aspect of the fairy tale is that it eases the pressures of childhood and gently teaches morality and virtuous traits. Learning these traits at a very young age, the child is able to grow up with a better understanding of good and bad. Fairy tales deal with and try to explain human existence; they deal with the ways people feel, believe, behave, think, hope, and fear; and they give reinforcement to the positive side of these ideas (Heuscher 5). They also improve the child's sense of identity, control, and connection (Vandergrift 14). This positive identity with self and peers will help him or her develop into a stronger individual. Bruno Bettelheim states that "fairy tales, unlike any other form of literature, direct the child to discover his identity and calling" (24). And Bettelheim feels that since fairy tales are dedicated to human situations, emotions, and inner pressures, the child learns to understand himself and others better (3). Learning to deal with society and its conditions is basic to learning to function as a capable person. The child who can learn this and other values

through this entertaining literature is one step ahead in becoming a competent adult.

The last value of the fairy tale is its ability to teach children about the world they live in and about the people who make up their world. While reading the fairy tale, children enter another world—a world that is like and unlike their world (Smith 51). Their heroes and heroines teach important lessons and assist children in understanding the world (Gibson 95). The concept of "world" is very hard for young children. By experiencing other worlds, space, and time, as illustrated in the fairy tale, children are able to gradually grasp this difficult concept. Because children are entertained by and enjoy these stories, they can perceive the world in different ways (Vandergrift 14). Fantasy helps reveal that we not only live in a world of facts, but also in a universe of spirit and mind (Egoff 81).

First, the fairy tale teaches about the world and its people, which helps to bring order and security into the child's inner self. Through the fairy tale, the child learns about the important relationships in life: relationships between brothers, sisters, parents, and grandparents (Gibson 96). This is one way the fairy tale can benefit children; they can learn the roles and characteristics of the people who surround and make up their lives. Children must learn the personalities and roles of the people around them in order to understand their individual positions in society. Through fairy tales, children witness good and bad people, identify with the hero, and want to be just like the good guy. They see the evil in villains and witness their danger and destruction and want to avoid

FAIRY TALES AND CHILDREN DO MIX, continued

their evil (Bettelheim 7). Children who hear or read fairy tales also get to view many positive and negative characteristics of people: selfishness, cleverness, greed, anger, trust, sharing, love, and hatred. Through the story, they can identify their own strong feelings and characteristics and feel assured that they are not the only ones who have experienced such feelings and emotions (Bettelheim 7).

The second way that fairy tales benefit children is by teaching and aiding them in developing positive perceptions and gaining successes in their own roles. Rudolf Ekstein tells us that "the social function of fairy tales traditionally has been to prepare the child for adult living" (7). Through the fairy tale, just as in a child's play, the child mimics the characteristics of those portrayed in the tale and learns to see their problems to assist in his present or future problems (Egoff 80). Gibson maintains that fairy tales "help the child by answering his questions about his role in the world and by showing him the different roles of his world" (96). He not only learns about the important roles within the family, but also about the roles of others who could influence his life. He views the roles of friends, enemies, guides, tempters, and other personalities. Viewing these roles allows her to build a base to categorize those who touch her life. To raise a child to be self-sufficient is the difficult task required of every parent. Fairy tales can assist the parent because, by reading these tales and sharing these stories with their children, parents show that they too believe in magic. In a painless manner, parents can teach their children about the difficult emotions and roles of childhood

(Ekstein 7). The secrets of fairy tales can unlock the child's secret self and help her enjoy herself and others more freely.

In conclusion, fairy tales are interpreted differently by different people. Some interpret fairy tales as violent, irrelevant, and bad for children; others disagree strongly with this interpretation. Those who look deeply at the actual and hidden messages that the tales hold find them not only safe for children but also a necessity for their growth. Fairy tales assist in the growth of the child in three ways. They assist the child by speaking on the child's level, by explaining the child's emotions, and by teaching about the world and people of the world. Fairy tale enchantment speaks not only to the child but to adults as well. Those who can enjoy the tales through the eyes of a child can learn about life. Without making demands, fairy tales give hope for the future and hold out the promise of a happy ending (Bettelheim 26).

WORKS CITED

Barry, Florence V. *A Century of Children's Books*. London: Metheren & Co., 1922.

Barthelme, Marion Knox. "The Eye of the Beholder." *Child*. Feb. 1987: 26 + .

Bettelheim, Bruno. *The Uses of Enchantment*. New York: Knopf, 1976.

Egoff, Sheila A. *Thursday's Child*. Chicago: American Library Association, 1981.

Ekstein, Rudolf. *Speaking the Truth Behind Fairy Tales*. Cassette. New York: McGraw-Hill, 1974.

Gibson, Janice T. "Who's Afraid of the Wicked Witch?" *Parent*. June 1986: 95–98.

FAIRY TALES AND CHILDREN DO MIX, continued

Heuscher, Julius E. *A Psychiatric Study of Fairy Tales*. Springfield: Thomas, 1963.

Mallet, Carl-Heinz. *Fairy Tales and Children*. Ed. Jochin Neugroschel. New York: Schocken, 1984.

Sadker, Myra; Pollock, David; and Miller, Dadker. *Now Upon a Time*. New York: Harper & Row, 1987.

Smith, Lillian H. *The Unreluctant Years*. Chicago: American Library Association, 1953.

Vandergrift, Kay E. *Child and Story*. Ed. Jane Anne Hannigan. New York: Neal-Schuman, 1980.

 ## JOURNAL SUGGESTIONS

Issues that you might write about in your journal include the following:

- How can you apply the writing skills you have practiced in this course to various writing tasks you perform? Think about writing that you do for other courses or as a part of your job.

- If you had to write a research paper, would you feel more confident about it now? Do you feel that you have a basic understanding of how to write a research paper?

- Have you ever had the opportunity to write using a computer and a word-processing program? If so, what was your reaction to using the computer for writing? Did writing on a computer make it easier for you to revise and edit?

- Has your writing changed as a result of studying composition? How has it changed? You might want to look back through your journal at some of your early journal entries before you respond to this issue.

- Has your attitude toward writing changed as a result of studying composition? Are you now more confident and more comfortable about your writing?

- How do you feel about your journal keeping? Is this an activity that you will enjoy continuing after you finish this course? What will you do differently if you continue journal keeping?

INDEX

Abbreviations, 148, 156, 164–166, 406
"About Men," 331
Abstract, 373, 374, 377
"A Busy Room," 180
Action verbs, 60, 63
Addition words, 66
American Psychological Association, 403
Anecdotal introduction, 78, 83–84
Anecdote, 83–84
Antecedent, 122, 125, 127–128
APA, *see* American Psychological Association
Apostrophe, 148, 156–157
Applications, 353
Audience, 14–19
    organization and, 44
    research paper and, 400
    revising and, 89–93, 105
    writing to learn and, 358

Balance, 261, 266–267, 295, 303
Bases of comparison or contrast, 295–297
"Beauty: A Definition," 36
Bibliography, 388–389, 391–392, 400, 402, 404–406

"Black Holes," 38
Body, 20
    conclusions and, 85–87
    paragraph and, 51–58
    research paper and, 402–405
    revision and, 92–105
    thesis and, 32–36
    unity and, 72
Brainstorming, 13
Britt, Suzanne, 310
Bullis, Dean, 302
"Buying a Pickup Truck," 279

Capitalization, 148, 161–163
Card catalog, 388–389
CBE (Council of Biology Editors), 403
Chatterton, Gordon, 202, 210
"China Still Lifes," 181
Chronological order, 44, 49, 256
"Cinematypes," 286
Class, 261, 267, 322
Classes, 266–267
Classification, 50, 259–291
Cliche, 108, 131, 132–133
Climactic order, 44, 45–46, 93
Clustering, 13–15, 28–29

Coherence, 43, 65–72, 92, 102, 103, 105
Colloquial, 131, 132
Colon, 147, 148, 149
Comma, 112–113, 147–153, 158–159, 402, 406
Comma splice, 110, 112–113
Communication transaction, 23
Comparison, 10, 293
Comparison and contrast, 50–51, 94, 293–318
Conclusion, 20–21, 77, 85–87, 371
Conclusion words, 66
Conner, Anne, 180
Connotative, 131–132
Contract, 24
Contrast, 32, 50, 67, 293, 326–327
Contrast introduction, 78, 79–82, 93
Contrast words, 66
Controlling idea, 24–25, 27, 28–29, 31, 33, 98
Coordinating conjunctions, 151
Council of Biology Editors, 403
"Courtship Through the Ages," 219
Critical reviews, 356, 373
Cubing, 10–13, 33–34

Dash, 147, 148, 153
Defining, 319, 320, 322–323
Definition, 50–51, 319–351
Denotative, 131
Description, 50–51, 171–197
Descriptive focus, 177
Details:
    chronological order and, 49
    coherence and, 65–67
    outline and, 368
    paragraphs and, 51–59
    revision and, 89–92
    spatial order and, 46
    support and, 178
Diction, 130–131, 400
Dictionary, 109, 119, 131, 153,
    322–323
Direct quotation, 151–152,
    158–160, 161, 375, 393–395,
    401–402
Dominant idea, 177
Double-entry notebook, 358–360

Editing, 92, 107–109, 110, 130,
    142, 147
Edwards, Flora Mancuso, 217
Egan, Irene, 247
Ehrlich, Gretel, 331
Elbow, Peter, 10
Ellipsis points, 148, 154, 402
"Elvira's Story," 217
Emphatic words and terms, 45–46
Essay examinations (*see* Exams),
    356, 367–368
Essay questions, 365–373
Essays, 356
Euphemisms, 108, 134
Example, 50–51, 199, 325–326
Example strategy (rhetorical),
    199–226
Exclamation point, 110, 147, 148
Extended definition, 322–323, 324,
    325
Extended example, 205

"Fairy Tales and Children Do
    Mix," 407
Faulty parallelism, 114–115
Faw, Sandi, 330
Final draft, 26, 107, 376, 403–404
Focus:
    cubing, 10–11

essay questions and, 366
focused freewriting, 7
focusing, 14–17, 357
guidelines and, 173
incorporating sources and, 399
inventory, 13
limiting the topic and, 387
prewriting and, 4, 358
reaction and, 378
reviews and, 381
support and, 178
working thesis and, 390–391
Focused freewriting, 7
Focused thesis statement, 25,
    32–42
    classification and, 267–268
    comparison and contrast and,
        303–304
    definition and, 324, 327–328
    example and, 206–207
    guidelines and, 173, 202,
        230–231, 261, 295
    process analysis and, 239
Focusing, 3, 14
Footnote, 404–405
Format, 368, 402–406
Fragments, 110, 111–112
Fredericks, Lynn, 306
"Freedom," 330
"Freedom of Speech: Another
    Look," 110, 202
Freewriting, 5–7, 8, 26, 398–399
"Friends, Good Friends—and Such
    Good Friends," 275
Function, 327
Funnel introduction, 78–79, 93

Gass, William, 181
General thesis statement, 24–31
    focus and, 176–177
    guidelines and, 202, 231, 261,
        295, 324
    thesis and, 206–207, 239,
        267–268, 303–304, 327–328
    thesis support and, 58
Global revision, 90–91
Greene, Bob, 192

"Hands," 306
Heck, Judith, 241, 301
Highlighting, 361
Howard, Martha, 274

"How to Cook Dried Pasta So You
    Can Taste It," 242
"How to Start an Intravenous
    Infusion," 241
Hull, Raymond, 212
Hyphen, 148, 153–154

Illustration words, 66, 68
Indefinite pronouns, 120–121,
    126–127
Indirect quotation, 158–159
Inform, 19, 20, 43
"Interstate Eating," 35
Introduction(s), 20, 24, 77–84, 85,
    88, 93, 105, 400
Introductory paragraph, 20
    introductions and, 77–85
    paragraphs and, 51–52
    revising and, 92–95, 105
    thesis statement and, 24–25
    writing a draft and, 400
Inventory, 13, 14
Inverted funnel conclusion, 86–87
Invoked audience, 16–18, 42
Irregular verbs, 119–120
Items in a series, 151–152

Jargon, 108, 135
Journal, 4–6, 16, 21
Journal suggestions, 21, 42, 74, 88,
    106, 167, 171, 200, 260, 293,
    320, 412

"Keeping Up with the Joneses,"
    301
Key ideas, 65, 362–363, 374, 378
Key words, 65
Kummer, Corby, 242

Local revision, 92
Looping, 8
Lyall, Donna H., 407

"Mail of the Species, The," 335
"Maker's Eye: Revising Your Own
    Manuscripts, The," 250
Mechanics, 112, 147–148
Mixed constructions, 144
Modern Language Association
    (MLA), 403
Modifiers, 110, 116–118
Multiple example, 202, 205

Murray, Donald M., 250
"My Father, the Prince," 188
"My Three Roles," 274

Note cards, 388–389, 391–397
Notes, 358, 386, 390, 391–397
Numbers, 148, 156, 165–166, 402–404

Oates, Joyce Carol, 339
"Ode to Makeup," 247
"On Boxing," 339
Organization, 8, 20–21
    comparison and, 299–300
    developing the essay and, 43–51, 204
    focusing and, 14
    notes and, 392
    process analysis and, 234
    reviews and, 382
    revising the essay and, 89–94
Outline, 362–364, 366, 367, 368, 392, 397–399, 402–403
Outlining, 362–364

"Paint," 302
Paragraph, 44–46, 51–56, 92, 105–107, 375–384, 393, 400
Paragraph-level unity, 72–74, 103–104, 105
Paragraph support, 57–60, 58, 94–95, 97–98, 105, 318
Parallelism, 110, 114–115
Paraphrase, 393–396, 405–406
Parentheses, 148, 155, 404–406
Parenthetical, 154, 155, 404–406
Peer revision, 90–92, 105
Performance order, 230, 256
Perrin, Noel, 279
Personal audience, 16
Persuasive, 19–20
Peter, Laurence J., 212
"Peter Principle, The," 212
Plan of development, 25, 32–41, 176–177, 206–207, 268, 304, 328, 400
Point, 23, 143
Point-by-point method, 299–301
Point of view, 16–18, 110
Precis, 374
Pretentious words, 133–139
Prewriting, 3–14, 42, 356–358

Principle of classification, 261, 263
Process, 227
Process analysis, 50, 227–257
Pronoun agreement, 110, 125–127
Pronoun reference, 110, 127–128
Pronouns, 65, 71, 120–121, 125–130, 378
Proofreading, 367, 371
Proper names, 162
Public audience, 18
Punctuation, 107–108, 110, 112, 147–166, 405
Purpose, 14, 19–20, 23, 42, 44, 50, 89, 90–92, 105, 357, 387, 390

Question mark, 110, 147–148, 159
Quotation, 149, 158, 393–396, 401–402, 404–405
Quotation mark, 148, 158–160, 161, 389, 393

Recopying, 361
Recursive, 4
Regular verbs, 119
Repetition, 65, 69–70
Reports, 356, 377–380
Research papers, 356, 383–412
Restricted universe, 261, 262
Review, 373, 381–383
Revision, 89–106
Revision checklist, 104–105
Rhetorical patterns, 49–50
Run-ons, 110, 112–113

Scott, Donald, 35
Semicolon, 112, 147, 148, 150
Sensory words, 60–64
Sentence, 110–111
Sentence interrupters, 151–152
Sexist language, 136
Slang, 130
Sources, 374, 387, 390–394, 397–406
Spatial order, 44, 46–49, 93–94
Specifics, 57–64, 65, 97–101, 105
Standard meaning, 324
Standard Written English (SWE), 108, 110, 147
Stover, Virginia, 36
Strategies of exposition, 44, 49–51
Style guides, 403

Subject-verb agreement, 110, 118–121, 125
Summary, 373–376, 377, 381–382, 393–394, 396
Summary conclusion, 85–86
Summary paragraph, 20
Support, 43, 51–60
    example and, 199, 202–203, 205–206
    focus, 176–178
    guidelines and, 173
    process analysis and, 233–234
    revising and, 89–105
Supporting paragraphs, 28
Swanson, William, 335
SWE (Standard Written English), 108, 110, 147
Synonyms, 65, 69–70, 131–132

Term, 322
Textbook outlining, 363
"That Lean and Hungry Look," 310
Theroux, Phyllis, 188
Thesis statement, 23–42
    applications and, 355
    example and, 199–200
    focus and, 176–177
    guidelines and, 173, 202, 261, 295, 324
    incorporating sources and, 401
    introduction and, 20, 78
    organization and, 204–205
    outline and, 397–399
    revising and, 90–93
    summary and, 394
    support and, 56–58, 178, 206–207
    thesis and, 239, 267–268, 303–304, 327–328
    topic and, 203, 231
    unity and, 72
    working thesis and, 391
Thesis support, 57–59, 95–97
Thurber, James, 219
Time order, 49
Time words, 66
Title page, 400, 402
Tone, 16–17, 11, 357, 375, 400
Topic, 24–25
    bibliography and, 388–389
    choosing and limiting, 385–387
    essay questions and, 366–368

Topic (*continued*)
   guidelines and, 173–174,
      202–203, 230–231, 261, 295,
      324
   prewriting and, 357
   reaction and, 378
   reviews and, 381
Topic sentence, 51–55, 97–99
Toth, Susan Allan, 286
"Transaction: Two Writing
   Processes, The," 308

Transitional words and phrases,
   see Transitions
Transitions, 65–69, 102, 105
"Twenty-Seven-Twenty-Two," 192

Unity, 43, 72–74, 92, 103–104, 105
Updike, John, 312

"Venezuela for Visitors," 312
Verb tense, 110, 119, 122–124, 129
Viorst, Judith, 275

Wagner, Dianne, 407
White, Frank, 38
Whole method, 299
Whole reading, 91
Wordiness, 131, 142–143
Working thesis, 390–391, 392
Works cited, 406, 411
Writing assignments, 355–356
Writing to learn, 358–364

Zinsser, William, 308